AUTHORITY, CONFLICT, AND THE TRANSMISSION OF DIVERSITY IN MEDIEVAL ISLAMIC LAW

STUDIES IN ISLAMIC LAW AND SOCIETY

EDITED BY

RUUD PETERS AND BERNARD WEISS

VOLUME 26

AUTHORITY, CONFLICT, AND THE TRANSMISSION OF DIVERSITY IN MEDIEVAL ISLAMIC LAW

BY

R. KEVIN JAQUES

BRILL
LEIDEN · BOSTON
2006

This book is printed on acid-free paper.

Library of Congress Cataloging-in-Publication Data

Jaques, R. Kevin.
Authority, conflict, and the transmission of diversity in medieval Islamic law / by R. Kevin Jaques.
p. cm. — (Studies in Islamic law and society, ISSN 1384-1130 ; v. 26)
Revision of the author's dissertation (doctorate) — Emory University, 2001.
Includes bibliographical references and index.
ISBN 90-04-14745-4 (alk. paper)
1. Ibn Qadi Shuhbah, Abu Bakr ibn Ahmad, 1377-1448. 2. Islamic law—Historiography. 3. Islamic Empire—History—1258-1517. I. Title. II. Series.

KBP275.I38J33 2006
340—dc22

2005057249

ISSN 1384–1130
ISBN 90 04 14745 4

PRINTED IN THE NETHERLANDS

For
Donna,
Jordan, and Joshua

CONTENTS

ACKNOWLEDGEMENTS

This book originated as a doctoral dissertation from Emory University's *West and South Asian Religions* program, in the Graduate Division of Religion (2001); although only three of the present eight chapters are in any way based on that work. Like most first books that result from a dissertation, however, this text has benefited from the help, support, and feedback of numerous family, friends, and colleagues. I would like to thank David Vishanoff for his friendship and fellowship through our joint efforts at Emory. David is a careful reader and was a tremendous sounding-board for ideas. His insights into *uṣūl al-fiqh* and al-Shāfiʿī's *al-Risālah* have been extremely helpful in the writing of this book. I would also like to thank Laurie Patton, Paul Courtright, Joyce Flueckiger, and Eric Reinders for challenging me to think in new ways. I would especially like to thank Vernon Robbins, whose Social Rhetorical Analysis project inspired much of my approach to *ṭabaqāt* texts. Vernon was always enthusiastic and encouraging in approaching texts in different ways.

This text would not have been possible without the kind support and efforts of Drs. Gordon Newby, Richard Martin, and Devin Stewart who guided the early stages of the project. Richard Martin has been a friend and advisor for almost twenty years and his help in exploring methods in the study of religion has been a constant source of inspiration. He also introduced me to the work of Fernand Braudel in the summer of 1993, which has had a profound impact on my understanding of history. Gordon Newby was always patient and was a true source of support throughout the rigors of graduate school.

Anyone who reads this book will notice the influence of George Makdisi on my understanding of the social institutions of medieval Muslim society. Although I never met Dr. Makdisi, Devin Stewart—his student and my teacher—transmitted to me the core of Makdisi's work. Devin and I worked for many hours through numerous Arabic texts and our educational relationship developed into one that reflected many of the styles of learning discussed in chapter four of the present work. My knowledge of Arabic is the result of Devin's many hours of effort, and while all mistakes in the text are purely mine, what I get right is largely because of his hard work. Later stages of this book have benefited from the advice of Christopher Melchert, another of Makdisi's students. Christopher read several drafts of each chapter and his insights and advice were always helpful. Both Devin and Christopher are extremely exact readers and consistently pressed me to work through my source texts and to improve my understanding of the material. While I did not always take their advice it was much appreciated nevertheless.

I would also like to thank a long list of professors and friends who convinced me to keep going over the years. Space, however, does not permit an inclusive list, but I would like to take this opportunity to mention a few who were especially encouraging and inspirational: Neil Merrell, Kurt Wenner, Dave Damrel, and especially Richard Wentz who was my first and most important guide in the study of religion. Furthermore, I would like to express my appreciation to my colleagues in the Department of Religious Studies at Indiana University, especially Steve Weitzman, Robert Campany, and Jerome Copulski who read several chapters and offered important comments.

I was able to complete this book due to the generous intellectual and financial support of the Department of Religious Studies and the RUGS program at Indiana University, which allowed me to take research leave in 2004–05 to complete the final draft. I would also like to thank my colleagues at the Oxford Centre for Islamic Studies at Oxford University who awarded me the al-Mutawa Visiting Research Fellowship in 2004–05. Ruba Kana'an, S. Hassan Abedin, and Muhammad Talib were extremely supportive during the period of my tenure there. I would also like to thank Farhan Nizami, the director of the centre, for his generous support.

I would like to close by thanking my parents Jimmie and Marjorie Jaques for their support over the years. My children Jordan and Joshua, to whom this book is dedicated, have been a great source of love and support. They can now stop asking why I am obsessed with Ibn Qāḍī Shuhbah. Finally, to my wife Donna, who read the final draft of the text and to whom this book is also dedicated, you have been with me for twenty-one years and without you none of this would have been possible. Like al-Muzanī, you are a 'pearl diver into the sea of knowledge.' Your insights into ritual, history, and social structures have always challenged me to wade into deeper waters.

It goes without saying that all of the errors and mistakes that follow are mine alone.

LIST OF FIGURES

LIST OF TABLES

INTRODUCTION: CRISIS, LEGAL DECLINE, AND THE *ṬABAQĀT* GENRE

A sense of crisis pervades Mamlūk period historiography. Wars, plagues, famines, political and religious corruption are all dominant themes. Although all of these phenomena were known before the Mamlūk period, what was different was the perception that they now occurred in combination and with devastating affect on Muslim society. These crises led to a pervasive sense that the past was better than the present and that all things contemporary paled in comparison with the glories of the earlier history of Islam. This is particularly apparent in histories written during the Circassian Mamlūk period (1382–1517). In works such as the *Kitāb al-sulūk li maʿrifat duwal al-mulūk* by Aḥmad b. ʿAlī al-Maqrīzī (d. 845/1441),[1] *al-Nujūm al-ẓāhirah fī mulūk miṣr wa ʾl-qāhirah* by Abū al-Maḥāsin Ibn Taghrī Birdī (d. 874/1470),[2] and the *Inbāʾ al-ghumr bi abnāʾ al-ʿumr* by Ibn Ḥajar al-ʿAsqalānī (852/1449)[3] there is, as William Popper says, "a pessimistic criticism of the present and [a] regret 'for the good old days.'"[4]

The perception of wide ranging historical, religious, political, and cultural catastrophes led to a crisis of intellectual leadership because Mamlūk society, as a religious cultural system, was founded on the assumption that scholars of divine law (*fuqahāʾ* sing. *faqīh*) had the ability to interpret sacred texts and thus guide people to live according to God's plan.[5] Islamic legal theory suggests that Muslims are a

---

[1] Aḥmad b. ʿAlī al-Maqrīzī, *Kitāb al-sulūk li-maʿrifat duwal al-mulūk*, ed. Saʿīd ʿAbd al-Fattāḥ ʿĀshūr, 4 vols. (Cairo: Maṭbaʿat dār al-kutub, 1972).

[2] Abū al-Maḥāsin Ibn Taghrī Birdī, *al-Nujūm al-ẓāhirah fī mulūk miṣr wa ʾl-qāhirah*, ed. William Popper, 7 vols. (Berkeley: University Press, 1909–1912).

[3] Ibn Ḥajar al-ʿAsqalānī, *Inbāʾ al-ghumr bi abnāʾ al-ʿumr*, ed. Sayyid ʿAbd al-Wahhāb Bukhārī, 9 vols. (Hyderabad: Dāʾirat al-maʿārif al-ʿuthmānīyah, 1975).

[4] William Popper, *Egypt and Syria under the Circassian Sultans: 1382–1468 A.D. Systematic Notes to Ibn Taghrī Birdī's Chronicles of Egypt* (Berkeley: University of California Press, 1955), 8.

[5] There have been a number of studies that have examined the role of jurists as authoritative interpreters. See for instance, Bernard Weiss, *The Spirit of Islamic Law* (Athens: University of Georgia Press, 1998); also see Wael Hallaq, *A History of Islamic Legal Theories* (Cambridge: University Press, 1997) and his *Authority, Continuity, and Change in Islamic Law* (Cambridge: University Press, 2001). For an excellent

special category of people because they 'submit' to the will of God. Submission requires people to do what God says; to obey the rules of the *sharīʿah.* According to medieval Muslim legal theory, however, the *sharīʿah* is not an explicit code of legal norms, but exists only in the mind of God. God indicates what the rules are through the texts of revelation (the Qur'an and the *sunnah*-the acts and statements of the Prophet Muḥammad which were thought to have been transmitted by pious individuals over the centuries and were later collected in written form in texts known as *aḥādith*, sing. *ḥadīth*). The *fuqahā'* claimed for themselves the exclusive right and ability to interpret the texts of revelation so that Muslims, common people and rulers alike, might know what God wants them to do in all walks of life.[6]

As the authoritative interpreters of revelation, the *fuqahā'* became, by virtue of their expertise, guides for the community.[7] They were judges, governmental advisors, administrators, and popular leaders.[8] When the crises of the 13th, 14th, and 15th centuries began to overwhelm the crumbling ʿAbbāsid state and the later Mamlūk Sulṭānate, blame was focused on the failure of the jurists to guide the community out of the problems that had overwhelmed it. Popular dissatisfaction with the ability of the jurists to guide the Muslim community was expressed, for example, in Ibn Taghrī Birdī's condemnation of the corruption of the jurists during one of several failed attempts at judicial reform in the early 9th/15th century[9] and in the public denunciation of Jamāl al-Dīn al-Suyūṭī (d. 909/1505) when he declared himself a *mujtahid* (authoritative interpreter of the texts of revelation) in the late Circassian period.[10]

---

medieval discussion of the role of the *fuqahā'* in Muslim society see Muḥyī al-Dīn b. Yaḥyā al-Nawawī, *al-Majmūʿ al-mudhahhab fī sharḥ al-muhadhdhab* (Beirut: Dār al-kutub al-ʿilmīyah, 1996), vol. 1, 67–75 and Tāj al-Dīn ʿAbd al-Wahhāb b. ʿAlī al-Subkī, *Muʿīd al-niʿam wa mubīd al-niqam* (Cairo: Maktabat al-khanjī, 1993).

6 Al-Nawawī, *al-Majmūʿ*, vol. 1, 13–110.

7 Ira Lapidus, "State and Religion in Islamic Societies," *Past and Present*, no. 5 (May 1996): 11–12.

8 For an excellent description of the kinds of positions jurists held in Damascus see Shams al-Dīn Ibn Ṭūlūn, *Quḍāt dimashq al-thaghir al-bassām fī dhikr man wulliya qaḍā' al-shām*, ed. Ṣalāḥ al-Dīn al-Munajjid (Cairo: Maṭbūʿāt al-majmaʿ al-ʿilmī al-ʿarabī, 1956). Also see Popper, *Egypt and Syria under the Circassian Sultans* and Bernadette Martel-Thoumian, *Les Civils et l'Administration dans l'état militaire mamlūk (IX/XV Siècle)* (Damascus: Institut Français de Damas, 1991).

9 Ibn Taghrī Birdī, *al-Nujūm*, vol. 6, 357.

10 Jamāl al-Dīn al-Suyūṭī, *Kitāb al-radd ʿalā man akhlad ilā al-arḍ wa jahil ann al-*

The crisis of leadership was also felt by the jurists themselves. As Wael Hallaq has demonstrated, the initial discussion of the so-called 'closing of the gate of *ijtihād*' (a metaphor for the end of independent legal reasoning) came about because jurists representing the established schools of Islamic law wanted to prevent new schools from arising. Legal theorists argued that the ability to develop new methods of textual interpretation came to an end after the deaths of the four eponymous founders of the Ḥanafī, Shāfiʿī, Mālikī, and Ḥanbalī schools. This theory, however, did not mean that the ability of jurists to 'discover' new rules in the texts of revelation came to a complete halt. To the contrary, Hallaq argues that jurists continued for centuries to employ various forms of independent legal discovery.[11]

In the Mamlūk period the discourse over the decline of legal expertise shifted as crises in close succession began to grip the Middle East. The Mongol invasion and destruction of the last vestiges of the ʿAbbāsid Empire in 1258 was interpreted as a direct challenge to the leadership of the *ʿulamāʾ* (community of religious authorities). Critics such as Ibn Taymīyah (d. 728/1328) began to argue that the abilities of jurists to guide the community had declined and that they were no longer suited to be the interpreters of revelation that they once claimed to be. It was their failure to provide the guidance necessary for the community to prosper that had brought about the invasion and destruction of Muslim lands by non-believers.[12]

Ibn Taymīyah called for a return to a basic form of piety and a legal method stripped of outside influences. Most importantly, he called for a return to *ijtihād* founded on a new infusion of basic legal and methodological education. Jurists, once re-educated in the fundamental elements of law would then lead a religious reconstruction of Muslim society, divesting it of the foreign corruptions that had caused it to fall prey to outside invasion and domination.[13]

---

ijtihād fī kull ʿaṣr farḍ, ed. Khalīl al-Mays (Beirut: Dār al-kutub al-ʿilmīyah, 1983), 11–16, 97–116.

[11] Hallaq, *Authority, Continuity, and Change*, 166–235.

[12] Ibn Taymīyah, *Majmūʿat al-rasāʾil wa ʾl-masāʾil* (Cairo: Lajnat al-turāth al-ʿarabī, 1976) vol. 1, 25–70.

[13] Ibn Taymīyah, *al-Siyāsah al-sharʿīyah* (Beirut: Dār al-kutub al-ʿarabīyah, 1966), 9–14; *Maʿārij al-wuṣūl ilā anna uṣūl al-dīn wa furūʿ ʿuhū qad bayyanahā al-rasūl* (Cairo: Quṣayy Muḥibb al-Dīn al-Khaṭīb, 1968), 13–20; and *Majmūʿat al-rasāʾil wa ʾl-masāʾil*, vol. 1, 149–181.

Historiography, eschatology, and the ideology of crisis

Although he was, in his time, marginal to the mainstream of medieval Muslim thinking, some of Ibn Taymīyah's ideas did find champions in the 'orthodox' schools of legal and theological thought, perhaps most importantly with the historians Shams al-Dīn Muḥammad b. Aḥmad al-Dhahabī (d. 748/1348) and Ismāʿīl Ibn Kathīr (d. 774/1373).[14] Al-Dhahabī's *Tārīkh al-islām*[15] and its abridgements *al-ʿIbar fī akhbār al-bashar mimman ʿabar* and *Kitāb tadhkirat al-ḥuffāẓ*,[16] and Ibn Kathīr's *al-Bidāyah wa ʾl-nihāyah*[17] became the main sources for Circassian period historians and served as the foundations for many abridgements and addendums.[18]

Al-Dhahabī was a staunch defender of Ibn Taymīyah and his ideas. He argued that jurists had allowed Islamic society to fall into crisis because they were too fixated on arguing about speculative legal method (*uṣūl al-fiqh*) to give adequate attention to the problems of the community (*ummah*). The juridical fixation on *uṣūl al-fiqh* resulted, according to al-Dhahabī, in a "spiritual disease" that weakened the *ummah*.[19] According to the historian and Shāfiʿī scholar Taqī al-Dīn al-Subkī (d. 749/1349), al-Dhahabī's bias against the jurists, especially Shāfiʿīs, and his predilection for the ideas of Ibn Taymīyah, contaminated his historical analyses and limited the usefulness of his work.[20] Later scholars writing during the Circassian Mamlūk period disagreed, arguing that al-Dhahabī was the greatest historian of the age.[21]

---

[14] Khān, vol. 3, 85.

[15] Shams al-Dīn Muḥammad b. Aḥmad b. ʿUthmān al-Dhahabī, *Tārīkh al-islām wa wafayāt al-mashāhīr wa ʾl-aʿlām*, ed. ʿUmar ʿAbd al-Salām Tadmurī, 58 vols. (Beirut: Dār al-kutub al-ʿarabī, 1999).

[16] *Kitāb tadhkirat al-ḥuffāẓ*, 2 vols. (n.p.: Dār al-fikr al-ʿarabī, n.d.).

[17] Ismāʿīl Ibn Kathīr, *al-Bidāyah wa ʾl-nihāyah*, ed. ʿAlī Muḥammad Muʿawwaḍ et al., 14 vols. (Beirut: Dār al-kutub al-ʿilmīyah, 1994).

[18] Carl Brockelmann, *Geschichte der Arabischen Litteratur*, G II, 46, 49, 56; S II, 45–47, 48–49.

[19] See al-Sakhāwī, *al-Iʿlan bi ʾl-tawbīkh li-man dhammah al-tārīkh* (Damascus: n.p., 1930), 42 as quoted by Franz Rosenthal, *The History of Muslim Historiography* (Leiden: E. J. Brill, 1968), 377. Also see Shams al-Dīn Muḥammad b. Aḥmad al-Dhahabī, *Bayān zaghal al-ʿilm wa ʾl-ṭalab*, ed. Muḥammad Zāhid al-Kawtharī (Damascus: al-Qudsī, 1929), 20–21. For his defense of Ibn Taymīyah see pp. 32–34.

[20] Rosenthal, *History of Muslim Historiography*, 371–75.

[21] Ibid., 375–78.

Ibn Kathīr, like al-Dhahabī, was very close to Ibn Taymīyah and was even buried in a grave next to his.[22] Ibn Kathīr, however, understood the decline of the period in apocalyptic terms and his treatment of the causes of the Mongol invasion and the destruction of the ʿAbbāsid Caliphate is an important window on to how medieval historians conceptualized the idea of social, political, and religious crisis.[23] He writes that the Muslim world had fallen into decline for almost a century before the Mongol assault. Political infighting and competition for power led political and religious leaders to neglect the community. For instance, in 589/1193 conditions were so abhorrent that when famine struck in ʿIrāq people resorted to cannibalism; the corpses of children were even consumed by the starving.[24] As these calamities persisted, Muslim leaders failed to find solutions to the problems but instead vied with each other for power.[25] Even the jurists in Baghdād and Damascus were more concerned with their internal struggles for power than they were for the plight of the Muslim community.[26] This situation persisted until 656/1258 when the Mongols attacked Baghdād.

Ibn Kathīr writes that the officials around the ʿAbbāsid Caliph Mustaʿṣim Billāh fled the city or collaborated with the advancing enemy. These included court officials, but also judges, jurists, Ṣūfīs, members of the noble houses (*aʿyān*), as well as common people. Tens of thousands were murdered, legal colleges were destroyed, their funds confiscated by the invaders, and books of learning were burned. While this was going on the Caliph, oblivious to the destruction of the city and the assault on his palace, occupied himself with concubines.[27]

In the end, Ibn Kathīr claims that over 80,000 people were killed in Baghdād alone, although he quotes unnamed informants that place the number at over a million. He clearly does not give credence to this fantastic figure but quotes it rhetorically to demonstrate just how horrible the event was.[28] For Ibn Kathīr, however, the importance

---

[22] Khān, vol. 3, 86.

[23] See his *al-Nihāyah fī al-fitan wa ʾl-malāḥim*, 2 vols., Muḥammad Aḥmad ʿAbd al-ʿAzīz (Beirut: Dār al-kutub al-ʿilmīyah, 1988) for an extended look at his views on eschatology.

[24] Ibn Kathīr, *al-Bidāyah*, vol. 13, 5–6.

[25] Ibid., 12–13.

[26] Ibid., 25–28; 33–35.

[27] Ibid., 235–42.

[28] Ibid., 238.

of the event is not the death toll, or even the destruction of the ʿAbbāsid Caliphate, but what it symbolizes with respect to the decline of moral conditions and the failure of the scholars to act as guides for the community. He says that "[God] caused to befall on the people of Baghdād that which happened to the children of Israel in Jerusalem."[29] He then quotes the Qurʾan, Sūrah 17:4–5, stating:

> And we decreed for the children of Israel in the book, Verily, you will work corruption in the earth twice, and you will become great tyrants. So when the time for the first of the two came, we brought against you our slaves of great power who ravaged the country. A promise was fulfilled.

He then says,

> Among the children of Israel a multitude were killed. The sons of the prophets were captured from among the people who prayed. Jerusalem was ruined [by] what [had happened to it] and it was inhabited by the slaves. The ascetics, scholars, and the prophets no longer occupied its thrones.[30]

Ibn Kathīr uses the Qurʾanic passage as a commentary on the events surrounding the Mongol invasion and the end of the Caliphate. He, in effect, argues that the causes of the first destruction of Jerusalem as depicted in the Qurʾan are the same as those that led to the destruction of Baghdād; both events he interprets as a manifestation of God's divine justice. In his analysis of Sūrah 17, Ibn Kathīr states that Israel had been destroyed the first time because the Israelites "had rebelled and killed many of the prophets and scholars (*ʿulamāʾ*)."[31] In other words, they had cut themselves off from those capable of interpreting revelation. The second destruction of Israel (which he attributes to the coming of Islam) occurred because the Israelites failed to learn the lessons of the first event, prompting God to send another army to punish them for their inequities.[32] The second destruction was followed by a period during which God provided for even more guidance through the prophetic office of Muḥammad. Ibn Kathīr indicates that this final dispensation of revelation was

---

[29] Ibid.
[30] Ibid.
[31] Ibn Kathīr, *Tafsīr al-qurʾān al-ʿaẓīm*, ed. Muḥammad Ḥusayn Shams al-Dīn (Beirut: Dār al-kutub al-ʿilmīyah, 1998), vol. 5, 44.
[32] Ibid., 44–45.

ignored, not just by the Israelites, but by humankind in general. This third and final rejection precipitates the day of resurrection and the end times, which for Ibn Kathīr coincided with his own period.[33]

Sūrah 17 begins with revelatory episodes associated with Moses and Muḥammad (verses 1–3). It then presents, and thrice repeats over the course of the chapter, a pattern of revelation, destruction, the return of revelation or guidance, and finally, the onset of the eschaton (16–59, 60–71, 72–100 respectively). In each instance, there is a cycle whereby a) God gives revelation to the people who then reject or corrupt it, b) they are punished through the destruction of life and property, c) they are given a second chance to obey the revelation, and d) when they ultimately fail, God destroys them a second time and introduces the day of judgement. In all cycles but the first (verses 1–15), the second destruction is conflated with the apocalypse.

By drawing an analogy between the first destruction of Israel and the sack of Baghdād, Ibn Kathīr argues that the Mongol attack began a period of eschatological turmoil and unless the community returns to obeying revelation and listens to those with knowledge (*ʿilm*),[34] God will unleash apocalyptic destruction that will ultimately lead to the day of resurrection.[35] Ibn Kathīr draws on centuries of apocalyptic ideas that forecast a time when foreign non-Muslim invaders would attack and overwhelm the Muslim world. Apocalypticists such as al-Ḥasan b. Muḥammad al-Daylamī (d. 8th/14th century) transmitted *ḥadīth* that foretold the end times. For instance, in one tradition, the Prophet Muḥammad states that

> the *ʿulamāʾ* are the guardians of the Messengers . . . [they are] faithful as long as they do not intermingle with the Sulṭān and (do not) have intercourse with the world. When they intermingle with the Sulṭān and have intercourse with the world, then they have betrayed the Messenger, and so be wary and afraid of them.[36]

According to David Cook, in his book *Studies in Muslim Apocalyptic*, the failure of the *ʿulamāʾ* to guide the community is a common theme

---

[33] Ibid., 45–47.
[34] Ibid., 69.
[35] Ibid., 82.
[36] Al-Ḥasan b. Muḥammad al-Daymalī, *Irshād al-qulūb fī al-mawāʿiẓ wa ʾl-ḥikam* (Najaf: al-Maṭbaʿah al-ḥaydarīyah, n.d.), vol. 3, 100 as quoted in David Cook, *Studies in Muslim Apocalyptic* (Princeton: The Darwin Press, 2002), 248.

in apocalyptic literature. Because the *ʿulamāʾ* fail to set aside their own interests and to focus on guiding the community, moral decay, described as 'ignorance' (*jahl*), sets in and God is forced to punish the *ummah*.[37] Ironically, those specializing in legal rules are not the subject of blame in apocalyptic literature, but, as with al-Dhahabī, people who focus on auxiliary areas of intellectual endeavour such as lexicography, grammar, Qurʾan recitation, and legal methodologies.[38]

Apocalypticists mention a number of groups that cause the destruction of the Muslim community, prominent among them the Turks. The Turks are describes as being among the "Arab's most deadly enemies."[39] A number of prophecies said to have originated with the Prophet Muḥammad foretell of a time when massive invasions from the east will overwhelm and destroy the Muslim community. For instance, one tradition states that

> the hour will not arrive until you fight a group with small eyes, wide faces, as if their eyes were the pupils of locust, as if their faces were beaten shields, wearing shoes made of hair. Taking up leather shields until they fasten their horses to palm trees in ʿIrāq.[40]

In another tradition, Ibn Tāwās (d. 664/1266), in his *al-Malāḥim wa ʾl-fitan* states

> The incomprehensible ones are coming, the incomprehensible ones are coming! They cut off your heads, steal your land-spoils, settle in your land, expose your shame, enslave the best of you, and humiliate your nobility. [They are] ugly of colour, [with] rough necks, renowned swords; their sticks peeled, and their whips knotted at the end. They will be harsher on my community than the Pharaoh was on the Children of Israel.[41]

In each instance, the invaders come as instruments of God's will to punish the moral decay of the Muslim community.[42]

Ibn Kathīr, and other Mamlūk period historians, drawing from these apocalyptic visions, understood their time to be the beginning

[37] Cook, 250–51.
[38] Ibid., 252–53.
[39] Ibid., 85.
[40] Ibid., 84–85.
[41] See ʿAlī b. Mūsā Ibn Tāwās, *al-Malāḥim wa ʾl-fitan* (Najaf: al-Maṭbaʿah al-ḥaydarīyah, 1946), as quoted by Cook, 86.
[42] Cook, 88.

of the eschaton, the beginning of the end.[43] They, however, clearly believed that there were ways to avoid the immediate end of creation. Ibn Kathīr, drawing from Sūrah 17:18–41, lists a number of things that must be done in order to prevent the eschaton; these include: worshipping God alone and without partners,[44] obeying and being respectful to ones parents,[45] maintaining ties of kinship,[46] spending ones money carefully,[47] prohibiting the killing of children,[48] prohibiting adultery and fornication,[49] prohibiting homicide,[50] prohibiting the unlawful use of moneys provided for orphans,[51] and fulfilling contractual obligations.[52] Each of these requires religious leadership and it is the *ʿulamāʾ* that becomes the focus of Mamlūk period ideas about the preservation of Muslim society in the context the coming eschaton. Central to Ibn Kathīr's eschatology is that the *ʿulamāʾ* failed in its role as guides and interpreters of revelation.

Biography and the discourse of legal and moral decline

Although the apocalypicists did not specifically blame the jurists for the moral decline of the community, the jurists themselves had argued for centuries that they had failed to adhere to their own standards. Al-Nawawī (d. 676/1277), for instance, argued in the midst of the Mongol invasion that legal standards had declined because they had failed to develop an understanding of legal history, especially the lives of the great jurists of the past in the contexts of their own times. He states that

> an acquaintance with the elite [jurists of the past] establishes a kind of relationship between them and those who know them. On the Day of Resurrection, such a relationship will be helpful in securing intercession. Now the relationship of a scholar to his pupil is like the

[43] Also see, Remke Kruk, "History and Apocalypse: Ibn al-Nafī's Justification of Mamluk Rule," *Der Islam* 72, no. 2 (1995): 324–37.
[44] Ibn Kathīr, *Tafsīr al-qurʾān*, vol. 5, 59.
[45] Ibid., 59–62.
[46] Ibid., 63.
[47] Ibid., 63–66.
[48] Ibid., 66.
[49] Ibid., 66–67.
[50] Ibid., 67–68.
[51] Ibid., 68–69.
[52] Ibid.

> relationship between a father and his son, in fact, it is something more sacred. A pupil who does not know his teacher is like a son who does not know his father, in fact, he is even more wrong. A jurist who is asked, for instance, about al-Muzanī and al-Ghazālī and does not know the interval of time between them and the distance between the places where they lived certainly reveals a truly disqualifying lack of knowledge. Certainly the transmitters of traditions, the *ḥadīth* scholars have long appreciated the truth of this and drawn the consequences: they have written monographs on personality criticism, and they have also dealt with this subject in works which go under the title of *history*. The jurists, on the other hand, have ceased to realize (the importance of) this subject. Thus, their previous awareness of the different degrees of accuracy and accomplishment among their leaders and experts ceased to exist.[53]

Here, al-Nawawī articulates a potent critique of the legal profession that would shape the development of a genre of legal biographical historical text over the next 300 years. He argues that the crisis of the period *was* a crisis of authority that can chiefly be blamed on a failure to maintain the teachings of the great jurists of previous generations.

Al-Nawawī's critique came to dominate the internal discourse of the legal schools, especially the Shāfiʿīs and Ḥanafīs. Internal to the schools there was an attempt to sort out the problems of legal interpretation by seeking to delineate the chains by which authoritative knowledge was passed from generation to generation. The root of the problem, according to this view, was that jurists had drifted away from the core methods and doctrines of the schools of law; that they had become influenced by ideas and intellectual traditions that led jurists away from the purpose of the legal profession: to articulate rules for the guidance of the community. This view of the decline of legal abilities is expressed most fully in the genre of biographical historical dictionaries known as *ṭabaqāt* (literally, generations or ranks).

An overview of the development of the ṭabaqāt *genre*

According to H. A. R. Gibb, Arab Islamic historiography embraces both annals and biography.[54] In fact, biographies were so compre-

[53] Rosenthal, 303.

[54] See his *Studies on the Civilization of Islam*, ed. Stanford J. Shaw and William R. Polk (Boston: Beacon Press: 1962), 108.

hensive by the Mamlūk period that, "biography *was* history in the view of many of its practitioners."[55] This view is shared by most scholars who have examined the biographical genre.[56] *Ṭabaqāt* texts,

[55] Tarif Khalidi, *Arabic Historical Thought in the Classical Period* (Cambridge: University Press, 1994), 210.

[56] There has been extensive work done on and with biographical literature in the Islamic tradition. The following represents a brief list of texts that are important examinations and applications of the genre. See Michael Cooperson, *Classical Arabic Biography: The Heirs of the Prophet in the Age of al-Maʾmūn* (Cambridge: University Press, 2000); Jonathan P. Berkey, *The Transmission of Knowledge in Medieval Cairo: A Social History of Islamic Education* (Princeton: University Press, 1992); Richard W. Bulliet, "A Quantitative Approach to Medieval Muslim Biographical Dictionaries," *The Journal of Economic and Social History* 13 (1970): 195–211, also see his *Conversion to Islam in the Medieval Period: An Essay in Quantitative History* (Cambridge: Harvard University Press, 1979) and his *Islam: The View from the Edge* (New York: Columbia University Press, 1994); Claude Cahen, "History and Historians," in *Cambridge History of Arabic Literature*, ed. M. J. L Young, et al., vol. 3 (Cambridge: University Press, 1990), 188–233, and his "Editing Arabic Chronicles: A Few Suggestions," *Islamic Studies* 1, no. 3 (1962): 1–25; Michael Chamberlain, *Knowledge and Social Practice in Medieval Damascus, 1190–1350* (Cambridge: University Press, 1994); Hartmut Fähndrich, "The Wafayat al-Aʿyan of Ibn Khallikan: A New Approach," *Journal of the American Oriental Society* 93 (1973): 432–445; H. A. R. Gibb, "Islamic Biographical Literature," in *Historians of the Middle East*, ed. B. Lewis and P. M. Holt, (London: Oxford University Press, 1962), 54–58; Ibrahim Hafsi, "Recherches sur le genre *Tabaqat* dans la littérature arabe," *Arabica* 23 (September 1976): 227–65; 24 (February 1977): 1–41; 24 (June 1977): 150–86; Tarif Khalidi, *Arabic Historical Thought in the Classical Period*; Donald P. Little, *An Introduction to Mamluk Historiography: An Analysis of Arabic Annalistic and Biographical Sources for the Reign of an-Malik al-Nasir Muhammad ibn Qala'un* (Wiesbaden: Franz Steiner, 1970), and see his *History and Historiography of the Mamluks* (London: Variorum Reprints, 1986), and "Historiography of the Ayyubid and Mamluk Epochs," in *The Cambridge History of Egypt*, ed. Carl F. Petry, vol. 1: Islamic Egypt, 640–151 (Cambridge: University Press, 1998); Otto Loth, "Die Ursprung und Bedeutung der Tabaqat," *Zeitschrift der Deutschen Morgenländischen Gesellschaft* 23 (1869): 593–614; George Makdisi, "*Ṭabaqāt*-Biography: Law and Orthodoxy in Classical Islam," *Islamic Studies* 32 (1993): 371–96; Carl F. Petry, *The Civilian Elite of Cairo in the Later Middle Ages* (Princeton: University Press, 1981); William Popper, trans. *History of Egypt: An Extract from Abī l-Maḥāsin Ibn Taghrī Birdī's Chronicle* (New Haven: American Oriental Society, 1967); Wadad al-Qadi, "Biographical Dictionaries: Inner Structure and Cultural Significance," in *The Book in the Islamic World: The Written Word and Communication in the Middle East*, ed. George N. Atiyeh (Albany: State University of New York Press, 1995), 93–122; Ruth Roded, *Women in Islamic Biographical Collections* (Boulder Co.: Lynne Rienner Publishers, 1994); Franz Rosenthal, "On Medieval Authorial Biographies: Al-Ya'qubi and Ibn Hajar," in *Literary Heritage of Classical Islam: Arabic and Islamic Studies in Honor of James A. Bellamy*, ed. Mustansir Mir (Princeton: Darwin Press, 1993), 255–74, and especially his *A History of Muslim Historiography*, 93–95, 100–06; Devin Stewart, "Capital, Accumulation, and the Islamic Academic Biography," *Edebīyat* 7 (1997): 346–62; Ferdinand Wüstenfeld, *Academien der Araber und ihre Lehrer* (Göttingen: Vandenhoeck und Ruprecht, 1837); M. J. L. Young, "Arabic Biographical Writing," in *The Cambridge History of Arabic Literature: Religion, Learning and Science in the ʿAbbasid Period*, ed. M. J. L. Young, J. D. Latham and R. B. Serjeant (Cambridge: University Press, 1990), 168–87; and Chase Robinson, *Islamic Historiography* (Cambridge: University Press, 2003), 72–74.

however, are different from other forms of biography because of their focus on authority, especially in disciplines of knowledge thought to have originated with the Prophet Muḥammad. *Ṭabaqāt* texts map the chains by which authoritative knowledge is transmitted from generation to generation and in doing so present readers with overviews of trends in the development of different scholarly traditions and schools of thought. The authors of *ṭabaqāt* texts present their histories by retelling the lives of individuals; by linking scholars, concepts, intellectual traditions, events, alliances, and conflicts together through the use of a range of rhetorical strategies. Historical understandings are therefore presented in the details of each biographical entry, which when taken as a whole, show the ebbs and flows of intellectual development and how the authors of *ṭabaqāt* works understood historical contexts to have influenced the development of Islamic thought.

The earliest extant biographical dictionary is *al-Ṭabaqāt al-kubrā* by Ibn Saʿd (d. 230/845).[57] This *ṭabaqāt* text was first analyzed by Otto Loth in a short work published in 1869.[58] Ibn Saʿd's *ṭabaqāt* examines the Companions of Muḥammad who transmitted sayings from the Prophet, who also fought in the battle of Badr (circa 2/624), as well as those who later migrated to various areas of the newly emerging Islamic world.[59] According to Loth, as traditionists began to develop a science that focused on those who transmitted *ḥadīth*, they started to develop biographical dictionaries that catalogued the qualities, qualifications, and localities of those who transmitted traditions of the Prophet.[60] For Loth, H. A. R. Gibb, and others, biographical genres developed as a sub-genre of *ḥadīth* science.[61]

Ibrahim Hafsi, in his monumental "Recherches sur le Genre '*Ṭabaqāt*,'" one of the few analyses devoted solely to the *ṭabaqāt* genre, observes that *ṭabaqāt* texts are the highest expression of the bio-

---

[57] Hamilton Gibb, "Islamic Biographical Literature," 54; also see Ibrahim Hafsi, "Recherches sur le Genre '*Ṭabaqāt*,'" (September 1976): 242.

[58] Otto Loth, "Die Ursprung und Bedeutung der Tabaqat," 593–614.

[59] Ibn Saʿd, *al-Ṭabaqāt al-kubrā*, 9 vols. (Beirut: Dār al-masīrah, 1957–1968); Gibb, 54–55.

[60] Cooperson, 1; Gibb, "Islamic Biographical Literature," 54–55.

[61] Cooperson, 1; Gibb, "Islamic Biographical Literature," 55–56. This view has been the standard by which biographical dictionaries, including *ṭabaqāt*, have been analyzed for over a century. For a more contemporary restatement of this thesis see Devin Stewart, "Capital, Accumulation," 47.

graphical focus of *ḥadīth* specialists.[62] For Hafsi, "le genre *ṭabaqāt* est né dans le cadre du *ḥadīṯ* et en est inséparable."[63] Hafsi argues that *ḥadīth* science not only influenced the origins of the *ṭabaqāt* genre but also came to dominate the later development of the tradition as it was used by other professional groups.[64]

According to George Makdisi, however, the origins of the *ṭabaqāt* genre and its later development may not have been influenced by *ḥadīth* science.[65] While he does not explore the origins of the *ṭabaqāt* genre, his misgivings about the genre's origins stem from W. Heffening's argument that the origins of the *ṭabaqāt* genre have more to do with the "interest of the Arabs in genealogy and biography" than with *ḥadīth* studies.[66] Michael Cooperson and Tarif Khalidi agree with Heffening's assessment and locate the origins of biographical dictionaries in Arab genealogies.[67] One of the shortcomings of their analyses for present purposes is that they fail to distinguish between *ṭabaqāt* and other kinds of biographical work.[68] It is difficult to ascertain the accuracy of their theories for the development of *ṭabaqāt* since they address only the broad outlines of biographical literature while Loth, Makdisi, and Hafsi look more narrowly at the *ṭabaqāt* genre.

Khalidi argues that the origins of the biographical genre lie in pre-Islamic times.[69] Interest in biography was motivated by the dominant cultural passion for genealogies and poetry. As Khalidi contends,

> genealogy and the chain of poetic transmission (*riwāyah*) were both well-established pre-Islamic cultural interests. Short biographies of the Prophet's Companions were intended to authenticate the history of the early community as these Companions carried with them the guarantee of truth into far corners of the empire.[70]

---

[62] Hafsi, 23 (1976), 227–29.
[63] Ibid., 228.
[64] Ibid., 228–29.
[65] Makdisi, "*Ṭabaqāt,*" 372–73.
[66] W. Heffening, "Ṭabaqāt," in *Encyclopedia of Islam,* 1st ed. Also see Makdisi, "*Ṭabaqāt,*" 372.
[67] Cooperson, 1–8; Tarif Khalidi, 205.
[68] Cooperson points out that the lines between different biographical genres are blurred, with many biographical texts being confused with annalistic histories, even by medieval Muslim writers (p. 18). The blurring of biographical genres has made studies of particular kinds of biographical texts, such as *ṭabaqāt,* difficult since many of the qualities found in these texts are also found in other biographical and historical texts.
[69] Khalidi, 205.
[70] Ibid.

Later, as the bureaucratic structure of the Umayyads and ʿAbbāsids took shape biographical dictionaries became more important as there was a need to catalogue warriors and their descendants who were due state stipends for military service.[71] Only later did traditionists appropriate the genre for their own purposes.

Traditionists were only one in a series of groups that came to use the genre to provide a trans-generational record of their memberships. Khalidi, departing from other scholars, argues that the single most important group that contributed to the development of the genre were the Ṣūfīs. He contends that biographical dictionaries are concerned with mapping chains of descent in the transmission of 'truth.' *Silsilah* (conceived as a spiritual chain of transmission), not *isnād* (a scholarly chain of transmission) is the prime motivation behind biographical method.[72] By Mamlūk times, Khalidi argues, the need to map the history of the transmission of 'truth' became the main motive behind the writing of biographical texts.[73]

The problem with Khalidi's theory is that the first Ṣūfī *ṭabaqāt* work postdates (by a century) the production of the earliest *ṭabaqāt* works. As Makdisi and Hafsi point out, the earliest *ṭabaqāt* texts were written by the rationalist Wāṣil ibn ʿAṭāʾ (d. 131/748) and by the traditionalist al-Muʿāfā b. ʿImrān b. Nawfal al-Mawṣilī[74] (d. 184/800); although Chase Robinson has called into question al-Mawṣilī's role into the formation of the genre.[75] The first Ṣūfī *ṭabaqāt* was written

[71] Ibid.

[72] Khalidi, 206.

[73] Ibid.

[74] *Kitāb ṭabaqāt al-muḥaddithīn.* Hafsi, 23 (1976), 241; Makdisi, "*Ṭabaqāt,*" 374. It is important not to confuse the difference between "traditionists" and "traditionalists." A traditionist is a scholar who specializes in the transmission and collection of *ḥadīth.* A traditionalist, in the context of early Islam, is a scholar who opposes rationalist theological and juridical thought. The confusion arises from the use of the term *ahl al-ḥadīth* (the people of tradition) that was used in Islamic texts to refer to both *ḥadīth* specialists and *ḥadīth* specialists who oppose rational speculation. Certain *ṭabaqāt* texts are referred to as traditionalist in orientation because they emphasize the authority of scholars who oppose rationalist theology and legal thought. Virtually all traditionalist *ṭabaqāt* texts focus on *ḥadīth* science as a genre of knowledge which leads to a further confusion as to the use and meaning of the terms. Where the difference is discernable, the following will refer specifically to traditionalists when it is clear that the individual opposed rationalism. Otherwise, the term traditionist will be used to refer to *ḥadīth* specialists for whom no known affiliation exists.

[75] Hafsi, 24 (1977), 28. See Chase F. Robinson, "al-Muʿāfā b. ʿImrān and the Beginnings of the *Ṭabaqāt* Literature," *Journal of the American Oriental Society* 116, no. 1 (Jan.–March, 1996): 114–120.

by Muḥammad b. ʿAlī b. Ḥasan al-Tirmidhī[76] (d. 285/898), and follows the format of the previous eleven traditionist *ṭabaqāt*.[77] If, as these dates suggest, the first *ṭabaqāt* was that compiled by Wāṣil, the purported founder of the Muʿtazilī school of theology,[78] it would suggest that the genre grew out of the rationalist/traditionalist debate, and only secondarily as a form specific to Ṣūfīs.[79]

Cooperson agrees with Khalidi that the origins of the biographical genre predate the formation of traditionalist groups. For Cooperson, however, the purpose of biography is to identify those responsible for the transmission of knowledge, not 'truth.' Following Heffening, Cooperson argues that most biographical collections devoted to fields other than *ḥadīth* studies are, for the most part, at least as old as those of *ḥadīth*.[80] He contends that the oldest biographical collections are those devoted to the life of the Prophet Muḥammad. These biographies were written by *akhbārī*s (collectors of reports), who become an identifiable group as early as the Caliphate of Muʿāwiyah (29/661–48/680). The oldest collections were, however, written before the specialization of professions began to take place.[81] *Akhbārī*s would include the genealogies of Companions and others who were important in Muḥammad's story as they recounted the life of the Prophet. These genealogies often included a brief narrative about the lives of those included in the list of ancestors. The narrative collections of genealogies were the earliest kind of biography.[82]

Cooperson argues that Ibn Saʿd's *al-Ṭabaqāt al-kubrā* has been misidentified as a work about *ḥadīth* transmitters. The text, after all, contains much that one does not find in later traditionist works, most importantly the biography of the Prophet. Ibn Saʿd's text nevertheless influenced how later traditionists constructed their biographical dictionaries. It is, however, the dominance of the *isnād* as the primary vetting agent that sets traditionist biographies apart from *akhbārī* texts, especially after al-Shāfiʿī.[83] In *ḥadīth* science, examinations of

[76] *Ṭabaqāt al-ṣūfiyah*.
[77] See Hafsi, 23 (1976) for a complete list of these texts.
[78] There is reason to believe that Wāṣil ibn ʿAṭā' did not actually compose a biographical text. The text is not mentioned in any early bibliographic dictionary, nor is it mentioned in any later Muʿtazilī *ṭabaqāt* work.
[79] Makdisi. "*Ṭabaqāt*," 373.
[80] Cooperson, 1.
[81] Ibid., 1–2.
[82] Ibid., 2–3.
[83] Ibid., 5–6.

the chain of transmission became the most important avenue for evaluating the worth of *ḥadīth*. Scholars examined such variables as the general knowledge of each member in the chain, their reputations for truthfulness, histories of mental illness, and whether or not it would have been physically possible for each link in the chain to have met and passed on the tradition.

Cooperson's chief insight into the genre is the idea that biography becomes central to Islamic historical literature because the notion of descent (here metaphorical, not literal) from the Prophet Muḥammad becomes one of the most important concepts in Islamic intellectual thought. As specialization in religious professions becomes more distinct (by the 2nd/8th century) so does the need to map out the chains through which the Prophet's knowledge was communicated to different professional groups.[84] The idea that different professional groups are heirs to specific kinds of knowledge particular to that group lies at the heart of the biographical genre.[85]

The idea that specialized disciplines of knowledge originate with the Prophet Muḥammad is based on a *ḥadīth* which states that "scholars are heirs to the prophets."[86] Over time, as various disciplines of specialized knowledge formed (law, theology, grammar, lexicography, medicine, even poetry) their practitioners began to assert that their authority originated with knowledge passed on to them from the Prophet.[87] As specialization in religious professions became more distinct (by the 2nd/8th century) so did the need to map out the chains through which the Prophet's knowledge was communicated to different professional groups.[88]

According to George Makdisi, as religious vocations became more professionalized, *ṭabaqāt* works, which had been concerned with authority, began to focus on outlining 'orthodoxies' within each religious

[84] Ibid., 7–8.
[85] Ibid., 13–14.
[86] Al-Khaṭib al-Baghdādī, *Kitāb al-faqīh wa 'l-mutafaqqih*, vol. 1 (Beirut: Dār al-kutub al-ʿilmīyah, 1980), 17; for a discussion of the various arguments for juridical authority, see Devin Stewart, *Islamic Legal Orthodoxy: Twelver Shiite Responses to the Sunni Legal System* (Salt Lake City: University of Utah Press, 1998), 215. For an excellent discussion on the importance of descent in medieval Muslim culture, see Roy Mottahedeh, *Loyalty and Leadership in an Early Islamic Society* (New York: I. B. Tauris, 2001), 98–104.
[87] Stewart, *Islamic Legal Orthodoxy*, 215.
[88] Cooperson, 7–8.

profession.[89] While biographical histories such as *Tārīkh baghdād* by al-Khaṭīb al-Baghdādī (463/1071)[90] may contain biographies of jurists and other members of professional groups, *ṭabaqāt* works are specifically dedicated to listing only those whose opinions can be considered authoritative in the formation of orthodoxy, regardless of the field of specialization.[91] Makdisi goes on to argue that because *ṭabaqāt* texts are central in delimiting the boundaries of permissible opinion, they mark off the peripheries of different professional schools of thought. This, he argues, is particularly important for understanding the history of Islamic legal institutions.[92] *Ṭabaqāt* works, therefore, not only demarcate the boundaries of permissible opinion; they can also tell us something about the internal debates and struggles of legal schools.

Ṭabaqāt *and the crisis of authority during the Mamlūk period*

By the Mamlūk period, because of the crises that shook the Muslim community in the Middle East, the *ṭabaqāt* genre became a manifestation of the crisis of religious authority. Because it had previously been used to map the contours of authoritative knowledge in each of the religious sciences, *ṭabaqāt* texts became the locus of intellectual debates over how the crisis of authority had arisen and the kinds of curatives that were needed to repair the situation.

The use of the *ṭabaqāt* genre as a vehicle for debating the crisis of authority during the Mamlūk period is demonstrated by the explosion in the production of texts beginning in the 7th/14th centuries. As figure 1.1 demonstrates, the number of *ṭabaqāt* works produced declines steadily after the initial formation of the genre in the 3rd/9th century. This decline continues until the period following the Mongol invasion in the mid 7th/13th century. In the 8th/14th and 9th/15th centuries the production of the genre increases, doubling the total number of texts produced just two centuries earlier, before steadily declining once again in the 10th/16th century.

---

89 George Makdisi, "*Ṭabaqāt*," 372–73.

90 Al-Khaṭīb al-Baghdādī, *Tārīkh baghdād aw madīnat al-salām*, 16 vols., ed. (Beirut: Dār al-kutub al-ʿilmīyah, n.d.).

91 Makdisi, "*Ṭabaqāt*," 373.

92 Ibid., 379–82.

Figure 1.1. Total number of *ṭabaqāt* texts produced by century

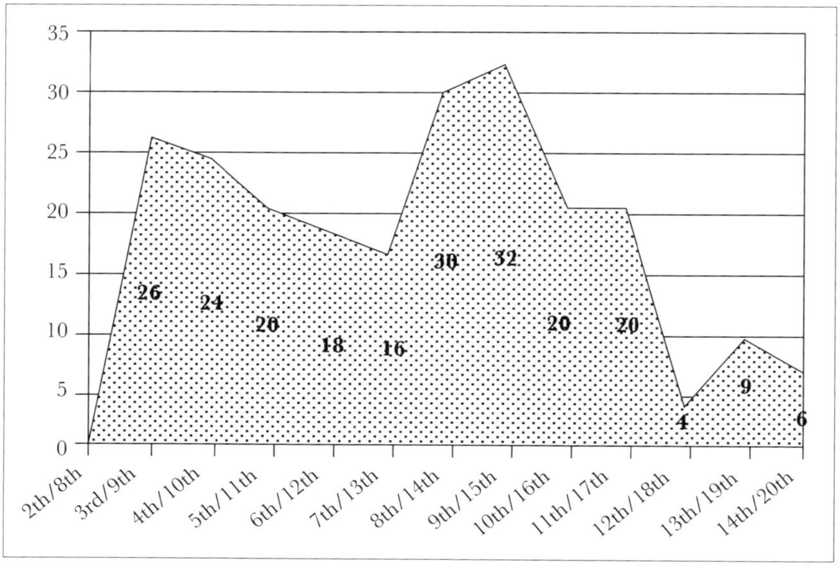

Source: Data from Ibrahim Hafsi, "Recherches sur le genre *Tabaqat* dans la littérature arabe," *Arabica* 23 (September 1976): 227–65; 24 (February 1977): 1–41; 24 (June 1977): 150–86.

Besides the Mongol destruction of the ʿAbbāsid Empire in 1258, the Middle East was subjected to the outbreak of the plague in 749/1348, which reoccurred every 10–12 years until 1516.[93] The plague was extremely traumatic for Muslims living in Egypt and Syria. While the sometimes fantastic death tolls listed by medieval Muslim historians, ranging into the hundreds of thousands, have been discredited by medieval and modern researchers,[94] they speak to the horror that the plagues caused. Additionally, the region continued to be invaded from the east and the north until finally being conquered

---

[93] See Lawrence I. Conrad, "*Ṭāʿūn* and *Wabāʾ*: Conceptions of Plague and Pestilence in Early Islam," *Journal of the Economic and Social History of the Orient* 15, pt. 3 (1982): 268–307 and his "Arabic Plague Chronologies and Treatises: Social and Historical Factors in the Formation of a Literary Genre," *Studia Islamica*, no. 54 (1981): 51–93. Also see Michael Dols, "Plague in Early Islamic History," *Journal of the American Oriental Society* 94, no. 3 (1974): 371–83 and his *The Black Death in the Middle East* (Princeton: University Press, 1977) which remains the only detailed analysis of the plague in the region.

[94] Conrad, "Arabic Plague Chronologies," 65–66.

by the Ottomans in 1517. The invasions of Tīmūr (d. 1405)[95] and other Turko-Mongol states along with pressure from the Franks,[96] impressed upon the people of the Mamlūk period that the Muslim community was in serious danger.

Internally, the Mamlūk state was extremely chaotic. The first half of the era, known as the Baḥrī period, lasted from 1260 to 1382. Over the course of little more than a century, the Sulṭānate changed hands 24 times. The second half of the period was dominated by the violent rise of the Circassian Mamlūks who saw the Sulṭānate change 27 times between 1382 and 1517. With each change of Sulṭān there would follow purges of political authority at all levels of administration. By the middle of the 9th/15th century these purges became extremely violent with mass executions and mutilations as new leaders sought to consolidate their control.

The jurists were intimately involved in these political upheavals. Siding with different contenders to the throne, jurists frequently suffered punishments for falling in with defeated groups, losing wealth, and suffering torture and sometimes even death.[97] The crisis of authority lead jurists to think seriously about how their circumstances had changed so radically from a past that was, especially in comparison to present conditions, valorized as a golden period of enlightenment, security, and intellectual vitality. Legal *ṭabaqāt* works (those dedicated to the legal profession) become increasingly important sources for sorting out the roots of the declining fortunes of jurists and in mapping out chains of authority that were still considered valid given the perception that most jurists were no longer capable of interpreting the texts of revelation directly.

As figure 1.2 demonstrates, the crisis of authority was primarily expressed in legal *ṭabaqāt* and not in texts devoted to other religious disciplines. Figure 1.2 shows that there had been a steady increase in the number of legal *ṭabaqāt* works written since the 3rd/9th century, even as non-legal *ṭabaqāt* texts declined in production. The

---

[95] See Beatrice Forbes Manz, *The Rise and Rule of Tamerlane* (Cambridge: University Press, 1989).

[96] Norman Housley, *The Later Crusades 1274–1580: From Lyons to Alcazar* (New York: Oxford University Press, 1992), 178–203.

[97] See for instance, Ibn Taghrī Birdī, *al-Nujūm*, vol. 5, 533–34; Ibn Ṭūlūn, *Quḍāt dimashq*, 119; Ibn Qāḍī Shuhbah, *Tārīkh*, ed. ʿAdnān Darwīsh (Damascus: Institut Français de Damas, 1997), vol. 1, 391–92.

Figure 1.2. The production of legal *ṭabaqāt* compared to other genres of knowledge

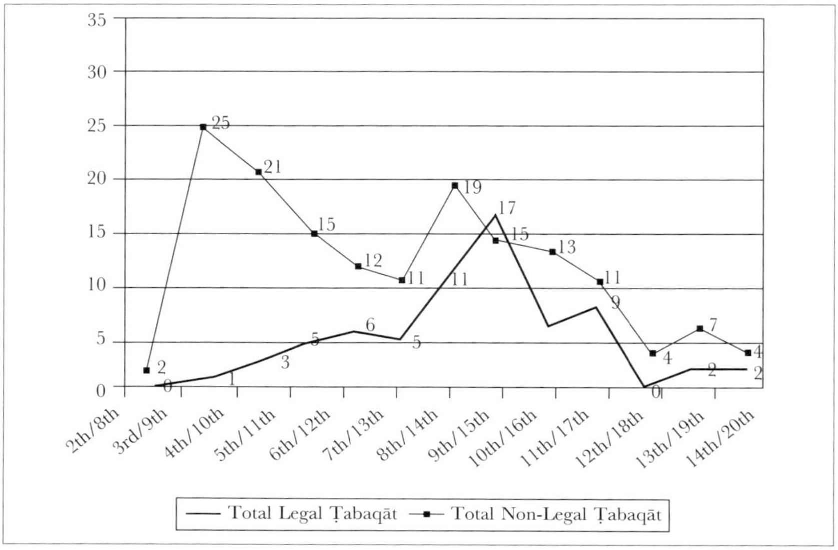

Source: Data from Ibrahim Hafsi, "Recherches sur le genre *Tabaqat* dans la littérature arabe," *Arabica* 23 (September 1976): 227–65; 24 (February 1977): 1–41; 24 (June 1977): 150–86.

increase, however, was slow until the 7th/13th and 8th/14th centuries. While there was an initial jump in the production of all texts in the century following the Mongol invasion and during the formation of the Mamlūk Sulṭānate and the outbreak of the plague, the production of non-legal *ṭabaqāt* began to decline after this, while the production of legal texts continued to increase for the next century. Figure 1.2 indicates that there may have been a widespread sense of crisis across most of the religious disciplines in the early Mamlūk period, but that there was a prolonged sense of crisis in the legal profession.

But was the sense of crisis spread across the entire legal profession or was it restricted to certain schools? The Mālikīs and the Ḥanbalīs seem to have been largely unaffected by crises of the Mamlūk period. Mālikī production never rises above one text in any century and the Ḥanbalīs never produce more than two.[98] Both the

[98] Hafsi, "Recherches sur le genre Tabaqat," 24 (February 1977): 1–41.

Figure 1.3. The production of *ṭabaqāt* texts for the Ḥanafī and Shāfiʿī schools of law

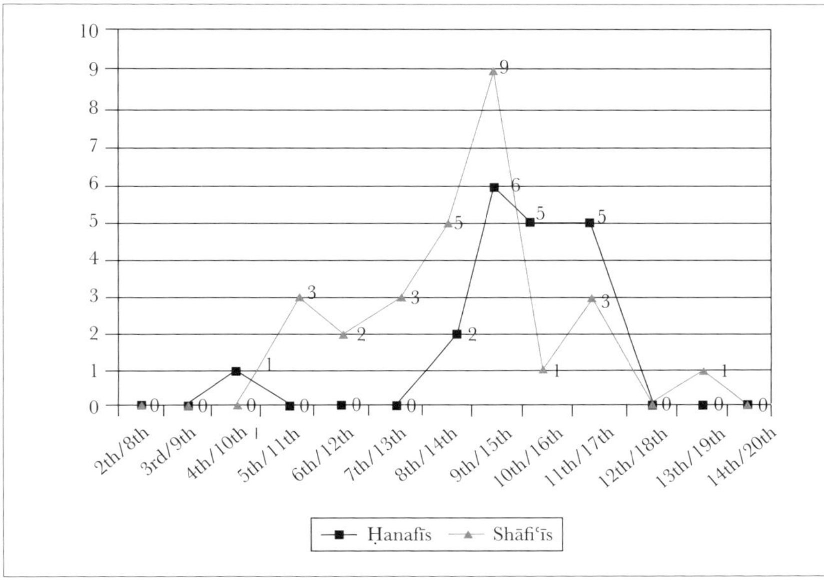

Source: Data from Ibrahim Hafsi, "Recherches sur le genre *Tabaqat* dans la littérature arabe," *Arabica* 23 (September 1976): 227–65; 24 (February 1977): 1–41; 24 (June 1977): 150–86.

Mālikīs and the Ḥanbalīs were marginal in the Mamlūk state, neither having much influence with the officials at court or the public at large.[99]

As figure 1.3 shows, the situation was much different for the Shāfiʿīs and the Ḥanafīs. The Shāfiʿīs were the dominant school under the Mamlūks with but few exceptions, as when the Ḥanafīs held greater influence at court during the brief reign of al-Mālik al-Ẓāhir Ṭaṭar (d. 824/1421).[100] Because of the role that the Shāfiʿīs and the Ḥanafīs

[99] See Joseph Escovitz, "The Establishment of the Four Chief Judgeships in the Mamlūk Empire," *Journal of the American Oriental Society* 102, no. 3 (July-October, 1982): 529–32 and his *The Office of Qāḍī al-Quḍāt in Cairo under the Baḥrī Mamlūks* (Berlin: Klaus Schwarz Verlag, 1984); A. Allouche, "The Establishment of the Four Chief Judgeships in Fatimid Egypt," *Journal of the American Oriental Society* 105 (1985): 317–20; and Sherman Jackson, "The Primacy of Domestic Politics: Ibn Bint al-Aazz and the Establishment of Four Chief Judgeships in Mamluk Egypt," *Journal of the American Oriental Society* 115, no. 1 (January–March, 1995): 52–65.

[100] Ibn Taghrī Birdī, *al-Nujūm*, vol. 6, 517.

played in Mamlūk society was much greater they also bore the heavier burden when the crises struck and the challenges to their authority were thus more pronounced. It is also important to note that the majority of *ṭabaqāt* were produced in the Circassian Mamlūk period when the greatest number of challenges to Muslim society occurred and the need to sort out the crisis of authority was the greatest.

Ṭabaqāt al-fuqahā' al-shāfiʿīyah *and the crises of the Circassian period*

This book will examine *Ṭabaqāt al-fuqahā' al-shāfiʿīyah* (The Generations of the Shāfiʿī Jurists) written by Abū Bakr b. Aḥmad Ibn Qāḍī Shuhbah (d. 851/1448), a text written during the worst of the Circassian Mamlūk period, and will test the thesis that *ṭabaqāt* works were used to sort out the causes for the declines of the Muslim community during the Mamlūk era.[101] Ibn Qāḍī Shuhbah's *Ṭabaqāt* contains the biographies of 784 jurists laid out chronologically, beginning with the students (*ṣāḥib* pl. *aṣḥāb*) of Imām Muḥammad b. Idrīs al-Shāfiʿī (d. 204/820), the eponym of his school, and continuing down 29 generations to 840/1436, or to Ibn Qāḍī Shuhbah's own time. Ibn Qāḍī Shuhbah was one of the most important jurists of his day and was trained not only in law but also in history. It is argued that Ibn Qāḍī Shuhbah wrote his *Ṭabaqāt* out of his concern for the decline of legal training among Shāfiʿī jurists. Working within the theoretical framework of the hierarchy of legal authorities outlined by al-Nawawī in his *al-Majmūʿ fī sharḥ al-mudhahhab*, Ibn Qāḍī Shuhbah sought to demonstrate that while *ijtihād* continued on a limited basis, the majority of jurists had simply become memorizers of substantive rules handed down from earlier times. This is not to say that he was troubled by this state of affairs; to the contrary, he sees this as the natural consequence of the political, economic, and environmental decay of the late ʿAbbāsid and Mamlūk periods.

The original title of this book, *He Died in Prison and in Chains*, was a quotation from Ibn Qāḍī Shuhbah's text which refers to the death of Abū Yaʿqūb al-Buwayṭī (d. 231/846). Al-Buwayṭī, al-Shāfiʿī's clos-

[101] There have been three published editions of the *Ṭabaqāt al-fuqahā' al-shāfiʿīyah*: the ʿAlī Muḥammad ʿUmar edition [2 vols. (Cairo: Maktabat al-thaqāfah al-dīnīyah, 1993–98)]; and two editions produced by al-Ḥāfiẓ ʿAbd al-ʿAlī Khān [4 vols. (Hyderabad: Dā'irat al-maʿārif al-ʿuthmānīyah, 1978–80) and 4 vols. (Beirut: ʿĀlam al-kutub, 1987). The following analysis is based on the Khān 1987 edition and will be referred to in the notes as "Khān."

est disciple and transmitter, is presented as dying prematurely due to the inquisition (*Mihna* c. 833–850) which attempted to force on the Muslim community a single theological conception of revelation. Because of al-Buwayṭī's death at the hands of the government, Ibn Qāḍī Shuhbah argues that two sub-schools of thought emerged in Shāfiʿī jurisprudence: one devoted to the faithful transmission of al-Shāfiʿī's original ideas and methodologies and another that sought to expand the limits of acceptable opinion through the use of widely divergent ideas. Over time, according to Ibn Qāḍī Shuhbah, these opinions become catalogued in two massive commentaries written by Abū al-Qāsim al-Rāfiʿī (d. 623/1226), and al-Nawawī, which, he argues, reach the highest level of authority because they transmit the widely ranging opinions of the masters of the Shāfiʿī school. The authoritative authors of divergent opinion therefore provide a protective barrier for the *madhhab* by guarding it from the insertion of legal rulings by less qualified jurists. In addition, and perhaps more importantly, these texts show jurists secondary approaches to legal reasoning that permitted them to continue discovering new legal rules without having to make recourse to *ijtihād* so that the law did not become static after the decline of legal capabilities.

Overview of the study

Ultimately, the purpose of the *Ṭabaqāt* is to demonstrate to Shāfiʿī jurists who believed they were living in a time of eschatological crisis, not only who the holders of diverging opinions were, but also what kinds of opinions they held and how they thought about the law. As is discussed throughout this book, Ibn Qāḍī Shuhbah sought to describe the causes of legal decline and curatives that jurists could turn to in times of crisis. It was meant by its author to be a textbook for jurists to use as a companion to the great *ikhtilāf* texts of the time; to fulfill the directive issued by al-Nawawī 200 years earlier.

Chapter one looks at the life of Ibn Qāḍī Shuhbah and the events that shaped his life and worldview. In particular, the chapter examines the events surrounding the publication of the text and gives an overview of the major themes he seeks to develop in his work. It then looks at his rise as a judge and the publication of the final three editions of the *Ṭabaqāt* before closing with a description of his final years and death.

Chapter two looks at how Ibn Qāḍī Shuhbah utilizes his source material and the extent to which authors of *ṭabaqāt* texts had control over the composition of their biographies. It has been argued that biographical writers merely regurgitated source material and that they had little ability to manipulate their texts to make specific arguments about history or religious authority. The chapter demonstrates that while authors were bound closely to their source material, the biographical traditions that developed around many historical figures were extremely diverse, and that authors such as Ibn Qāḍī Shuhbah had extensive control over what they used and how they combined and manipulated information.

Chapter three explores various rhetorical strategies that *ṭabaqāt* authors use to create histories of Islamic intellectual traditions. It focuses of the use of assorted forms of allusion, causation, hypertextual referencing, and forms of paronomasia. It then looks at how Ibn Qāḍī Shuhbah uses these micro-textual rhetorical strategies to prefigure the major themes of his text: the importance of sudden death on the creation of new historical trends and the centrality of *ikhtilāf* in the formation of Islamic law.

Chapter four focuses on analytical techniques useful in understanding both the rhetoric of *ṭabaqāt* works and how they depict trends in the development of Islamic legal history. These techniques will examine how terms for the acquisition of knowledge are ranked and classified, repeated, and progressively developed over the course of the text, exposing trends in the rise and fall of various classes of educative associations (*akhadha, ishtaghala/ashghala, ḥaṣṣala, baḥatha, takharraja, darasa/darrasa*, and *tafaqqaha*). The chapter then compares Ibn Qāḍī Shuhbah's depiction of education to theories presented by such scholars as George Makdisi, J. Gilbert, Jonathan Berkey, and Michael Chamberlain. It argues that Ibn Qāḍī Shuhbah presents a picture of medieval Islamic learning that emphasizes both institutional styles of education (the *madrasah*) typified by references to *darasa/darrasa, ishtaghala/ashghala*, and *takharraja*, and highly personal modes of learning exemplified by *akhadha*. Ibn Qāḍī Shuhbah, however, presents *tafaqqaha* as the preferred mode of acquiring knowledge of law and argues that because of its decline, the abilities of legal scholars to produce new rules declines as well.

Chapter five examines Ibn Qāḍī Shuhbah's description of the transmission of various genres of religious knowledge (*ʿilm*, plural *ʿulūm*) and compares his depiction of the historical development of legal authority to modern debates concerning the decline of *ijtihād*. It argues that he was largely unconcerned with the kinds of issues that so interest modern scholars: whether the gate of *ijtihād* closed. Instead, he is interested in the development of levels of juridical authority and especially of the ability of low and middle level 'affiliated' jurists to discover new rules in the texts of revelation. He describes a process whereby legal abilities decline, but one in which high level *mujtahid*s continue to exist to answer questions of special need. For Ibn Qāḍī Shuhbah, low and middle level jurists are the ones most responsible for maintaining the law, and their decline prompts the rise of a class of memorizers of legal dicta that do not have the ability to carry-out basic legal functions, thus threatening the existence of the community and precipitating the crises of the period.

Chapter six examines the role of *uṣūl al-fiqh* and allied sciences in the development of Islamic law. It challenges the idea that the ability to discover new rules in the texts of revelation was tied to expertise in speculative legal methodologies. Instead, it argues that, according to Ibn Qāḍī Shuhbah, basic methods of legal discovery, derived from the method of al-Shāfiʿī, are the only tools necessary to produce law. Ibn Qāḍī Shuhbah argues, through the progressive development of his text, that knowledge of basic legal method was communicated through *tafaqqaha* educational relationships to the exclusion of other forms of learning, and with its decline the ability of low and middle level jurists to discover law was seriously challenged. He also argues that as the legal profession became more specialized, jurists were attracted to speculative legal methodologies and other kinds of 'expedient' sciences that had little to do with the discovery of law. With the Mongol invasion in the thirteenth century and the outbreak of the plague in the fourteenth, the ranks of jurists were so severely devastated that there were few scholars left who could use the basic methods necessary for the day-to-day functioning of the law.

Ibn Qāḍī Shuhbah's text is not just a description of the development and decline of Islamic law; it also seeks to point contemporary and future jurists toward curatives for the collapse of legal ability among low and middle level jurists. He mentions 2058 texts over the course of his work, but describes 32 as being especially important for the continuing maintenance of the school. Eight texts represent the core doctrine (*madhhab*) of the school, thirteen refer to the central sources of divergent opinion, and the remaining eleven are sources that Ibn Qāḍī Shuhbah considers to be the most authoritative in disciplines such as *uṣūl al-fiqh*, grammar, lexicography, and history. Chapter seven examines these texts and the kinds of authority they impart on those who use them. It also explores the kinds of basic legal methods that the doctrinal and divergent opinions texts present for low and middle level jurists.

The final chapter returns to the context in which Ibn Qāḍī Shuhbah wrote his text. It argues that he was not only concerned with depicting the rise of law, the crises that were interwoven with its decline, and the texts that could point a way out of the morass, but that he was also interested to using the text as an intellectual autobiography that would legitimize his claim on the leadership of the Shāfiʿī school. Ibn Qāḍī Shuhbah produced four editions of the text, each written in the context of his rise to the position of chief Shāfiʿī judge of Damascus. One of the purposes of the text was to give him an intellectual lineage to establish his place in the highest levels of Shāfiʿī legal authority and thus mark him as a leader of the school who was uniquely qualified to guide it through the troubled waters of the Mamlūk period.

CHAPTER ONE

A BRIEF BIOGRAPHY OF IBN QĀḌĪ SHUHBAH

Early life and family

Taqī al-Dīn Abū Bakr b. Aḥmad b. Muḥammad b. ʿUmar b. Muḥammad b. ʿAbd al-Wahhāb b. Muḥammad b. Dhu'ayb b. al-Asadī al-Shuhbī al-Dimashqī al-Shāfiʿī, better known by his family name, Ibn Qāḍī Shuhbah, was born on I Rabīʿ 14, 779 (July 22, 1377) in Damascus.[1] His family was a well known, though largely minor member of the elite households of the city. His grandfather Muḥammad b. ʿUmar (d. 782/1380) had been a leading legal scholar and educator in Damascus for most of the 8th/14th century, teaching at a number of colleges and initiating many people into the ranks of the *ʿulamāʾ*. He was particularly well known as a scholar of *ḥadīth* and grammar, writing a number of books on those subjects, and on the law.[2] Besides his grandfather, the most famous person in the family was his great-uncle ʿAbd al-Wahhāb b. Muḥammad (d. 726/1326). ʿAbd al-Wahhāb was an important scholar of Arabic, grammar, and lexicography and appears to have been a well known teacher who produced a large number of students.[3]

Ibn Qāḍī Shuhbah's uncle, Yūsuf b. Muḥammad (d. 789/1388), studied law from his father Muḥammad and other scholars in Damascus and taught at several legal schools. He appears not to have been well known outside Syria and is not mentioned by al-Maqrīzī or other authors from the period.[4]

Ibn Qāḍī Shuhbah's father Aḥmad b. Muḥammad (d. 790/1388), studied alongside his brother Yūsuf with their father Muḥammad and other jurists of the age. He taught at the Umayyad Mosque and a number of colleges, and was a specialist in inheritance law, on

[1] Shams al-Dīn Muḥammad b. ʿAbd al-Raḥmān al-Sakhāwī, *al-Ḍawʾ al-lāmiʿ li-ahl al-qarn al-tāsīʿ* (Beirut: Manshūrāt dār maktabat al-ḥayāh, 1966), vol. 11, 21.

[2] Khān, vol. 3, 173. Also see his death notice in al-Maqrīzī, *al-Sulūk*, vol. 3, 407.

[3] Khān, vol. 2, 267. Also see Ibn Taghrī Birdī, *al-Manhal al-Ṣāfī wa 'l-mustawfī baʿad al-wāfī*, ed. Saʿīd ʿAbd al-Fattāh ʿĀshūr (Cairo: n.p., 1984), vol. 2, 263.

[4] Khān, vol. 3, 183.

which he wrote several books. He was also given a permission to issue legal opinions by his father Muḥammad b. ʿUmar.[5] Ibn Qāḍī Shuhbah's father died when he was just eleven years old and he appears to have been reared by his father's friend Shihāb al-Dīn Ibn Ḥijjī (d. 816/1413). Ibn Ḥijjī was a jurist of some note and served as a deputy judge of Damascus and chief preacher of the Umayyad Mosque on several occasions.[6] Ibn Ḥijjī was, however, primarily an historian whom Ibn Qāḍī Shuhbah describes as being a disciple (*tilmīdh*) of Ibn Kathīr.[7]

The relationship between Ibn Ḥijjī and Ibn Qāḍī Shuhbah was quite close. In passages that mention him, Ibn Qāḍī Shuhbah always speaks in the first person, indicating that he was present with Shihāb al-Dīn when various events took place. They were so close that in 803/1401, when Damascus was sacked and burned by Tīmūr, Ibn Qāḍī Shuhbah fled the city with Shihāb al-Dīn to Jerusalem.[8] He also seems to have been close to Najm al-Dīn Ibn Ḥijjī (d. 830/1427), Shihāb al-Dīn's brother. When Najm al-Dīn was appointed chief Shāfiʿī judge of Damascus in 820/1417, Ibn Qāḍī Shuhbah served as his deputy,[9] a position he held under Najm al-Dīn several times.[10] Ibn Qāḍī Shuhbah may have even followed his mentor to Cairo when Najm al-Dīn served as confidential secretary to the Sulṭān in 827/1424.[11]

Education and life as a scholar

Ibn Qāḍī Shuhbah also studied with a long list of scholars including ʿUmar b. Muslim al-Qurashī (d. 793/1391), who was tortured and killed by Sulṭān Barqūq (d. 801/1399) after the jurist sided with rebels who had seized Damascus in 792/1390.[12] Additionally, Ibn Qāḍī Shuhbah studied under Muḥammad b. Sulaymān Shams al-Dīn

[5] Khān, vol. 3, 148.
[6] Ibn Ṭūlūn, *Quḍāt dimashq*, 127; al-ʿAsqalānī, *Inbāʾ al-ghumr*, vol. 6, 65.
[7] Khān, vol. 3, 56, 86.
[8] Ibn Qāḍī Shuhbah, *Tārīkh*, vol. 4, 161–62.
[9] Ibn Ṭūlūn, *Quḍāt dimashq*, 133, 151.
[10] Ibid., 128–29.
[11] Ibid., 139; Ibn Taghrī Birdī, *al-Nujūm*, vol. 6, 577–78.
[12] Ibn Taghrī Birdī, *al-Nujūm*, vol. 5, 533–34; Ibn Qāḍī Shuhbah, *Tārīkh*, vol. 1, 391–92.

Abū ʿAbdallāh al-Ṣarkhadī (d. 792/1390), Aḥmad b. Ṣāliḥ b. Aḥmad b. Khaṭṭāb b. Marḥam al-Zuhrī (d. 795/1392), Maḥmūd b. Muḥammad b. Aḥmad b. Muḥammad b. Aḥmad al-Sharīshī (d. 795/1393), Muḥammad b. Aḥmad b. ʿĪsā b. ʿAsākīr b. Saʿd al-Suwadī, better known as Ibn Maktūm (d. 797/1395), ʿĪsā b. ʿUthmān b. ʿĪsā Sharaf al-Dīn Abū al-Rawḥ al-Ghazzī (d. 799/1397), ʿAbd al-Raḥmān b. Muḥammad b. Aḥmad al-Dhahabī, better known as Abū Hurayrah (d. 799/1397), Aḥmad b. Rāshid b. Ṭurkhān Shihāb al-Dīn Abū al-ʿAbbās al-Malkāwī (d. 803/1401), ʿUmar b. Raslān al-Bulqīnī (d. 805/1403), and Jamāl al-Dīn ʿAbdallāh b. Muḥammad al-Ṭaymānī (d. 815/1412).[13]

Ibn Qāḍī Shuhbah's own authority as a historian of law was built on intensive study in both areas. His work would not have been considered as important by later scholars had he not been able to claim knowledge and an intellectual lineage that linked him with the great historians and legal scholars of the past. One scholar who was tremendously influential in establishing his chain of transmission from the great historians of the previous century was ʿAbd al-Raḥmān b. Muḥammad b. Aḥmad al-Dhahabī, better known as Abū Hurayrah, the grandson of al-Dhahabī the famous biographer.[14] Abū Hurayrah was a specialist in *ḥadīth* and it is likely that Ibn Qāḍī Shuhbah heard traditions and historical information from him. Besides Shihāb al-Dīn Ibn Ḥijjī, al-Dhahabī is one of the most commonly cited sources of information used by Ibn Qāḍī Shuhbah in his *Ṭabaqāt*.

Throughout his *Ṭabaqāt* and other historical writings, Ibn Qāḍī Shuhbah most usually introduces the information cited in his text with the expression "so and so said" instead of using the formula "so and so said in his book," even though the material originated centuries earlier. In each instance where he uses the former expression he can be demonstrated to have a direct link through a chain of transmission to the individual who originally produced the information. Although it is unlikely that the specific material presented was actually transmitted orally to him, Ibn Qāḍī Shuhbah uses the authority gained by the personal link to the original author to establish his own legitimacy as a historian by saying "so and so said," implying rhetorically that the originating author said it directly to

[13] Al-Sakhāwī, *al-Ḍawʾ al-lāmiʿ*, vol. 11, 26.
[14] Ibid., vol. 4, 45; vol. 11, 21.

him. The importance of the attribution has nothing to do with modern historiographical concerns with first-person documentation versus second-hand and third-hand material. Instead, the use of the more interactive expression originates in the culture of medieval Muslim learning that placed a premium on the 'living word' and discouraged education through a 'dead' text.[15]

As is discussed in the following two chapters, medieval Muslim learning took many forms. One of the most important was referred to as *qaraʾa* (reading out loud). In medieval Muslim education there was an "interplay between orality and literacy."[16] Learning through the recitation of texts was highly ritualized and was used in some instances by the intellectual elites to initiate people into their ranks.[17] The ideology of auditory reading was drawn from *ḥadīth* transmission where one sought to "establish a tangible link between the auditor and the Prophet."[18] But the purpose was greater than simply creating a line of transmission that placed the individual in intellectual proximity to the originating source. It also had to do with experiencing the mystical presence of the source by recreating the existence, and in some ways the charisma and spiritual subsistence, of the original speaker.

One of the important mystical purposes of the oral transmission of *ḥadīth* was the reception of spiritual blessings (*barakāt* sing. *barakah*) that were thought to originate with the Prophet and were then communicated from individual to individual over time. *Barakāt* emanate from the presence of God and adhere to individuals and objects. The blessings can then 'rub off' onto other people or objects and are thus passed from person to person through contact that can be physical or aural. In North African Ṣūfī groups, the reception of spiritual blessing creates a "*barakah* status" that can be gained even by women who are barred from formal ceremonies and who only hear the recitation of texts through walls.[19] The creation of *barakah* status, however, goes beyond the mere transmission of blessings. It

---

[15] See Robinson, *Islamic Historiography*, 171.
[16] Ibid., 174.
[17] Chamberlain, *Knowledge and Social Practice in Medieval Damascus*, 133–51.
[18] Ibid., 139; also see Eerik Dickinson, "Ibn al-Ṣalāḥ al-Shahrazūrī and the Isnād," *Journal of the American Oriental Society* 122 (2002): 481–505; and William A. Graham, "Traditionalism in Islam," *Journal of Inter-disciplinary History* 23 (1992–93): 495–522.
[19] Richard J. A. McGregor, "A Sufi Legacy in Tunis: Prayer and the Shadhiliyya," *International Journal of Middle Eastern Studies* 29 (1997): 260.

also is thought to create the presence of the individuals from whom the blessings are received and to give authority to those who obtain their teachings.[20]

By stating that "so and so said," Ibn Qāḍī Shuhbah is claiming the authority of the original speaker which could only be attained through study with someone in the chain of transmission. It is more than a simple argument of location; it is also a claim to the personal presence of the original speaker through his words. As is discussed below, Ibn Qāḍī Shuhbah did not 'write' his texts, but recited them to scribes and students who wrote down the oral transmission of the material so that they could then read the texts out-loud and thus recreate the presence of the speaker. Each recitation of the text regenerated the spiritual and intellectual substance of the person and functioned to convey a form of *barakah* that stuck to the hearers of the text. Having a personal link to the original speaker was the only way of recreating the presence of the author, and having the grandson of al-Dhahabī as a source, who had actually heard the words of the author, was an important and intimate conduit of his intellectual and spiritual essence.

Beside his relationships to Shihāb al-Dīn Ibn Ḥijjī and Abū Hurayrah, Ibn Qāḍī Shuhbah was quite well connected to Ibn Kathīr and al-Dhahabī through his own family. Both historians studied with Ibn Qāḍī Shuhbah's great-uncle ʿAbd al-Wahhāb;[21] and his grandfather, ʿUmar b. Muḥammad Ibn Qāḍī Shuhbah, studied with Ibn Kathīr.[22] Thus his claim on the presence and authority of the great scholars was a powerful support to his legitimacy as a historian.

His reputation as a historian of Shāfiʿī law was also based on his work with those claiming intellectual descent from the great jurists of the past. His most important teacher in this regard was the great Egyptian jurist ʿUmar b. Raslān al-Bulqīnī (d. 805/1403).[23] Al-Sakhāwī states that Ibn Qāḍī Shuhbah studied the writings of al-Bulqīnī with al-Ṭaymānī[24] but Jamāl al-Dīn al-Suyūṭī claims that he studied (*tafaqqaha*) directly with the Egyptian scholar.[25] Ibn Qāḍī Shuhbah describes al-Bulqīnī as

---

[20] Ibid., 261.
[21] Khān, vol. 3, 85.
[22] Ibid., 174.
[23] Ibid., 148.
[24] Al-Sakhāwī, *al-Ḍawʾ al-lāmiʿ*, vol. 11, 26.
[25] Jamāl al-Dīn al-Suyūṭī, *Naẓm al-ʿiqyān fī aʿyān al-aʿyān*, ed. Phillip K. Hitti (New York: Syrian-American Press, 1927), 94.

> a leader of the jurists and of the traditionists, of the memorizers [of *ḥadīth*] and commentators on the Qur'an, of the *uṣūlīs* (specialists in legal methodology), the *mutakallims* (theologians), of the grammarians, the lexicographers, the logicians, the rhetoricians. He was an expert on divergent opinions and a skillful debater. He was the master of Islam, the remainder (*baqīyah*) of the *mujtahidīn*. He was peerless (*munqaṭiʿ al-qarīn*), unique, [and] a wonder of the time (*uʿjūbat al-zamān*).[26]

Al-Bulqīnī died when Ibn Qāḍī Shuhbah was in his early twenties and he continued to study his work under the assistance of al-Ṭaymānī, who was his disciple.

As Ibn Qāḍī Shuhbah rose as a legal authority his experiences studying the writings of al-Bulqīnī, as well as his work with his other teachers, would have become an important source of legitimacy as a scholar.[27] By the time al-Ṭaymānī was killed during the civil war of 815/1412, Ibn Qāḍī Shuhbah had begun teaching at a number of legal colleges, including the Surūrīyah, Amjadīyah, Mujāhidīyah, al-Ẓāhirīyah, Nāṣirīyah, ʿAdhrāwīyah, and Ruknīyah *madrasahs*, and he became a deputy headmaster (*nāʾib fī tadrīs*) at the Shāmīyah al-Barrānīyah and the Shāmīyah al-Jūwānīyah schools.[28] By 820/1417 Ibn Qāḍī Shuhbah began teaching at the Umayyad Mosque and continued to teach there periodically until his death.[29] In these schools he taught law and sometimes grammar and he amassed a large and important following of students, not just in the Shāfiʿī school, but also in the Ḥanafī and Ḥanbalī *madhhab*s as well.[30]

Outside the context of the legal college it appears that he also had a large number of students whom he initiated into the ranks of the *ʿulamāʾ* through informal *akhadha* education.[31] These included: Aḥmad al-ʿAwfī al-Ḥuwwārī al-Dimashqī al-Shāfiʿī (d. 889/1484),

---

[26] Khān, vol. 4, 36.

[27] See Devin Stewart, "Capital, Accumulation, and the Islamic Academic Biography," 356–60.

[28] Al-Sakhāwī, *al-Ḍawʾ al-lāmiʿ*, vol. 11, 22.

[29] Ibn Ṭūlūn, *Quḍāt dimashq*, 168. Also see ʿAbd al-Qādir b. Muḥammad al-Nuʿaymī, *al-Dāris fī tārīkh al-madāris* (n.p.: Maktabat al-thaqāfah al-dīnīyah, 1988), vol. 1, 263, 308, 394, 405.

[30] Ibn Ṭūlūn, *Mutʿat al-adhhān min al-tamattuʿ bi ʾl-iqrān bayna tarājim al-shuyūkh wa ʾl-aqrān* (Beirut: Dār Ṣādir, 1999), vol. 1, 267; vol. 2, 614, 748; al-Sakhāwī, *al-Ḍawʾ al-lāmiʿ*, vol. 10, 39–40; al-Nuʿaymī, *al-Dāris fī tārīkh al-madāris*, vol. 2, 59; 105.

[31] See the next chapter on how *akhadha* is characteristic of a specific kind of educational relationship. For an analysis of some of the social functions of knowledge see Michael Chamberlain, *Knowledge and Social Practice in Medieval Damascus*.

who studied closely with him;[32] Aḥmad b. Muḥammad b. Jabrīl al-Amawī al-Ḥārī al-Dimashqī al-Shāfiʿī (d. 896/1491);[33] Aḥmad b. ʿUmar b. ʿUthmān b. ʿAlī al-Shihān (?) al-Khwārzimī al-Dimashqī al-Shāfiʿī, better known as Ibn Qarāʾ;[34] Ibrāhīm al-Rabbāṭ al-Biqāʿī al-Maqdisī al-Miṣrī al-Dimashqī al-Shāfiʿī (d. 885/1480);[35] Ibrāhīm b. Mufliḥ al-Rāmīnī al-Ṣāliḥī al-Ḥanbalī (d. 884/1479); ʿAlī al-Baṣrawī al-Dimashqī al-ʿAkatī al-Shāfiʿī (d. 905/1500);[36] Muḥammad b. al-Khiḍr al-Dimashqī al-Ḥanbalī (d. 893/1488);[37] Muḥammad al-Balbīsī al-Maqdisī al-Shāfiʿī (d. 888/1483);[38] Muḥammad ʿIzz al-Dīn b. al-Ḥamrāʾ al-Dimashqī al-Ḥanafī (d. 894/1489);[39] and Muḥammad b. Muḥammad b. ʿAbdallāh b. Abī Bakr al-Balāṭansī al-Shāfiʾī, (d. 898/1493).[40]

Because recitation was central to the acquisition of knowledge and authority, books were important to Ibn Qāḍī Shuhbah. In his *Ṭabaqāt*, he mentions over 2000 texts written over the history of the Shāfiʿī school, and his writings would have been an important aspect of Ibn Qāḍī Shuhbah's reputation as a scholar. Over the course of his adult life he composed over thirty texts. He wrote five works on law, including two commentaries on the *Tanbīh* by Abū Isḥāq al-Shīrāzī and two commentaries on the *Minhāj* by al-Nawawī,[41] both of which he came to see as a foundational texts of law; and a work on the *Muhimmāt* by al-Isnawī.[42] He also wrote a commentary on the Qurʾan.[43]

His most numerous compositions, however, were on history. He wrote twenty-four histories, seven of which were biographical histories (four being *ṭabaqāt*) and seventeen chronicles. Four of his chronicles were short works or continuations of *Tārīkh al-islām* by al-Dhahabī,[44]

---

[32] Ibn Ṭūlūn, *Mutʿat*, vol. 1, 47.
[33] Ibid., vol. 1, 147.
[34] Ibid., vol. 1, 189. Also see al-Sakhāwī, *al-Ḍawʾ al-lāmiʿ*, vol. 2, 54.
[35] Ibn Ṭūlūn, *Mutʿat*, vol. 2, 261.
[36] Ibid., vol. 1, 540.
[37] Ibid., vol. 2, 614.
[38] Ibid., vol. 2, 647.
[39] Ibid., vol. 2, 748; also see *al-Ḍawʾ al-lāmiʿ*, vol. 10, 39–40.
[40] Ibn Ṭūlūn, *Mutʿat*, vol. 2, 758.
[41] Kātip Çelebi, *Kashf al-ẓunūn ʿan asāmī al-kutub wa ʾl-funūn* (London: R. Bentley for the Oriental Translation Fund of Great Britain and Ireland, 1835–1858), 492.
[42] Ibid., 1914, which states that it is not a work on the text by al-Isnawī, but a commentary on the *Rawḍah* by al-Nawawī, the full title of which is *al-Muhimmāt ʿalā al-rawḍah fī al-furūʿ*. Al-Sakhāwī does not mention the work. Khān, the editor of the 1978 and 1987 editions of the *Ṭabaqāt*, states that it is a commentary on al-Isnawī's text [Khān (1987), vol. 1, 26].
[43] *Kashf al-ẓunūn*, 438.
[44] Brockelmann, G II, 51; S II, 50; Khān (1987), vol. 1, 27; al-Ziriklī, *al-Aʿlam:*

and a number of his chronicle-like texts were composed of *muntaqā* (selected passages) from other historical works that he may have planned to incorporate into his own writings at some point.[45] His most lasting contribution to chronicle writing was his *Tārīkh*, which may have been an extension of his *Dhayl* (continuation) of the history his teacher Shihāb al-Dīn Ibn Ḥijjī composed.[46] The *Tārīkh* written by Ibn Ḥijjī was, in turn, a continuation of the histories written by al-Dhahabī, Ibn Kathīr, and al-Birzālī (d. 739/1338).[47] Ibn Qāḍī Shuhbah's *Tārīkh* was extensively quoted by other Circassian- and early Ottoman-period historians such as Ibn Ṭūlūn (d. 953/1546), al-Sakhāwī (d. 902/1497, who studied with Ibn Qāḍī Shuhbah),[48] and al-Nuʿaymī (d. 927/1521). After Shihāb al-Dīn Ibn Ḥijjī died in 816/1413, Ibn Qāḍī Shuhbah took it upon himself to continue the work of his teacher. He did this by keeping a daily diary of current events and, little by little, he built up his history of the Circassian period. According to al-Sakhāwī, he continued to compose his diary until the moment of his death, on which he was working when the "pen fell from his hand."[49]

Unfortunately, his *Tārīkh* is no longer extant past the year 813/1407,[50] although Ibn Ṭūlūn and al-Nuʿaymī quote passages from it as late as the 840s. An important contribution to the study of Damascus in the Circassian period would be a reconstruction of the *Tārīkh* from references in other texts.[51] These passages, however, only refer to the activities of scholars and judges in Damascus and would therefore limit its impact to a fairly narrow historical understanding.

Ibn Qāḍī Shuhbah's biographical texts were also important to later Muslim scholars. His *Manāqib al-imām al-shāfiʿī* (*The Virtues of Imām al-Shāfiʿī*) included a brief biography of the eponymous founder

---

qāmūs tarājim li-ashhar al-rijāl wa 'l-nisā' min al-ʿarab wa 'l-mustaʿribīn (Beirut: Dār al-ʿilm li 'l-malāyīn, 1990), vol. 3, 35.

45 Khān (1987), vol. 1, 27–28.

46 Al-Ziriklī, vol. 3, 35; David C. Reisman, "A Holograph MS of Ibn Qāḍī Shuhbah's '*Dhayl*'," *Mamluk Studies Review* 2 (1998): 22; also see *Tārīkh ibn qāḍī shuhbah*. So far, only a small section of Ibn Ḥijjī's text has been published. See Shihāb al-Dīn Ibn Ḥijjī, *Tārīkh ibn ḥijjī*, ed. Abū Yaḥyā ʿAbdallāh al-Kazarī, 2 vols. (Beirut: Dār Ibn Ḥazm, 2003).

47 Reisman, "A Holograph MS of Ibn Qāḍī Shuhbah's '*Dhayl*'," 22.

48 Al-Sakhāwī, *al-Ḍaw' al-lāmiʿ*, vol. 11, 22.

49 Ibid., 24.

50 Reisman, "A Holograph MS of Ibn Qāḍī Shuhbah's '*Dhayl*'," 30, 44.

51 For the value of such work, see Claude Cahen, "Editing Arabic Chronicles: A Few Suggestions," 1–25.

of the Shāfiʿī school as well as biographies of notable Shāfiʿī scholars up to the year 597/1201.[52] As with several of his chronicles, the text is based entirely on the death notices found in al-Dhahabī's *Tārīkh al-islām*.[53] Additionally, he wrote four *ṭabaqāts*, one for the Ḥanafī school, which is no longer extant,[54] one on grammarians and lexicographers whose name begin with Muḥammad,[55] a short commentary on *Ṭabaqāt fuqahāʾ al-yaman* by al-Jaʿdī (d. 546/1152),[56] and the subject of the present study, *Ṭabaqāt al-fuqahāʾ al-shāfiʿīyah*.

Professional career

Ibn Qāḍī Shuhbah was also active outside the realm of scholarship. As mentioned above, he had served as a deputy judge under Najm al-Dīn Ibn Ḥijjī on several occasions, including when he was the confidential secretary to Sulṭān Barsbāy between 827 and 828. The confidential secretary was one of the most powerful positions that a non-Mamlūk could hold within the Mamlūk state and gave the official uncommon access to the Sulṭān. He was responsible for reading official documents to the Sulṭān, drafting responses, and for managing access to information. He also had a seat in the Palace of Justice (*Dār al-ʿAdl*), where he acted as the Sulṭān's representative in adjudicating disputes. The confidential secretary was second only to the *wazīr* in power among the non-military elite.[57] Working as Najm al-Dīn's assistant in Cairo would have given Ibn Qāḍī Shuhbah access to the halls of power and insights into the inner-workings of Mamlūk government and of the judiciary. Unfortunately, his record of those experiences is no longer extant.

In the years following the death of Shihāb al-Dīn Ibn Ḥijjī in 816, Ibn Qāḍī Shuhbah fell increasingly under the shadow of Najm al-Dīn. Although being so closely linked to Najm al-Dīn offered many advantages for the young jurist, it also bore a heavy price.

---

[52] Ibn Qāḍī Shuhbah, *Kitāb manāqib al-imām al-shāfiʿī*, ed. ʿAbd al-ʿAzīz Fayyāḍ Ḥarfūsh (Damascus: Dār al-bashāʾir li l-ṭibāʿah wa l-nashr wa l-tawzīʿ, 2003).

[53] Ibid., 19.

[54] Al-Sakhāwī, *al-Ḍawʾ al-lāmiʿ*, vol. 11, 22.

[55] *Ṭabaqāt al-nuḥāh wa ʾl-lughawīyīn* (Najaf: Maṭbaʿat al-nuʿmān, 1974).

[56] Khān (1987), vol. 1, 29; ʿUmar b. ʿAlī al-Jaʿdī, *Ṭabaqāt fuqahāʾ al-yaman*, ed. Fuʾād al-Sayyid (Beirut: Dār al-qalam, n.d.).

[57] Popper, *Egypt and Syria under the Circassian Sultans*, 97.

Najm al-Dīn had, over the course of his life, gained a number of powerful enemies; he was, it seems, a rather difficult character. Ibn Qāḍī Shuhbah chronicles a number of conflicts between Ibn Ḥijjī and other scholars and Mamlūks, including, at one point, a brawl that involved maces.[58]

As his mentor grew older his conflicts with others in authority became more serious and he was eventually arrested on II Jumādā 10, 828 (April 29, 1425) because he failed to pay the Sulṭān the full 10,000-*dīnār* fee required for his appointment to the office of confidential secretary.[59] He was returned to Damascus a few days later, and when they arrived Ibn Qāḍī Shuhbah was forced to submit to questioning by a panel of judges who gathered to investigate the charges against Najm al-Dīn.[60]

During the following fifteen months Ibn Qāḍī Shuhbah worked as a deputy *muftī* (jurist consult) in the Palace of Justice of Damascus until he was replaced by Najm al-Dīn's son Bahā' al-Dīn (d. 850/1446) in Dhū al-Qaʿdah, 829 (September/October, 1426).[61] The Palace of Justice of Damascus was originally established in the 6th/12th century and was a place where the ruler or his representatives would hear and address grievances held between individuals or groups.[62] Little is known about the institution or its role in the administration of justice during the Mamlūk period.[63] It appears, however, that scholars who worked in the Palace functioned more as administrators of governmental decrees than as judges hearing disputes[64] and there is a sense in later texts, such as *Quḍāt dimashq* by Ibn Ṭūlūn, that work in the institution was seen as being less important and less prestigious than work as a deputy judge.[65]

Around the time that Ibn Qāḍī Shuhbah was replaced at the Palace of Justice, Najm al-Dīn was required to return to Cairo and,

---

58 Ibn Ṭūlūn, *Quḍāt dimashq*, 134.

59 Ibn Taghrī Birdī, *al-Nujūm*, vol. 6, 585–86; al-Maqrīzī, *al-Sulūk*, vol. 4, 685.

60 Ibn Ṭūlūn, *Quḍāt dimashq*, 151.

61 Ibid., 169.

62 Nasser O. Rabbat, "The Ideological Significance of the *Dār al-ʿAdl* in the Medieval Islamic Orient," *International Journal of Middle Eastern Studies* 27 (1995): 3–28.

63 Ibid., 4–5.

64 S. M. Stern, "Petitions from the Mamluk Period: Notes on the Mamluk Documents from Sinai," *Bulletin of the School of Oriental and African Studies* 29, no. 2 (1966): 233–76, especially 243.

65 See Ibn Ṭūlūn, *Quḍāt dimashq*, 149 and 169 for an indication of the prestige of these offices.

although he attempted to attain a legal writ allowing him to remain in Damascus, he was forced to leave the city on Dhū al-Qaʿdah 23, 829 (September 26, 1426). Although Ibn Qāḍī Shuhbah did not travel with him on this trip, he reports that by the end of Muḥarram, 830 (November, 1426), Najm al-Dīn was returned to the office of chief Shāfiʿī judge in a turn of fortunes that is characteristic of the Circassian period;[66] he was even given a gift of 500 *dīnārs* by the Sulṭān.[67] Unfortunately, the sources do not indicate whether Ibn Qāḍī Shuhbah returned to office as his deputy or whether he simply retired to teaching during this period.

The situation following his arrest and reappointment as chief judge was especially tense because several individuals resented the good treatment Najm al-Dīn received from the Sulṭān. On Dhū al-Qaʿdah 1, 830 (August 24, 1427) Najm al-Dīn was murdered by two assailants, in what was at the time one of the most notorious crimes of the century.[68] Although the actual perpetrators of the crime are unknown, it is clear that most historians believed that political and judicial rivalries were the motive.[69]

Following the murder, Bahāʾ al-Dīn Ibn Ḥijjī was appointed to take his father's place as chief Shāfiʿī judge[70] and a few months later Ibn Qāḍī Shuhbah was appointed to be one of his deputies.[71] Over the course of the following twenty years Bahāʾ al-Dīn eclipsed Ibn Qāḍī Shuhbah as his career path took him from chief Shāfiʿī judge to controller of the armies of Syria and Egypt, and eventually to confidential secretary of Damascus. Ibn Qāḍī Shuhbah claimed that his initial success as due to the guilt felt by the Sulṭān over the murder of Najm al-Dīn.[72] He was aided, however, by his marriage to the daughter of the powerful Shāfiʿī jurist Kamāl al-Dīn al-Bārizī in 835/1431.[73] Al-Bārizī would later become one of the most important and influential confidential secretaries in the Circassian period to Sulṭān Barsbāy and later to Sulṭān Jaqmaq[74] and he proved to

[66] Ibid., 141.
[67] Ibid., 142.
[68] Ibn Taghrī Birdī, *al-Nujūm*, vol. 6, 623; al-Maqrīzī, *al-Sulūk*, vol. 4, 750; Ibn Ṭūlūn, *Quḍāt dimashq*, 142.
[69] Ibn Ṭūlūn, *Quḍāt dimashq*, 142.
[70] Ibn Taghrī Birdī, *al-Nujūm*, vol. 6, 623; al-Maqrīzī, *al-Sulūk*, vol. 4, 751.
[71] Ibn Ṭūlūn, *Quḍāt dimashq*, 169.
[72] Ibid., 142–43.
[73] Ibid., 158.
[74] Ibn Taghrī Birdī, *al-Nujūm*, vol. 6, 680; vol. 7, 53.

be a powerful ally to Bahā᾽ al-Dīn, and ultimately an enemy to Ibn Qāḍī Shuhbah. It is not known if Ibn Qāḍī Shuhbah lost his position as deputy judge when Bahā᾽ al-Dīn was promoted to become the controller of the army in II Jumādā, 832 (March, 1429),[75] although he appears to have remained in Damascus until 837/1434 when he went on the pilgrimage to Mecca.[76]

Crisis and the first edition of the Ṭabaqāt

The years that followed appear to have been important for Ibn Qāḍī Shuhbah, although we have no direct evidence of what he went though during the period. By the winter of 841/1437–38 he seems to have reached near to the top of both of his roles as scholar and judge. Sometime during the late fall of 841/1437 he began working on *Ṭabaqāt al-fuqahā᾽ al-shāfiʿīyah*. By this time he was esteemed as the "remnant of the *mujtahids*" (*baqīyat al-mujtahidīn*) by ʿIzz al-Dīn Abū Yaʿlā Ḥamzah al-Ḥusaynī (d. 874/1469), his student and scribe.[77] His legal abilities were such, according to al-Sakhāwī who studied under him, that Ibn Qāḍī Shuhbah rose to be the leader of all of the Shāfiʿīs of Syria. He goes on to say that Ibn Qāḍī Shuhbah even had the capability of disagreeing with al-Shāfiʿī on legal problems, and in fact saw things that al-Shāfiʿī had failed to see, but that he reframed from issuing opinions that diverged from the established rules found in the quasi-canonical Shāfiʿī texts for fear of a public reaction.[78]

It is also important to note that at the very peak of his success as a scholar, and on the eve of his appointment as chief Shāfiʿī judge of Damascus the following year, he decided to write a *ṭabaqāt* of the Shāfiʿī school when at the same time the Middle East was facing a series severe of crises. In Rajab, 841 (December/January, 1437/38), plague appeared in Egypt, quickly spreading as far south as the Sudan,[79] and by the end of Shaʿbān (February), it had spread to

---

[75] Ibid., 157.
[76] Al-Sakhāwī, *al-Ḍaw᾽ al-lāmiʿ*, vol. 11, 23.
[77] Ibid., vol. 3, 163–64; Khān, vol. 4, 114.
[78] Al-Sakhāwī, *al-Ḍaw᾽ al-lāmiʿ*, vol. 11, 23.
[79] Muḥammad b. Aḥmad Ibn Iyās al-Ḥanafī, *Badā᾽iʿ al-zuhūr fī waqā᾽iʿ al-duhūr*, ed. Muḥammad Muṣṭafā (Cairo: Dār iḥyā᾽ al-kutub al-ʿarabīyah, 1972), vol. 2, 181.

Syria.[80] By the conclusion of the following month, the plague had become so bad that Sulṭān Barsbāy began to fear that it was a punishment from God.[81] The outbreak of the plague was also accompanied by the onset of the Sulṭān's own illness that would prove fatal within a few months.

Barsbāy and others in the Sulṭān's court blamed the plague on the moral decay of Muslim society. They reasoned that Muslims had fallen so far from the good grace of God that God had sent the plague to remind the people of their duties. The jurists in his court argued that the chief cause of the moral turpitude was the unbridled access of women to public spaces. Women, it was maintained, with their painted faces and unrestricted movements, were the cause of fornication. They argued that God would lift the plague only if they prevented women from moving about in public.[82] Sulṭān Barsbāy ordered that all women in Cairo were to be restricted to their homes, including servants and children. He also freed large numbers of prisoners as a sign of mercy.[83]

Whether or not similar policies were followed in Damascus is not known. The plague was quite severe there and attitudes toward women were likely to have been little different. At the very least, it is likely that the *ʿulamāʾ* of Damascus would have looked upon the new rules in Cairo with approval.

Al-Maqrīzī reports that just as the plague intensified a severe winter storm struck the region around the end of the month of Ramaḍān. He states that

> On the night of the feast (Shawwāl 1) the coldness of the winter increased in Syria. It came from Palestine to the people of Damascus, Hamāh, Aleppo, and Dayār Bakr to Arzinkān. [It was so cold that] the frost covered their trees so that all their green leaves blackened. The trees of willows and the nuts fell. [The frost killed] the cultivated bean, and the barley, *al-bīqīyāʾ*, the Sparrowgrass, and all of the vegetables. In their affliction [from the plague], the frost bestowed on them abundant [harm] and caused twice as many people to die. . . . In Ṣafad a cold wind caused the people and the animals, as well as the plants and the trees, to perish; as God wills.

[80] Al-Maqrīzī, *al-Sulūk*, vol. 4, 1031.
[81] Ibn Taghrī Birdī, *al-Nujūm*, vol. 6, 760; al-Maqrīzī, *al-Sulūk*, vol. 4, 1031–33; Ibn Iyās, *Badāʾiʿ al-zuhūr*, vol. 2, 182–83.
[82] Ibn Taghrī Birdī, *al-Nujūm*, vol. 6, 760; al-Maqrīzī, *al-Sulūk*, vol. 4, 1032.
[83] Ibn Taghrī Birdī, *al-Nujūm*, vol. 6, 761; al-Maqrīzī, *al-Sulūk*, vol. 4, 1032–33.

> It came to pass also on the night of the ʿĪd al-Fiṭr a violent cold wind hit the city of Fez and the North African countries, along with a very great torrent. It blew down and the destroyed several houses. It was a horrible matter and a horrible accident.[84]

As the cold increased, the rivers froze, causing water shortages in Damascus. As people became weak from the cold, and from the lack of food and water, the plague became worse, causing even greater numbers to die.[85]

Through the early part of the month of Shawwāl (late March/early April) Barsbāy's condition became worse as rumors spread across the region about his health. As always happened in times of such political crises, contenders for the Sulṭānate began to jockey for position. In Damascus, the viceroy Amīr Īnāl al-Jakamī, who had been in control of the city for two years, began to plot in the eventuality of Barsbāy's death. Barsbāy, fearing a coup or revolt, began to move Amīrs and attempted to establish a basis of legitimacy for his fourteen year old son Yūsuf to succeed him.[86]

In the week following the onset of the late winter storm a rumor began to spread that on Shawwāl 9 (April 4) the world would end. A number of historians from the period record the event, which varies depending on where they were at the time, but it seems that it was a widely circulated rumor that was taken seriously by common people and intellectual and political elites alike.[87] On the 9th, men gathered at their local Mosques waiting for the end to arrive. At al-Azhar Mosque in Cairo, where the historians Ibn Taghrī Birdī and al-Maqrīzī were in attendance, pandemonium broke out when, in the middle of his sermon, the preacher collapsed causing fears that the end was indeed at hand.[88]

In the weeks that followed it must have seemed that the world actually was ending. The plague in Syria became even worse, rival-

[84] Al-Maqrīzī, *al-Sulūk*, vol. 4, 1035–36.
[85] Ibid.
[86] Ibid., 1032–40.
[87] See Ibn Taghrī Birdī, *al-Nujūm*, vol. 6, 764–65; al-Maqrīzī, *al-Sulūk*, vol. 4, 1038–40; Ibn Iyās, *Badāʾiʿ al-zuhūr*, vol. 2, 182–85; Ibn Ḥajar al-ʿAsqalānī, *Inbāʾ al-ghumr*, vol. 9, 8–9; al-Qāḍī ʿAbd al-Bāsiṭ, *Kitāb akhbār al-duwal wa āthār al-uwal*, vol. 2. MS Hunt. 610 (Bodliean Library Manuscript), fol. 7b. Note: Brockelmann [G II 47, 54] identifies the author as ʿAbd al-Bāsiṭ b. Khalīl b. Shāhīn al-Malaṭī al-Ḥanafī (d. 920/1514). He does not provide the title of the text. The manuscript lists the name of the author as al-Qāḍī ʿAbd al-Bāsiṭ al-Mūrraj, or possibly al-Mawraj.
[88] Ibn Taghrī Birdī, *al-Nujūm*, vol. 6, 764–65; al-Maqrīzī, *al-Sulūk*, vol. 4, 1038–40.

ing the one that struck the region in 833/1429–30, which was one of the worst pandemics to strike the Middle East since the plagues first began the previous century. Famine also increased as the crops that had just begun to be harvested were destroyed by the biting cold and frost.[89]

By the early weeks of Dhū al-Qaʿdah (late April), rumors of Barsbāy's impending death began to race across Mamlūk territories. By the 4th, Barsbāy decided that he should install his son Yūsuf as the next Sulṭān and to form a coalition of loyal Amīrs who would support him. He appointed Amīr Jaqmaq as regent and then gave a speech blaming the plagues of 833 and 841 on his purchased Mamlūks who had continually rebelled against his authority and caused much turmoil in Cairo.[90] Upon receiving the position, Jaqmaq began to maneuver so that he could seize power once Barsbāy died.

Sometime during this month, Ibn Qāḍī Shuhbah completed the first edition of his *ṭabaqāt*. Throughout the past three to four months, through the outbreak of plague, famine, devastating cold, political turmoil, and rumors of the end of the world, Ibn Qāḍī Shuhbah sat in a room with several students who transcribed his text. He says in an *ijāzah* (permission to teach) that he appended to the cover of the text for his student al-Ḥusaynī, that he intended his book to be studied, in other words, to be used as a textbook.[91] Sometime during the following four years al-Ḥusaynī carried the text to Egypt where he read it with the famous scholar Ibn Ḥajar al-ʿAsqalānī. Ibn Ḥajar made copious notes in the margins of the text, which appear upside down in the original manuscript held by the British Museum.[92] It appears that al-Ḥusaynī read the text to Ibn Ḥajar who sat across from the student, and who then made comments and corrections.

Overview of the text

In the introduction to his text, Ibn Qāḍī Shuhbah says that he wrote the text in order to describe "the generations of the Shāfiʿī jurists."[93] He says

[89] Al-Maqrīzī, *al-Sulūk*, vol. 4, 1040–45.
[90] Ibn Iyās, *Badāʾiʿ al-zuhūr*, vol. 2, 187–88; al-Maqrizī, *al-Sulūk*, vol. 4, 1043–45; Ibn Taghrī Birdī, *al-Nujūm*, vol. 6, 767–68.
[91] Ibn Qāḍī Shuhbah, *Ṭabaqāt al-fuqahāʾ al-shāfiʿīyah*, Arabic Manuscript Collection, The British Library, Or. Mus. 3037, fol., 1a.
[92] See Or. Mus. 3037.
[93] Khān, vol. 1, 53–54.

> I limit myself in it to the biographies of [scholars] with a known name, [who are] remembered due to their fame, and whose situation needs be known by the students of legal science, or to those whom al-Rāfiʿī and others transmitted from in their well known compiled works. This in reality is what is meant by [the phrase] 'the generations of the Shāfiʿī jurists.' I do not mention any but the famous scholars and others who happen to have been transmitted from, even though excellence in legal science, or the teaching of law at the *Niẓāmīyah* or another *madrasah* might [also] be attributed to them. For the abundant supply of those biographies is too much for the student of the law [to understand] and [it would] confuse the purpose of [this work] with other things. I might mention in [this work] a few biographies in whom are not found the condition for some reason which made this necessary. Glance at the biographies, and the wisdom behind their mention will become apparent to the one who examines his biography. It is ordered into twenty-nine generations. The first generation are those who studied with Imām al-Shāfiʿī, may God be pleased with him and bless him. Second, [I mention] the [Imām's] disciples (*aṣḥāb*) up to the year 300. After that, I mention one generation for every twenty years, even if this requires a few to be placed after the people of their generation due to the extension of their lives, or a few of them to be mentioned with the generation of their master teachers because of the suddenness of their early deaths. Necessity forced me to cite them thus. Without a doubt the last of every generation is close to the first of the generation which follows it. I ordered each generation according to the letters of the alphabet, for convenient reference.[94]

Here Ibn Qāḍī Shuhbah is only concerned with those jurists who are remembered for their fame, which he ties directly to their roles in the transmission of substantive law. In this transmission Abū al-Qāsim Muḥammad al-Rāfiʿī (d. 623–24/1226) stands out as the most important compiler of divergent substantive legal rulings, but Ibn Qāḍī Shuhbah also mentions that 'others' who composed substantive law texts are important in the transmission of these rules. It is significant that Ibn Qāḍī Shuhbah nowhere mentions *ijmāʿ* (consensus) as a criterion for being included in his *Ṭabaqāt*. This approach is very different from Abū Isḥāq al-Shīrāzī, whose main goal in his *Ṭabaqāt* was to establish those "whose opinions are considered authoritative in arriving at consensus and whose disagreements are to be taken into account."[95]

---

[94] Ibid.

[95] George Makdisi, *The Rise of Colleges* (Edinburgh: University Press, 1981), 107.

Considering that Ibn Qāḍī Shuhbah mentions 784 biographies drawn from over 600 years of history, it is clear that a wide range of opinions must be included in the material transmitted over time. Again, the main criterion for inclusion is the legal opinions that have been transmitted in authoritative legal works down to Ibn Qāḍī Shuhbah's time for which each jurist is known. While Ibn Qāḍī Shuhbah does not seem intent to catalogue those whose voices are directly involved in the formation of consensus, he is specifically making an argument for the importance of disagreement (*ikhtilāf*) over legal rules, and for locating those whose voices in disagreement should be considered authoritative. As al-Shīrāzī implies, *ikhtilāf* is simply the opposite of *ijmāʿ*. Only one who is considered by the tradition to be authoritative in the formation of *ijmāʿ* is authoritative in the formation of *ikhtilāf*. By placing an emphasis on the *transmission of diverging opinions*, Ibn Qāḍī Shuhbah is asserting a powerful argument about the history of Shāfiʿī law and the state of the law in his time.

If Ibn Qāḍī Shuhbah's text is compared with earlier Shāfiʿī legal *ṭabaqāt*, an emerging concern with identifying and establishing those who count in the development of acceptable legal diversity is observed. Part of this focus is on paring down and limiting to a specific few those whose opinions should be counted. For instance, one of the earliest Shāfiʿī *ṭabaqāt* is al-ʿAbbādī's (d. 458/1066) *Ṭabaqāt al-fuqahāʾ al-shāfiʿīyah*.[96] Al-ʿAbbādī lists only those jurists he considered authoritative in the first six generations of the Shāfiʿī school. In those six generations, he lists 234 jurists (46 in the first generation, 36 in the second, 26 in the third, 80 in the fourth, 30 in the fifth, and 14 in the sixth). Admittedly, many of the jurists listed, especially in the fourth generation, are considered the students of certain master jurists. In fact, the text indicates that they, because of their associations with master jurists, should also be counted in the body of authoritative jurists. In many respects, al-ʿAbbādī seeks to expand the ranks of authority to as many people as possible.

Ibn Qāḍī Shuhbah, on the other hand, seeks to restrict the number of jurists in each generation to a select few. In the first six generations, he lists only 113 biographies (17 in the first generation, 13 in the second, 20 in the third, 20 in the fourth, 21 in the fifth, and 22 in the sixth). Of these, Ibn Qāḍī Shuhbah attempts to discredit

---

[96] Abū ʿĀṣim Muḥammad b. Aḥmad al-ʿAbbādī, *Kitāb ṭabaqāt al-fuqahāʾ al-shāfiʿīyah*, ed. Gösta Vitestam, no. 21 (Leiden: E. J. Brill, 1964).

al-Muḥāsibī (d. 243/857) as an authority on the grounds that he did not really study with al-Shāfiʿī.[97] Of the remaining 112 jurists, 67 are specifically mentioned as having their opinions included in al-Rāfiʿī's text, and of these, 27 are involved in the transmission of *ikhtilāf*. Clearly, Ibn Qāḍī Shuhbah seeks to limit the scope of divergent opinions by restricting inclusion to specific authorities.

He does, nevertheless, include 45 jurists in the first six generations who are not mentioned in al-Rāfiʿī's text or who are not directly mentioned as being involved in *ikhtilāf*. If Ibn Qāḍī Shuhbah's sole purpose was to count those who are authoritative in the transmission of divergent opinions, why include the other thirty jurists? As Ibn Qāḍī Shuhbah says in his introduction, "I might mention in [this work] a few biographies in whom are not found the condition for some reason which made this [their mention] necessary." In other words, Ibn Qāḍī Shuhbah is arguing that he specifically includes jurists who are not authoritative in the formation of divergent opinions.

The hypertextual nature of legal *ṭabaqāt* is mentioned in the next chapter. An important aspect of hypertextual thinking is keeping chains of authority in mind when evaluating the character, abilities, and qualifications of jurists. Ibn Qāḍī Shuhbah must make an argument for the transmission of *ikhtilāf* down to his own time and a justification for why certain jurists should be counted in that transmission. Hypertextually, Ibn Qāḍī Shuhbah weaves his biographies together into a tapestry of intellectual history. Each thread is a line connecting individual jurists to other jurists, and ultimately into the tapestry as a whole. Since knowledge is passed through each thread, Ibn Qāḍī Shuhbah must list jurists who, while not being directly involved in the transmission of *ikhtilāf*, are nonetheless important in establishing the authority of transmitters of *ikhtilāf* in the overall fabric of the history of law.

The transmission of *ikhtilāf* is also why Ibn Qāḍī Shuhbah is very concerned with the chronological placement of jurists in specific periods. He mentions the problem of chronological placement twenty-six times in his text, usually in the early generations, and most often in disputing the placement of certain jurists by previous writers of *ṭabaqāt* texts. His main concern seems to be to fix reliable dates and places of death. For instance, he argues that al-Shīrāzī's placement

[97] Khān, vol. 1, 59–60.

of Isḥāq b. Khuzaymah (d. 321/933) in the second generation is incorrect. Al-Shīrāzī based his placement on the assertion that Ibn Khuzaymah studied with al-Muzanī (d. 264/878) and al-Rabīʿ (d. 270/884), jurists of the first generation. Instead, Ibn Qāḍī Shuhbah places him in the third generation, arguing that the main criterion for placement is not with whom he studied, but his date of death.[98] Establishing clear demarcations of generational boundaries, and those included in each, does not, however, seem to be the only motive in placing Ibn Khuzaymah in the third generation. Ibn Surayj (d. 306/918), the most important jurist of the third generation, is mentioned as a contemporary of Ibn Khuzaymah, who is not listed as either a student of, or a teacher of, Ibn Surayj.[99] Thus, because Ibn Qāḍī Shuhbah is very conscious of establishing a correct and exact history in the transmission of *ikhtilāf*, he must make sure that jurists are placed in their proper generations.

As discussed above, the stamp of *ḥadīth* science was firmly embedded in the *ṭabaqāt* genre from an early period. Ibn Qāḍī Shuhbah himself was very active in *ḥadīth* science and collection. Indeed, outside of historical writing, one of his chief occupations seems to have been *ḥadīth* collection.[100] It is not surprising, then, that methods and standards in the collection of *ḥadīth* (i.e., the exact fixing of dates of death, the reliability of transmitters, and the probability that jurists could have met each other given their dates of death and geographical regions) would predominate in Ibn Qāḍī Shuhbah's *Ṭabaqāt*.

Ibn Qāḍī Shuhbah's interest in fixing accurate ranges of dates is further demonstrated by the periods he set for each generation. Ibn Qāḍī Shuhbah states in his introduction that each generation lasts twenty years, which, however, does not agree with his actual periodization of the generations. For instance, the twelfth generation lasts 29 years (470/1077–499/1106), the thirteenth generation 19 years (501/1108–520/1127), and the eighteenth generation 14 years (606/1209–620/1223). The average period of each generation is approximately 23 years. His attention to accurate date ranges suggests that Ibn Qāḍī Shuhbah took great care to order each generation with respect to the preceding and following generations because

[98] Khān, vol. 1, 68–69.
[99] Ibid.
[100] Al-Sakhāwī, *al-Ḍawʾ al-lāmiʿ*, vol. 11, 22–23.

mapping out the chronological development of the transmission of *ikhtilāf* is central to his purposes.[101]

As discussed above, the centrality of the transmission of divergent opinion is why Ibn Qāḍī Shuhbah lists jurists who are not directly mentioned as being involved in the formation of authoritative divergent opinions: they are a part of the fabric of intellectual transmission that ties jurists and periods together. They are partially authoritative, in that they needed to possess a definite level of knowledge in order to be able to transmit certain kinds of divergent substantive legal opinions. It is therefore clear that not every jurist listed would be a voice in either *ijmāʿ* or *ikhtilāf*. They are simply intermediaries between authorities. But since part of Ibn Qāḍī Shuhbah's task is historical, he is forced to include certain jurists to demonstrate unbroken lines of intellectual descent *and* to maintain the historical narrative.

Because Ibn Qāḍī Shuhbah lists a number of jurists (approximately 60%) who are not authoritative holders of divergent opinions (and thus conversely voices in *ijmāʿ*), he is able to construct a broader history of Shāfiʿī law than he would otherwise be able to. Al-Isnawī (d. 772/1370–71), like Ibn Qāḍī Shuhbah, wrote a *ṭabaqāt* that sought to catalogue those jurists listed in al-Rāfiʿī's *al-ʿAzīz* and al-Nawawī's *al-Rawḍah*, as well as other jurists who transmitted divergent opinions.[102] In doing so, he includes the biographies of 1289 jurists up to his own time. The nature of his work, however, is different because it is divided alphabetically, not chronologically. Where Ibn Qāḍī Shuhbah can develop a diachronic historical narrative built on a chronological telling of Shāfiʿī history, al-Isnawī's text, while certainly containing historical elements, does not develop a similar narrative.

The historiographic model for Ibn Qāḍī Shuhbah's text is Abū Isḥāq al-Shīrāzī's *Ṭabaqāt al-fuqahāʾ*. Written in the eleventh century, al-Shīrāzī's *Ṭabaqāt* chronologically develops the history of Islamic law from the time of the Prophet Muḥammad, up to his own generation. His project is, however, broader than a telling of Shāfiʿī legal history. Al-Shīrāzī charts the development of law and the emer-

---

[101] Internally within each generation the biographies are listed alphabetically. Ibn Qāḍī Shuhbah says in his introduction that this is done to make reference more easy, but it was also likely done because fixing a chronology within such short expanses of time would have been more difficult.

[102] ʿAbd al-Raḥīm al-Isnawī, *Ṭabaqāt al-shāfiʿīyah*, ed. Kamāl Yūsuf al-Ḥūt (Beirut: Dār al-kutub al-ʿilmīyah, 1987), vol. 1, 13–17.

gence of authoritative holders of *ijmāʿ* and *ikhtilāf* from the companions of the Prophet (*ṣaḥābah*), through their successors (*tābiʿūn*) in nine different geographical areas of the Islamic world, to the jurists that came after them in Baghdād and Khurāsān, and then finally through the five legal schools that were established in his time. *Ijmāʿ* and *ikhtilāf* are thus broader and more narrow for al-Shīrāzī; broader in that *ijmāʿ* included those things on which all jurists agreed (although this, by no means, should be taken to indicate that there were, or indeed are, a wide range of rules that have achieved anything near consensual agreement) and more narrow in that he was interested in listing the major thinkers in each school and period who held divergent opinions. Ibn Qāḍī Shuhbah clearly understands his history to be building on al-Shīrāzī's, whom he quotes more frequently (by a percentage of citations) than any other writer (91 times in the 199 biographies prior to that of al-Shīrāzī), including in his text all but nine Shāfiʿī jurists mentioned by al-Shīrāzī in his *Ṭabaqāt*.[103]

Al-Shīrāzī tells his history through the way he structures his text. Not only is it chronological, but it is also divided into categorical segments that create a historical argument. Thus he does not need a great deal of narrative to convey the idea that legal knowledge originated with the Prophet Muḥammad and has been passed down and expanded on by pious authorities ever since.

Ibn Qāḍī Shuhbah, however, is limited in telling his history since he restricts himself to the Shāfiʿī school and does not segment his text by region. Because the text includes the biographies of 784 jurists spanning 29 generations and approximately 650 years, each biography is relatively brief, with the average biographical notice running approximately 15 lines; the shortest being just five lines[104] and the longest being just 93 lines.[105] Most citations include the jurist's full name, his *kunyah* (patronymic), generally his date of birth, place of birth, his qualities and characteristics, his specialties in legal education and in the legal profession, his teachers, his students, the institutions in which he studied, possible political or historical controversies he was involved in, his date of death, place of death, cause

[103] Al-Shīrāzī's text covers only the first 199 jurists mentioned in Ibn Qāḍī Shuhbah's *Ṭabaqāt*. Al-Shīrāzī is listed as the 200th jurist in Ibn Qāḍī Shuhbah's text, and the first of the eleventh generation.

[104] Khān, vol. 1, 98.

[105] Ibid., 472–477.

of death, place of burial, and any notable opinion for which he is remembered. In cases where the author feels the jurist should not be included in the Shāfiʿī school, there is generally a short argument to that effect.[106] Ibn Qāḍī Shuhbah relates his history through the construction of individual biographies, by the combination of qualities, abilities, teachers, students, historical circumstances, and so forth, which are then implicitly or explicitly related to other biographies. To tease out this history one has to look at the work from the level of the text, using the information contained in each biography in relation to all other biographies, to construct a historical overview of the school.

Ibn Qāḍī Shuhbah's rise and fall and the final editions of his Ṭabaqāt

In the weeks and months following the completion of the first edition of the *Ṭabaqāt*, Ibn Qāḍī Shuhbah became embroiled in the political maneuverings of rival Amīrs following the death of Barsbāy on Dhu al-Ḥijjah 13 (June 6).[107] Although Amīr Jaqmaq had sworn fealty to Barsbāy's son Yūsuf, he deposed the boy on I Rabīʿ 19, 842 (September 9, 1438).[108] Following the deposition, Jaqmaq reshuffled the judiciary of Egypt, especially the Shāfiʿī judges because they were important in shaping the opinion of the elite households.[109] Jaqmaq also issued orders to reorganize the judiciary of Damascus, moving chief Shāfiʿī judge Kamāl al-Dīn al-Bārizī to Cairo to become his new confidential secretary. As a replacement he appointed Burhān al-Dīn Ibrāhīm Ibn al-Bāʿūnī as chief Shāfiʿī judge.[110]

In Damascus, the viceroy Amīr Jakamī refused to recognize the deposition or the reorganization orders and went into revolt. On I Jumādā 15 (November 3) Amīr Jakamī appointed Ibn Qāḍī Shuhbah as chief Shāfiʿī judge, charging him 1000 *dīnār*s as a fee.[111] He also

---

[106] For instance see vol. 1, 28–29.

[107] Ibn Taghrī Birdī, *al-Nujūm*, vol. 6, 771; al-Maqrīzī, *al-Sulūk*, vol. 4, 1049.

[108] Ibn Taghrī Birdī, *al-Nujūm*, vol. 7, 31; al-Maqrīzī, *al-Sulūk*, vol. 4, 1085.

[109] Ibn Iyās, *Badāʾiʿ al-zuhūr*, vol. 2, 203; al-Qāḍī ʿAbd al-Bāsiṭ, *Kitāb akhbār* vol. 2, MS Hunt. 610, fols. 15–17.

[110] Al-Maqrīzī, *al-Sulūk*, vol. 4, 1100.

[111] Badr al-Dīn Maḥmūd b. Aḥmad al-ʿAynī, *ʿIqd al-jumān fī tārīkh ahl al-zamān*, ed. ʿAbdallāh al-Ṭanṭāwī al-Qarḥūṭ (Cairo: al-Zahrāʾ liʾ l-iʿlām al-ʿarabīyah, 1989), 528–29.

appointed Ibn al-Bāʿūnī as chief preacher of the Umayyad Mosque, a role customarily given to the chief Shāfiʿī judge.[112] The position of chief preacher to the Umayyad Mosque was an important one because government edicts were issued there as part of the Friday sermon. It was a position that was also used by Sulṭāns and rebel Amīrs to broadcast propaganda to the people in support of claims to authority in times of political crisis. Ibn al-Bāʿūnī must not have proven loyal to Jakamī because he was shortly replaced by Ibn Qāḍī Shuhbah, resulting in lasting resentment between the two jurists.[113]

Jakamī claimed that he was loyal to the memory of Barsbāy and to his son, the rightful Sulṭān, Yūsuf. He ordered Ibn Qāḍī Shuhbah to give the Friday sermon in Yūsuf's name, in effect proclaiming him Sulṭān.[114] Ibn Qāḍī Shuhbah must have known that this was a dangerous move. His own teacher al-Qurashī had been tortured to death for siding against Barqūq in a failed revolt. He could have refused the order and forced Jakamī to find a new chief judge and preacher, but he did not. Sometime before Ramaḍān 20 (most likely the 13th) Ibn Qāḍī Shuhbah gave the Friday sermon in the name of Yūsuf in the Umayyad Mosque. The immediate affect of the sermon was to link Ibn Qāḍī Shuhbah to the revolt, making him an enemy of the new Sulṭān, Jaqmaq.[115]

Upon receiving the news, Jaqmaq relieved Jakamī as viceroy of Damascus on Ramaḍān 23, 842 (March 9, 1439), appointing in his place Amīr Āqbughā al-Timrāzī.[116] Jakamī immediately released a number of prisoners who had earlier sworn loyalty to Jaqmaq in a move meant to distance himself from the revolt implied by the sermon.[117] Jaqmaq, using Bahāʾ al-Dīn Ibn Ḥijjī as an intermediary,[118] began to work behind the scenes to remove support in Damascus for the revolt. As Jakamī lost ground to Jaqmaq he decided to arrest Ibn Qāḍī Shuhbah on Shawwāl 29 as a sign of loyalty to the new

112 Ibn Ṭūlūn, *Quḍāt dimashq*, 168.

113 al-Sakhāwī, *al-Ḍawʾ al-lāmiʿ*, vol. 1, 26–29.

114 Ibn Taghrī Birdī, *al-Nujūm*, vol. 7, 63–64; al-Maqrīzī, *al-Sulūk*, vol. 4, 1112; Ibn Ṭūlūn, *Iʿlām al-warā*, 49–50.

115 Ibid.

116 Ibn Ṭūlūn, *Iʿlām al-warā bi-man wullīya nāʾiban min al-atrāk bi-dimashq al-shām al-kubrā*, ed. Muḥammad Aḥmad Duhmān (Damascus: al-Maṭbaʿah wa ʾl-jarīdah al-rasmīyah, 1964), 51–52; al-Maqrīzī, *al-Sulūk*, vol. 4, 1112.

117 Ibn Taghrī Birdī, *al-Nujūm*, vol. 7, 64–65; al-Maqrīzī, *al-Sulūk*, vol. 4, 1113.

118 Ibn Taghrī Birdī, *al-Nujūm*, vol. 7, 69–81; al-Maqrīzī, *al-Sulūk*, vol. 4, 1115–23.

Sulṭān.[119] He was replaced by Bahāʾ al-Dīn Ibn Ḥijjī,[120] who, in an unusual move, traveled to Cairo to receive his new appointment, although not from the Sulṭān, but from the Sulṭān's confidential secretary, Ibn Ḥijjī's father in-law, Kamāl al-Dīn al-Bārizī.[121]

On Dhū al-Qaʿdah 3 (April 18) forces loyal to Jaqmaq marched into Damascus and took control of the city.[122] Jakamī was executed several weeks later and his head was carried to Cairo along with Ibn Qāḍī Shuhbah who was taken to Egypt as a prisoner.[123] It is not known what happened to Ibn Qāḍī Shuhbah over the next several months. He appears to have been returned to Damascus sometime in 843 where he again took up teaching and writing. On II Rabīʿ 29, 843 (October 9, 1439) Ibn Qāḍī Shuhbah completed the second edition of his *Ṭabaqāt*. This text was a copy of the version he produced the previous year. On Ramaḍān 10, 843 (February 15, 1440) Ibn Qāḍī Shuhbah completed a third edition of the *Ṭabaqāt*.[124] This too was a copy of the text produced in 841 and appears to have received few significant changes. Both texts appear to be the result of dictations given by Ibn Qāḍī Shuhbah to students who were then required to read the text back to the teacher in order to receive an *ijāzah* like the one issued to al-Ḥusaynī after completing the 841 text. *Ijāzah*s were an important part of the educational process that certified the student to teach a specific range of subjects or disciplines.[125] As is discussed in the conclusion of this book, Ibn Qāḍī Shuhbah may have used his *Ṭabaqāt* as a kind of extended *ijāzah*, in effect, certifying his students to teach the wealth of knowledge transmitted by the entire text.

Eight days after the completion of the third edition, Ibn Qāḍī Shuhbah was rehabilitated enough in the eyes of Sulṭān Jaqmaq to be reappointed chief Shāfiʿī judge of Damascus. He replaced Shams

[119] Al-ʿAynī, *ʿIqd al-jumān*, 528–29. Al-Maqrīzī gives the date as Dhū al-Qaʿdah 3. See al-Maqrīzī, *Sulūk*, vol. 4, 1135.

[120] Al-Sakhāwī, *al-Ḍawʾ al-lāmiʿ*, vol. 11, 22; Ibn Ṭūlūn, *Quḍāt dimashq*, 169.

[121] Ibn Ṭūlūn, *Quḍāt dimashq*, 158.

[122] Ibn Taghrī Birdī, *al-Nujūm*, vol. 7, 93–94; al-Maqrīzī, *al-Sulūk*, vol. 4, 1135–36.

[123] Al-ʿAynī, *ʿIqd al-jumān*, 528–29.

[124] Khān, vol. 4, 148–49.

[125] See Devin Stewart, "The Doctorate of Islamic Law in Mamluk Egypt and Syria," in *Law and Education in Medieval Islam: Studies in Memory of Professor George Makdisi*, ed. Joseph E. Lowry, Devin Stewart, and Shawkat M. Toorawa (Oxford: Gibb Memorial Trust, 2004), 51–54.

al-Dīn Muḥammad b. Ismāʿīl b. Muḥammad al-Wanāʾī (d. 849/1445), who had replaced Bahāʾ al-Dīn Ibn Ḥijjī five months earlier.[126] He was not, however, trusted to be the sole chief preacher of the Umayyad Mosque, as was customary for the chief Shāfiʿī judge. Instead he shared the position with Ibn al-Bāʿūnī who had proven loyal to Jaqmaq during Jakamī's revolt in 841.[127]

His rehabilitation, however, did not last long as he was ordered to be removed from both positions two months later, on Dhū al-Qaʿdah 15 (April 19).[128] He seems to have remained in the position until his replacement, Sirāj al-Dīn al-Ḥimṣī (d. 861/1456–57), arrived in Damascus from Cairo on Muḥarram 3, 844 (June 5, 1440).[129] For reasons that are not clear, on the 12th of that month, al-Ḥimṣī was removed and Ibn Qāḍī Shuhbah was reinstalled as chief Shāfiʿī judge. When al-Ḥimṣī received the news he immediately traveled to Cairo and pressed his case with court officials. He seems to have made a convincing plea because on Muḥarram 20 the Sulṭān fired Ibn Qāḍī Shuhbah and returned al-Ḥimṣī to office.[130]

Final years

In the midst of the turmoil of his appointment and firing, Ibn Qāḍī Shuhbah completed the fourth and final edition of his *Ṭabaqāt* on Muḥarram 14.[131] Following the completion of this version, which differs little from the 841 original, and after his final removal from office, Ibn Qāḍī Shuhbah tired of public life and became a mendicant traveling to tombs around Syria and in Jerusalem collecting *ḥadīth*.[132] Over the final years of his life, Ibn Qāḍī Shuhbah continued to travel, to teach, and to write. Each Ramaḍān he traveled to Jerusalem and stayed at the Ṭūlūnīyah *madrasah* where scholars and

---

[126] al-ʿAynī, *ʿIqd al-jumān*, 547; al-Maqrīzī, *al-Sulūk*, vol. 4, 1128, 1183. Ibn Iyās (*Badāʾiʿ al-zuhūr*, vol. 2, 222) lists the name of the jurist as al-Wanādī.
[127] Ibn Ṭūlūn, *Quḍāt dimashq*, 168.
[128] Al-Maqrīzī, *al-Sulūk*, vol. 4, 1188; Ibn Ṭūlūn, *Quḍāt dimashq*, 168.
[129] Al-ʿAynī, *ʿIqd al-jumān*, 552.
[130] Al-Maqrīzī, *al-Sulūk*, vol. 4, 1201.
[131] Khān, vol. 4, 149.
[132] Al-Sakhāwī , *al-Ḍawʾ al-lāmiʿ*, vol. 11, 22.

common people visited him to hear his recitation and analysis of the *Ṣaḥīḥ* of al-Bukhārī. During these trips his reputation as an intellectual continued to grow; and according to his student al-Sakhāwī, he was even compared to the renowned Ibn Ḥajar al-ʿAsqalānī.[133]

In 851/1447 he made his last visit to Jerusalem. He went back to Damascus in Dhū al-Qaʿdah (January, 1448) and returned to his teaching in the Taqawīyah *madrasah*. On Thursday, the 10th of that month, while he was teaching, a debate broke out among his students concerning the religious problems caused by a sudden death. According to his son Badr al-Dīn, who related the story to al-Sakhāwī, Ibn Qāḍī Shuhbah said that sudden death was preferred. As he left the school Badr al-Dīn noticed that his father did not sit up straight on his mule. Ibn Qāḍī Shuhbah is then quoted as saying in a tired tone of voice, "O my son, what remains of our youth?"[134]

He then went to the Nāṣirīyah *madrasah* where again the discussion turned to death. The following day (Dhū al-Qaʿdah 11) Ibn Qāḍī Shuhbah was sitting with his son Badr al-Dīn working on his diary of current events, a journal he had kept since his days studying with Shihāb al-Dīn Ibn Ḥijjī. According to Badr al-Dīn, Ibn Qāḍī Shuhbah placed his pen in the ink well and leaned on his pillow. As he did so his head turned slightly and his son, fearing that something was amiss, reached for his hand and found that he had died. His death was sudden and painless, "like bleeding to death but without the blood."[135]

Following his death, Badr al-Dīn reported that people had pleasant dreams of his father, a point al-Sakhāwī uses to buttress the piety and goodness of his beloved teacher.[136] The foreshadowing of Ibn Qāḍī Shuhbah's death, the tale of its sudden and painless onset, and the stories of the dreams that people claimed to have had of him after his demise are all meant to convey his special status as a man of God and a scholar of outstanding repute. They are used rhetorically to shape the reader's opinion of Ibn Qāḍī Shuhbah. Al-Sakhāwī used rhetoric in a way that was common in biographical literature and his teacher Ibn Qāḍī Shuhbah used similar methods

[133] Ibid.
[134] Ibid., 24.
[135] Ibid.
[136] Ibid., 23.

of telling history through the lives of men and women in order to create a view of history that explained the role of God in the progress of time and how humans, through their own efforts, could shape that development.

CHAPTER TWO

A BRIEF *DISCURSUS* ON THE DIVERSITY OF SOURCE MATERIAL AND AUTHORIAL CHOICE

The current project seeks to build on previous analyses of *ṭabaqāt* texts by looking at an aspect of the genre that has often been overlooked. One of the underlying theses of this book is that *ṭabaqāt* works present (among other things) rhetorical interpretations of Islamic history and are therefore one of our most important sources of information on medieval Islamic thought. Before discussing the rhetorical strategies and methods used in *ṭabaqāt* texts, however, it is necessary to briefly examine how Ibn Qāḍī Shuhbah uses his sources in constructing his biographies and the extent to which he exercises control over the composition of biographical entries. It has frequently been assumed that *ṭabaqāt* authors were, to a large extent, simple compilers of pre-existing information who were inextricably bound to the materials from which they drew, and therefore, were unable to exercise conscious design in the shaping and constructing of their biographies. In other words, authors were restricted in what they said about historical figures to what had already been reported in previous texts. Coupled with this assumption is the idea that, although any particular individual may have been mentioned in many different texts over wide expanses of time, there was little real diversity in the details that were reported.

In many respects the first assumption generally applies, although to differing degrees. *Ṭabaqāt* authors were in the main bound to their sources and did attempt to faithfully quote their textual informants. The second assumption, that there was wide agreement in what authors record about their subjects, is, however, less true. There was, in fact, wide ranging diversity in the material transmitted about people that included not just differences in dates of death (the most common aspect of source inconsistency), but also in naming, professional qualifications, positions held, teachers, students, family relations, professional and religious classifications, places lived, places of death, the historical events in which individuals were thought to have (or have not) participated and their importance in understanding the life of the person. Not only this, but there was also a good deal of variation in the use of descriptive terms for such things as education, professional offices and positions, ranks of authority, and attributions of virtue and character (or the lack thereof).

The Formation of biographical traditions

For authors writing in the Mamlūk era, such as Ibn Qāḍī Shuhbah, the diversity of source material is more pronounced for biographies written about individuals who lived in the earlier periods of Islamic history. This is the case because, logically, there tend to be more biographies written for any given individual the earlier in time a person lived; and, over time, authors began to develop distinct biographical traditions that focused on different aspects of an individual's life story. As these biographical traditions came to include greater levels of diverse and sometimes conflicting detail, the amount of information available to later historians became larger.

Biographical traditions usually begin with reports from purported eyewitnesses; people who claimed to have known the individual, to have seen him or her do or say something of note, or to have had some kind of direct information. Although there are instances where the eyewitness is also the author, in most cases, reports were orally communicated by eyewitnesses to authors, or to secondary informants, and sometimes even by chains of informants, who then passed the information on to authors. In many *ṭabaqāt* works, however, the names of transmitters are rarely supplied because the brevity of an entry is one of the most common structural elements of the genre.[1]

Statements purported to come from eyewitnesses are far more important in *ṭabaqāt* works and are generally used for rhetorical purposes. If, for instance, an eyewitness is given his own biographical entry in the text, is described as being a reputable authority in the school, and is quoted as saying something positive about the subject of a biography, his quotation is used to buttress the authority of the subject. If, however, the eyewitness is not described in constructive terms, and is quoted as saying something positive about the subject,

[1] There are notable exceptions to this rule, most importantly Ibn Saʿd's *al-Ṭabaqāt al-kubrā*. As mentioned in the previous chapter, this text has many elements that are not usually found in texts typical of the genre.

such quotes are used rhetorically to diminish the authority of the subject. Providing a list of transmitters for such material, in most cases, would do nothing to alter the impression of the witness or the subject and is, therefore, usually removed from the text.

To the contrary, *wafayāt* and *tārīkh* texts typically supply the names of transmitters of material that the author seeks to present as being original to his work. This seems to be the case because 1) authors are generally unconcerned about the length of an individual biography; 2) many *wafayāt* and *tārīkh* works are heavily influenced by standards and methods common in *ḥadīth* transmission and, therefore, use *isnād*s (the chains of transmitters) to give credibility to the report, but not necessarily the subject of the report;[2] and 3) unlike *ṭabaqāt*, *wafayāt* and *tārīkh* are not committed to explicating the transmission of authority within a specific discipline of study, but instead focus on the integrity of the historical information itself.[3]

Irrespective of the historiographical genre, in virtually all instances, reports were not committed to writing until after the death of the subject, and in most cases, not for a period of years. These reports, like all orally communicated material, were subject to alteration and variation depending on the attitudes and opinions of the witnesses, transmitters, and authors. In many instances, there were multiple witnesses to specific events, especially if the person was important or if the event was considered momentous at the time.

Although an author committed a biography to paper, it did not end the transmission of oral reports about an individual or cause the expansion of the corpus of biographical information that was transmitted over time to cease. Because biographical writing was so popular since early in Islamic history, in any generation there could be several biographies written about a recently deceased person, each using different informants, or if using the same informant, utilizing different information about the subject, and thus rendering a different view of the individual's character, abilities, and importance.

In many instances, there was an overlap in the composition of biographical entries and the continued transmission of oral accounts concerning the subject's life. It was not uncommon for new oral transmissions to continue to appear in the written record twenty-five, fifty, or even more than one hundred years after the first written

[2] Robinson, *Islamic Historiography*, 68–71.
[3] Ibid., 71–72.

entry was published. Some of the best examples of this growth are the biographical traditions that formed around the life of Abū Ibrāhīm Ismāʿīl b. Yaḥyā al-Muzanī (d. 264/878), one of the most important and controversial members of the early Shāfiʿī school. New oral traditions were incorporated into his biographical corpus more than two hundred years after his death.[4]

Authors also tended to contribute to the growth of biographical traditions by emphasizing different attributes, abilities, and characteristics, particularly in traditions dedicated to members of different religious professions, especially the law, where there were frequent methodological and doctrinal debates (see chapter five for the development of sub-schools within the Shāfiʿī tradition). This is especially pronounced in *ṭabaqāt* texts because of the emphasis on doctrinal and hierarchical authority. Authors used biography to challenge or support the legitimacy of an idea or method by linking it to the qualities and qualifications of their originators and transmitters. One important arena of contestation was to attack or praise the training, abilities, and importance of the individual, and in less frequent instances, his or her morals and virtues.

Over the centuries even fairly unimportant scholars had many diverse and sometimes highly polemical biographical traditions devoted to them. By the Mamlūk period it was not uncommon for a scholar living in the 4th/10th century to have ten to twenty biographies devoted to his life, each possessing common elements, but also diverging on important issues of rank and qualification in order to portray structures of authority within intellectual traditions in certain ways (see chapters five and six).

Each biographical entry can be divided into individual passages that contain narrative elements representing or referring to specific

[4] Compare the biographies found in Ibn Abī Ḥātim, *Kitāb al-jarḥ*, vol. 2, 204; Ibn Yūnus, *Tārīkh al-miṣrīyīn*, vol. 1, 44; Abū ʿAbdallāh al-Ḥusayn b. ʿAlī al-Ṣaymarī, *Akhbār abī ḥanīfah wa aṣḥābihi* (Beirut: Dār al-kitāb al-ʿarabī, 1976), 162; al-Khalīlī, *Kitāb al-irshād*, vol. 1, 432; Abū Bakr al-Bayhaqī, *Manāqib al-shāfiʿī*, vol. 1, 347–48; Abū Isḥāq al-Shīrāzī, *Ṭabaqāt al-fuqahāʾ*, 142; Ibn ʿAsākir, *Tārīkh madīnat dimashq*, ed. Muḥibb al-Dīn Abī Saʿīd ʿUmar b. Gharāmah al-ʿAmrawī (Beirut: Dār al-fikr, 1995), vol. 5, 369; Ibn Khallikān, *Wafayāt al-aʿyān*, vol. 1, 217, 271–73, vol. 2, 75–76; al-Nawawī, *Tahdhīb al-asmāʾ wa ʾl-lughāt*, vol. 2, 312; al-Dhahabī, *Tārīkh al-islām*, vol. 20, 65–68; *Siyar aʿlām al-nubalāʾ*, vol. 12, 492–97; Tāj al-Dīn ʿAbd al-Wahhāb b. ʿAlī al-Subkī, *Ṭabaqāt al-shāfiʿīyah al-kubrā* (1999), vol. 1, 322–30; al-Isnawī, *Ṭabaqāt al-shāfiʿīyah*, vol. 1, 32 Ibn Ḥajar al-ʿAsqalānī, *Lisān al-mīzān*, ed. ʿĀdil Aḥmad ʿAbd al-Mawjūd and ʿAlī Muḥammad Muʿawwaḍ (Beirut: Dār al-kutub al-ʿarabīyah, 1996), vol. 1, 380–86.

phenomena. In many narrative elements, especially those depicting authority in some fashion, authors use descriptive terms that carry specific meanings. As is described in chapters three and four, most descriptive terms have very precise technical connotations and are used by authors with great care. The way that descriptive terms are used in relation with other terms and ideas provides indications of the implications that authors are attempting to convey in each narrative element. Furthermore, the way an author combines narrative elements provides additional evidence for the author's overall views of the subject of the biography.

Out of the growth of biographical traditions two primary types of variation in source material emerge: thematic variation and terminological variation. Thematic and terminological variation develops in a biographical tradition as authors add new material or recast earlier narrative elements by glossing previous information for the sake of brevity; by adding clarifying information such as dates, the names of witnesses, the names of those who testify to the attributes of the subject, or references to historical events that are designed to lend credibility to the report; by redacting specific terms, references, names, or events in order to change the meaning of the inherited material; or by using different technical terms because a) linguistic conventions changed and the original word no longer carries the same meanings that the original author is thought to intend, b) because the original word does not imply what the current author needs it to, c) because the current author simply prefers certain terms to others for artistic reasons (medieval authors frequently sought to attain particular poetic ideals), or d) for other reasons that are not necessarily clear from the context of the entry but may become apparent only by comparing terms across the whole of the work.

By the time that Ibn Qāḍī Shuhbah wrote his text he had at his disposal a wealth of highly diverse source material from which he could draw in order to shape each biographical entry to suit his particular rhetorical needs. He relies on twenty-eight primary texts in the composition of his *Ṭabaqāt* but utilizes, in total, over 300 different sources of biographical information. These sources were not only other *ṭabaqāt* (he utilizes twenty-six as source texts), but also annalistic histories (forty-five source texts), biographies (ten source texts), death notices (five source texts), numerous legal, theological, grammatical, methodological, and mystical texts, as well as various commentaries, addenda, and continuations. In most biographies, Ibn

Qāḍī Shuhbah is careful to refer to a few of the sources for the information he uses. On average, he provides three citations for each biographical entry, but in the majority of cases it can be demonstrated that he uses information from far more sources than he states (see below).

As figure 2.1 demonstrates, the average number of primary sources Ibn Qāḍī Shuhbah utilizes for each entry declines over the course of his text from an average minimum of twenty-eight in the first three generations to an average minimum of three in the twenty-sixth generation. (This is based on a survey of 100 biographies, chosen at random from the first 676 entries [the first twenty-six generations]. To arrive at the statistics represented by figure 2.1 a search was conducted of the available sources that Ibn Qāḍī Shuhbah used in his text for each of the individuals listed in the sample. Sources that are no longer extant were also included in instances where references to the biography in the lost source are mentioned in other texts.[5] As is discussed in more detail in the final section of this

Figure 2.1. The diversity of sources in the *ṭabaqāt* by generation

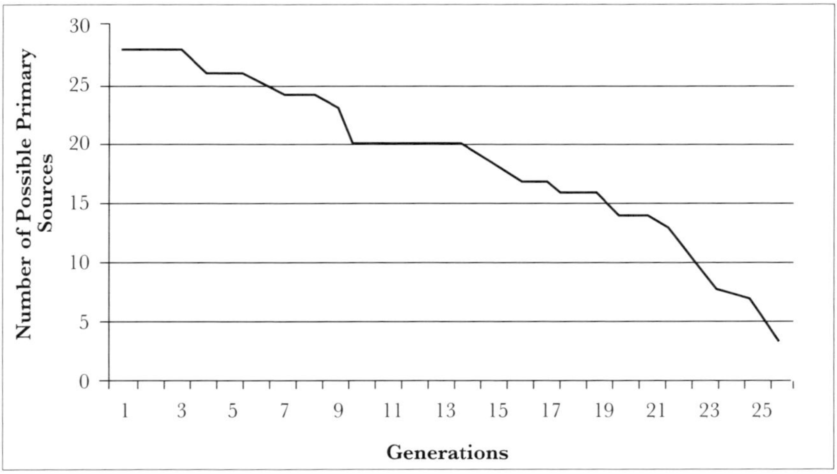

Source: Ibn Qāḍī Shuhbah, *Ṭabaqāt al-fuqahā' al-shāfi'īyah*, ed. al-Ḥāfiẓ 'Abd al-Alī Khān, 4 vols. (Beirut: 'Ālam al-kutub, 1987).

[5] It is likely, however, that the actual numbers are higher than stated in figure 2.1 because the search for biographies in all sources was not possible due to: 1) unavailability of texts, 2) incompleteness or inaccuracies of indexes in several bio-

chapter, the survey also involved searching a selected sample of source texts for thematic and terminological variations in the biographical traditions that developed for each of the selected scholars.) Following the twenty-sixth generation Ibn Qāḍī Shuhbah begins to utilize oral sources to an increasing degree until the final generation (the twenty-ninth) when he relies on his own eye-witness accounts in almost all biographies to supplement oral reports and a few textual sources (see figure 2.2).[6] In the final two generations the most

graphical collections, and 3) due to mistakes on my part in regards to the identification of citations due to variables in names. The most commonly used extant or clearly identifiable biographical texts are: Ibn Abī Ḥātim, *Kitāb al-jarḥ wa 'l-taʿdīl*, 9 vols. (Hyderabad: Dā'irat al-maʿārif al-ʿuthmānīyah, 1952–53; reprint, Beirut: Dār iḥyā' al-turāth al-ʿarabī, np); Ibn Yūnus, *Tārīkh al-miṣrīyīn*, ed. ʿAbd al-Fattāḥ Fatḥī ʿAbd al-Fattāḥ (Beirut: Dār al-kutub al-ʿarabīyah, 2000); Muḥammad al-Ḥākim, *Tārīkh nīsābūr*; Khalīl b. ʿAbdallāh al-Khalīlī, *Kitāb al-irshād fī maʿrifat ʿulamā' al-ḥadīth*, ed. Muḥammad Saʿīd b. ʿUmar, 3 vols. (Riyad: Maktabah al-rushd, 1989); al-ʿAbbādī, *Kitāb ṭabaqāt al-fuqahā' al-shāfiʿīyah*; Abū Bakr al-Bayhaqī, *Manāqib al-shāfiʿī*, ed. Aḥmad Ṣaqr, 2 vols. (Cairo: Maktabat dār al-turāth, 1971); al-Khaṭīb al-Baghdādī, *Tārīkh baghdād aw madīnāt al-salām*; Abū Isḥāq al-Shīrāzī, *Ṭabaqāt al-fuqahā'*; al-Samʿānī, *Kitāb al-ansāb*, 13 vols. (Hyderabad: Maṭbaʿat majlis dā'irat al-maʿārif al-ʿuthmānīyah, 1993); Ibn ʿAsākir, *Tārīkh madīnat dimashq*; Ibn al-Jawzī, *Al-Muntaẓam fī tārīkh al-mulūk wa 'l-umam*, ed. Muḥammad ʿAbd al-Qādir ʿAṭā, 18 vols. (Beirut: Dār al-kutub al-ʿilmīyah, 1992); Ibn al-Ṣalāḥ, *Ṭabaqāt al-fuqahā' al-shāfiʿīyah*, ed. Muḥyī al-Dīn ʿAlī al-Najīb, 2 vols. (Beirut: Dār al-bashā'ir al-islāmīyah, 1996); Muḥyī al-Dīn b. Yaḥyā al-Nawawī, *Tahdhīb al-asmā' wa 'l-lughāt*, 2 vols. (Cairo: Idārat al-ṭabāʿah al-munīrīyah, 1927); Abū al-ʿAbbās Aḥmad b. Muḥammad Ibn Khallikān, *Wafayāt al-aʿyān wa anbā' al-zamān*, ed. Iḥsān ʿAbbās, 6 vols. (Beirut: Dār Ṣādir, 1977); Ibn Qudāmah, *Ṭabaqāt ʿulamā'al-ḥadīth*, ed. Akram al-Būshī and Ibrāhīm al-Zaybaq, 4 vols. (Beirut: Mu'assasat al-risālah, 1997); al-Dhahabī, *Tārīkh al-islām*, ed. ʿUmar ʿAbd al-Salām Tadmurī, 58 vols. (Beirut: Dār al-kutub al-ʿarabī, 1999), also see his *Siyar aʿlām al-nubalā'*, 25 vols. (Beirut: Mu'assasat al-risālah, 1984), *Kitāb tadhkirat al-ḥuffāẓ*, 2 vols. n.p.: Dār al-fikr al-ʿarabī, n.d., and *al-ʿIbar fī khabar man ghabar*, 4 vols. (Beirut: Dār al-kutub al-ʿilmīyah, 1985); Ṣalāḥ al-Dīn Khalīl b. Aybak al-Ṣafadī, *Kitāb al-wāfī bi 'l-wafayāt*, ed. Muḥammad Yūsuf Najm et al, 29 vols. (Wiesbaden: Franz Steiner Verlag GMBH, 1971); ʿAbdallāh b. Asʿad b. ʿAlī al-Yāfiʿī, *Mir'āt al-jinān*, 4 vols. (Beirut: Dār al-kutub al-ʿilmīyah, 1997); Tāj al-Dīn al-Subkī, *Ṭabaqāt al-shāfiʿīyah al-kubrā*, 6 vols. (Beirut: Dār al-kutub al-ʿilmīyah, 1999); ʿAbd al-Raḥīm al-Isnawī, *Ṭabaqāt al-shāfiʿīyah*, ed. Kamāl Yūsuf al-Ḥūt, 2 vols. (Beirut: Dār al-kutub al-ʿilmīyah, 1987); Ismāʿīl Ibn Kathīr, *al-Bidāyah wa 'l-nihāyah*; Muḥammad b. Qāsim al-Nuwayrī, *Kitāb al-ilmān*, ed. ʿAzīz Surayl Atiya, 8 vols. (Hyderabad: Osmania Oriental Publications Bureau, 1979); Muḥammad b. ʿAbdallāh al-Qaysī, *Tawḍīḥ al-mushtabih*, ed. Muḥammad Nuʿaym al-ʿArqasūsī, 9 vols. (Beirut: Mu'assasat al-risālah, 1993); Ibn Ḥajar al-ʿAsqalānī, *Lisān al-mīzān*, ed. ʿĀdil Aḥmad ʿAbd al-Mawjūd and ʿAlī Muḥammad Muʿawwaḍ (Beirut: Dār al-kutub al-ʿarabīyah, 1996), and his *Inbā' al-ghumr*.

[6] In many instances, Ibn Qāḍī Shuhbah uses the phrase "Shihāb al-Dīn Ibn Ḥijjī said," which may indicate that he drew his information from his mentor's *Tārīkh*. In several biographies, however, what Ibn Qāḍī Shuhbah attributes to Ibn Ḥijjī

Figure 2.2. Types of sources (by percentage) for entries in the last three generations

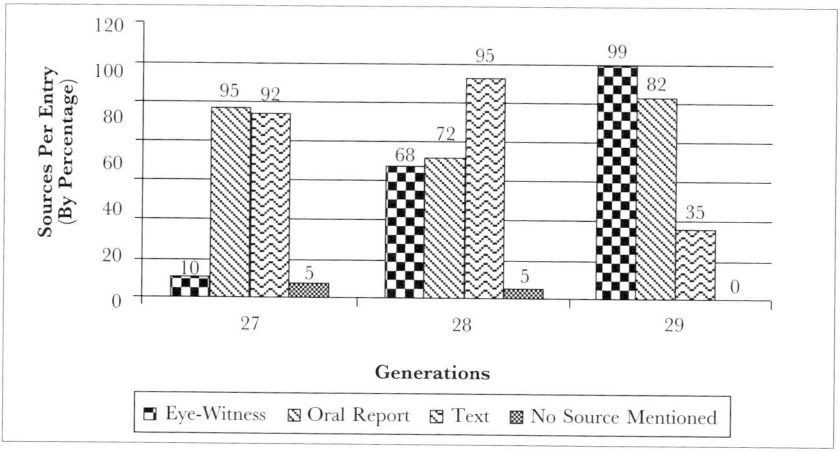

Source: Ibn Qāḍī Shuhbah, *Ṭabaqāt al-fuqahā' al-shāfiʿīyah*, ed. al-Ḥāfiẓ ʿAbd al-Alī Khān, 4 vols. (Beirut: ʿĀlam al-kutub, 1987).

important textual source is that of his contemporary Ibn Ḥajar al-ʿAsqalānī (d. 852/1449). Even in the case of Ibn Ḥajar, however, when Ibn Qāḍī Shuhbah quotes the historian it is unclear as to whether he is actually drawing his information from a written text or if he is basing his quote on an oral transmission. Ibn Qāḍī Shuhbah knew Ibn Ḥajar and may have exchanged information with the historian on more than one occasion.[7]

In only one generation, the twenty-sixth, does Ibn Qāḍī Shuhbah have recourse to fewer than seven sources of information. Following this generation his ability to draw from diverse sources and to control the content of each biography increases dramatically, until the

differs from how he is quoted in Ibn Qāḍī Shuhbah's *Dhayl* of Ibn Ḥijjī's text. It is assumed here that, because of their close relationship, when Ibn Qāḍī Shuhbah refers to Ibn Ḥijjī, these quotes were drawn from oral reports.

[7] Ibn Qāḍī Shuhbah and Ibn Ḥajar met at least once in 825/1422 when Ibn Ḥajar traveled to Damascus and gave lectures in the Umayyad mosque (Ibn Ṭūlūn, *Iʿlām al-warā*, 44). The Egyptian also appears to have carried out a lengthy correspondence with Shihāb al-Dīn Ibn Ḥijjī during the period in which Ibn Qāḍī Shuhbah was his student. In the exchange of letters, the two historians traded information that both used in their respective works. See Ibn Ḥijjī, *Tārīkh Ibn Ḥijjī*, vol. 2, 770. Additionally, as was discussed in the previous chapter, Ibn Qāḍī Shuhbah appears to have asked his student al-Ḥusaynī to take a copy of the *Ṭabaqāt* to Cairo so that Ibn Ḥajar could comment on his text.

last generation where he seems to exercise almost complete freedom in how he phrases and constructs each biography.

Thematic variation: The example of Abū al-Qāsim al-Dārakī

The expansion of, and thematic variation in, source material and how this enabled Ibn Qāḍī Shuhbah to shape his biographies can be exemplified with almost any entry in his text. Take, for instance, the biographical tradition that developed around Abū al-Qāsim al-Dārakī (d. 375/986), who was, in many respects, a fairly minor character in Shāfiʿī legal history. Between Dārakī's death and the time that Ibn Qāḍī Shuhbah wrote his text there were many biographies dedicated to the scholar in a variety of sources, including annalistic histories, death notices, and *ṭabaqāt*. To explore the kinds of thematic variation that are possible in a biographical tradition, the following examination will focus on eleven texts that contain entries for al-Dārakī (see figure 2.3). In these eleven texts al-Dārakī is presented

Figure 2.3. Selected textual sources for al-Dārakī

Author and Date of Death		Title
1. Muḥammad al-Ḥākim	405/1014	*Tārīkh nīsābūr*[8]
2. Abū ʿĀṣim al-ʿAbbādī	458/1066	*Kitāb ṭabaqāt al-fuqahāʾ al-shāfiʿīyah*[9]
3. al-Khaṭīb al-Baghdādī	463/1071	*Tārīkh baghdād*[10]
4. Abū Isḥāq al-Shīrāzī	476/1075	*Ṭabaqāt al-fuqahāʾ*[11]
5. ʿAbd al-Karīm al-Samʿānī	562/1166	*Kitāb al-ansāb*[12]
6. Ibn al-Jawzī	597/1201	*al-Muntaẓam fī tārīkh al-umam wa ʾl-mulūk*[13]
7. al-Nawawī	677/1278	*Tahdhīb al-asmāʾ wa ʾl-lughāt*[14]
8. Ibn Khallikān	681/1282	*Wafayāt al-aʿyān*[15]
9. Tāj al-Dīn al-Subkī	771/1370	*Ṭabaqāt al-shāfiʿīyah al-kubrā*[16]
10. Ibn Kathīr	774/1373	*Ṭabaqāt al-fuqahāʾ al-shāfiʿīyah*[17]
11. Jamāl al-Dīn al-Isnawī	776/1375	*Ṭabaqāt al-shāfiʿīyah*[18]

[8] The passage containing the biography for al-Dārakī in the *Tārīkh nīsābūr* is now lost. It is reconstructed here from al-Samʿānī's *Kitāb al-ansāb*, vol. 5, 276–78.
[9] Al-ʿAbbādī, *Kitāb al-ṭabaqāt*, 100.
[10] Al-Khaṭīb, *Tārīkh baghdād*, vol. 10, 463–65.
[11] Al-Shīrāzī, *Ṭabaqāt al-fuqahāʾ*, 117–18.
[12] Al-Samʿānī, *Kitāb al-ansāb*, vol. 5, 276–78.
[13] Ibn al-Jawzī, *al-Muntaẓam fī tārīkh al-mulūk wa ʾl-umam*, 314.
[14] Al-Nawawī, *Tahdhīb al-asmāʾ wa ʾl-lughāt*, vol. 2, 263.

in a number of ways: as a scholar of *ḥadīth*, law, and rhetoric; and as someone capable of the highest levels of legal reasoning who, according to others, fell outside the limits of Shāfiʿī legal orthodoxy.

Al-Ḥākim's Tārīkh nīsābūr

The earliest known biography for al-Dārakī was written by his contemporary Muḥammad b. ʿAbdallāh al-Ḥākim al-Nīsābūrī (d. 405/1014). Al-Ḥākim does not mention any source for his information, but he probably relied on eyewitness accounts, transmitted material, and possibly his own observations.[19] He gives al-Dārakī's name as ʿAbd al-ʿAzīz b. al-Ḥasan b. Aḥmad al-Dārakī, and states that he was better known as Abū al-Qāsim. All later scholars list al-Dārakī's name as ʿAbd al-ʿAzīz b. ʿAbdallāh,[20] or ʿAbd al-ʿAzīz b. ʿAbdallāh b. Muḥammad.[21] Al-Subkī, writing more than three centuries later, argues that the name Ḥasan b. Aḥmad refers to Abū al-Qāsim's maternal grandfather and that al-Ḥākim's error resulted from his poor knowledge of the scholars of Baghdād. Because of his inadequate familiarity, al-Subkī argues that al-Ḥākim conflated information concerning al-Dārakī's father and maternal grandfather with authentic material about ʿAbd al-ʿAzīz b. ʿAbdallāh.[22] Al-Subkī's argument, however, is somewhat misleading because al-Ḥākim wrote about the scholars of Nīsābūr, who would have included not only Abū al-Qāsim (for the first two-thirds of his life), but also his father and maternal grandfather. While it is reasonable to suggest that al-Ḥākim might have erred in his account of al-Dārakī's activities after

---

[15] Ibn Khallikān, *Wafayāt al-aʿyān*, vol. 2, 361.

[16] Al-Subkī, *Ṭabaqāt al-shāfiʿīyah al-kubrā* (1964–76), vol. 3, 330–31.

[17] Ibn Kathīr, *Ṭabaqāt al-fuqahāʾ al-shāfiʿīyīn*, ed. Aḥmad ʿUmar Hāshim (Cairo: Maktabah al-thaqāfah al-dīnīyah, 1993), vol. 1, 318–320.

[18] Al-Isnawī, *Ṭabaqāt al-shāfiʿīyah*, vol. 1, 245.

[19] Al-Samʿānī, *Kitāb al-ansāb*, vol. 5, 276–78. Tāj al-Dīn al-Subkī, in his entry for al-Dārakī, disputes the idea that al-Ḥākim knew al-Dārakī, insisting that the historian made numerous mistakes because he was unfamiliar with the scholar (*Ṭabaqāt al-shāfiʿīyah al-kubrā* [1964–76], vol. 3, 330).

[20] Al-ʿAbbādī, *Kitāb al-ṭabaqāt*, 100; al-Shīrāzī, *Ṭabaqāt al-fuqahāʾ*, 117; al-Nawawī, *Tahdhīb al-asmāʾ wa ʾl-lughāt*, vol. 2, 263.

[21] Al-Khaṭīb, *Tārīkh baghdād*, vol. 10, 463; al-Samʿānī, *Kitāb al-ansāb*, vol. 5, 276 (although he, in also quoting al-Ḥākim, provides the ʿAbd al-ʿAzīz al-Ḥasan b. Aḥmad variant); Ibn al-Jawzī, *al-Muntaẓam fī tārīkh al-mulūk wa ʾl-umam*, 314; Ibn Khallikān, *Wafayāt al-aʿyān*, vol. 2, 361; al-Subkī, *Ṭabaqāt al-shāfiʿīyah al-kubrā* (1964–76), vol. 3, 330; Ibn Kathīr, *Ṭabaqāt al-fuqahāʾ al-shāfiʿīyīn*, vol. 1, 318; al-Isnawī, *Ṭabaqāt al-shāfiʿīyah*, vol. 1, 245.

[22] Al-Subkī, *Ṭabaqāt al-shāfiʿīyah al-kubrā* (1964–76), vol. 3, 330.

he arrived in Baghdād, it is somewhat disingenuous to argue that his supposed deficiency might have influenced his report for scholars who lived in Nīsābūr.

According to al-Ḥākim, al-Dārakī and his father were *ḥadīth* experts.[23] Al-Subkī disputes this also, saying that it was al-Dārakī's maternal grandfather who was the *ḥadīth* specialist.[24] Al-Ḥākim, however, argues that al-Dārakī was so proficient in the study of *ḥadīth* that he, while living in Nīsābūr, led a group of scholars who specialized in the study of conflicting prophetic traditions (*mukhtalifah*), a contention that al-Subkī also implies is incorrect.[25]

Al-Ḥākim, provocatively in light of the later biographical tradition, does not ascribe to al-Dārakī any profound legal ability; he does not even mention any scholars with whom al-Dārakī was supposed to have studied. He states, however, that when al-Dārakī arrived in Nīsābūr in 353/964, from his native region in the vicinity of Iṣbahān, he taught law (*darrasa*) for two years before traveling to ʿIrāq. After he arrived in Baghdād, al-Ḥākim states that al-Dārakī rose to become a leader of the Shāfiʿī school, establishing his own *majlis*[26] in a Mosque founded by Daʿlaj b. Aḥmad b. Daʿlaj (d. 351/962) for teaching law.[27] Daʿlaj b. Aḥmad was, according to al-Dhahabī, a wealthy traditionist who became a patron to the community of *ḥadīth* scholars who lived and worked in Mecca, ʿIrāq, and Sijistān, from where Daʿlaj's family originated.[28] Al-Ḥākim goes on to say that after al-Dārakī arrived in Baghdād he developed a following of people who used to ask him to resolve legal problems.[29]

Al-Ḥākim presents al-Dārakī is as a specialist in *ḥadīth* who had unspecified training in law, but who, for reasons unstated in the biography, was able to develop a following within the general public and within sections of the Shāfiʿī school in Baghdād. Reference to Daʿlaj b. Aḥmad is used by al-Ḥākim to buttress the importance of *ḥadīth* scholarship for al-Dārakī, implicitly linking it to his role as a

[23] Al-Samʿānī, *Kitāb al-ansāb*, vol. 5, 276.
[24] Al-Subkī, *Ṭabaqāt al-shāfiʿīyah al-kubrā* (1964–76), vol. 3, 330.
[25] Al-Samʿānī, *Kitāb al-ansāb*, vol. 5, 276; al-Subkī, *Ṭabaqāt al-shāfiʿīyah al-kubrā* (1964–76), vol. 3, 330.
[26] Literally a 'sitting,' connoting a place where students would gather, usually in a large circle, to listen to al-Dārakī teach.
[27] Al-Samʿānī, *Kitāb al-ansāb*, vol. 5, 276–77.
[28] Al-Dhahabī, *Tārīkh al-islām*, vol. 25, 53–56.
[29] Al-Samʿānī, *Kitāb al-ansāb*, vol. 5, 276–78.

professor of law and as leader of the Shāfiʿī school. In fact, for al-Ḥākim, al-Dārakī's legal expertise and fame are tied directly to his authority in the study and transmission of *ḥadīth*.

Al-ʿAbbādī's Kitāb ṭabaqāt al-fuqahāʾ al-shāfiʿīyah

Between 450/1058 and 475/1083, almost a century following the death of al-Dārakī, three more biographies were written that drew on transmitted eyewitness accounts, although none appear to have relied on al-Ḥākim's text to any extent. The earliest of these was composed by the Shāfiʿī jurist and historian Abū ʿĀṣim al-ʿAbbādī, who says nothing about al-Dārakī's training, where he was from, or the subjects in which he specialized. In fact, al-ʿAbbādī provides almost no biographical information at all. Instead, he attempts to depict al-Dārakī as a jurist who was in the mainstream of the Shāfiʿī school by referring to al-Dārakī's opinion regarding the purity of vessels that contained wine that had turned to vinegar over time.

Al-Dārakī is quoted as arguing that wine vessels do not need to be purified after their contents had already turned to vinegar. In other words, he assumes that although wine is impure, vinegar, because it undergoes a change, loses its impurity. Therefore, if the vessel were to be used to hold another liquid, for instance, water used in ritual ablutions, no additional precautions need to be taken to ensure that the vessel does not communicate its previous impurity, gained from the wine, to the water. Al-ʿAbbādī goes on to say that other scholars, whom he does not mention, held that the vessel must be purified.[30]

Al-Nawawī, in his *al-Majmūʿ al-mudhahhab fī sharḥ al-muhadhdhab*, indicates that al-Dārakī's opinion reflects that of al-Shāfiʿī and other mainstream scholars in the school.[31] Al-ʿAbbādī quotes it to suggest that al-Dārakī represented orthodox school thought; and by contrasting his opinion with other, unnamed individuals who differed with his and al-Shāfiʿī's opinion, he is also arguing that al-Dārakī is not a voice in *ikhtilāf.* Although it is by no means certain from the context of the entry, it further implies that al-ʿAbbādī may have been reacting to a current of dissent that had formed around the

[30] Al-ʿAbbādī, *Kitāb al-ṭabaqāt,* 100.
[31] Al-Nawawī, *al-Majmūʿ*, vol. 2, 531.

reputation of the scholar, although he provides no specific clue as to what that might have concerned. By providing almost no details about al-Dārakī's life, al-ʿAbbādī seems to assume that his readers were already familiar with specifics of his biography. The only biographical information provided by al-ʿAbbādī concerns two of al-Dārakī's students, Maymūn al-Wāsiṭī and Abū Muḥammad al-Muqrīʾ, neither of whom was notable in the study of law.

Al-ʿAbbādī, in fact, does not provide a biography for al-Wāsiṭī, nor does he refer to him in any other biography in his text. Al-Isnawī, in his *Ṭabaqāt*, lists his full name as Maymūn b. Sahl al-Wāsiṭī and says that he was a student of al-Dārakī, although he bases this solely on al-ʿAbbādī. Al-Isnawī goes on to say that the scholar died in 428/1037.[32] Al-Dhahabī, however, lists his full name as Maymūn b. Sahl Abū Najīb al-Wāsiṭī al-Harawī and states that he died in Ramaḍān; he provides no other information.[33]

Likewise, al-ʿAbbādī does not present a biography for Abū Muḥammad Ismāʿīl b. Ibrāhīm al-Muqrīʾ, although he does refer to him in his entry for Aḥmad b. ʿAlī al-Ikhshād. Al-ʿAbbādī does not give any biographical details of al-Muqrīʾ's life beyond stating that he was "the student (*ṣāḥib*) of Abū al-Qāsim al-Dārakī."[34] Al-Samʿānī, in his *Kitāb al-ansāb*, states that Abū Muḥammad al-Muqrīʾ studied in Khurāsān and ʿIrāq and that he was "among the people of the house and the people of *ḥadīth*;" he does not supply the date of his death.[35] Al-Subkī, as with al-Samʿānī, states that al-Muqrīʾ was a descendant of the Prophet, but he adds that al-Shāfiʿī was also his ancestor, for whom he wrote a *Manāqib* (a text dedicated to outlining al-Shāfiʿī's virtues). He further depicts the jurist as studying law (*tafaqqaha*) with al-Dārakī and as hearing *ḥadīth* from al-Ḥākim. Al-Subkī lists his date of death as 424/1033.[36]

Al-ʿAbbādī crafts al-Dārakī's biography in such a way as to make the scholar appear in the mainstream of the Shāfiʿī school who, in the overall history of its development, made little overall impact. Like al-Ḥākim, although with less direct emphasis, al-Dārakī is

[32] Isnawī, *Ṭabaqāt*, vol. 2, 305.
[33] *Tārīkh al-islām*, vol. 28, 247.
[34] Al-ʿAbbādī, *Kitāb al-ṭabaqāt*, 32.
[35] *Kitāb al-ansāb*, vol. 12, 401.
[36] *Ṭabaqāt* [1964–76], vol. 4, 266–68.

presented as being a minor scholar whose students were unknown as authorities in the law, but who had some abilities in the collection and transmission of prophetic traditions.

Abū Isḥāq al-Shīrāzī's Ṭabaqāt al-fuqahā'

At around the same time that al-ʿAbbādī wrote his text, Abū Isḥāq al-Shīrāzī was writing his *Ṭabaqāt.* He, unlike al-Ḥākim and al-ʿAbbādī, focuses more specifically on al-Dārakī's role as student and teacher of law. He describes al-Dārakī as "an accomplished jurist," who

> studied law (*tafaqqaha*) with Abū Isḥāq al-Marwazī; he rose to the level of *tadrīs* (headmaster) in Baghdād. *Shaykh* Abū Ḥāmid al-Isfarā'īnī studied with him after the death of Abū al-Ḥasan b. al-Marzubān. In general the masters (*shuyūkh*) of Baghdād and others besides them among the people of distant lands studied (*akhadha*) with him.[37]

In this passage, al-Shīrāzī makes no mention of al-Dārakī's reputation as a scholar of *ḥadīth*, emphasizing instead his role in legal education. In his clarification of the 'mistakes' committed by al-Ḥākim, al-Subkī describes al-Shīrāzī's biography as the more accurate account, using it to emphasize al-Dārakī's role as a jurist and to distance the scholar from claims that he specialized in *ḥadīth.* While al-Shīrāzī states that al-Dārakī was an accomplished jurist he does not describe him as a leader of the school in ʿIrāq and he makes no mention of any controversy surrounding his opinions.

Al-Shīrāzī is also the first writer to refer to Abū Isḥāq al-Marwazī (d. 340/952) as al-Dārakī's legal instructor. Al-Marwazī was an important early Shāfiʿī jurist who was considered by most Shāfiʿī scholars to represent the *madhhab*, or the collection of opinions that are reflective of the collective thought of the school.[38] Al-Marwazī was well known in his time and it is significant that neither al-ʿAbbādī nor al-Ḥākim makes reference to the relationship, especially since al-ʿAbbādī presents al-Marwazī as one of the greatest Shāfiʿī jurists of all time.[39] If al-Marwazī were truly the teacher of al-Dārakī it would only serve to raise al-Dārakī's reputation in the school and

---

[37] Al-Shīrāzī, *Ṭabaqāt al-fuqahā'*, 117–18.

[38] See Hallaq, *Authority, Continuity, and Change in Islamic Law*, 155–60. Also see chapter five of the present work.

[39] Al-ʿAbbādī, *Kitāb al-ṭabaqāt*, 68–69.

contribute to his authority as a legal scholar. If, on the other hand, al-Dārakī was considered by some to be less reputable or too controversial, describing such a relationship would only serve to diminish al-Marwazī's standing, something al-ʿAbbādī appears reluctant to do.

Al-Shīrāzī does not describe the circumstances in which al-Marwazī and al-Dārakī were supposed to have met. Al-Marwazī died in 340/952, twelve years before al-Dārakī arrived in Nīsābūr and began to work as a teacher, according to al-Ḥākim's chronology.[40] Additionally, in his biography for al-Marwazī, al-Shīrāzī states that at some point before 340/952, al-Marwazī traveled to Egypt, where he remained until his death. Al-ʿAbbādī clarifies this point by stating that al-Marwazī was in Egypt during the "year of the Qarāmaṭah," the Ismāʿīlī sect that had engaged in a protracted struggle with proto-Sunnī authorities in much of the Middle East in the 3rd/9th and 4th/10th centuries.[41] Al-Dhahabī indicates that the "year of the Qarāmaṭah" most likely refers to the year 317/929 when the Qarmaṭīs attacked Mecca and carried off the Black Stone.[42] Al-Dhahabī, al-ʿAbbādī, and al-Shīrāzī indicate that after al-Marwazī left for Egypt he did not return to the east, although it is possible that he did and they were either unaware of it, or that it did not, from their point of view, merit any mention. If al-Dārakī and al-Marwazī did study together, it most likely occurred before 317/929, when al-Dārakī would still have been quite young. Although al-Marwazī appears to have made several trips to the region around Iṣbahān before 317/929, he does not seem to have spent extended periods in the area.[43] Any study between the two would, therefore, have been quite brief.

Al-Shīrāzī's work is, however, not the only source during the period that place the two scholars together. Abū Isḥāq al-Māwardī (d. 450/1058), in his legal text *al-Ḥāwī al-kabīr*, states that al-Dārakī transmitted several legal opinions from al-Marwazī (interestingly, al-Māwardī does not relate any opinion that originated with al-Dārakī).[44]

[40] Al-Samʿānī, *Kitāb al-ansāb*, vol. 5, 276.

[41] Al-ʿAbbādī, *Kitāb al-ṭabaqāt*, 68–69.

[42] Al-Dhahabī, *Tārīkh al-islām*, vol. 23, 380–82. A less probable date is 332/944–45, when the Qarmaṭī leader Abū Ṭāhir died (*Tārīkh al-islām*, vol. 25, 13–17).

[43] Ibid., vol. 23, 380–82.

[44] Abū al-Ḥasan al-Māwardī, *al-Ḥāwī al-kabīr fī fiqh madhhab al-shāfiʿī wa huwa sharḥ mukhtaṣar al-muzanī*, ed. ʿAlī Muḥammad al-Muʿawwaḍ et al. (Beirut: Dār al-kutub al-ʿilmīyah, 1994), vol. 10, 260, 468; vol. 11, 121, 321.

It may be that al-Shīrāzī describes the relationship based on al-Māwardī, or on an emerging legal tradition in which al-Dārakī transmitted legal opinions from al-Marwazī; a tradition of which al-ʿAbbādī was unaware.

Al-Shīrāzī is also the first to claim that Abū Ḥāmid al-Isfarāʾīnī (d. 406/1016) studied law from al-Dārakī. According to al-Shīrāzī, Abū Ḥāmid was an important scholar, to whom he devotes one of his longest biographies. He describes Abū Ḥāmid as "rising to become a leader in Baghdād in temporal matters and in religion."[45] According to al-Shīrāzī, Abū Ḥāmid was a specialist in law and legal method (*uṣūl al-fiqh*); he even wrote a commentary on the *Mukhtaṣar* of al-Muzanī, one of the most important sources of *ikhtilāf* in the Shāfiʿī school. In his biography for al-Isfarāʾīnī, however, al-Shīrāzī does not mention al-Dārakī as one of Abū Ḥāmid's teachers. As described in the next two chapters, *ṭabaqāt* writers were careful to combine information in an entry in order to create images of authority for particular individuals. Al-Shīrāzī's reference to Abū Ḥāmid in his entry for al-Dārakī is meant to give credibility to al-Dārakī as a scholar of law. Conversely, his decision not to mention al-Dārakī as a teacher in the biography of Abū Ḥāmid indicates that al-Shīrāzī did not think that such a reference would contribute anything to Abū Ḥāmid's standing in the school, and for reasons discussed below, might actually damage it.

Al-Shīrāzī may have gone to such lengths to build al-Dārakī's image as an authority for personal reasons. According to Ibn Qāḍī Shuhbah, later biographical traditions for al-Shīrāzī maintained that three of his four closest teachers, Abū Aḥmad Ibn Rāmīn (d. 430/1039),[46] Abū ʿAbdallāh al-Bayḍāwī (d. 424/1033),[47] and Abū al-Ṭayyib al-Ṭabarī (d. 450/1058)[48] studied directly with al-Dārakī; a fourth instructor, Abū Ḥātim al-Qazwīnī (d. 440/1048 or 1049)[49] is said to have studied with Abū Ḥāmid al-Isfarāʾīnī who, as men-

---

[45] *Intahat ilayhi riʾāsat al-dunyā wa ʾl-dīn bi-Baghdād* (*Ṭabaqāt*, 124).

[46] Khān, vol. 1, 213.

[47] Ibid., 215–16.

[48] Ibid., 226–28. Abū al-Ṭayyib al-Ṭabarī was, according to al-Khaṭīb al-Baghdādī, a great Shāfiʿī jurist who heard *ḥadīth* from many people, including al-Dāraquṭnī. He also studied law with many people in Khurāsān and Baghdād. He was trustworthy in *ḥadīth*, knowledgeable in *uṣūl al-fiqh*, and he studied *ikhtilāf* (al-Khaṭīb, *Tārīkh baghdād*, vol. 9, 358–60).

[49] Khān, vol. 1, 218.

tioned above, is supposed to have studied with al-Dārakī. Because intellectual lineage was an important component in the construction of legal authority, much of al-Shīrāzī's reputation as a jurist would have rested on how he configured the abilities and reputation of al-Dārakī.

Al-Khaṭīb al-Baghdādī's Tārīkh baghdād

The third and most extensive biography written during the period was composed by al-Khaṭīb al-Baghdādī. Unlike other biographies dedicated to al-Dārakī up to his time, al-Khaṭīb al-Baghdādī provides a list of transmitters for much of the information he cites, although there is still a great deal of material that is provided without stating who his sources are. Al-Khaṭīb states that al-Dārakī

> went down to Nīsābūr for two years and taught law (*darrasa*) there. He then transferred to Baghdād and lived there until the time of his death. There, he transmitted *ḥadīth* from his maternal grandfather al-Ḥasan b. Muḥammad al-Dārakī. He used to teach in Baghdād in the *masjid* of Daʿlaj b. Aḥmad. . . .

In this section of the biography, al-Khaṭīb follows the general outline of al-Ḥākim's text, except that he does not mention, as al-Ḥākim does, that al-Dārakī led of group of *ḥadīth* scholars who studied conflicting prophetic traditions. He also indirectly clarifies al-Dārakī's name by specifying that Ḥasan b. Muḥammad was his grandfather, which is the most likely to source for al-Subkī's critique of al-Ḥākim. But it also reinforces the view, presented by al-Ḥākim, that al-Dārakī was an authority in *ḥadīth*.

Al-Khaṭīb then says that al-Dārakī

> had a circle in the grand Mosque of the city for the issuance of legal opinions and [for the study of] rhetoric.

This passage seems to refer to the narrative element found in al-Ḥākim that states that al-Dārakī formed his own *majlis* (council) in which the people turned to him for legal consultations. It may also refer to the narrative element in al-Shīrāzī's biography that states that al-Dārakī became a *mudarris* (headmaster) in the study of law while in Baghdād. Furthermore, al-Khaṭīb states for the first time in the al-Dārakī biographical tradition that the scholar had a circle in the grand mosque of Baghdād; implying a certain level of authority with the public and with ʿAbbāsid officials. He also states that al-Dārakī taught rhetoric, suggesting a higher level of legal training than previously indicated by al-Ḥākim, al-ʿAbbādī, or al-Shīrāzī. Immediately following this brief description of legal authority, al-Khaṭīb returns to al-Dārakī's role as a scholar of *ḥadīth*, stating that

> Al-Ḥusayn b. Bakr al-Qāḍī,[50] Abū Ṭālib ʿUmar b. Ibrāhīm the jurist,[51] Abū al-Qāsim al-Azharī,[52] Abū Muḥammad al-Khilāl,[53] ʿAlī b. Muḥammad b. al-Ḥasan al-Ḥarbī,[54] ʿAbd al-ʿAzīz al-Azjī,[55] al-ʿAtīqī,[56] and al-Tanūkhī[57] reported to us [that] he was reliable.
>
> Abū Ṭālib ʿUmar b. Ibrāhīm [transmitted a tradition] from Abū al-Qāsim al-Dārakī, the Shāfiʿī jurist, who corrected [the tradition] and dictated it to al-Dāraquṭnī.[58] [He said] "[I] transmitted from my grandfather Abū ʿAlī al-Ḥasan b. Muḥammad from Muḥammad b. Ḥumayd from ʿAbdallāh b. Mubārak from Ḥumayd al-Ṭawīl from Anas b. Mālik who said, 'The Prophet of God said, "I am commanded to fight

[50] Al-Ḥusayn b. Bakr b. ʿUbaydallāh b. Muḥammad b. ʿUbayd Abū al-Qāsim (d. 433/1042). According to Khaṭīb al-Baghdādī he heard *ḥadīth* from al-Dārakī (al-Khaṭīb, *Tārīkh baghdād*, vol. 8, 26).

[51] ʿUmar b. Ibrāhīm b. Saʿīd b. Ibrāhīm b. Muḥammad b. Bajād b. Mūsā b. Saʿd b. Abī Waqqāṣ Abū al-Ṭālib al-Zuhrī (d. 434/1042). Al-Khaṭīb lists him as a Shāfiʿī jurist who heard *ḥadīth* from al-Dārakī (al-Khaṭīb, *Tārīkh baghdād*, vol. 11, 274).

[52] Abū al-Qāsim ʿUbaydallāh b. Aḥmad b. ʿUthmān b. al-Faraj b. al-Azharī (d. 445/1053). Al-Samʿānī says that he was a source for al-Khaṭīb al-Baghdādī (al-Samʿānī, vol. 1, 190).

[53] Al-Dhahabī, in his *Kitāb al-muʿīn fī ṭabaqāt al-muḥaddithīn*, ed. Hammām ʿAbd al-Raḥīm Saʿīd (ʿAmmān: Dār al-furqān, 1984) lists his full name as Abū Muḥammad al-Ḥasan b. Muḥammad b. al-Ḥasan al-Khilāl of Baghdād (p. 127). Al-Khaṭīb states he transmitted *ḥadīth* from many of his generation but does not list al-Dārakī as one of them. He died in 439/1047 (*Tārīkh baghdād*, vol. 7, 425).

[54] Al-Ḥarbī is not listed in al-Samʿānī, al-Dhahabī, or al-Khaṭīb al-Baghdādī.

[55] Abū al-Qāsim ʿAbd al-ʿAzīz b. ʿAlī b. Aḥmad b. al-Faḍl b. Shakr b. Bakrān al-Azjī (d. 356/967) (al-Samʿānī vol. 1, 180). Al-Khaṭīb says that ʿAbd al-ʿAzīz heard *ḥadīth* from al-Dārakī (*Tārīkh baghdād*, vol. 10, 468).

[56] Abū al-Ḥasan Aḥmad b. Muḥammad b. Aḥmad b. Muḥammad b. Manṣūr al-ʿAtīqī (b. 367, d. 441/1049–50 in Baghdād). According to al-Samʿānī, he was a source for al-Baghdādī (al-Samʿānī, vol. 9, 233). According to al-Khaṭīb al-Baghdādī, al-ʿAtīqī was born in Baghdād and heard *ḥadīth* there from a variety of people, including al-Dārakī (al-Khaṭīb, *Tārīkh baghdād*, vol. 4, 379).

[57] Abū al-Qāsim ʿAlī b. Muhasin b. ʿAlī b. Muḥammad Abū al-Fahm al-Tanūkhī (d. 443/1051 in Baghdād) (al-Samʿānī, vol. 3, 95–96). Al-Khaṭīb lists his biography but does not state that he studied with al-Dārakī (*Tārīkh baghdād*, vol. 12, 115).

[58] According to al-Khaṭīb al-Baghdādī, Abū al-Ḥasan al-Ḥāfiẓ ʿAlī b. ʿUmar al-Dāraquṭnī heard *ḥadīth* from many people, although he does not list al-Dārakī as one of them. He transmitted *ḥadīth* to many of al-Khaṭīb's sources, including al-ʿAtīqī, al-Tanūkhī, al-Azharī, al-Azjī, al-Ṭabarī, al-Khilāl, and al-Barqānī. He was also a source for al-Ḥākim. He was one of the greatest jurists of Baghdād and was an expert in law, *ḥadīth*, Qurʾan recitation, and *ikhtilāf*. He died in 385/995 (al-Khaṭīb al-Baghdādī, *Tārīkh baghdād*, vol. 12, 34–40).

the people until they say that there is no god except God and that Muḥammad is the Prophet of God, and they face our *qiblah* (direction of prayer), and they eat what we slaughter, and they pray our prayers. When they do that [then] their blood (meaning lives) and their properties are forbidden to us except what is ours by right. Their reckoning is with God." '"[59]

That al-Khaṭīb would emphasize *ḥadīth* is not a surprise given his own profound interests in the subject. He uses references to specific *ḥadīth* throughout his text to highlight the importance of the discipline for the great scholars of Baghdād. After establishing the centrality of *ḥadīth* scholarship and transmission for al-Dārakī, al-Khaṭīb then moves, as does al-Ḥākim, to link his expertise in prophetic traditions to his authority as a scholar of law. He states that:

> It is reported to us by the judge Abū al-Ṭayyib Ṭāhir b. ʿAbdallāh al-Ṭabarī, he said, "I heard Abū Ḥāmid al-Isfarā'īnī say, 'what I saw from al-Dārakī I agree with.'"
>
> I heard ʿĪsā b. Aḥmad b. ʿUthmān al-Hamadhānī[60] say, "If ʿAbd al-ʿAzīz b. ʿAbdallāh al-Dārakī was asked to issue a legal opinion on an issue, he would reflect [on it] a long time, and then he would issue an opinion. Sometimes his legal opinion differed from the opinion (*madhhab*) of al-Shāfiʿī and Abū Ḥanīfah. It is said he held to that by saying, 'decide on [what] was reported by so and so from so and so from the Prophet of God according to this or that [event]. The acceptance of the *ḥadīth* from the Prophet is more worthy than the acceptance of the statements of al-Shāfiʿī and Abū Ḥanīfah, if it contradicts [his report].'"
>
> Or, it is like what was said, reported to us by Ibn al-Tawzī[61] from Muḥammad b. Abū al-Fawāris[62] who said, "ʿAbd al-ʿAzīz b. ʿAbdallāh al-Dārakī was trustworthy in [the transmission of] *ḥadīth*. He used to believe in seclusion. I heard nothing from him that was novel or that was obscure. . . . I am blessed that I heard things from him. . . ."
>
> It is reported to us by al-ʿAtīqī who said, "In the year 375 Abū al-Qāsim al-Dārakī, the master of the Shāfiʿīs, died on the day of Friday

[59] Sunan Abī Dāwūd 2635.

[60] He is not listed in al-Samʿānī, *Ṭabaqāt al-muḥaddithīn* by al-Dhahabī, al-Khaṭīb al-Baghdādī, al-Isnawī, Ibn Qāḍī Shuhbah, Ibn al-Ṣalāḥ, or al-Subkī (although he is quoted in the biography of Abū Aḥmad b. Abū Muslim al-Faraḍī (d. 406/1015–16), (*Tārīkh baghdād*, vol. 5, 234).

[61] Unable to locate based on name.

[62] Muḥammad b. Aḥmad b. Muḥammad b. Fāris b. Sahl Abū al-Fatḥ b. Abū al-Fawāris was born in 338. He was primarily a *ḥadīth* expert who traveled throughout ʿIrāq, Iran, and Khurāsān collecting traditions. Al-Barqānī heard *ḥadīth* from him, as did al-Ṭabarī. He died in 412/1021 (al-Khaṭīb al-Baghdādī, *Tārīkh baghdād*, vol. 1, 352–53).

> the 13th during the passing of the night in the month of Shawwāl. He was trustworthy and reliable. He rose to the level of leader of the Shāfiʿī school." It is reported to us by al-Barqānī[63] who said, "Abū al-Qāsim al-Dārakī, the jurist, died in Dhū al-Qaʿdah in the year 375." It is sounder that he died during Shawwāl.[64]

The above quote is interesting for a number of reasons and needs to be deconstructed in order to understand the full impact of its claims on the al-Dārakī biographical tradition.

Al-Khaṭīb al-Baghdādī begins the passage by foreshadowing his statement about al-Dārakī's claims to independence from al-Shāfiʿī and Abū Ḥanīfah by using Abū Ḥāmid al-Isfarāʾīnī's authority as a jurist—as a scholar of law, legal method, and prophetic traditions—as testimony to the correctness of al-Dārakī's approach by saying "what I saw from al-Dārakī I agree with." Phrases denoting agreement are used by al-Khaṭīb in a number of biographical entries as a means of creating the impression that there was near unanimity among scholars on a wide range of doctrinal and methodological issues. Such phrases are used to create 'circles of authority' by suggesting that like-minded scholars were grouped together in the pursuit of common goals. For instance, in his biography for Abū Ṭayyib al-Ṭabarī, al-Khaṭīb quotes Abū Muḥammad al-Bāfī as saying "Abū al-Ṭayyib al-Ṭabarī agreed with Abū Ḥāmid al-Isfarāʾīnī." He also quotes al-Isfarāʾīnī as saying, "Abū al-Ṭayyib al-Ṭabarī agreed with Abū Muḥammad al-Bāfī."[65] By attributing a testimony of agreement to Abū Ḥāmid, al-Khaṭīb suggests that al-Isfarāʾīnī, al-Ṭabarī, al-Bāfī, and the other scholars to whom he attributes such statements of agreement all held the same opinion regarding the priority of *ḥadīth* over the opinions of al-Shāfiʿī and Abū Ḥanīfah.

It may seem, however, somewhat surprising that al-Khaṭīb would suggest that al-Dārakī would openly disagree with both al-Shāfiʿī and Abū Ḥanīfah, arguing that his own interpretation of *ḥadīth* outweighed their opinions. Not only this, but by creating a circle of authority around al-Dārakī in the previous section, al-Khaṭīb suggests that many other scholars held to that view as well. According to al-Subkī, al-Khaṭīb studied law (*tafaqqaha*) with Abū Ṭayyib al-

---

[63] Abū Bakr Aḥmad b. Muḥammad b. Aḥmad b. Ghālib al-Barqānī (d. 425/1034) was a famous *ḥadīth* transmitter, jurist, and Qurʾan scholar. He transmitted information to al-Khaṭīb (al-Samʿānī, vol. 2, 168–69).

[64] Al-Khaṭīb al-Baghdādī, *Tārīkh baghdād*, vol. 10, 463–65.

[65] Ibid., vol. 9, 358–60.

Ṭabarī and Abū Naṣr Ibn al-Ṣabbāgh (d. 447/1055), both important authorities in the transmission of divergent opinion within the Shāfiʿī school.[66] Al-Subkī goes on to argue that one of the sources of al-Khaṭīb's ability to contribute to divergent opinion, and indeed one loci of his authority to do so, was his claim to expertise in *ḥadīth*. Al-Khaṭīb held strict theological views that tended away from rationalism, and his understanding of the importance of near-literalist interpretations of *ḥadīth* was a major factor in his own legal methodology.[67] Al-Khaṭīb's description of al-Dārakī may therefore be interpreted as a statement of the historian's own views; attributions of agreement are thus used as evidence of the appropriateness of his own particular ideas as well as those of al-Dārakī.

As discussed above, however, it would appear that there was some controversy surrounding al-Dārakī and his opinions; al-ʿAbbādī implied as much when he presented al-Dārakī's opinion on the purity of wine vessels without any biographical or historical context. As with al-ʿAbbādī, al-Khaṭīb seeks to blunt such apparent criticisms, not by quoting a legal opinion, but through the testimony of contemporary legal authorities. Al-Khaṭīb quotes Abū al-Fawāris (d. 412/1021) as saying that the scholar heard "nothing from him (al-Dārakī) that was novel or that was obscure." Although little is known about Abū al-Fawāris beyond his role as a *ḥadīth* specialist from whom al-Khaṭīb heard prophetic traditions,[68] it is clear that al-Khaṭīb placed great trust in Abū al-Fawāris and uses the quotation to establish the correctness of such a *ḥadīth*-centered approach.

Additionally, there is a noticeable lacuna in al-Khaṭīb's presentation of al-Dārakī when compared with the biography provided by al-Shīrāzī. Although al-Khaṭīb mentions Abū Ḥāmid al-Isfarā'īnī in creating a circle of authority around al-Dārakī's legal method, he does not describe Abū Ḥāmid as his student, nor, significantly, does he refer to al-Marwazī as his teacher. He, in fact, gives no specific information regarding who al-Dārakī's teachers or students were. One reason for this paucity of educational information is that, because al-Khaṭīb was not interested in describing specific structures of legal authority within the Shāfiʿī school, he was less concerned with listing teachers and students than he was in specifying those with whom

[66] See chapter seven.
[67] Al-Subkī, *Ṭabaqāt al-shāfiʿīyah al-kubrā* (1999), vol. 2, 362–69.
[68] Al-Khaṭīb, *Tārīkh baghdād*, vol. 1, 352–53.

al-Dārakī was involved in the transmission of *ḥadīth*. Al-Khaṭīb normally is rather careful in listing teachers and students, especially if they were important people in their own rights, as were al-Marwazī and Abū Ḥāmid. If al-Dārakī was closely linked to either scholar in his mind, it is likely that he would have mentioned some affiliation. This suggests that although al-Dārakī may have worked with both scholars, their relationships may not have been as close or as important as al-Shīrāzī wants them to appear, indicating that their specification in his entry was done to support his own claims to authority.

Al-Khaṭīb goes much further in his depiction of al-Dārakī than either al-ʿAbbādī or Abū Isḥāq. Part of this has to do with the nature of the texts. Al-Khaṭīb al-Baghdādī was writing a history of the notable people of Baghdād and, as a *ḥadīth* scholar, emphasized training, expertise, and use of prophetic traditions in many of his biographies. He was also less concerned with discussing specific issues of legal authority within the Shāfiʿī school, a central issue for both al-ʿAbbādī and Abū Isḥāq. Because al-Shīrāzī and al-ʿAbbādī were writing *ṭabaqāt* texts, they were concerned with describing the parameters of Shāfiʿī thought; and both sought to present the scholar as the archetypal representative of the mainstream of the Shāfiʿī school. Although al-Shīrāzī may have done so in part to clarify his own intellectual heritage, both scholars wanted to describe the boundaries of permissible thought within the school, and both hoped to ignore any reputation for controversy or for diverging from the opinion of al-Shāfiʿī.

Thematic variation and Ibn Qāḍī Shuhbah's biography

Over the next 400 years a number of narrative themes emerge in the al-Dārakī biographical tradition that are, for the most part, rooted in the biographies discussed above. As figure 2.2 shows below, there are approximately fifty narrative elements that appear in the eleven biographies written about al-Dārakī up to Ibn Qāḍī Shuhbah's time (although there are probably more given the likelihood that there were additional biographies written about him). These elements can be grouped into eight general thematic clusters that are emphasized by different writers to create specific representations of al-Dārakī's authority. The narrative elements within these themes vary widely, some describing al-Dārakī as a representative of the *madhhab* and other emphasizing his aberrant (*gharīb*) legal opinions; some focusing on his specialization in prophetic traditions and others in the law.

Figure 2.4. Narrative elements in the al-Dārakī biographical tradition

Narrative Element	Sources
Demographic Elements	
1. Name Tradition 1: ʿAbd al-ʿAzīz b. ʿAbdallāh	Kh, Sh, S, J, N, IKh, Sb, IK, I, IQ
2. Name Tradition 2: ʿAbd al-ʿAzīz b. Ḥasan	Ḥ, S, Sb
3. Clarification of the Spelling of Dārak	S, N, IKh, I, IQ
4. Location of Dārak	S, N, IKh, Sb, IK, I, IQ
5. Place of Burial	Kh, J, I
6. Died in Dhū al-Qaʿdah	Kh, N, IKh, I, IQ
7. Died in Shawwāl, 375	Ḥ, Kh, S, N, Sb, IQ
8. Died on the 13th of Shawwāl, 375	Kh, N, IKh, IK, I
9. He was more than 70 years old when he died	Kh, J, N, IKh, I, IQ
10. May God have mercy on him (*raḥimahu Allāh*)	IQ
Learning	
1. Study law (*tafaqqaha*) with al-Marwazī	Sh, N, Sb, IK, I, IQ
2. Study (*akhadha*) with al-Marwazī	IKh
Teaching	
1. Taught law (*darrasa*) in Nīsābūr for a period	IK, IQ
2. Taught law (*darrasa*) in Nīsābūr for two years	Kh, S, J, N, Sb, I
3. Taught law (*darrasa*) in Nīsābūr between 353 and 355	Ḥ, S, IKh
4. The *shaykh*s of Baghdād and the people of distant lands studied (*akhadha*) with him	Sh, N, IKh, Sb, IK, IQ
5. Held position of *mudarris* (headmaster)	Sh, N, IKh, Sb
6. Taught law (*darrasa*) in the Mosque of Daʿlaj b. Aḥmad	Ḥ, Kh, S, J, IKh
7. Circle in the Grand Mosque for the issuance of legal opinions and the study of rhetoric	Kh, S, J, N, IKh
8. Maymūn al-Wāsiṭī his disciple (*talāmidh*)	ʿA

Figure 2.4 (*cont.*)

Narrative Element	Sources
9. Abū Muḥammad al-Muqrī᾽ his disciple (*talāmidh*)	ʿA
10. al-Dāraquṭnī studied (*qara᾽a*) Qur᾽an with him	IK
11. Abū al-Ḥusayn al-Ṭabarī studied law (*tafaqqaha*) with him	IK
12. al-Isfarā᾽īnī studied law (*tafaqqaha*) with him	Sh, N, IKh, Sb, IK, IQ
Role as Leading Jurist	
1. *Ri᾽āsah* (leadership) of the Shāfiʿīs	Ḥ, Kh, S, J, N, Sb, IK, I, IQ
2. Circle for the issuance of legal opinions	IK, IQ
3. Held a *majlis* in the Grand Mosque of Baghdād	Ḥ, S, Sb
4. Could perform *ijtihād*	IK
5. Had the ability to carry-out *ijtihād*-like operations	Ḥ, Kh, J, N, Sb
6. Opinions disagreed with those of al-Shāfiʿī and Abū Ḥanīfah	Kh, J, N, IKh
7. Held divergent opinions (*ikhtilāf*)	IK, N
8. Held aberrant (*gharīb*) opinions	N
9. Citation of *ḥadīth* in support of his *ikhtilāf*	IK
10. Quoted by al-Rāfiʿī	N
11. He had a new approach to legal issues in the school	IKh
12. Provides citation in support of his divergence from al-Shāfiʿī and Abū Ḥanīfah	Kh, J, N, IKh, IK
13. His opinions were reflective of those of al-Shāfiʿī	ʿA
Ḥadīth Scholar	
1. al-Dārakī as a trustworthy transmitter (*thiqah*)	IKh, S, Sb, IQ
2. Father as *ḥadīth* specialist	Ḥ, S, IKh, Sb, IK, I
3. He was a *ḥadīth* specialist (*muḥaddith*)	Ḥ, Sb (disputes claim)
4. Held a group for the study of contradictory traditions (*mukhtalifah*)	Ḥ, S, Sb

Figure 2.4 (*cont.*)

Narrative Element	Sources
5. al-Dārakī transmitted *ḥadīth* from his grandfather	Kh, S, IKh, Sb, IK
6. al-Dārakī transmitted *ḥadīth* in Nīsābūr and Baghdād	Ḥ, S, J
7. al-Dārakī as a reliable (*amīnan*) transmitter	Kh, J
Reputation	
1. Abū Ḥāmid al-Isfarāʾīnī's testimony for al-Dārakī	Kh, S, J, N, IKh, Sb, IK, I, IQ
2. Al-Dārakī as among the great Shāfiʿī jurists	Ḥ, S, IKh, Sb (disputes claim)
3. There was nothing new in his legal opinions	Kh
4. al-Dārakī held odd or strange opinions	N, IK
5. Mentioned in legal texts	N, Sb
Religious Attributes	
1. al-Dārakī as a practitioner of seclusion (*iʿtizāl*)	Kh, S, N, IKh, IK

Note: Ḥ = al-Ḥākim, ʿA = al-ʿAbbādī, Kh = Khaṭīb al-Baghdādī, Sh = al-Shīrāzī, S = al-Samʿānī, J = Ibn al-Jawzī, N = al-Nawawī, IKh = Ibn Khallikān, Sb = al-Subkī, IK = Ibn Kathīr, I = al-Isnawī, IQ = Ibn Qāḍī Shuhbah.

Although there are a wide array of narrative clarifications and amendments that occur over the 400 years between the beginnings of the al-Dārakī tradition and Ibn Qāḍī Shuhbah's text, there are a number of key variations that are important for understanding how Ibn Qāḍī Shuhbah composed his entry. Out of the fifty narrative elements listed above, Ibn Qāḍī Shuhbah utilizes only fourteen in the construction of his biography.[69] In his entry for the scholar, Ibn Qāḍī Shuhbah states that al-Dārakī

[69] Ibn Qāḍī Shuhbah may have used additional sources that are no longer extant or ones for which a biography for al-Dārakī could not be located due to inconsistencies in naming.

> taught (*darrasa*) in Nīsābūr for a period then he lived in Baghdād. He used to have a circle for [issuing] legal opinions. He rose to become the leader (*riʾāsah*) of the school in Baghdād. He studied law (*tafaqqaha*) with Abū Isḥāq al-Marwazī. The *shaykh* Abū Ḥāmid studied law (*tafaqqaha*) with him after the death of *shaykh* Abū al-Ḥasan b. al-Marzubān. He said "what I saw from him I agreed with." Abū Isḥāq said in his *Ṭabaqāt*, "in general the masters (*shuyūkh*) of Baghdād and others besides them among the people of distant lands studied (*akhadha*) with him." Al-Khaṭīb said, "He was trustworthy [and] al-Dāraquṭnī relied on him." He died in the year 375 in the month of Shawwāl, some say in the month of Dhū al-Qaʿdah, in excess of 70 years of age; may God have mercy on him. Dārak [is spelled with] a *fatḥ* over the *rāʾ* and is among the villages of Iṣbahān.[70]

In his entry, Ibn Qāḍī Shuhbah skillfully draws together elements from the biographies of Abū Isḥāq al-Shīrāzī and al-Khaṭīb al-Baghdādī, although it is immediately evident by his clarification of the spelling and location of the village of Dārak that he also consulted at least one, and possibly other entries that he does not cite. Furthermore, since he utilizes biographical information in other entries in his text from each of the eleven sources mentioned above, it is likely that he could have drawn on any of the narrative elements listed in figure 2.2 had he chosen to do so.

The first aspect of his biography that stands out is just how careful Ibn Qāḍī Shuhbah is to combine information from the previous texts to shape the impression of al-Dārakī, and how this cautious structuring subtly changes the image of the jurist. He begins by quoting Ibn Kathīr's statement that al-Dārakī "taught (*darrasa*) in Nīsābūr for a period." Ibn Qāḍī Shuhbah also glosses al-Khaṭīb's statement that after al-Dārakī taught in Nīsābūr for two years, "he then transferred to Baghdād and lived there until the time of his death," with the simple statement that "then he lived in Baghdād."

Ibn Qāḍī Shuhbah then returns to Ibn Kathīr, stating that al-Dārakī "used to have a circle for [issuing] legal opinions," which is itself a gloss on earlier references to al-Dārakī's circle for the issuance of legal opinions and for the study of rhetoric in the Grand Mosque of Baghdād mentioned by al-Khaṭīb, and later by al-Samʿānī, Ibn Jawzī, al-Nawawī, and Ibn Khallikān (all of which are, in turn, glosses on al-Ḥākim). Ibn Qāḍī Shuhbah follows this with a quotation from al-Shīrāzī, although without attribution, with his comment

[70] Khān, vol. 1, 141.

that al-Dārakī "studied law (*tafaqqaha*) with Abū Isḥāq al-Marwazī. The *shaykh* Abū Ḥāmid studied law (*tafaqqaha*) with him after the death of *shaykh* Abū al-Ḥasan b. al-Marzubān." Significantly, Ibn Qāḍī Shuhbah does not include al-Shīrāzī's statement that al-Dārakī "rose to the level of *tadrīs* in Baghdād," and, in fact, chooses to say nothing about his rank as a teacher.

Following his statement that Abū Ḥāmid al-Isfarāʾīnī studied with al-Dārakī, Ibn Qāḍī Shuhbah interpolates into his entry Abū Ḥāmid's statement, found in al-Khaṭīb, that "what I saw from him I agreed with." By combining al-Shīrāzī's claim that Abū Ḥāmid was al-Dārakī's student with al-Khaṭīb's use of Abū Ḥāmid's testimony of agreement, Ibn Qāḍī Shuhbah shapes the biography to give al-Dārakī a definition of authority that is absent in either of the two biographies from which he drew his quotations. As discussed above, al-Shīrāzī listed Abū Ḥāmid as al-Dārakī's student to give additional credibility to al-Dārakī; but by not listing him as a teacher in his entry for al-Isfarāʾīnī, al-Shīrāzī sought, at the same time, to distance the teacher's reputation from that of his supposed student. Al-Khaṭīb, who does not describe a student/teacher relationship at all, used the testimony of agreement not to give credibility to al-Dārakī as a legal expert, but instead to create a circle of authority for his approach to law, for which al-Khaṭīb appears to have had some sympathy.

Ibn Qāḍī Shuhbah, however, takes a different approach to the relationship between the two scholars. Unlike al-Shīrāzī, he describes al-Dārakī as a teacher in his entry for Abū Ḥāmid;[71] and therefore does not imply that there is anything about al-Dārakī that might lessen the importance of al-Isfarāʾīnī if a strong association exists between them. Ibn Qāḍī Shuhbah describes Abū Ḥāmid as "the *shaykh* of the Shāfiʿīs of ʿIrāq," who "studied widely (*ishtaghala*) in the religious sciences," and from whom the "legal scholars and religious leaders of Baghdād studied (*akhadha*)."[72] Overall, Ibn Qāḍī Shuhbah describes Abū Ḥāmid as one of the great Shāfiʿīs of the age who was an expert in law, legal method, divergent opinion, and *ḥadīth* science and transmission. By interpolating Abū Ḥāmid's statement of agreement into al-Dārakī's entry next to a reference to their educational relationship, Ibn Qāḍī Shuhbah is asserting that the full

---

[71] Khān, vol. 1, 172.
[72] Ibid., 172–73.

weight of al-Isfarāʾīnī's authority as a scholar of law stands as testimony for the legal authority of al-Dārakī; implying that much of what Abū Ḥāmid knew grew out of his study with Abū al-Qāsim.

Ibn Qāḍī Shuhbah, after creating an image of al-Dārakī as a scholar on a par with Abū Ḥāmid, inserts al-Shīrāzī's comment "in general the masters (*shuyūkh*) of Baghdād and others besides them among the people of distant lands studied (*akhadha*) with him." Adding this quote into the entry at this point has two outcomes: 1) by citing Abū Isḥāq directly, he seeks to add al-Shīrāzī's authority to the image of greatness that Ibn Qāḍī Shuhbah is creating around al-Dārakī, and 2) it is meant to imply that not only did Abū Ḥāmid recognize Abū al-Qāsim's authority as a teacher, but so did the leading Shāfiʿī scholars of the period from around the Muslim world.

Following this, Ibn Qāḍī Shuhbah folds into his narrative a direct citation from al-Khaṭīb when he states al-Dārakī "was trustworthy [and] al-Dāraquṭnī relied on him." This passage is interesting for several reasons, not least of all because it demonstrates how Ibn Qāḍī Shuhbah developed his biographical entries. The passage just quoted was not drawn from al-Khaṭīb al-Baghdādī's entry for al-Dārakī, but from his biography for ʿAlī b. ʿUmar al-Dāraquṭnī (d. 385/995).[73] It indicates that while Ibn Qāḍī Shuhbah relied primarily on the primary or core biographical tradition written for an individual, he also drew material from parallel biographies written for other people that contained information about his subject. Using sources from outside the main biographical traditions gives Ibn Qāḍī Shuhbah an even greater range of diverse sources from which to draw and provides him with more creativity and freedom in how he shapes each entry.

In its original context, al-Khaṭīb referred to al-Dārakī in al-Dāraquṭnī's entry to lend support for al-Dāraquṭnī's authority as a *ḥadīth* transmitter. Ibn Qāḍī Shuhbah, conversely, uses the reference to al-Dāraquṭnī to give credibility to al-Dārakī's authority as a scholar of *ḥadīth* and also to blunt claims that al-Dārakī might somehow be outside the orthodox boundaries of the *madhhab*. Al-Nawawī and Ibn Kathīr both assert that al-Dārakī held opinions that put him at odds with the mainstream of the school. In some cases, this is meant to imply that al-Dārakī was the author of divergent opinion within the

[73] Al-Khaṭīb, *Tārīkh baghdād*, vol. 12, 34–40.

school, which for Ibn Qāḍī Shuhbah is a positive attribute. But tinged with the appellation of *ikhtilāf* is a more negative contention that al-Dārakī, in his independence, went too far. Al-Nawawī, for instance, while claiming that al-Dārakī was for the most part reputable, goes so far as to say that he also held aberrant (*gharīb*) opinions.[74]

It is significant that Ibn Qāḍī Shuhbah does not make any reference to al-Dārakī's claim to disregard the opinions of al-Shāfiʿī based on his independent reading of *ḥadīth*, even though it is mentioned by al-Khaṭīb al-Baghdādī, as well as by Ibn al-Jawzī, al-Nawawī, and Ibn Khallikān. By specifically citing al-Khaṭīb in his reference to al-Dāraquṭnī in the context of *ḥadīth*, Ibn Qāḍī Shuhbah appears to be drawing the reader to the debate; but in drawing attention to al-Dāraquṭnī and his 'reliance' on al-Dārakī, the reader is pushed to come a far different conclusion.

The key to deciphering the subtext of this issue is in how Ibn Qāḍī Shuhbah describes al-Dāraquṭnī. According to Ibn Qāḍī Shuhbah, al-Dāraquṭnī was "preeminent in his age in memorization (of *ḥadīth*), in comprehension, and *waraʿ*."[75] '*Waraʿ*' means 'piety,' 'piousness,' but also 'caution;' it connotes a fear of God that results in careful contemplation and timidity. Here, Ibn Qāḍī Shuhbah links it with the science of prophetic traditions to suggest that al-Dāraquṭnī was extremely careful in his use and transmission of *ḥadīth* due to an understanding of the theological consequences of misusing *ḥadīth*. He also quotes al-Khaṭīb, who, quoting Abū Ṭayyib al-Ṭabarī, says that al-Dāraquṭnī was the "*amīr al-muʾminīn* of *ḥadīth*."[76] The term '*amīr al-muʾminīn*' (literally 'the commander of the faithful') was the title given to the Caliphs and describes their symbolic role as the paramount religious leader. Ibn Qāḍī Shuhbah creates an image of al-Dāraquṭnī as an extremely well respected and pious religious and scholastic leader who was guided by a deep sense of religious piety, born of his fear of the punishment of God. He then ends his entry by mentioning that al-Nawawī cites al-Dāraquṭnī's legal opinions in his chapter on rules outlining the proper conduct of judges. This suggests that not only was al-Dāraquṭnī an authority on *ḥadīth*, but that he was also a notable jurist who held important opinions worthy

---

[74] Al-Nawawī, *Tahdhīb al-asmāʾ*, vol. 2, 263.
[75] Khān, vol. 1, 161–62.
[76] Ibid., 162.

of note in one of the most important legal collections in the history of the Shāfiʿī school.

By stating that al-Dāraquṭnī relied on al-Dārakī, Ibn Qāḍī Shuhbah suggests that al-Dārakī was also a reputable, trustworthy, and God-fearing scholar of prophetic traditions, and, in effect, that al-Dāraquṭnī was in some sense derivative of al-Dārakī. But Ibn Qāḍī Shuhbah also seeks to draw important contrasts between the two scholars. Although al-Dārakī is described by al-Nawawī and others as a source of divergent opinion, even being mentioned by al-Rāfiʿī in the *ʿAzīz sharḥ al-wajīz*, Ibn Qāḍī Shuhbah makes no reference to this fact, which, given the main purpose of his text, has extremely important implications. He is expressly seeking to distance the scholar from any imputation of independence from al-Shāfiʿī, or that he held views that took him outside the school. By omitting to mention the wide ranging literature that refers to al-Dārakī's contributions to *ikhtilāf*, he attempts to disassociate him from any controversy surrounding his legal methods or opinions; and by linking him with al-Dāraquṭnī, Ibn Qāḍī Shuhbah aims to draw al-Dārakī away from the margins and into the center of school affiliation and participation.

The overall image that Ibn Qāḍī Shuhbah casts of al-Dārakī is as a reputable, highly trained, and important scholar, who had many important and well regarded students, and who contributed to the growth of the *madhhab* of the school. He is in no way presented as challenging the ideas of al-Shāfiʿī or Abū Ḥanīfah, or as someone who had anything more than a professional interest in *ḥadīth* studies. He is also not referred to as someone who possessed the ability to independently examine the texts of revelation in order to discover, on his own, new legal dicta. Although al-Ḥākim, al-ʿAbbādī, al-Khaṭīb al-Baghdādī, Ibn al-Jawzī, al-Nawawī, al-Subkī, and Ibn Kathīr all imply or directly assert that he had this ability, Ibn Qāḍī Shuhbah makes no reference to it at all.

Terminological variation and authorial choice

As the biographical tradition that developed around the life of al-Dārakī suggests, thematic variation in source material is quite extensive, giving authors great license in how they shape an entry. As discussed above, one aspect of thematic variation is deviation in the use of descriptive terminology. Not all narrative elements contain descriptive terms, although many do. Terms describe numerous types of phenomena that relate to structures of authority, classes of professional activities, and kinds of religious and moral characteristics that all contribute to the portrayal of the biographical subject. One of the most common complexes of technical descriptive terms in *ṭabaqāt* works, as is exemplified by the al-Dārakī tradition, involve education and learning. As is explained in chapter four in some detail, these terms describe not just the subjects studied, but also teacher/student relationships, levels and intensities in the acquisition of knowledge, and the extent to which a student or a teacher achieved distinction in learning in a particular field. Because terms denoting modes of learning are so common in biographical entries, and so important in constructing images of authority in *ṭabaqāt* texts, they are a useful tool for measuring terminological variation and, in particular, in assessing Ibn Qāḍī Shuhbah's ability to control the selection of individual terms in the composition of his work.

Ibn Qāḍī Shuhbah's text is quite detailed, although *ṭabaqāt* works such as that produced by al-Subkī are far more extensive in the range of scholars listed and the size and detail of the citation provided for each individual. Ibn Qāḍī Shuhbah, for instance, mentions 1,333 educational relationships and describes over 5,000 links in the transmission of legal dicta and prophetic traditions from one scholar to another. Al-Subkī lists 1419 biographies and depicts nearly twice as many educational relationships and transmissive links as Ibn Qāḍī Shuhbah. Ibn Qāḍī Shuhbah also lists over 2,000 student/teacher relationships without using a term that outlines a specific mode of learning; using instead terms that denote discipleship such as *ṣāḥib* (pl. *aṣḥāb*, *ṣaḥb*, *ṣaḥābah*, and *ṣuḥbah*) and *tilmīdh* (pl. *talāmīdh*).

As stated earlier, 100 biographies were selected at random from the first twenty-six generations of Ibn Qāḍī Shuhbah's text. To test the extent to which terms for modes of learning vary from text to text, and thus the level of variation Ibn Qāḍī Shuhbah had access to, each biography was compared with entries found in ten earlier texts.[77] In total, 511 biographies were surveyed from the core

[77] The texts used in the survey are: al-ʿAbbādī, *Kitāb ṭabaqāt al-fuqahāʾ al-shāfiʿīyah*; al-Khaṭīb al-Baghdādī, *Tārīkh baghdād aw madināt al-salām*; Abū Isḥāq al-Shīrāzī, *Ṭabaqāt al-fuqahāʾ*; Ibn ʿAsākir, *Tārīkh madīnat dimashq*; al-Nawawī, *Tahdhīb al-asmāʾ wa ʾl-lughāt*; Ibn Khallikān, *Wafayāt al-aʿyān wa anbāʾ al-zamān*; al-Dhahabī, *Siyār aʿlām al-nubalāʾ*; Tāj al-Dīn al-Subkī, *Ṭabaqāt al-shāfiʿīyah al-kubrā*; Ibn Kathīr, *al-Bidāyah wa ʾl-nihāyah*; Ibn Ḥajar al-ʿAsqalānī, *Lisān al-mīzān*.

biographical traditions that were devoted to each scholar in the sample and 832 parallel entries were examined for references to modes of learning. The survey looked only for terms that specified learning such *akhadha, ishtaghala, ashghala, qaraʾa, takharraja, ḥaṣṣala, baḥatha, darasa*, and *darrasa* and did not look at other linkages or at references to discipleship. Because of the sheer size of the survey, the figures that follow represent only a preliminary assessment and a more detailed analysis will need to be done for a future publication.

The survey demonstrated that the most important tool that writers have is choice. Authorial choice is demonstrated in the al-Dārakī biographical tradition (see figure 2.5 below) from which Ibn Qāḍī Shuhbah only drew on four of twelve possible educational associations. He does not refer to al-Dārakī's position as *mudarris* in Baghdād, that he taught law (*darrasa*) in the Mosque of Daʿlaj b. Aḥmad, that he taught rhetoric, that al-Dāraquṭnī studied (*qaraʾa*) Qurʾan with him, that Abū al-Ḥusayn al-Ṭabarī studied law (*tafaqqaha*) with al-Dārakī, nor does he refer to any of the students mentioned by al-ʿAbbādī. Ibn Qāḍī Shuhbah's choice of only a few narrative elements demonstrates that authors could control terminological variation in a text simply through a process of authorial selection. The writer thus has enormous power in managing the use of terms by his ability to remove from the record any reference to a specific term or complex of terms. According to the survey, Ibn Qāḍī Shuhbah chooses to describe only about 33% of all possible educational relationships mentioned in earlier texts.

Figure 2.5. Modes of learning in the al-Dārakī biographical tradition

1. Study law (*tafaqqaha*) with al-Marwazī†	Sh, N, Sb, IK, I, IQ
2. Study (*akhadha*) with al-Marwazī†	IKh
3. Taught law (*darrasa*) in Nīsābūr	Ḥ, Kh, S, J, IKh, N, IK, Sb, I, IQ
4. The *Shaykh*s of Baghdād and the people of distant lands studied (*akhadha*) with him	Sh, N, IKh, Sb, IK, IQ
5. Held position of *mudarris* (headmaster)††	Sh, N, IKh, Sb
6. Taught law (*darrasa*) in the Mosque of Daʿlaj b. Aḥmad	Ḥ, Kh, S, J, IKh

Figure 2.5 (*cont.*)

7. Circle in the Grand Mosque for the issuance of legal opinions and the study (*akhadha*) of rhetoric	Kh, S, J, N, IKh
8. Maymūn al-Wāsiṭī his disciple (*talāmidh*)	ʿA
9. Abū Muḥammad al-Muqrīʾ his disciple (*talāmidh*)	ʿA
10. al-Dāraquṭnī studied (*qaraʾa*) Qurʾan with him	IK
11. Abū al-Ḥusayn al-Ṭabarī studied law (*tafaqqaha*) with him	IK
12. al-Isfarāʾīnī studied law (*tafaqqaha*) with him	Sh, N, IKh, Sb, IK, IQ

Note: Ḥ = al-Ḥākim, ʿA = al-ʿAbbādī, Kh = Khaṭīb al-Baghdādī, Sh = al-Shīrāzī, S = al-Samʿānī, J = Ibn al-Jawzī, N = al-Nawawī, IKh = Ibn Khallikān, Sb = al-Subkī, IK = Ibn Kathīr, I = al-Isnawī, IQ = Ibn Qāḍī Shuhbah.

† See chapter four for a discussion of the significance of Ibn Qāḍī Shuhbah's use of *tafaqqaha* instead of *akhadha*. See chapter eight for its importance in relation to al-Dārakī's biography and Ibn Qāḍī Shuhbah's configuration of his own authority.

†† The term used in the biographies is '*tadrīs*,' usually in the context of al-Dārakī rising to the rank of one who undertakes *tadrīs*.

Of the associations he does list, Ibn Qāḍī Shuhbah is able to choose from at least two possible terms 46% of the time (the most common being *tafaqqaha* and *akhadha* as with the descriptions of the relationship between al-Dārakī and al-Marwazī), three terms in 9% of instances, and four or more terms in .8% of cases; with most variations originating in the texts of al-Subkī, Ibn Khallikān, and Ibn Kathīr who each seemed to have been less constrained by the received traditions they inherited.[78] If one factors in the variations in terminological

[78] Absolute variation is much lower when Ibn Qāḍī Shuhbah's redactions are factored out. In absolute terms, in the 1343 biographies surveyed there were 2148 references to education. In only 29% of instances was there a choice between two terms (again the two most commonly used were *tafaqqaha* and *akhadha*), in 8% of cases there were three possible terms, and in just .2% for four or more terms. These percentages would likely change if the survey included a greater number of texts, although it is unclear if they would be substantially altered. Also, the survey did not take into account variations in manuscript editions of the various texts and thus actual numbers may be different and not exactly reflective of the range of choices at Ibn Qāḍī Shuhbah's disposal.

usage in parallel biographies, these numbers increase by an average of 12% for two terms, 2% for three terms, and .04% for four or more terms. While these figures do not indicate that Ibn Qāḍī Shuhbah exercised absolute freedom of choice in the terms he decides to use over the course of his text, it does demonstrate that he did have some control of the terms he used and thus how they progressed over the course of his text in the majority of instances.

The wealth of information on al-Dārakī, who in the larger view of Shāfiʿī legal history was a relatively minor figure, demonstrates that Ibn Qāḍī Shuhbah has great latitude in what he presents and how he does so. He is bound by the received biographical traditions that developed around al-Dārakī and other scholars but because there was, in actuality, great diversity of information and opinion about their lives, careers, and abilities, Ibn Qāḍī Shuhbah has immense freedom in how he mixes information. As is discussed in the following chapter, *ṭabaqāt* authors combined the information originating from previous examinations and, using a range of rhetorical strategies and methods, sought to create impressions of history through a retelling of biographies that are linked together across the whole of the text.

CHAPTER THREE

MICRO-TEXTUAL RHETORICAL STRATEGIES IN IBN QĀḌĪ SHUHBAH'S TEXT: AUTHORITY, DEATH, AND THE ORIGINS OF *IKHTILĀF* IN THE SHĀFIʿĪ *MADHHAB*

A socio-rhetorical analysis of ṭabaqāt

Ṭabaqāt authors were able to draw from rich traditions of biographical material giving them great freedom in shaping their texts. As in the case of Abū al-Qāsim al-Dārakī, *ṭabaqāt* writers such as Ibn Qāḍī Shuhbah were able to construct entries by combining received information and then selectively mixing, removing, interpolating, and recasting passages, and thus altering material to imply ideas that may not have been intended by their original authors. In some instances, later writers drew rhetorical arguments verbatim from earlier texts. In these situations, however, it should not be assumed that the implications of the original arguments were lost on these authors. To the contrary, writers frequently strengthened arguments through the combination of new rhetorical elements not previously employed. Because most writers were careful and rather masterful manipulators of previous material, even in situations where they present whole sections of earlier texts, it is more proper to talk about 'their arguments' than it is to refer to a passage as belonging to some other writer. *All authors exercise choice in what they include and how they do so.* When a *ṭabaqāt* writer presents a quotation or a selection from a previous work, whether it is attributed to another author or not, he does so because it conveys the ideas he sees as important. He *chooses to make the selection*, an aspect of *ṭabaqāt* composition that cannot be overemphasized.

Compositional choices are made initially at the level of the individual biographical entry, which is the most fundamental element of a *ṭabaqāt* work. Writers craft every entry to suggest specific ideas not just about the nature of that person's authority, but about authority in general and the historical development of authority structures in specific disciplines of religious knowledge. Each biographical entry contains a kind of curriculum vitae for scholars who belong to certain professional categories or sub-categories.[1] According to Tarif Khalidi a typical entry contains a scholar's

> name and surname, then *kunya*, then connection to a town, then descent, then school of law, then the person's particular knowledge, craft, power, position or principality. The teachers of a person are well to the fore. Scholars are described either as *ʿallāma* or else as *ḥāfiẓ, imām, shaykh, faqīh* and then *uṣūlī, naḥwī, manṭiqī* and so forth, where applicable. The date of birth, or more commonly of death, is given and the general character estimate comes at the end. With particularly important entries, the biographers often devoted a final section to an assessment of the personality as seen by other biographers, by themselves if they possessed first-hand information or by collating several authoritative opinions. Information in a 'typical' entry included, in addition to the standard data, a résumé of a person's career, a few anecdotes to illustrate virtues or skills and often a personal touch, e.g. 'he kept himself aloof from others', 'he was much given to laughter', 'he was miserly', and so forth. These touches illuminate a character, especially when information is first hand.[2]

In *ṭabaqāt* texts the order of elements varies from biography to biography depending on how the author seeks to shape the impression of the jurist. Elements are combined and arranged in such a way as to shape the history and the various attributes of the person examined. As entries are assembled and combined, authors then use common rhetorical elements across the whole of the text to manipulate the presentation of historical development. By reading a *ṭabaqāt* text at both the macro (the overall text) and micro (the individual entry) level—by attempting to discern an author's overall argument—modern scholars can glean information from the text that yields important indications of how medieval authors understood Islamic history.

A close 'inner-textual' reading of the text is central to understanding the rhetorical arguments presented in *ṭabaqāt* works.[3] The inner-textual approach is one of five approaches to discerning the socio-rhetorical texture of religious texts outlined by Vernon Robbins in his *Exploring the Texture of Texts*. Socio-Rhetorical analysis was invented to examine the multiple discourses of Mediterranean culture

[1] Makdisi, "*Ṭabaqāt*," 373.
[2] Khalidi, 210.
[3] Vernon Robbins in his *Exploring the Texture of Texts: A Guide to Socio-Rhetorical Interpretation* (Valley Forge: Trinity Press International, 1996), 7–39.

evident in the New Testament. While many of Robbins' approaches are more suited to the study of the New Testament, his emphasis on finding ideas that progressively develop throughout an entire book is particularly useful for looking at *ṭabaqāt* works.

Inner-textual reading focuses on how ideas relate to each other as they develop over the course of an entire text. On a functional level, with texts as large as many *ṭabaqāt*, this requires plotting ideas, concepts, historical events, and terms on a spread sheet to see how these phenomena progressively develop over the span of the work.[4] Inner-textual approaches are typically designed to deal with short sections or passages, not entire texts. As is discussed below, the present configuration of inner-textual analysis developed additional techniques of plotting the development of ideas throughout the body of the text.

Micro-textual rhetorical strategies

Inner-textual readings of *ṭabaqāt* texts show that authors utilize a large number of rhetorical techniques and strategies that function on two levels: the macro-text and the micro-text. Macro-textual strategies link biographies to larger themes and trends in the text as a whole. Micro-textual strategies function more narrowly; they serve to create impressions and communicate meanings by linking ideas and individuals in each biography and between biographies in the same generation (*ṭabaqah*). Understanding the macro-textual rhetorical strategies of *ṭabaqāt* texts illuminates larger themes and issues that authors seek to present. While these themes are extremely important to the

[4] This approach is not unique to medieval biographical material. For instance see Leen Breure, "In Search of Mental Structures: A Methodological Evaluation of Computerized Text Analysis of Late Medieval Religious Biographies," *History and Computing* 11 (1999): 61–78. The approach outlined by Breure differs from the method used in this study in that Breure created quantitative variables for various phrases and words used in death notices written about members of the Modern Devotion movement in the Netherlands in the 15th century. He then used computerized algorithms to produce statistical models that projected certain attitudes toward death. In doing so, Breure relied heavily on theories from depth psychology and by doing so assumed that the authors of the two texts he reviewed would have shared mental attitudes toward death with the individuals described in their biographies. For an excellent discussion of the use of databases in the analysis of prosopography and onomastics, see the volume by K. S. B. Keats-Rohan, ed., *Resourcing Sources*, vol. 7, *Prosopographica et Genealogica* (Oxford: Occasional Publications of the Unit for Prosopographical Research, 2002).

purposes of composing a *ṭabaqāt* work, authors wrote in the genre because of the desire to understand the role of the individual as an instrument of God's will in history. History develops through God's creative power as God manifests God's self in the lives of individual humans. Historical understandings cannot be undertaken, according to medieval Muslim thought, without understanding the way in which God uses humans as instruments of divine will.[5]

Medieval Muslims also believed that God imbued certain people with extra-ordinary abilities who should serve as models for the community. This idea seems to have predated the rise of Islam and was 'Islamized' by the notion of Muḥammad's *sunnah* (example). With the development of the Muslim community the idea of *sunnah* continued to be a potent cultural motif. The rise of various biographical genres, including *ṭabaqāt,* is in no small measure due to the dominance of the idea in Arabic Islamic society.

Because the lives of individuals served as important carriers of cultural meaning, authors of biographies used various rhetorical methods and strategies to create models for normative behavior when they retold the lives of famous or infamous people. The *ṭabaqāt* genre appears to have developed a number of rhetorical strategies that may have also been used in other biographical forms. A survey of over thirty *ṭabaqāt* works has led to the discovery of a range of micro-textual rhetorical strategies. The following will discuss rhetorical strategies used in Ibn Qāḍī Shuhbah's text such as general allusion (sometimes referred to as *kināyah*), evocative allusion (*taʿrīḍ*), allusions to secret or special knowledge used to establish the authority of individuals or ideas (pl. *rumūz,* sing. *ramz*), causative association, hyper-textual referencing, and forms of *tajnīs* (paronomasia). Additional micro-textual rhetorical strategies will be discussed in other sections of the book as needed.

It should be noted here that many of the following conclusions concerning the use of rhetorical strategies in *ṭabaqāt* works is still speculative. Authors do not explicitly say that they use or borrow techniques from other genres or that they have created new techniques for use in the *ṭabaqāt* genre. At most, we see similarities in the way that techniques are described in various genres of rhetoric and their use in *ṭabaqāt.* Additional studies will need to be done to

[5] Robinson, *Islamic Historiography,* 129–31.

further explore the use of rhetorical strategies to create Islamic histories in biography.

Allusion: kināyah, taʿrīḍ *and* ramz

As stated above, *ṭabaqāt* texts seek to establish authority in specific disciplines of knowledge, while historical texts and even some other forms of biography seek to list notable individuals who are known, not just for their expertise in particular fields, but for their general contributions to Islamic historical development. Additionally, *ṭabaqāt* texts, using specific rhetorical strategies and devices, seek to map out the historical development of authority in specific fields of specialization in such a way that gives legitimacy to certain kinds of authority (both in terms of people and ideas) within professional groups.

According to M. L. J. Young, the biographical genre also gave scholars more flexibility to shape history to conform to the "priorities and the assumptions of the age which produced it."[6] Although writers went to great lengths to "achieve accuracy"[7] in the information they reported, scholars were attracted to biography because they could create a history of a particular group employing methods and assumptions that went beyond the boundaries of historiographical method. While admitting that there are important similarities between the two genres, Michael Cooperson has distilled three areas that make biography distinct from historiography:

1) biography assumes the reader is knowledgeable about the history surrounding the life of the person referred to in the biography (this allows the writer to gloss certain areas and combine events in such a way that creates a unique historical view, as was demonstrated in the last chapter in the various biographies dedicated to Abū al-Qāsim al-Dārakī);
2) biography allows the writer to express opinions about history and people's character, about personal philosophical development, and can do so without having to fix dates to the development of certain ideas or philosophies (giving the writer more license than in historical writing); and
3) the authority to report information derives from the writer's ability to provide secret or otherwise unknown information, which

6 Young, 178.
7 Ibid.

> gives the report an air of veracity that a historical writer could not employ.[8]

In *ṭabaqāt* works, the first two categories appear to be combined in the form of general allusion (*kināyah*) to events or activities. In medieval rhetorical texts, *kināyah* is an important element in making effective arguments. While scholars differed over the kinds of allusion that were permissible in rhetorical argumentation, and indeed over what constituted a true allusion,[9] Abū Yaʿqūb Yūsuf b. Abī Bakr al-Sakkākī (d. 626/1229), in his *Miftāḥ al-ʿulūm*, presents a discussion of allusion that most closely resembles its use by Ibn Qāḍī Shuhbah and other *ṭabaqāt* writers.

Al-Sakkākī distinguishes between metaphor (*istiʿārah*) and allusion by arguing that the object of an allusive reference must have existed in reality.[10] While metaphor and allusion are both important in rhetorical argumentation, allusion becomes more important in *ṭabaqāt* texts because it allows the author to refer to specific events and phenomena by using a form of 'shorthand' that carries specific meanings but in minimal space. The events and ideas referred to in allusions were considered so important and so well known that authors did not feel the need to discuss them in detail because they assumed all readers would understand their larger contexts. While they may frequently appear to be casual asides to modern readers, and thus too frequently overlooked, allusions are an extremely important mode of argumentation in *ṭabaqāt* texts.

An example of a general allusion to a historical event that is designed to open vistas of meaning for the reader occurs in the biography of Muḥammad b. Muḥammad Ibn al-Bārizī (d. 828/1425). Ibn Qāḍī Shuhbah states that Ibn al-Bārizī

> was appointed chief judge of Aleppo after al-Muʾayyad was appointed governor of it. He then went with him to Cairo. He was established as the confidential secretary.[11]

Ibn Qāḍī Shuhbah provides no other historical information that would contextualize this passage. He provides no dates for when Ibn

[8] Cooperson, 22–23.
[9] *Encyclopedia of Islam*, 2nd ed., s.v. "Kināya."
[10] Abū Yaʿqūb Yūsuf b. Muḥammad al-Sakkākī, *Miftāḥ al-ʿulūm* (Beirut: Dār al-kutub al-ʿilmīyah, 2000), 513.
[11] Khān, vol. 4, 107.

al-Bārizī or al-Mu'ayyad were in Aleppo, who al-Mu'ayyad was or his importance, when or why they went to Cairo, or why the reference to al-Bārizī's appointment as confidential secretary (*kātib al-sirr*) is significant. He is able to write in such terse prose because he assumes that the reader understands the larger context to which he is referring. Ibn Qāḍī Shuhbah expects that the reader will know, for instance, that al-Mu'ayyad refers to the Mamlūk Sulṭān al-Mu'ayyad Shaykh (d. 824/1421), who, in a protracted civil war that lasted eight years, attempted to seize control of the Sulṭānate from Faraj b. Barqūq.

Between 807/1404 and 815/1412, Shaykh, Sulṭān Faraj, and the rebel Amīr Nawrūz (d. 817/1414) were locked in a conflict that devastated major cities such as Aleppo and Damascus, and almost ruined the economies of Egypt and Syria as each side was forced to extort financial resources from the population to pay for the prolonged struggle. It also witnessed increasing pressure on members of the *'ulamā'* to take sides and to sponsor various contenders for the Sulṭānate. Perhaps most instrumental in this was Amīr al-Mu'ayyad Shaykh who appointed a number of chief judges based not just on their qualifications but also on their loyalty to his cause. Ibn al-Bārizī, Ibn Qāḍī Shuhbah's mentor Najm al-Dīn Ibn Ḥijjī, and other scholars (later known as the 'Mu'ayyadīyah')[12] were appointed to various judgeships because of their willingness to side with Shaykh against Sulṭān Faraj and Amīr Nawrūz. Whenever Shaykh controlled a town, either as the lawfully appointed governor or as a rebel, he appointed judges to that city's administration to serve not just on the judiciary, but also as controllers of the local army, markets, hospitals, treasuries, financial bureaus, and different trusts. He also appointed judges to serve as his confidential secretaries and to other positions where he could extend his influence and thus gain the support of the elites of the city.[13] Faraj and Nawrūz did the same, which resulted in the rampant politicization of the judiciary and the *'ulamā'*, leading to their increasing dependence on the various contenders for the incomes that came from their political involvement. The allusive phrase "he

[12] Ibid.

[13] See Ibn Ṭūlūn, *Quḍāt dimashq*, 129 and 131. Also see Ibn Ayyūb, *Nuzhat al-khāṭir*, vol. 2, 105, 107; Ibn Ḥijjī, *Tārīkh ibn ḥijjī*, vol. 2, 769, 807; and Ibn Ḥajar al-'Asqalānī, *Inbā' al-ghumr*, vol. 6, 65–66, 88–89 for evidence of this.

was appointed chief judge of Aleppo after al-Mu'ayyad was appointed governor of it" is meant to call these events to mind.

Over the course of the civil war, Sulṭān Faraj had been forced to invade Syria in pursuit of the two rebels on several different occasions and had nearly succeeded in defeating his opponents. As was custom, whenever the Sulṭān left Egypt for an invasion of Syria he brought along with his army an entourage that was designed to give his rule an air of legitimacy. Most importantly, he took with him the four chief judges of Egypt and the Caliph who was taken out of virtual house arrest and forced to ride at the head of the army.[14]

During a confused battle outside the gates of Damascus in Muḥarram, 815 (April–May, 1412) that pitted Faraj and the army of Egypt against the combined forces of Shaykh and Nawrūz, Sulṭān Faraj lost control of not only the four chief judges and the Caliph, but also of his treasury, which by a happy turn of fortune for Shaykh, fell into his hands. When Faraj realized what had happened he retreated to the citadel of Damascus where he carried out a protracted defense as his support began to drain away.[15]

Shaykh, with the advice of a number of close associates, Ibn al-Bārizī among them, devised a plan that would destroy any remaining support for the Sulṭān. In a daring move, they offered oaths of loyalty to Caliph Mustasʿīn Billāh (d. 833/1430) and proclaimed him Sulṭān. Shaykh then forced the four chief judges of Egypt, and all other judges loyal to him, Ibn al-Bārizī included, to draft a statement saying that opposition to the Caliph was tantamount to apostasy. Within days, all support for Faraj was exhausted and he was forced to surrender. Shaykh then ordered the four chief judges to convict Faraj of crimes against religion, resulting in his execution on 16 Ṣafar, 815 (28 May, 1412).[16]

Over the next six months Shaykh, with the help of Ibn al-Bārizī and other loyalists, plotted to seize the throne from the Caliph, which they accomplished on 1 Shaʿbān, 815 (6 November, 1412). As soon as Shaykh took the Sulṭānate, he appointed Ibn al-Bārizī his confidential secretary. Ibn al-Bārizī went on to become one of the most influential confidential secretaries in Mamlūk history, serving Shaykh on several occasions.[17]

---

[14] Al-Maqrīzī, *Kitāb al-sulūk*, vol. 4, 87–88.
[15] Ibn Taghrī Birdī, *al-Nujūm al-ẓāhirah*, vol. 6, 266–68.
[16] Ibid., 268–70. Also see Ibn Ḥajar al-ʿAsqalānī *Inbā' al-ghumr*, vol. 7, 54–60.
[17] Ibn Ṭūlūn, *Quḍāt dimashq*, 129–30.

The power of such allusions to historical events (in what are, in most cases, very brief references), is that in the space of just fifteen words, Ibn Qāḍī Shuhbah is able to encapsulate over twenty years of history and to contextualize not just the career of Ibn al-Bārizī, but also to call to mind the role of the judiciary in Mamlūk politics. Not only this, but he is also able to revive memories of the restoration of the Caliphate and Ibn al-Bārizī's role in its eventual destruction as a participant in the group of loyalists who owed their positions to al-Mu'ayyad Shaykh. Thus he is able to allude to an entire shift in judicial authority, to collateral changes in the role of the *ʿulamāʾ* as guides for the community and as political powers, without ever referring to either phenomenon directly. This ability not only frees the author from long and detailed explanations, but also allows him to create layers of meaning in the minds of a knowledgeable audience.

Some allusions, however, go further, carrying with them meanings that go beyond the apparent significance of the reference and are important for understanding the grammar of medieval Islamic cultural discourse. Al-Sakkākī and other rhetoricians referred to such 'evocative' allusions as a sub-category of *kināyah* known as *taʿrīḍ* (literally 'to hint'). *Taʿrīḍ* is a form of allusion that refers to events, as well as to qualities and abilities of which the reader is assumed to have a general knowledge but which also 'hints' at a deeper religious or mystical meaning.[18] According to ʿAbd al-Ghanī al-Nābulsī (d. 1143–44/1731), it is "an indirect indication of the speaker's intention, the sense being understood neither from the use of words in their literal meaning nor through transference, but from the general tenor of the discourse."[19] It is, therefore, an allusion to an event or thing that carries a meaning that goes beyond the temporal explanation for the phenomenon, the one normally or superficially attributed to the referent; a meaning that is revealed over the course of an entire work. By reading—and in *ṭabaqāt* plotting—the repetition of evocative allusions and their relationship to the overall development of the discourse one can ascertain the oblique meanings the author is attempting to evoke. For instance, in Ibn al-Mulaqqin's

[18] Al-Sakkākī, 411.

[19] Pierre Cachia, *The Arch Rhetorician or the Schemer's Skimmer: A Handbook of late Arabic Badīʿ drawn from ʿAbd al-Ghanī an-Nābulsī's Nafaḥāt al-azhār ʿalā nasamāt al-asḥār* (Wiesbaden: Harrassowitz, 1998), 66–67.

Ṭabaqāt al-awliyāʾ (*The Generations of the Saints*), one of the most common evocative allusions is to miracles (pl. *karāmāt*, sing. *karāmah*) performed by God through a saint.[20] In approximately 70% of the biographies listed in the text, *karāmāt* are attributed to the individuals listed, and are, therefore, a sign of his or her authority. The term nevertheless evokes a range of meanings that simple definition does not convey.

According to Frederick Denny, *karāmah* establishes a link between the saint and the Prophet Muḥammad; showing that just as Muḥammad possessed the ability to perform miracles, which confirmed his special relationship with God, saints likewise are designated as God's chosen spiritual leaders through their demonstration of *karāmāt*. Saints demonstrate that they are spiritual heirs to the Prophet, and owners of his special spiritual knowledge, by having miracles attributed to them. *Karāmah* also ties saints into a network of popular meanings as a result of the vast literature that developed describing the 'tales of the prophets.'[21] These popular stories relate myriad miracles attributed not only to Muḥammad but also to many of the pre-Islamic prophets. In a sense, references to *karāmāt* make the saints equals, if not in some cases superior, to Biblical and Qurʾanic prophets by attributing to them abilities that figures such as Moses and Muḥammad did not possess.[22]

Historical events that carry great meaning for both writer and reader are also the subject of *taʿrīḍ*. As demonstrated above, although general allusion to historical events are common in *ṭabaqāt* works, evocative allusions are different in that they are intended to bring to mind symbolic meanings that have greater religious value. Where a general allusion to a historical event is designed to allow the writer to truncate a passage and still communicate a range of historical trends and events and at the same time indicate something about their importance for understanding the context of an individual,

---

[20] See ʿUmar b. ʿAlī Ibn al-Mulaqqin, *Ṭabaqāt al-awliyāʾ* (Cairo: Maktabat al-khānjī, 1973).

[21] For an excellent example of this see *ʿArāʾis al-majālis fī Qiṣaṣ al-anbiyāʾ or "Lives of the Prophets" as Recommended by Abū Isḥāq Aḥmad Ibn Muḥammad Ibn Ibrāhīm al-Thaʿlabī*, trans. William M. Brinner (Boston: Brill, 2002), especially the story of al-Khiḍr (pp. 361–82).

[22] Frederick Denny, "'God's Friends': The Sanctity of Persons in Islam," in *Sainthood: Its Manifestations in World Religions*, ed. Richard Kieckhefer (Berkeley: The University of California Press, 1988), 84.

evocative allusions are designed to go past the apparent historical context and to convey deeper, and more fundamentally more important metaphysical meanings.

In late medieval *ṭabaqāt* texts one of the most evocative allusions is to the plague. The plague first broke out in the Middle East in 748–49/1348–49, and continued until the early sixteenth century, re-occurring on fairly regular cycles; and, as seen in the introduction to this book, greatly affecting the lives of peoples in the region. There is, however, little direct discussion of the plague in most *ṭabaqāt* works. For instance, Ibn Qāḍī Shuhbah does not enter into a detailed direct discussion of the plague or its impact. Rather, he alludes to the plague indirectly through evocative references such as when he states that Ibn al-Babāʾī died as a martyr (*shahīd*) in the year 749/1349.[23] Other times he refers directly to death by plague, as with the biography of Shams al-Dīn Abū al-Thanāʾ al-Iṣfahānī, who is described as "dying as a martyr from the plague in the year 749."[24] The use of the term '*shahīd*' in reference to death by plague may seem odd to those familiar with discussions of the pandemic in medieval Europe.[25] In the medieval Islamic Middle East, plague was seen as a blessing for the Muslims and a curse for unbelievers. It was, according to Ibn Ḥajar al-ʿAsqalānī, part of God's plan that should not be avoided. Therefore, following justifications found in both the Qurʾan and *ḥadīth*, jurists argued that Muslims were forbidden to flee an area afflicted by plague.[26] To do so would be an act of impiety and a sign that the individual did not trust in the will of God. In one sense, death from plague was therefore construed to indicate the ultimate submission to God's will and a sign of great piety, especially among the pious juridical community. Martyrdom from plague was also an additional sign of the individual's authority to discover and transmit legal rulings—piety and authority being intimately related.

---

[23] Khān, vol. 3, 70–71.

[24] Ibid., 3, 72.

[25] There are a number of excellent analyses of the plagues in Europe. See Robert S. Gottfried, *The Black Death: Natural and Human Disaster in Medieval Europe* (New York: Free Press, 1983); Philip Ziegler, *The Black Death* (Godalming: Bramley, 1998); and William Naphy and Andrew Spicer, *The Black Death: and the History of Plagues 1345–1730* (Charleston, S.C.: Tempus, 2000).

[26] Ibn Hajar al-ʿAsqalānī, *Badhl al-māʿūn fī faḍl al-ṭāʿūn* (Riyad: Dār al-ʿāṣimah, 1991), 229–35.

Furthermore, Ibn Ḥajar quotes a *ḥadīth* that states that "plague is a martyrdom for all who obey the will of God" (i.e., the Muslims).[27] This is based on the idea that death by plague is similar to death on a battle field. The similarity arises from the lexical relationship between the idea of being pierced (*ṭaʿn*) by a spear or cut by a sword while fighting 'in the path of God,' thus making one a martyr, and death by plague (*ṭāʿūn*).[28] Plague is therefore seen as a piercing that one endures while holding fast to God's command not to flee. During the various plague outbreaks that medieval Muslims in the Middle East and Central Asia endured (during the fourteenth through early sixteenth centuries), the pandemic took a heavy toll on the population. This had a tremendous impact on the worldviews of medieval Muslims. Evocative allusions to the plagues, thus assumes a network of symbolic meanings that carried important cultural and religious connotations beyond the word itself.

In *ṭabaqāt* texts, references to secret or special knowledge frequently take the form of allusions to unusual or supernatural phenomena that go beyond empirical observation but are, nevertheless, believed to exist in reality. Allusions of this type are not commonly found in the standard rhetorical collections. They are, however, common in Ṣūfī literature and are referred to as *rumūz* (sing. *ramz*, a symbol or a secret sign, literally 'winking or to signal with your eyes and eyebrows').[29] In Ṣūfī thought, *ramz* is taken to be a kind of coded speech that conveys hidden messages apparent only to initiates.[30] *Ramz* is used by Ibn Qāḍī Shuhbah and other *ṭabaqāt* writers as a form of allegorical language that uses obscure symbols and references to allude to hidden, usually religious and mystical qualities in order to establish the authority of specific individuals or traditions of thought by appealing to supernatural sources.

In real terms the differences between *taʿrīḍ* and *ramz* may appear to be few. In the al-Sakkākī rhetorical tradition, where both terms are to be found as a sub-category of *kināyah, ramz* is an allusion to something that is more obscure than in *taʿrīḍ*.[31] In Ibn Qāḍī Shuhbah's text, they are distinguished by the fact that while both may refer to

[27] Ibid., 179.
[28] Ibid., 180.
[29] *Encyclopedia of Islam*, 2nd ed., s.v. "Ramz."
[30] Ibid.
[31] Ibid.; also see al-Sakkākī, 411.

phenomena with supernatural symbolic meaning, and do so in such a way as to support or establish authority, *rumūz* specifically refer to allusions to dreams, prophecy, and other methods of paranormal communication. Secondly, although *taʿrīḍ* may refer to supernatural phenomena, it also alludes to actual historical events as well as characteristics and ideas that carry meanings that become clear through their repeated use over the course of a text. *Ramz* alludes only to supernatural events and does so specifically to establish authority. If there is a deeper meaning, and indeed there may be, it is not as easy to discern because *ramz* allusions occur far less frequently and are thus difficult to analyze using progressive or repetitive analysis (see chapter four).

A citation from Ibn Qāḍī Shuhbah's *Ṭabaqāt* demonstrates how *kināyah, taʿrīḍ*, and *ramz* are used. He presents al-Buwayṭī, a disciple of al-Shāfiʿī, as follows:

> Yūsuf b. Yaḥyā al-Qurashī Abū Yaʿqūb al-Buwayṭī al-Miṣrī, the jurist. (He was) one of the great legal scholars from among the students of al-Shāfiʿī and (among) the leaders of Islam. Al-Rabīʿ said, "He held a high status with al-Shāfiʿī. Men sometimes used to ask [al-Shāfiʿī] about questions and he would say 'Ask Abū Yaʿqūb,' and when he had answered, he [al-Shāfiʿī] would then say, 'It is as he said.' Sometimes the chief of police would come to al-Shāfiʿī, [and] al-Shāfiʿī, turning and pointing to Abū Yaʿqūb, would say, 'This is my spokesman.'" He succeeded al-Shāfiʿī in his circle after him. Al-Shāfiʿī said, "No one is more deserving of my *majlis* than Abū Yaʿqūb. And no one among my students is more knowledgeable than he." Al-Nawawī said in the introduction to a commentary on *al-Muhadhdhab*, "Abū Yaʿqūb was greater than al-Muzanī and al-Rabīʿ al-Murādī." Al-Ḥākim said, "I heard Abū al-ʿAbbās al-Aṣamm say, 'I saw my father in a dream, and he said to me, 'Consult the book of al-Buwayṭī, for of the books of the Shāfiʿīs, there is no book with fewer errors than his." He used to fast and recite the Qur'an. He hardly passed a day and night without completing the entire Qur'an; this, in spite of doing good deeds for the people. Ibn Abī al-Jārūd said, "Al-Buwayṭī was my neighbor. I was unable to get up at any hour of the night without hearing him reciting and praying." He died in Baghdād in prison and in chains during the Inquisition in the month of Rajab, in the year 231. Ibn Yūnus said (he died) in the year 232.[32]

In the above biography, we see aspects of each of the rhetorical devices outlined above. The Ibn Qāḍī Shuhbah assumes that the

[32] Khān, vol. 1, 70–72.

reader is familiar with allusions to such historical references as the *miḥnah* (Inquisition, 218/833–237/850), which also evocatively draws parallels between al-Buwayṭī's story and that of Aḥmad Ibn Ḥanbal (d. 241/855). Ibn Qāḍī Shuhbah also exhibits the use of *ramz* by including the story of Abū al-ʿAbbās al-Aṣamm's dream, where his dead father tells him to read al-Buwayṭī's books. Understanding that forms of allusion are used in *ṭabaqāt* texts, however, does not go far enough in helping us read and understand the importance of the above citation and the meanings Ibn Qāḍī Shuhbah is seeking to communicate. To understand why the allusions are meaningful and what they indicate about Ibn Qāḍī Shuhbah's larger thesis, it is necessary to read them in the context of the text as a whole.

Causation in legal ṭabaqāt

Ibn Qāḍī Shuhbah's text, like other *ṭabaqāt* detailing the development of juridical authority, is presented as a companion to legal texts.[33] For instance, al-ʿAbbādī states in his *Kitāb ṭabaqāt al-fuqahāʾ al-shāfiʿīyah* that he includes jurists who are famous for their knowledge, who are known in their countries, and who are the authors of legal rulings (*aṣḥāb al-fatāwī*).[34] Abū Isḥāq al-Shīrāzī, in his *Ṭabaqāt al-fuqahāʾ*, argues that he writes his text in order to describe only those jurists who can be considered authoritative in the formation of legal consensus and who are to be regarded as authoritative in disputed questions or points of law (*khilāf*).[35] Similarly, al-Isnawī (d. 772/1370) argues in the introduction to his *Ṭabaqāt* that he wrote his text to list those jurists found in the two foundational *fiqh* texts, the *ʿAzīz fī sharḥ al-wajīz* and the *Rawḍat al-ṭālibīn*.[36] Ibn Qāḍī Shuhbah likewise argues that one of the reasons he wrote his text was so that legal scholars could easily make reference to the jurists listed in the *ʿAzīz* and the *Rawḍah*.[37] These examples demonstrate one of the most important characteristics of legal *ṭabaqāt*, namely that they are designed and created for the express purpose of being used by jurists in the pursuit of discovering new rules of law or in ascertaining the verac-

---

[33] Norman Calder, "Law," in *History of Islamic Philosophy*, ed. Seyyed Hossein Nasr and Oliver Leaman, vol. 1 (New York: Routledge, 2001), 982.
[34] Al-ʿAbbādī, *Kitāb ṭabaqāt al-fuqahāʾ al-shāfiʿīyah*, 1.
[35] Abū Isḥāq al-Shīrāzī, *Ṭabaqāt al-fuqahāʾ*, 31.
[36] Al-Isnawī, vol. 1, 17.
[37] Khān, vol. 1, 53–54.

ity of earlier rules through an appraisal of the characters and abilities of their authors. They are unlike other kinds of biographical histories in that they have the juridical community as their specific audience and are not intended to be read by others outside that group. Because many legal *ṭabaqāt* were written by jurists for jurists, the knowledge contained and communicated through *ṭabaqāt* is determined by the legal culture in which the community of jurists participated. Legal *ṭabaqāt* works were written by jurists who had interests in a variety of areas. As George Makdisi has pointed out, if one wanted to engage in an intellectual discipline, the law was, outside medicine, one of the few fields open. The importance of legal training for intellectual pursuits indicates that the influence of legal cultural grammars may be important for understanding non-legal *ṭabaqāt* as well. The current project, however, is more narrowly focused on legal texts; further research is necessary to ascertain the overall importance of legal cultural grammars on the genre as a whole.[38]

Legal ṭabaqāt *as an expression of a jurisprudential historiography*

Legal training had an effect on the composition of legal and paralegal *ṭabaqāt* works. 'Paralegal *ṭabaqāt*' refers to *ṭabaqāt* texts devoted to genres of knowledge that were ancillary to the legal profession such as lexicography, grammar, Qur'an commentary, and *ḥadīth*. If legal *ṭabaqāt* are legal biographical histories written by jurists, they are best understood as juridically shaped. In other words, the methods and assumptions that inform the composition of *fiqh* (legal rules) texts also shape legal *ṭabaqāt*.

Fiqh texts were not intended to be read by the unqualified general public. The advice advanced in these texts is composed in such a way that is understandable only to those who have actual experience in the practice of certain activities that the texts seek to clarify. This point was made clear to me in 1996 when I participated in the slaughter of a bull for the purpose of obtaining *ḥalāl* (ritually slaughtered and thus acceptable) meat. The men who carried out the slaughter were four Muslim graduate students who had never slaughtered an animal before and did so in this instance solely because

[38] For an interesting discussion of the influence of legal training on medieval Muslim intellectual life, see George Makdisi, *The Rise of Humanism in Classical Islam and the Christian West: with Special Reference to Scholasticism* (Edinburgh: University Press, 1990), 48–66.

of the high price of *ḥalāl* meat in the area. In preparation, they read only *ḥadīth* and a few legal treatises as guides for the slaughter. The result was that they knew almost nothing of the practical aspects of slaughter such as how to catch the animal, transport it to the slaughter floor, how to tie it down, and the modality of actually cutting the throat beyond the very limited descriptions found in *ḥadīth* and legal treatises, not to mention how the animal was to be butchered after death. *Fiqh* and *ṭabaqāt* texts mention only those things that are under dispute or are necessary to know to fulfill the minimum requirements of a particular act. Thus, they mention only what is deemed to be important so that an act or ruling will be in conformance with the will of God.

Methodologically, *fiqh* texts are based on the location of causation, or *ʿillah*. The *ʿillah* is the motivating factor that gives rise to a certain set of conditions. Finding the *ʿillah* is the first step in legal reasoning that makes the use of *qiyās* (analogy) possible.[39] For instance, the first chapter of almost every *fiqh* text is a discussion of *ṭahārah* (ritual purity). Ritual purity is the gateway to almost every aspect of religious observance in Islam, and the lack of purity prevents Muslims from participating in most religious activities such as prayer, pilgrimage, or even touching, and in some cases reading, the Qurʾan.

In the *Minhāj al-ṭālibīn*, one of the most widely read and frequently memorized texts of Shāfiʿī law, al-Nawawī argues, based on a citation from the Qurʾan, that water is essential for the kinds of ritual cleansing necessary to become ritually pure. Because water is so important, the purity of water becomes the central, first question that must be clarified before describing the other steps in becoming ritually pure. Only water that has not been altered by any other substance can be considered 'water' in the proper sense of the word. Anything that alters the substance of water, such as saffron, renders the water impure and not proper for use in purification. A body that does not change the substance of the water, such as sand, does not render the water impure. The difference between saffron and sand is that saffron cannot be removed from the water whereas sand, or other hard non-dissolving substances, can be filtered out, return-

[39] Hallaq, *A History of Islamic Legal Theories*, 84–95; Weiss, *The Search For God's Law*, 555–56. I translate the term as 'motivating factor' instead of '*ratio legis*' (Hallaq) or 'occasioning factor' (Weiss) because neither term conveys the sense of causality that is fundamental to Islamic law.

ing the water to its original condition.[40] Thus, the motivating factor in deciding whether a foreign substance renders water impure is whether it can be removed.

This leads to a secondary argument as to whether dead insects that fall into water render it impure. It is generally held that corpses of any kind are impure. Contact with dead animals causes the highest level of ritual impurity, requiring a full bath (*ghusl*) to return the individual to a pure state.[41] Al-Nawawī states, however, that some jurists held that a bloodless dead insect in water does not render it (the water) impure.[42] Thus the *ʿillah*, or motivating factor, in determining whether a dead animal can cause impurity is not the fact of death itself, but the possible exposure to bodily fluids, which, when mixed with the water, cannot be removed. Since a bloodless insect cannot render water impure by the loss of fluids, once it is removed (as is required of other hard non-dissolving substances), the water is rendered pure.[43] Thus we see that causation leads to a series of implications that follow logically from the initial motivating factor.

Causation is also the most basic assumption in the legal historical approach used by many jurists in legal *ṭabaqāt* texts. Jurist/historians do not just assume that 'A' leads to 'B,' but that 'A' causes 'B' in such a way that without 'A' there would be no 'B.' Causative assumptions control not only the writing of individual biographies but the whole of the *ṭabaqāt* work.

Returning to the biographical notice of al-Buwayṭī, Ibn Qāḍī Shuhbah states that:

> He used to fast and recite the Qurʾan. He hardly passed a day and night without completing the entire Qurʾan; this, in spite of doing good deeds for the people. Ibn Abī al-Jārūd said, "Al-Buwayṭī was my neighbor. I was unable to get up at any hour of the night without hearing him reciting and praying."[44]

While this may seem like a testimony to al-Buwayṭī's piety and thus his character—and on one level it is—Ibn Qāḍī Shuhbah places it

[40] Al-Nawawī, *Minhāj al-ṭālibīn* (Beirut: Dār al-kutub al-ʿilmīyah, 1996), 5.
[41] Ibid., 7–8.
[42] Ibid., 5–6.
[43] Al-Nawawī holds that the entire discussion is actually fruitless, apparently due to the fact that the amount of impurity caused by the inclusion of an insect's bodily fluids falls below the level of pollution required to render a body of water impure (al-Nawawī, *Minhāj al-ṭālibīn*, 5–6).
[44] Khān, vol. 1, 71.

next to the following sentence: "he died in Baghdād in prison and in chains during the inquisition in the month of Rajab, in the year 231."[45] Ibn Qāḍī Shuhbah assumes that the reader would know that the *miḥnah* involved the persecution of those who refused to confess that the Qur'an was created (clearly an evocative allusion). Additionally, he seeks to establish a causative association between piety, especially al-Buwayṭī's devotion to the Qur'an, and its direct result, imprisonment and death. Ibn Qāḍī Shuhbah juxtaposes piety and martyrdom with the dangers of extremist rationalism. Ibn Qāḍī Shuhbah assumes rationalism (the context of the causation) to exist. It is a fact as impurity is a fact. In the face of the fact of rationalism, there are multiple possible historical outcomes depending on which causative relationship occurs. The account assumes that if al-Buwayṭī had not been devoted to the Qur'an and to prayer he would not have refused to betray the traditionalist view of the eternality of the Qur'an. Similarly, it assumes that al-Buwayṭī's extreme piety led directly to the outcome of imprisonment and death—martyrdom—a positive outcome in the Islamic scheme.

The hypertextual nature of ṭabaqāt *texts*

On the level of the text, causative association and allusion are extremely important for understanding the overall ethos that authors attempt to convey. *Ṭabaqāt* are not meant to be used only as biographical dictionaries; they are not designed simply to be used as reference tools to which jurists can turn to find information on individual figures of the past. They are *hypertextual* by nature, and thus tell a constructed story of the author's view of history. The term 'hypertextual' is used specifically to bring to mind the way that pages link and cross-reference on a website. *Ṭabaqāt* texts refer to people, events, and concepts, assuming that readers will link them together to form a mental picture of the whole text, as well as the relationships between individual biographies and events. Since *ṭabaqāt* texts were frequently memorized, it is likely that scholars could call to mind many different networks of meaning depending on the item under review. To understand what the author is attempting to convey, the reader must understand the relationships the author draws

[45] Ibid., 71–72.

between individual biographies and the information contained in them, and their importance. Thus hypertextual referencing is macro-textual and micro-textual. Ibn Qāḍī Shuhbah demonstrates the use of hypertextual referencing in his biographical citation for al-Buwayṭī. He says that,

> He (al-Buwayṭī) had a high status with al-Shāfiʿī. The men sometimes used to ask [al-Shāfiʿī] about questions and he would say "Ask Abū Yaʿqūb," and when he answered, he [al-Shāfiʿī] would then say, "It is as he said." Sometimes the chief of police came to al-Shāfiʿī, [and] al-Shāfiʿī, while turning and pointing to Abū Yaʿqūb, would say, "This is my spokesman (*lisān*)."[46]

Ibn Qāḍī Shuhbah goes on to say that

> He (al-Buwayṭī) succeeded al-Shāfiʿī in his circle after him. Al-Shāfiʿī said, "No one is more deserving of my *majlis* than Abū Yaʿqūb. And no one among my students is more knowledgeable than he."[47]

Finally, Ibn Qāḍī Shuhbah quotes al-Nawawī as stating, "Abū Yaʿqūb was greater than al-Muzanī and al-Rabīʿ al-Murādī."[48]

To understand the significance of these statements we must also read Ibn Qāḍī Shuhbah's biographical entries for al-Muzanī and al-Rabīʿ al-Murādī. Ibn Qāḍī Shuhbah gives the following biographical notice regarding al-Muzanī:

> [He was a] leading jurist, an author of works arranged by chapter. He studied (*akhadha*) with al-Shāfiʿī and he used to say, "I am a creation from the qualities of al-Shāfiʿī (*anā khalq min akhlāq al-Shāfiʿī*)." Shaykh Abū Isḥāq mentions him as the first student of al-Shāfiʿī. He said, "he was an ascetic, a legal scholar, a jurist of independent reason (*mujtahid*), an intense debater and argumentative, and he dove into the sea of precise meanings. He wrote many books." Al-Shāfiʿī said, "Al-Muzanī is the champion of my school of thought." He was born in the year 175 and died during Ramaḍān, some say during I Rabīʿ, in the year 264. His prayers were answered. Al-Rāfiʿī, in the chapter on ritual ablutions, said, "According to al-Muzanī the combing of the beard is obligatory." Ibn Kajj transmitted this from one of the students (of al-Shāfiʿī), "(Then) al-Muzanī's unique positions should not be considered as being representative of (al-Shāfiʿī's) range of acceptable rules, when he did not derive it according to the jurisprudential method of al-Shāfiʿī." But al-Rāfiʿī transmitted, in the chapter on

46 Khān, vol. 1, 71.
47 Ibid.
48 Ibid.

> divorce on the insistence of the wife, from the Imām [al-Shāfiʿī] that he said, "'I consider every choice from al-Muzanī to be derivative (*takhrījan*) [of my opinion/legal method],' for he does not contradict the jurisprudential method of al-Shāfiʿī. Unlike Abū Yūsuf and Muḥammad, for they contradict the jurisprudential method [of Abū Ḥanīfah] a great deal." Al-Isnawī said, "I saw in *al-Nihāyah*, as if he, in the violation of rules for ritual ablutions, gave the opposite of what al-Rāfiʿī cited from him concerning divorce on the insistence of the wife. He said that he derived a subsidiary legal ruling, and his derivation (*takhrīj*) was more deserving than the derivation (*takhrīj*) of others besides him." Otherwise, he would be the master of an independent school of thought.[49]

Much of this biographical citation is consumed with justifying al-Muzanī's inclusion in the Shāfiʿī school. As Norman Calder has pointed out in his *Studies in Early Islamic Jurisprudence*, whether al-Muzanī held opinions independent from those of al-Shāfiʿī, especially regarding legal method, has been a hotly debated issue throughout Shāfiʿī legal history.[50] Clearly, Ibn Qāḍī Shuhbah presents quotations that argue for his inclusion. He compares al-Muzanī's thought with that of Abū Yūsuf (d. 182/798) and Muḥammad b. al-Ḥasan al-Shaybānī (d. 189/805), both students of Abū Ḥanīfah (d. 150/767), the eponymous founder of the Ḥanafī school of law. He argues that, although there is controversy, al-Muzanī is attested to have derived his method from al-Shāfiʿī's and therefore must be considered a member of the school.

Ibn Qāḍī Shuhbah does not want to claim that al-Muzanī was as close to al-Shāfiʿī as was al-Buwayṭī. Although al-Muzanī is the 'champion' of al-Shāfiʿī's school of thought, he is not represented as enjoying the intimacy that al-Buwayṭī did. Al-Buwayṭī is described as being the heir to al-Shāfiʿī, as his most knowledgeable student; while al-Muzanī is described as being 'a creation from the qualities' (*khalq min akhlāq*) of al-Shāfiʿī.

In fact, the rhetorical use of the phrase *khalq min akhlāq* is reminiscent of a rhetorical device used in poetry known as *jinās al-kāfī* (imperfect paronomasia). There are a number of categories of *tajnīs* described in manuals of rhetoric. Essentially, *tajnīs* occurs when a writer seeks to create an allusion to one concept by using another

---

[49] Khān, vol. 1, 58–59.

[50] Norman Calder, *Studies in Early Islamic Jurisprudence* (Oxford: Clarendon Press, 1993), 86–104.

word that is phonetically similar.[51] *Jinās al-kāfī* happens when the term or concept alluded to occurs in the same sentence and is either phonetically the same or approximate to it.[52] Ibn Qāḍī Shuhbah creates a *jinās al-kāfī* between the terms *akhlāq* (qualities) and *khalq* (creation). Ibn Qāḍī Shuhbah is saying that al-Muzanī is the creation of al-Shāfiʿī; a product of his intellect, a manifestation of his opinion. The use of *tajnīs*, however, does not appear to end there.

The central controversy of the *miḥnah* was the issue of the created versus eternal Qurʾan. The ʿAbbāsid state issued a decree in 218/833 that required all state-paid officials to publicly articulate belief in the created nature of the Qurʾan (*khalq al-Qurʾān*). The issue had fundamental theological and political implications. If one assumed the Qurʾan was created then the rules found in the text were thought to have limited applicability beyond the time the revelation occurred. If one assumed the text was eternal-and this is the view that became the norm following the end of the Inquisition in 235/850—then the rules, both explicit and implied, had permanent validity for all people at all times. The state sponsored the created position because it placed the power of law squarely in its hands since revelation had little legal value.[53]

Ibn Qāḍī Shuhbah is seeking to create a comparison between al-Muzanī as the creation of al-Shāfiʿī and al-Buwayṭī as his spokesman (*lisān*) by using the phonetic similarity of *akhlāq* to *khalq* to create an allusion to the controversy of the created Qurʾan as a context. In this case the paronomasia is referred to as *jinās al-tāmm* (perfect paronomasia), or an allusion made between two terms that have the same phonetic sound.[54] *Lisān* means 'spokesman' but it also means 'speech' or 'language.' The Qurʾan refers to itself as 'clear Arabic language' (*lisānun ʿarabīyun mubīn*).[55] Not only is al-Buwayṭī held up as a martyr in the struggle over defending the eternality of the Qurʾan but he is rhetorically associated with the eternal text itself. The allusion here is clear: just as the Qurʾan is a manifestation of the essence of God so to is al-Buwayṭī a manifestation of al-Shāfiʿī. By referring to al-Muzanī as *akhlāq*, Ibn Qāḍī Shuhbah is attempting

[51] Cachia, 19.
[52] Ibid., 21.
[53] *The Encyclopedia of Islam*, 2nd ed., s.v. "Miḥnah."
[54] Cachia, 21.
[55] 16:103.

to carefully define him as close to al-Shāfiʿī, but not so close as al-Buwayṭī; as knowledgeable in the legal method, but not so knowledgeable as al-Buwayṭī. Ultimately, Ibn Qāḍī Shuhbah is attempting to create a picture of al-Muzanī as dependent and derivative of the eponym; and to base his legal method on that of al-Shāfiʿī (to be his creation), but finally, like all created things, to have a separate essence from the creator.

But why go to such rhetorical lengths to create a picture of al-Muzanī's place in the *madhhab*, and to comparing him with al-Buwayṭī? To answer that question it is first necessary to look at Ibn Qāḍī Shuhbah's notice for al-Rabīʿ al-Murādī:

> A student of al-Shāfiʿī and his servant (*khādim*); [He was] a transmitter of his later [literally 'new'] books. Shaykh Abū Isḥāq said, "It was he who transmitted the books of al-Shāfiʿī." Al-Shāfiʿī said, "Al-Rabīʿ is my transmitter." Al-Dhahabī said, "Al-Rabīʿ was more knowledgeable than al-Muzanī in *ḥadīth*, and al-Muzanī was much more knowledgeable in law than he. It was as if the former knew only *ḥadīth*, and the latter knew only law." He was born in 173 or 4 and he died in Shawwāl in the year 270. Al-Shāfiʿī said of him, "He is the best memorizer of my students." People traveled to him from all corners of the earth to get al-Shāfiʿī's knowledge and to transmit his books. Al-Quḍāʿī said, "Al-Rabīʿ was the last who transmitted from al-Shāfiʿī in Egypt."[56]

The most salient aspect of this synopsis is al-Rabīʿ's importance as al-Shāfiʿī's chief transmitter. Al-Rabīʿ's specialization in *ḥadīth*, and not in law, is meant to convey that he transmitted al-Shāfiʿī's opinion without interpretation or manipulation. As Calder has pointed out, al-Rabīʿ is, according to tradition, thought to have been the primary transmitter of al-Shāfiʿī's most important *fiqh* text *Kitāb al-umm*.[57]

Secondly, as he did with the hypertextual references between the biographies of al-Muzanī and al-Buwayṭī, Ibn Qāḍī Shuhbah uses *tajnīs* as a rhetorical ploy to create an impression of al-Rabīʿ as the faithful and truthful possessor and transmitter of al-Shāfiʿī's authentic opinion. Here Ibn Qāḍī Shuhbah employs a rhetorical strategy similar to *jinās al-muḍāriʿ* (variant paronomasia) used in poetry. In

[56] Khān, vol. 1, 65–66.

[57] Although Calder argues that it is the result of the collaborative efforts of his students and intellectual descendents who wrote in his name over several generations. See his *Studies in Early Islamic Jurisprudence*, 67–85; 97–101.

*jinās al-muḍāri*ʿ, one of the consonants in the trilateral root is changed but remains in the same phonetic category.[58] The purpose is to create an allusion, between two words in the same passage, using terms that sound similar. In this situation, unlike in normal *jinās al-muḍāri*ʿ, the use of *khādim* (servant) is meant to allude to the absent term *qadīm* (eternal). In the context of the allusion to the *miḥnah* found in the biography of al-Buwayṭī and the use of *tajnīs* to recall notions of createdness for al-Muzanī, Ibn Qāḍī Shuhbah uses a type of variant paronomasia to create a comparison between al-Muzanī and al-Rabīʿ.

Here, al-Rabīʿ is equated with the eternal or orthodox view of the Qurʾan and al-Muzanī with the created Book. By referring to al-Rabīʿ as *khādim* Ibn Qāḍī Shuhbah is seeking to evoke notions of orthodoxy, permanence, and accuracy. Just as the Qurʾan is understood to be the eternal unerring word of God, so too are the texts from al-Shāfiʿī that al-Rabīʿ transmitted. Al-Muzanī is the creation of al-Shāfiʿī, al-Rabīʿ his unchanging word.

Analysis and recognition of the causative associations and evocative allusions stemming from the hypertextual nature of the *Ṭabaqāt* allows us to identify two central themes: 1) Ibn Qāḍī Shuhbah is making an argument for the importance of political and historical events on the development of law, and, 2) he is prefiguring what will become his most important theme: *ikhtilāf* (disagreement over legal rulings).

Ibn Qāḍī Shuhbah makes an intricate argument about the importance of historical events as determinants in the history of Islamic law. It is recalled that he reports that al-Buwayṭī was 'greater' than either al-Muzanī or al-Rabīʿ and that he was al-Shāfiʿī's designated heir after the latter's death in 204/820. He also states that al-Buwayṭī died in prison as a result of the Inquisition. One naturally assumes that al-Buwayṭī, given his high standing in Shāfiʿī history, would also be listed by Ibn Qāḍī Shuhbah as an important transmitter of al-Shāfiʿī's thought. To the contrary, Ibn Qāḍī Shuhbah does not list him as being a teacher or transmitter of information to any other scholar. This is surprising given that al-Buwayṭī is mentioned by al-Nawawī as being preferable to both al-Rabīʿ and al-Muzanī as a transmitter of al-Shāfiʿī's opinion, and al-Subkī, in his *Ṭabaqāt*, lists

[58] Cachia, 28.

a number of rulings he transmitted from his master.[59] Why does Ibn Qāḍī Shuhbah choose not to mention al-Buwayṭī as a transmitter or as having any students?

The hypertextual nature of the work is extremely important in understanding the argument that Ibn Qāḍī Shuhbah attempts to make regarding legal history. An examination of the biographies of the next several generations produces no mention of al-Buwayṭī as having a single student. His books are mentioned only once, in the biography of Ibn al-ʿIfrīs (d. early fifth/eleventh century), and then not by title.[60] Al-Muzanī and al-Rabīʿ, on the contrary, have twenty-five students (15 for al-Muzanī and 10 for al-Rabīʿ), founded the two major early sub-schools within the *madhhab*, and (in the case of al-Muzanī) authored major works that became part of the core curriculum of the school. Then why elevate al-Buwayṭī above the others?

By elevating al-Buwayṭī above al-Muzanī and al-Rabīʿ, Ibn Qāḍī Shuhbah is establishing one of the major motifs of his text: the importance of premature death (either sudden natural death or death due to political, economic, or environmental causes), for the development of Islamic law. In almost every instance where a jurist in mentioned as dying from imprisonment, war, plague, murder, or suddenly, Ibn Qāḍī Shuhbah indicates that lines in the transmission of knowledge, which are central to his argument, are cut short. In his text, the occurrence of unusual death marks the formation of new trends in Islamic law; turning points in the movement from one stage of Shāfiʿī legal history to the next. Unusual death is the sign of God's hand in history.

The second ramification of the comparison between al-Muzanī and al-Rabīʿ is the formation of sub-schools in the *madhhab* founded on divergent opinions (*ikhtilāf*) concerning rules reflective of God's will. By contrasting al-Muzanī, the specialist in law who, though following al-Shāfiʿī's method, nonetheless derives divergent rules, with al-Rabīʿ, the faithful transmitter of al-Shāfiʿī's opinion, Ibn Qāḍī Shuhbah sets out the earliest instance of authorized divergent opinions. Ibn Qāḍī Shuhbah's use of al-Shāfiʿī's statement about the authority of al-Muzanī to derive divergent rules is extremely impor-

[59] Al-Nawawī, *al-Majmūʿ*, vol. 1, 111; al-Subkī, *al-Ṭabaqāt al-shāfiʿīyah al-kubrā*, vol. 2, 162–170.
[60] Khān, vol. 1, 139.

tant in this respect. From these divergent opinions concerning rules, though not methods (at least until later), Ibn Qāḍī Shuhbah indicates that sub-schools form that reflect differing legal and intellectual views. Over time these sub-schools split into new intellectual schools dedicated to legal, religious, and theological theory and speculation.

Ibn Qāḍī Shuhbah also establishes the authority for textual divergences by contrasting these two early authorities. They establish the earliest textual traditions that embody the type of disagreement seen to extend over the entire history of the school. For instance, the last jurist mentioned by Ibn Qāḍī Shuhbah as commenting on al-Muzanī's *Mukhtaṣar* is Ibn al-ʿAdlān, who died in 748/1347, a mere century before Ibn Qāḍī Shuhbah completed his *Ṭabaqāt*.[61]

Beyond al-Muzanī and al-Rabīʿ, Ibn Qāḍī Shuhbah mentions jurists involved in some form of *ikhtilāf* in 60% of 784 biographies (this includes not only jurists mentioned as deriving divergent opinions, but those who are also mentioned in authoritative texts that catalogue their divergent opinions). Divergent legal opinion is one of the core foci of Ibn Qāḍī Shuhbah's text, which attempts to catalogue those who are authorized to hold diverging opinions.

Conclusion

The preceding analysis has attempted to highlight some of the insights that a close inner-textual reading of *ṭabaqāt* texts may yield. It has demonstrated through an examination of allusion, causative associations, and hypertextuality, that the medieval Muslim authors of *ṭabaqāt* texts made rhetorical arguments about the nature and historical development of authority structures in various genres of knowledge.

The use of rhetorical methods should indicate to historians of Islamic intellectual thought that *ṭabaqāt* texts must be used with caution. Typically, these texts are used as nothing more that sources of data on the lives on individual jurists, traditionists, doctors, and other scholars of interest. It is clear, however, that the way authors chose to structure individual biographies, and whole texts, can tell us much about how they saw the nature of authority and history and, in the end, may not contain completely accurate information on the actual

[61] Khān, vol. 3, 54.

historical development of Islamic thought and law. *Ṭabaqāt* texts must, therefore, be understood primarily as snapshots of historical and intellectual thought as they existed at the time the texts were written. While *ṭabaqāt* texts can still be used as sources of information on individual lives and careers, historians must first attempt to understand and account for the rhetorical purposes of the texts to ensure that they develop accurate pictures of Islamic history.

CHAPTER FOUR

MACRO-TEXTUAL RHETORICAL STRATEGIES: TRENDS IN LEARNING AS INDICATORS OF INTELLECTUAL DEVELOPMENT

Although medieval Muslim biographers were interested in the lives of individuals, they believed that historical development resulted from God's involvement with humans on both an individual and community level. People do not live in isolation from one another, but live in societies that bind them together through networks of loyalty, dependence, and ultimately law. Describing history therefore involved understanding not just how individuals lived but how they interacted. Ultimately, medieval Muslim historians attempted to describe historical trends as manifestations of multiple human activities.

One of the functions of *ṭabaqāt* works is to describe the development of trends in intellectual history. To do this, authors utilized a number of macro-textual rhetorical strategies that indicate how writers understood the progress of movements over time. There are at least three macro-textual rhetorical strategies that are common in *ṭabaqāt* texts that each rely on observing how themes, ideas and terms repeat over the course of the text: 1) ranking and classification, 2) terminological repetition, and 3) progression (patterns of repetition). Each macro-textual strategy works in concert with micro-textual strategies to create views of historical and intellectual development and is therefore difficult to describe in isolation.

It is necessary, however, before looking in detail at macro-textual rhetorical strategies, to briefly return to the discussion of terminological variation described in chapter two. As mentioned above, authors had enormous control over how they manipulated source material, but because most authors felt bound to the information presented in the sources, they usually did not attempt to change specific terms. There are, however, instances where terminological variation does creep into the historical record because of changes in lexical usage, personal preference, or through errors. As the survey of 100 biographies drawn from the first twenty-six generations of Ibn Qāḍī Shuhbah's text demonstrates, terminological variation was actually fairly common, occurring in 37% of cases where a specific educational relationship was described within the core biographical traditions. It is not possible to know why, in each instance, an author introduced a different term without a close examination of the text in which the variation occurs.

Because Ibn Qāḍī Shuhbah exercises the ability to remove from his biographies a large amount of information that he has access to in the source material, he is able to control the kinds of terms he uses to a much greater degree than one might otherwise assume. He, for instance, refers only to 33% of all educational relationships mentioned in the source material. He thus selectively removes a vast number of terms and associations from his text and is therefore able to shape the development of certain structures of authority by not creating linkages between students and teachers or by not using specific terms to describe those linkages. Furthermore, as mentioned above, in the 33% of educational associations he does mention, there is a much higher percentage of variation available to him (variation in terms occurs in 37% of core biographies and 58% of core and parallel biographical traditions for each scholar).

Because the vast majority of these variations are between only two terms (46%), Ibn Qāḍī Shuhbah is still restricted a great deal in how he describes a particular educational relationship. The trends discussed over the course of this book need, therefore, to be nuanced to appreciate their implications for understanding Ibn Qāḍī Shuhbah's view of Islamic history and actual trends that may have occurred throughout Islamic history as they were described by the historians he uses as sources. As is discussed below, it is clear that Ibn Qāḍī Shuhbah uses the power to withhold information to create specific impressions of Islamic history, especially in his infrequent use of terms denoting the ability to perform *ijtihād* and *ijtihād*-like operations. In other instances, as in the use of educational terms, it is difficult to know, without a large-scale examination of the biographical traditions surrounding each entry, how Ibn Qāḍī Shuhbah's profound ability to withhold information or his more limited power to select between terms, influences his presentation of history.

Ultimately, Ibn Qāḍī Shuhbah controlled the terms he decided to use. He had the choice not to use a term, to simply describe a relationship in another way (for instance, by referring to discipleship between student and teacher), or, in instances were variation existed, to select between terms for the one that most closely indicated the meaning he was attempting to convey. As the example of al-Dārakī demonstrates, Ibn Qāḍī Shuhbah was careful in selecting from the source material to create a specific image of the scholar and his place in history; Ibn Qāḍī Shuhbah does not use terms randomly or without consideration. The following will therefore describe the repetition and progressive development of terms and concepts as manifestations of Ibn Qāḍī Shuhbah's historical understandings. While they may also indicate something about actual historical trends, making such claims requires an extensive analysis of source material from each period of Islamic history and goes beyond the scope of the present study.

Ranking and classification

Ranking and classification are two of the most fundamental aspects of the *ṭabaqāt* genre. Among other meanings, the primary definition of '*ṭabaqah*' is 'rank,' or 'class.'[1] Ranking and classification serve two primary functions: they establish models for hierarchies of authority within each discipline and they serve to portray the panorama of authority structures thought to have actually existed at any one time in different localities. The presentation of ranks or classes of authority *as models of and models for* intellectual professions portrays a tension in *ṭabaqāt* texts between what was supposed to exist and an author's understanding of—and frequent dissatisfaction with—the reality of intellectual development.

The authors of *ṭabaqāt* works imply a preexisting ranking of authority by excluding some scholars from their works while including others. By including specific scholars they assert that those authorities mentioned in the text deserve special attention due to some quality or attribute that they possess or are associated with, but not necessarily because of their own positions of authority. As stated in chapter one, Ibn Qāḍī Shuhbah argues that he includes famous jurists who deserve mention because of their authority, and thus fame, but he does not provide a biography for everyone that deserves such attention. Instead, he asserts that

[1] Makdisi, "*Ṭabaqāt*," 371.

> I limit myself... to the biographies of [scholars] with a known name, [who are] remembered due to their fame, and whose situation needs to be known by the students of legal science, or to those from whom al-Rāfiʿī and others transmitted in their well known compiled works.[2]

Thus, while fame and ability are important in establishing the qualities that permit inclusion in the text, Ibn Qāḍī Shuhbah implies that abilities alone do not establish their qualification. Instead he includes authorities 1) who might serve as an example for jurists and 2) those who transmitted divergent legal opinions that are recorded in *al-ʿAzīz sharḥ al-wajīz* by al-Rāfiʿī and other texts (such as *Rawḍāt al-ṭālibīn* by al-Nawawī) that present divergent legal opinions (*ikhtilāf*) from a range of scholars. *Ikhtilāf* is important to Ibn Qāḍī Shuhbah because, as is discussed in chapters five, six, and seven, as Islamic law fell into decline the majority of jurists were no longer able to turn to the texts of revelation to 'discover' new rules and thus, according to him, had to turn to the catalogues of diverse opinions found in works such as the *ʿAzīz sharḥ al-wajīz* and *Rawḍāt al-ṭālibīn*. Ranking is therefore not exclusively about establishing the top authorities in a discipline but also, and more importantly for Ibn Qāḍī Shuhbah, it is about establishing a hierarchy of ideas and philosophies.

Authors often include individuals not because they are authorities in their own right, but because they transmit ideas and concepts that are authoritative. Ibn Qāḍī Shuhbah includes a wide range of jurists that he does not characterize as being specialists in any particular discipline of knowledge or who are notable for anything beyond their role as bridges in the transmission of *ikhtilāf* and other ideas and concepts from the authorities of the past to those of later generations. Establishing links in the transmission of knowledge is what necessitates their inclusion.

The quality of an idea or concept is also implicitly connected to the rank of the person who transmits it from one generation to the next. People who are characterized as being involved in events or movements that are disreputable, who have low levels of education, or who do not demonstrate important qualities, by implication diminish the ideas they communicate. Their negative attributes 'rub off' on the philosophies, rules, and methodologies they convey. Conversely, scholars characterized as possessing superior qualities, teachers, ideas, and students are likely to be described as promoting and transmit-

[2] Khān, vol. 1, 53.

ting opinions that reach the highest levels of authority. Ideas are thus frequently the subject of ranking, not just the people.

Ibn Qāḍī Shuhbah ranks and compares a variety of legal methodologies and sub-disciplines such as grammar, theology, and lexicography. The ranking of ideas and concepts, for Ibn Qāḍī Shuhbah, serves the primary purpose of establishing the importance of legal diversity in the historical development of Shāfiʿī law. Ibn Qāḍī Shuhbah understood legal history as a progression of trends that, over time, led to an attenuation in the abilities of jurists to utilize formal methods of legal discovery. In other words, he creates a picture of legal history that began with periods of vital and original legal discovery, which gave way to periods of consolidation where originality, while still occurring, is limited by a reduction in methodological capabilities. This led to periods closer to his own where originality was rare, and when jurists turned to the opinions of previous generations as guides for new legal development. Ibn Qāḍī Shuhbah, therefore, attempts to increase the reservoir of opinions that jurists could cite in new legal discovery by specifying those scholars who were authoritative voices in legal diversity.

The diversity that Ibn Qāḍī Shuhbah seeks to rank and thus map is, however, not limited to divergent legal opinions, but also extends to diverse intellectual sub-schools of thought that make up the overall Shāfiʿī *madhhab*. He maps a spectrum of jurists whose primary concerns were extra-*fiqh*, such as *kalām* (theology), and genres of legal methodology that included heavily *kalām*-oriented approaches, as well as very restricted forms of methodological thinking. He catalogues six primary forms of legal methodology (*uṣūl al-fiqh*): 1) restricted methods that were originally narrowly based on those thought to originate from al-Shāfiʿī, 2) modes of legal reasoning that incorporate methodologies of logic (*manṭiq*), 3) less restricted modes of legal reasoning that are configured not just as *uṣūl al-fiqh*, but also as a defense of religion (*uṣūl al-dīn*), 4) theologically oriented modes of legal reasoning that are configured as an extension of theological debates, 5) *kalām*-oriented jurisprudential methodologies which are philosophically influenced and contain aspects of Muʿtazilī thought, and 6) non-specified genres of legal methodology which are not described as belonging to any specific sub-school of thought. In the end, the diversity of legal methodology is evidence, for Ibn Qāḍī Shuhbah, of the decline of legal thought, because speculative methodologies draw jurists away from the purpose of law: the rules themselves.

The focus on legal diversity, however, should not blind us to the real need in Islamic law for consensus and commonality. An important aspect of Ibn Qāḍī Shuhbah's argument is the centrality of core legal, methodological, and theological texts in Shāfiʿī legal thought. He lists 2058 texts written by various jurists over the course of the history of the school. Of these 2058, only 32 are mentioned as having been used, commented on, studied, or memorized by two or more jurists. These 32 core texts, utilized by over half of the jurists included in the work, represent for Ibn Qāḍī Shuhbah the curriculum of Shāfiʿī legal, methodological, and theological thought. The word 'curriculum' is specifically used to describe these 32 core texts because Ibn Qāḍī Shuhbah implies that they represent, in various periods, the standard text books in a regularized system of study. Of these 32 texts, 21 are legal texts which contain the range of legal opinion that Ibn Qāḍī Shuhbah argues is so important to the longevity of the school. While the present study seeks only to understand Ibn Qāḍī Shuhbah's opinion, an important line of inquiry in future studies would be to ascertain the importance of these texts for other jurists during the medieval period.

Repetition

Ranking and classification, however, is rarely explicit. While authors do frequently use terms that denote positions of authority such as '*raʾīs*,' '*imām*,' and '*shaykh*,' the importance of these terms relative to other terms is not always clear. One of the rhetorical strategies that authors of *ṭabaqāt* works use to establish the relative rank of individuals and ideas is repetition, which serves as the foundation of most macro-textual rhetorical strategies.

As demonstrated above, biographies in *ṭabaqāt* texts are usually brief, frequently just a few lines, although in some texts they can be quite extensive. Because of the small amount of space devoted to each biographical entry, authors use terms and phrases with great care. As Jonathan Z. Smith notes, words are "notoriously difficult and slippery affairs."[3] While there is the tendency to treat words as containing or relating facts that speak for themselves, "all speech is

[3] Jonathan Z. Smith, *Drudgery Divine: On the Comparison of Early Christianities and the Religions of Late Antiquity* (Chicago: The University of Chicago Press, 1994), 54.

mediated and necessarily indirect, and . . ., therefore, all speech requires translation, whether we are treating with interpersonal, intra-cultural or intercultural communication."[4]

Repetition of key terms or concepts over the course of an entire text is, on one level, unavoidable; there is, after all, a limited semantic and lexical range to describe any particular phenomenon. But, as with any language, Arabic possesses a lexical and semantic array that is broad enough to describe analogous categories of phenomena. Once a range of analogous terms or phrases has been identified, it becomes necessary to understand why a term is repeated in a specific way, how authors link terms with particular concepts and motifs, and what its selection, instead of some other analogous term or phrase, implies for understanding the meaning of the text.

The linking of terms with particular concepts and motifs is complicated by the fact that *ṭabaqāt* texts draw their material from other sources, many of which were written centuries before in decidedly different cultural contexts. It is frequently unclear whether, or the extent to which, authors understood how earlier writers may have used specific words and whether they intended to use them in the same way. There have been copious studies of semantic and lexical shifts in grammatical, philosophical, theological, and legal terminology in the medieval period.[5] These studies indicate that there was

[4] Ibid., 55.

[5] See Ariel A. Bloch, *Studies in Arabic Syntax and Semantics* (Wiesbaden: Otto Harrassowitz, 1991), 102–136; Margaret Larkin, *The Theology of Meaning: ʿAbd al-Qāhir al-Jurjānī's Theory of Discourse* (New Haven, Conn.: American Oriental Society, 1995), 5–23; S. A. Bonebakker, *Materials for the History of Arabic Rhetoric from the Ḥilyat al-Muḥāḍara of Ḥātimī* (Napoli: Istituto Orientale di Napoli, 1975), 15–18; Adrian Gully, *Grammar and Semantics in Medieval Arabic: A Study of Ibn Hisham's 'Mughni l-Labib'"* (Richmond, UK: Curzon Press, 1995), 27–72; also see his "*Taḍmīn*, 'Implication of Meaning' in Medieval Arabic," *Journal of the American Oriental Society* 117, no. 3 (July–Sept., 1997): 466–80, especially important in this regard see pages 467–71; Gerhard Endress, "The Language of Demonstration: Translating Science and the Formation of Terminology in Arabic Philosophy and Science," *Early Science and Medicine* 7, no. 3 (2002): 231–254; Naphtali Kinberg and Fahid Abu-Khadra, "Casual and Adversative Meanings of the Particle *Lākin* in Arabic," *Journal of the American Oriental Society* 107, no. 4 (Oct.–Dec., 1987): 761–65; Bernard Weiss, "Subject and Predicate in the Thinking of Arabic Philologists," *Journal of the American Oriental Society* 105, no. 4 (Oct.–Dec., 1985): 605–22; also see his *The Search for God's Law* (Salt Lake City: University of Utah Press, 1992), 135–50; Jaroslav Stetkevych, "Arabic Hermeneutical Terminology: Paradox and the Production of Meaning," *Journal of Near Eastern Studies* 48, no. 2 (April, 1989): 81–96; M. A. S. Abdel Haleem, "Grammatical Shift for Rhetorical Purposes: *Iltifāt* and Related Features in the Qur'ān," *Bulletin of the School of Oriental and African Studies* 55, no. 3 (1992): 407–432, and "Early Islamic Theological

little standardization in the use of important theoretical terms in disciplines such as law, philosophy, legal theory, or grammar. Given that there appears to have been little consistency in the use of key terms from author to author and period to period, it is therefore likely that similar changes in the meaning and usage of descriptive terminology also took place in historical and biographical works.

The lexical complexity of *ṭabaqāt* works can be demonstrated by looking at a number of conceptual categories. For instance, as discussed above, one of the most common elements of a biographical entry is the description of the transmission of knowledge from teacher to student or from generation to generation. Frequently, terms and phrases used to describe the transmission of information are concerned with the acquisition of knowledge. Terms such as *akhadha, ishtaghala, ashghala, qaraʾa, takharraja, ḥaṣṣala, baḥatha, darasa, darrasa,* and *tafaqqaha* are widespread in *ṭabaqāt* works and describe the process of teaching and studying. It would be difficult to ascertain a ranking of levels or classification of types of learning by examining these terms in isolation, but by looking at how authors repeat these terms, the contexts in which terms are used, and the ideas to which authors repeatedly link terms, it is possible to develop a relative ranking and typology of learning in any *ṭabaqāt* work.

---

and Juristic Terminology: *Kitāb al-ḥudūd fī ʾl-uṣūl* by Ibn Fūrak," *Bulletin of the School of Oriental and African Studies* 54, no. 1 (1991): 5–41; Nabil Shehaby, "*ʿIlla* and *Qiyās* in Early Islamic Legal Theory," *Journal of the American Oriental Society* 102, no. 1 (Jan.–March, 1982): 27–46 (this article provides an excellent example of lexical shifts in key legal theoretical terms); Ramzi Baalbaki, "Reclassification in Arab Grammatical Theory," *Journal of Near Eastern Studies* 54, no. 1 (January, 1995): 1–13; Aryeh Levin, "The Grammatical Terms *al-Musnad, al-Musnad ʾIlayhi* and *al-Isnād*," *Journal of the American Oriental Society* 101, no. 2 (April–June, 1981): 145–65. Wael Hallaq has written extensively on lexical changes in legal terminology, see his *Authority, Continuity, and Change in Islamic Law*, especially pages 1–17; *A History of Islamic Legal Theories: An Introduction to Sunnī Uṣūl al-Fiqh*; "Was the Gate of *Ijtihad* Closed?" *International Journal of Middle Eastern Studies* 16 (1984): 3–41 (this article is an important examination of the changes in meaning of the term '*ijtihād*' from the 3rd to the 5th Islamic century); "Notes on the Term *Qarīna* in Islamic Legal Discourse," *Journal of the American Oriental Society* 108, no. 3 (July–Sept., 1988): 475–80; Kees Versteegh, "Linguistic Contacts Between Arabic and Other Languages," *Arabica* 68 (2001): 470–508; Jonathan Owens, "Models for Interpreting the Development of Medieval Arabic Grammatical Theory," *Journal of the American Oriental Society* 111, no. 2 (April–June, 1991): 225–38; and M. Y. I . H. Suleiman, "On the Underlying Foundations of Arabic Grammar: A Preliminary Investigation," *Bulletin of the British Society for Middle Eastern Studies* 16, no. 2 (1989): 176–85.

Table 4.1. The Frequency of reference to modes of learning in Ibn Qāḍī Shuhbah's *Ṭabaqāt*

Mode of Learning	Number of Biographies in which a Mode is Mentioned	Percentage of Total Biographies in which a Mode is listed (out of 469)
Darasa/Darrasa	294	63%
Akhadha	296	63%
Tafaqqaha	256	55%
Ishtaghala/Ashghala	208	44%
Qaraʾa	154	33%
Takharraja	71	15%
Ḥaṣṣala	48	10%
Baḥatha	6	1%

Source: Ibn Qāḍī Shuhbah, *Ṭabaqāt al-fuqahāʾ al-shāfiʿīyah*, ed. al-Ḥāfiẓ ʿAbd al-Alī Khān, 4 vols. (Beirut: ʿĀlam al-kutub, 1987).

Akhadha

In Ibn Qāḍī Shuhbah's text there are 784 biographies, of which 469 describe the process of learning using one of the terms listed in table 4.1. The term that occurs most frequently is '*akhadha*,' which literally means 'to take.'[6] In Ibn Qāḍī Shuhbah's text, *akhadha* represents the lowest and most general level of learning and is used in reference to the study of twenty different fields of knowledge (see table 4.2). Biographies can include multiple references to learning and frequently list one or more modes of learning, subjects studied or taught, and a list of teachers or students. In biographies that use *akhadha* to describe a mode of learning, 168 references do not define a field of knowledge. Law (*fiqh*), which in Ibn Qāḍī Shuhbah's text most usually refers to rules of law and not jurisprudence (the study of legal methodology) is referred to 49 times as the subject of study. The next most frequently appearing subjects are *naḥw* (grammar) and *uṣūl al-fiqh* (legal methodology).

In 98% of instances in which *akhadha* is used to describe the process of learning, a student/teacher relationship is defined. Students are described as '*akhadha ʿan*' (taking from) a teacher or, frequently, a list

[6] Makdisi, *The Rise of Colleges*, 113.

of teachers. In 80% of biographies that list *akhadha* as a mode of learning, students are described as becoming teachers and as having students of their own who then 'take' knowledge from them. Use of the term *akhadha* thus becomes an important component in the creation of networks that map intellectual relationships across generations. That over half of the relationships do not refer to a subject studied also implies that for Ibn Qāḍī Shuhbah, the transmission of specific fields of knowledge, while important, was secondary to the nature of the student/teacher dynamic defined by *akhadha*.

Table 4.2. *Akhadha* as the mode of learning

Field of Study	Number of References	Percentage of Total References to *Akhadha* (out of 269)
No Field Listed	168	57%
Fiqh	49	17%
Naḥw (Grammar)	23	7%
Uṣūl al-Fiqh (Legal Methodologies)	20	7%
ʿIlm (Religious Sciences)	13	4%
Ḥadīth	12	4%
Arabic	7	2%
Qirāʾah (Variant Recitations of the Qurʾan)	6	2%
Lughah (Lexicography)	6	2%
Kalām (Theology)	5	2%
Tafsīr (Qurʾanic Commentaries)	5	2%
Uṣūlayn (Legal and Theological Methodologies)	4	1%
The Study of Specific Texts	4	1%
Adab al-Qāḍī (Rules for Judges)	3	1%
Manṭiq (logic)	2	.06%
Sufism	2	.06%
Farāʾiḍ (Inheritance Law)	2	.06%
Al-ʿUlūm al-ʿAqlīyah (Rational Sciences)	2	.06%
Medicine	1	.003%
Ḥifẓ (Memorization of Texts)	1	.003%
Preaching	1	.003%
History	1	.003%

Source: Ibn Qāḍī Shuhbah, *Ṭabaqāt al-fuqahāʾ al-shāfiʿīyah*, ed. al-Ḥāfiẓ ʿAbd al-Alī Khān, 4 vols. (Beirut: ʿĀlam al-kutub, 1987).

According to Michael Chamberlain, medieval educational practices were aimed at creating cultural capital that was then converted into economic wealth and used to create bonds of loyalty and social cohesion. Elite households (*aʿyān*) ritualized the acquisition of knowledge and tied it to notions of beneficence, service, spiritual blessings, and imitation as a means of enforcing its role in the social hierarchy of the medieval Muslim Middle East.[7] An important aspect of *aʿyān* social maintenance was the production of biographical dictionaries that charted lines of intellectual descent and facilitated claims to social status.[8] As seen from this point of view, Ibn Qāḍī Shuhbah uses *akhadha* relationships to specify the chains of student/teacher connections which bolstered *aʿyān* authority. Understanding what this meant *for* Ibn Qāḍī Shuhbah requires comparing how he uses other terms for the acquisition of knowledge over the course of his text.

Ishtaghala/Ashghala

Ishtaghala and *ashghala*, like *akhadha*, occur fairly frequently, or in 44% (208) of the biographies that mention a mode of learning (see table 4.1). *Ishtaghala* and *ashghala* are derived from the trilateral root *sh gh l*, which means to 'to occupy' or 'to take up' a particular task. It also connotes an image of activity, of widely ranging effort. *Ishtaghala* is the eighth form of the verb and means to intensively study, usually under someone else's direction. *Ashghala* is the fourth form of the verb and means 'to occupy or engage' another person. Ibn Qāḍī Shuhbah uses these two verbs to indicate a higher, more broadly ranging level of study or teaching that involved 20 different fields of knowledge (see table 4.3). *Ishtaghala* and *ashghala* are meant to create an impression of a larger volume of subjects studied, a greater number of teachers from whom one takes instruction, and more time spend in learning. Ibn Qāḍī Shuhbah, for instance, describes Badr al-Dīn al-Ṭanbidhī (d. 809/1406) as studying many subjects over a long period of time (*ishtaghala kathīran*) and attending (*lāzam*) a number of teachers.[9]

---

[7] Chamberlain is specifically interested in Damascus during the late Ayyūbid and early Mamlūk period. He suggests, however, that his analysis holds true for other areas of the Middle East during the period. His study is of particular interest for the present discussion because Ibn Qāḍī Shuhbah lived in Damascus during the century following the period of Chamberlain's examination. See Michael Chamberlain, *Knowledge and Social Practice in Medieval Damascus*, 108–30. Also see Roy Mottahedeh, *Loyalty and Leadership in an Early Islamic Society*, 142–47.

[8] Chamberlain, 149–50.

[9] Khān, vol. 4, 16–17.

Table 4.3. *Ishtaghala* and *ashghala* as modes of learning

Field of Study	Number of References	Percentage of Total References to *Ishtaghala* and *Ashghala* (out of 208)
No Field Listed	107	50%
ʿIlm (Religious Sciences)	34	16%
Fiqh	21	10%
Funūn ʿIlm (Diverse Religious Sciences)	10	5%
Arabic	7	3%
Ḥadīth	6	3%
Farāʾiḍ (Inheritance Law)	6	3%
The Study of Specific Texts	5	2%
Naḥw (Grammar)	4	2%
Uṣūl al-Fiqh (Legal Methodologies)	3	1%
Lughah (Lexicography)	2	1%
Al-ʿUlūm al-ʿAqlīyah (Rational Sciences)	2	1%
Khilāf (Divergent Legal Opinions)	2	1%
Kalām (Theology)	1	.05%
Qirāʾat (Variant Recitations of the Qurʾan)	1	.05%
Manṭiq (logic)	1	.05%
Tafsīr (Qurʾanic Commentaries)	1	.05%
Preaching	1	.05%
History	1	.05%
ʿIbādāt (Ritual Rules)	1	.05%

Source: Ibn Qāḍī Shuhbah, *Ṭabaqāt al-fuqahāʾ al-shāfiʿīyah*, ed. al-Ḥāfiẓ ʿAbd al-Alī Khān, 4 vols. (Beirut: ʿĀlam al-kutub, 1987).

Ishtaghala is different from *akhadha* in several other important aspects. First, *ishtaghala* and *ashghala* are both used in their infinitive (*maṣdar*) forms in a number of instances as descriptors of achievement in learning and teaching. Ibn Qāḍī Shuhbah uses them in this way when he describes Ibrāhīm b. Hibatallāh al-Isnawī (d. 721/1321) as being "persistent in studying and teaching" (*mulāziman li ʾl-ishtighāl wa ʾl-ishghāl*).[10] Secondly, in instances where a teacher/student rela-

[10] Ibid., vol. 2, 245.

tionship is defined, second generation educational relationships that create impressions of intellectual transmission over time are rarely present. *Ishtaghala* and *ashghala* appear to be used by Ibn Qāḍī Shuhbah to create impressions of intense and diverse study but not to promote the dissemination of knowledge or *aʿyān* authority. They are thus signifiers of individual achievement in learning and teaching but not generally descriptors of intellectual pedigree. As with *akhadha* relationships, 50% of references to *ishtaghala* and *ashghala* do not refer to the study of a particular field of knowledge. Unlike *akhadha* relationships, however, when a field is not specified neither is an educational partner. In other words, when a field is absent as a complementary term, the *maṣdar* forms of *ishtaghala* or *ashghala* are used as signifiers of achievement or are used without listing a specific teacher.

The use of *ishtaghala* as a signifier of achievement in study, especially in comparison to *akhadha*, is also demonstrated in the number of references to excellence (*barāʿah*), elevated knowledge (*maʿrifah*), or skill (*mahārah*) an individual is described as possessing in a particular field of knowledge after engaging in either practice. Excellence, knowledge, and skill are attributed to only four individuals as a result of *akhadha* whereas 75 individuals are referred to as possessing these qualities as a result of *ishtaghala* (or 36% of the time). This indicates that Ibn Qāḍī Shuhbah may have understood learning to involve the transmission of knowledge as a means of cultural capital (as is implied by his presentation of *akhadha* relationships) *and* as the transmission of important religious knowledge that was central to the maintenance of Islamic society through the application of the law. Knowledge was not simply a means of social promotion and maintenance for Ibn Qāḍī Shuhbah. As will be demonstrated throughout this book, knowledge was a means of survival that had deeply religious connotations. Changes in intellectual development and the impact that these had on the maintenance of Islamic law was the heart of the matter.

Table 4.4. *Qara'a* as a mode of learning

Field of Study	Number of References	Percentage of Total References to *Qara'a* (out of 154)
The Study of Specific Texts	30	19%
Uṣūl al-Fiqh (Legal Methodologies)	29	18%
No Field Listed	25	16%
Qirā'āt (Variant Recitations of the Qur'an)	25	16%
Naḥw (Grammar)	24	15%
Fiqh	14	9%
Arabic	12	8%
Kalām (Theology)	6	3%
Ḥadīth	5	3%
Khilāf (Divergent Legal Opinions)	5	3%
ʿIlm (Religious Sciences)	2	1%
Uṣūlayn (Legal and Theological Methodologies)	2	1%
Manṭiq (logic)	2	1%
Bayān (Rhetoric)	2	1%
Riwāyah (Poetic Transmission)	2	1%
Adab al-Qāḍī (Rules for Judges)	2	1%
Tafsīr (Qur'anic Commentaries)	2	1%
Farā'iḍ (Inheritance Law)	2	1%
Uṣūl al-Dīn (Theology)	1	.06%
Jadal (Debate)	1	.06%
Maʿānī (Rhetoric)	1	.06%
Lughah (Lexicography)	1	.06%
Tawrāh and *Injīl* (The Torah and Gospels)	1	.06%

Source: Ibn Qāḍī Shuhbah, *Ṭabaqāt al-fuqahā' al-shāfiʿīyah*, ed. al-Ḥāfiẓ ʿAbd al-Alī Khān, 4 vols. (Beirut: ʿĀlam al-kutub, 1987).

Qara'a

Qara'a is the next most frequent kind of instruction mentioned by Ibn Qāḍī Shuhbah and occurs in 33% (154) of biographies that refer to a mode of learning (see table 4.1). As described in the introduction, *qara'a* had multiple and important social, educational, ritual, and even mystical purposes. In Ibn Qāḍī Shuhbah's text it specifically refers to the study of a particular book or to the recitation of a particular text, usually under someone's direct supervision, but in a number of instances by oneself.[11] Lane, in his *Arabic English Lexicon*, states that the most basic meaning of the word is 'to recite,'[12] and George Makdisi states that "the verb qarāʾa . . . meant to read, to recite, to recite from memory, to study. It was used primarily in connection with the Koran; but it was used for other subjects, including . . . in law."[13]

The relationship between reading and recitation was important in the pre-modern world. As William Graham has pointed out in his *Beyond the Written Word*, throughout the medieval world reading and writing were oral exercises. Graham, quoting M. T. Clanchy, argues that

> medieval writing was mediated to the non-literate by the persistence of the habit of reading aloud and by the preference, even among the educated, for listening to statements rather than by scrutinizing the script.[14]

As Chamberlain points out, *qaraʾa* also served an important social role in the medieval Muslim Middle East. He states that,

> public reading was one of the major forms of cultural production. . . . Books were also emblems of prestige for the elite. Rulers tried to write books and to memorize them. . . . Shaykhs also gained prestige by learning, reciting, copying or composing books, to the extent that a shaykh's nickname could refer to a book he had memorized. . . . Finally, books had talismanic power as carriers of *Baraka* [spiritual blessings].[15]

Qaraʾa, for Chamberlain, augments the acquisition of cultural capital by promoting bonds of loyalty and social prestige. But he also argues that books were "held in suspicion" and that while they were "'tools of knowledge,'" they were also derided by scholars who argued that "'knowledge is not gained from books, which are some of the most damaging of all corruptions.'" Chamberlain goes on to state that

---

[11] See, for instance Khān, vol. 2, 211–12; vol. 3, 52–54; 125–26; 164–65; 180; vol. 4, 14–15; 27–28.
[12] *Lane's Arabic English Lexicon*, s.v. "qaraʾa."
[13] *The Rise of Colleges*, 143.
[14] M. T. Clanchy, *From Memory to Written Record: England 1066–1307* (Cambridge, Mass.: Harvard University Press, 1979), 150; quoted in William Graham, *Beyond the Written Word: Oral Aspects of Scripture in the History of Religion* (Cambridge: University Press, 1993), 38.
[15] Chamberlain, 135–37.

> there were ways of acquiring *ʿilm* [knowledge] that bypassed the mediation of written texts. Most people experienced the Qur'an and *ḥadīth* as oral performances rather than texts, and indeed the memorization of the Qurʾan has long been central to the education of children.[16]

In the end, Chamberlain argues that books as sources of knowledge were devalued because the increasing focus on written transmission of knowledge threatened the very nature of *aʿyān* authority. Reading books disconnected students from the ritual complex that arose around learning that allowed for the continuance of *aʿyān* control of cultural capital. It, according to his view, "threatened the monopoly of the shaykhs over the transmission of knowledge."[17]

Indeed, Chamberlain is right in his assessment that there were ways that the masses could acquire knowledge outside textual transmission; and it is clear that education developed many profound ritual structures. But the kinds of *ʿilm* that Ibn Qāḍī Shuhbah presents are far more specialized than the general level of religious and pious knowledge that Chamberlain describes. Furthermore, books, especially their recitation in the presence of a master of the discipline, were a potent part of the learning process that vested the student with deeper levels of authority.

Books, for Ibn Qāḍī Shuhbah, carry the knowledge of the masters of the school. As stated above, he lists 2058 texts in the course of his work. Out of this collection only 32 are commented on, studied, or memorized by more than two jurists. Over 60% of the jurists utilize these 32 texts (the remaining 2026 texts are mentioned only as part of the bibliography of an individual jurist). Of these 32 texts, 8 are *fiqh* texts and 13 are *fiqh* texts which contain *ikhtilāf.* The remaining texts are *ḥadīth* texts, grammars, lexicographies, theological texts, and legal methodologies (see chapter seven for a more detailed discussion of the importance of these texts). As stated above, one of the purposes of writing the *ṭabaqāt* is to list those jurists whose opinions are found in the *ʿAzīz sharḥ al-wajīz* by al-Rāfiʿī, a text that, in his estimation, forms the foundation of Shāfiʿī legal knowledge.

As Table 4.4 shows, Ibn Qāḍī Shuhbah refers to *qaraʾa* as the study of a specific text in 30 biographies that use it to describe a mode of learning. The next most frequent references to *qaraʾa* occur

[16] Ibid., 138.
[17] Ibid., 140.

in the study of legal methodologies, variant recitations of the Qur'an (which is oral by nature),[18] grammar, *fiqh* (when listed as a discreet field of study), and then Arabic. *Qara'a* implies a more professional relationship between student and teacher and is frequently augmented by reference to the issuance of an *ijāzah* (permission to teach or transmit) by a teacher to a student. *Ijāzah*s are referred to in 70% of biographies where *qara'a* is mentioned as a mode of learning.

Chamberlain downplays the importance of *ijāzah*s in medieval Islamic education. He cites numerous examples of fraudulent and frivolous *ijāzah*s and argues that they had little to do with establishing the authority of scholars.[19] George Makdisi and Devin Stewart, who see education as far more standardized and institutionalized than does Chamberlain, argue that the issuance of an *ijāzah* was considered to be equivalent to a certificate of graduation from a *madrasah*.[20] For Makdisi and Stewart, an *ijāzah* was central to establishing the credentials of scholars in their fields of knowledge and must be taken seriously when looking at the development of Islamic education.[21] As is discussed below in the examination of *darasa* and *darrasa*, Makdisi's view of the importance of the *ijāzah* is very similar to the way Ibn Qāḍī Shuhbah presents it in his text.

Assuming that *ijāzah*s are important in the construction of authority, *qara'a* would thus appear to be a bridge between the very personal aspects of *akhadha* and the more professional and intensified aspects of *ishtaghala*. It is, for Ibn Qāḍī Shuhbah, central to the development of professional authority as a jurist. Unlike *akhadha* and *ishtaghala*, which are used over 50% of the time without reference to a field of study, *qara'a* is used in conjunction with a particular area of knowledge 86% of the time. This suggests that Ibn Qāḍī Shuhbah saw it as an important aspect of professionalization.

Takharraja

Like *qara'a, takharraja* appears to be an important term referring to the professionalization of scholars. It occurs in 71 biographies that refer to a mode of learning (see table 4.1) and is based on the root

[18] See Graham, 99–100.
[19] Chamberlain, 88–90.
[20] Makdisi, *The Rise of Colleges*, 271.
[21] Stewart, "The Doctorate of Islamic Law," 45–48.

kh r j, meaning 'to go out' or 'to leave.' *Takharraja* is the fifth form of the verb and in modern Arabic means 'to study, to be educated, or to graduate.' *Takharraja* is lexically related to the term '*takhrīj*' (a type of legal reasoning that will be discussed in more detail in chapter five) but in Ibn Qāḍī Shuhbah's text appears to represent a completely different concept (in fact, *takhrīj* is mentioned in only six biographies as a category of reasoning in his *ṭabaqāt*).[22]

Table 4.5. *Takharraja* as a mode of learning

Field of Study	Number of References	Percentage of Total References to *Takharraja* (out of 71)
No Field Listed	50	70%
Ḥadīth	7	10%
Funūn ʿIlm (Diverse Religious Sciences)	4	6%
Fiqh	3	4%
Uṣūl al-Fiqh (Legal Methodologies)	2	3%
Kalām (Theology)	1	1%
Manṭiq (logic)	1	1%
Adab al-Qāḍī (Rules for Judges)	1	1%
Ḥifẓ (Memorization of Texts)	1	1%
Lughah (Lexicography)	1	1%
Naḥw (Grammar)	1	1%
Khilāf (Divergent Legal Opinions)	1	1%

Source: Ibn Qāḍī Shuhbah, *Ṭabaqāt al-fuqahā' al-shāfiʿīyah*, ed. al-Ḥāfiẓ ʿAbd al-Alī Khān, 4 vols. (Beirut: ʿĀlam al-kutub, 1987).

As table 4.5 shows, 70% of references to *takharraja* do not specify a topic of study. In fact, the majority of biographies that use *takharraja* as a descriptor of learning do not even specify a student/teacher relationship at all. Only 16 of 71 entries mention a specific teacher or student. In 45 of 71 biographies (63%) an unnamed group is described as graduating from the individual. Group size, in fact,

[22] See Sherman Jackson, *Islamic Law and the State: The Constitutional Jurisprudence of Shihāb al-Dīn al-Qarāfī* (New York: E. J. Brill, 1996), 91–96; Wael Hallaq, "*Takhrīj* and the Construction of Juristic Authority," in *Studies in Islamic Legal Theory*, ed. Bernard Weiss (Boston: Brill, 2002), 317–35; and his *Authority Continuity and Change in Islamic Law*, especially pages 43–56.

varies. For instance in his biography of Qāḍī Jamāl al-Dīn al-Ḥamawī (d. 697/1298), Ibn Qāḍī Shuhbah states that "many [literally 'a group'] were graduated from him" (*takharraja bihi jamāʿah*),[23] whereas in his biography of Muḥammad b. Yūnus al-Irbilī (d. 608/1212) "the people" (*khalq*) are described as having graduated from him (*takharraja bihi*).[24] Ibn Qāḍī Shuhbah also states that the "Egyptians graduated" (*takharraja bihi al-miṣrīyūn*) from Abū ʿAbdallāh al-Iṣfahānī (d. 688/1289)[25] and the "people of the country (of Yemen)" (*takharraja bihi ahl al-balad*) were graduated from Aḥmad b. Abī Bakr al-Yamānī (d. 815/1412).

Takharraja would therefore appear to be very dissimilar from *akhadha* or *qaraʾa* with their emphasis on personal educational relationships. How Ibn Qāḍī Shuhbah views the nature of *takharraja* is, however, not clear. In two instances he describes people as being "graduated from the hand" (*takharraja ʿalā yad*) of a teacher.[26] It is also not clear whether or not *takharraja* refers to an individualized form of learning as with *akhadha* or whether there is an institutional connotation. In three instances, students are listed as graduating from a teacher specifically in relation to study at a *madrasah*,[27] and 34 (48%) individuals are described as graduating students and teaching at a *madrasah* at that same time. Furthermore, of the 21 instances where a specific field of knowledge is mentioned, 17 are described as occurring in conjunction with study at a school. It appears that when Ibn Qāḍī Shuhbah uses *takharraja* as a descriptor of learning he means some form of group work, as in a *ḥalqah* (discussion circle) or in a *madrasah* where large numbers of students attend lectures. Use of the term seems to signify a form of certification of learning that takes place in a group context and, therefore, appears to be less important than *ishtaghala* or *qaraʾa*. In none of the 71 instances where *takharraja* is used does he describe the knowledge gained as being superior in any way.

---

[23] Khān, vol. 2, 195.
[24] Ibid., vol. 2, 67.
[25] Ibid., vol. 2, 201.
[26] Ibid., vol. 1, 64; 155.
[27] Ibid., vol. 2, 66; 92; 112.

Table 4.6. *Ḥaṣṣala* as a mode of learning

Field of Study	Number of References	Percentage of Total References to *Ḥaṣṣala* (out of 48)
No Field Listed	39	81%
Fiqh	1	2%
Uṣūl al-Fiqh (Legal Methodologies)	3	6%
Arabic	1	2%
Naḥw (Grammar)	1	2%
Funūn ʿIlm (Diverse Religious Sciences)	1	2%
Farāʾiḍ (Inheritance Law)	1	2%

Source: Ibn Qāḍī Shuhbah, *Ṭabaqāt al-fuqahāʾ al-shāfiʿīyah*, ed. al-Ḥāfiẓ ʿAbd al-Alī Khān, 4 vols. (Beirut: ʿĀlam al-kutub, 1987).

Ḥaṣṣala *and* baḥatha

Ḥaṣṣala and *baḥatha* occur less frequently than other terms for learning and most usually refer to achieving a high level of learning and not to specific subjects studied. Of the 48 times *ḥaṣṣala* occurs in the text it refers to a general achievement in learning in 39 instances (see table 4. 6). When *ḥaṣṣala* is mentioned with a specific discipline of knowledge it most usually emphasizes the level of expertise the individual attained in that field. For instance, in his biography of Abū al-Qāsim al-Rāzī (d. 522/1128), Ibn Qāḍī Shuhbah states that al-Rāzī "attainted a high level of knowledge (*ḥaṣṣala*) of the *madhhab* and *khilāf*"[28] and in his biography of Imām al-Ḥaramayn al-Juwaynī (d. 478/1085) he states that the jurist and theologian "learned theology (*uṣūl al-dīn*) and legal methodologies completely (*ḥaṣṣala*)."[29]

Similarly, *baḥatha* (or sometimes in its noun form: *baḥth*), which occurs in only six biographies, is used to indicate especially high levels of achievement in learning and never occurs in conjunction with a specific field of study. In each instance, it occurs only in the biography of a scholar in Ibn Qāḍī Shuhbah's intellectual pedigree and is used to establish the superior credentials of the individual.

[28] Khān, vol. 1, 307.
[29] Ibid., vol. 1, 255.

Darasa/Darrasa *and* Tafaqqaha

Darasa means 'to study' and *darrasa* 'to teach.' In modern Arabic they are the most commonly used words to refer to basic levels of instruction. According to Makdisi, *darasa* and *darrasa*, when used "without a complement" always referred to the study of law.[30] Indeed, in Ibn Qāḍī Shuhbah's text *darasa* and *darrasa* (which occur in 294 biographies) seem to always refer to the study of law except when they are modified by complementary terms such as '*ḥadīth*' or '*tafsīr*' (see table 4.7). Perhaps more important for understanding Ibn Qāḍī Shuhbah is the context in which the terms occur.

Darasa and *darrasa* occur in 228 biographies that link the terms to institutions of learning, most usually a *madrasah*. In only 41 instances are the terms used to refer to educational relationships between teacher and student, or as independent descriptors of learning, that are not somehow connected to an institution.

Table 4.7. *Darasa* and *darrasa* as modes of learning

Field of Study	Number of References	Percentage of Total References to *Darasa* and *Darrasa* (Out of 294)
No Complementary Term	269	91%
Fiqh	8	2%
Tafsīr (Qur'anic Commentaries)	6	2%
Ḥadīth	4	1%
Qirā'āt (Variant Recitations of the Qur'an)	1	.03%
The Study of Specific Texts	1	.03%
Iftā' (the study of legal rulings)	1	.03%
Uṣūl al-Fiqh (Legal Methodologies)	0	0%

Source: Ibn Qāḍī Shuhbah, *Ṭabaqāt al-fuqahā' al-shāfi'īyah*, ed. al-Ḥāfiẓ 'Abd al-Alī Khān, 4 vols. (Beirut: 'Ālam al-kutub, 1987).

Tafaqqaha, which occurs in 256 biographies, on the other hand, almost always refers to personal educational relationships between teacher and student that are usually discussed without reference to an institution. In only 12 biographies are institutions of learning mentioned

[30] Makdisi, *The Rise of Colleges*, 113.

in relation to *tafaqqaha*, and in half of those a teacher and student are mentioned by name.

Tafaqqaha is the fifth form verb of the root *f q h*, which means 'to understand.' The word '*fiqh*,' which is normally translated as 'law,' actually means 'an understanding of God's will that is indicated in the texts of revelation and 'discovered' through an application of particular methods of textual analysis.' *Tafaqqaha* means to teach to someone else what the understandings of God's will are, in other words, at least in the way the term is used by Ibn Qāḍī Shuhbah, it refers specifically to teaching the rules of the law and not necessarily to methods of legal discovery.

In comparing the ways in which *darasa/darrasa* and *tafaqqaha* are used in the text, it is clear that the personal educative relationship is more highly prized by Ibn Qāḍī Shuhbah than institutional learning. As noted above, Ibn Qāḍī Shuhbah uses three qualifiers that attribute superiority or excellence to different modes of learning (excellence [*barāʿah*], elevated knowledge [*maʿrifah*], and skill [*mahārah*]). In only four biographies does Ibn Qāḍī Shuhbah attribute any of these levels of superiority to knowledge gained from *darasa* or *darrasa*.[31] In 67 biographies, superiority of knowledge of *fiqh* is directly linked to *tafaqqaha*; in 54 of these *tafaqqaha* is linked with the highest level of superiority: *barāʾah*. For instance, in his biography of Abū Naṣr al-Fatāwī (d. 518/1134), Ibn Qāḍī Shuhbah states that Abū Naṣr "studied law (*tafaqqaha*) with the Imām al-Ḥaramayn. Ibn al-Samʿānī said, 'he excelled (*baraʿa*) in *fiqh*.'"[32]

While it is unclear the extent to which the legal education gained by jurists after the late fifth/eleventh century would have been held in an institution, it is important to note that Ibn Qāḍī Shuhbah seeks to create two pictures of legal learning, one personal and the other institutional. This depiction of learning is common in *ṭabaqāt* works and has influenced the way scholars present views of legal education. Makdisi, along with scholars such as Devin Stewart, Richard van Leeuwen, and J. Gilbert, have focused on the large number of references to legal colleges and have developed theories of medieval Islamic legal education that interpret it as highly structured and standardized, with regular systems of promotion and grad-

[31] Khān, vol. 3, 145; 146; 267; 300.
[32] Ibid., vol. 1, 310.

uation.[33] Other scholars, such as Chamberlain, Jonathan Berkey, Roy Mottahedeh, and A. L. Tibawi, see medieval Islamic education as a set of highly informal relationships that have more to do (except for the top scholars) with constructing networks of loyalty and mutual support than they do with inculcating knowledge in any particular area. Because learning was highly informal and personalized, they see the *madrasah* as being extraneous to the development of Islamic thought. Instead, to the extent that *madrasahs* were important at all, they simply served as one of a number of conflict sites between various social groups.[34]

Ibn Qāḍī Shuhbah depicts a system where close personal educational connections took place both inside and outside the *madrasah*. *Akhadha* relationships appear to have existed outside the *madrasah* system and are portrayed by Ibn Qāḍī Shuhbah as private teacher/student relationships whereby authority was acquired, not so much due to the information learned, but due to the relationship that formed out of the contact. *Tafaqqaha* relationships, while personal, were concerned with learning *fiqh*. By attributing excellence to many of the *tafaqqaha* educational connections Ibn Qāḍī Shuhbah is attempting to creating a *model for* the ideal legal learning environment. It is not, however, a relationship that is described as producing certificates (*ijāzahs*) for issuing legal opinions (*ijāzah bi 'l-iftā'*). But it is the *ideal* relationship for producing knowledge of legal rules.

[33] Richard Bulliet disagrees with much of what Makdisi sees as the institutionalization of learning, although he does contend that the *madrasah* system, largely unimportant in Central Asia, did attempt to create a regularized system of teaching. See his *The Patricians of Nishapur: A Study in Medieval Islamic Social History* (Cambridge: Harvard University Press, 1972), 48–50 and his *Islam: A View from the Edge* (New York: Columbia University Press, 1994), 145–52; also see Devin Stewart, *Islamic Legal Orthodoxy*, 95–97; Richard van Leeuwen, *Waqfs and Urban Structures: The Case of Ottoman Damascus* (Boston: Brill, 1999), 82; J. Gilbert, "The 'Ulama' of Medieval Damascus and the International World of Islamic Scholarship," Ph.D. Diss. (University of California-Berkeley, 1977), 58–60; and "Institutionalization of Muslim Scholarship and Professionalization of the *'Ulamā'* in Medieval Damascus," *Studia Islamica* 52 (1980): 105–34.

[34] A. L. Tibawi, "Origin and Character of "*al-Madrasah*," *Bulletin of the School of Oriental and African Studies* 25, no. 1/3 (1962): 225–38; Jonathan Berkey, "Women and Islamic Education in the Mamluk Period," in *Women in Middle Eastern History*, ed. Nikki Kedde and Beth Baron (New Haven: Yale University Press, 1991), 143–57, and his *The Transmission of Knowledge in Medieval Cairo: A Social History of Islamic Education* (Princeton: University Press, 1992), 20–27; Roy Mottahedeh, *Loyalty and Leadership*, 135–50.

Ishtaghala and *ashghala*, when they function as signifiers of accomplishment, along with *ḥaṣṣala* and *baḥatha*, create a *model of* the ideal scholar. Study with a large number of scholars in a wide variety of subjects is clearly prized as an attribute of success. *Ishtaghala* and *ashghala* also serve to describe educational relationships that are less individual than with *akhadha* and *tafaqqaha*. Students who are described as *ishtaghala* study a broad range of topics, spending less time with any one teacher and by necessity studying with more scholars. Ibn Qāḍī Shuhbah presents this as being connected to the rise of the *madrasah* in that there is only one reference to *ishtaghala/ashghala* prior to the rise of the *madrasah* system and in 128 of 208 biographies that refer to *ishtaghala/ashghala*, learning in a *madrasah* is also mentioned. Ibn Qāḍī Shuhbah, therefore, implies that this mode of learning occurred in an institutionalized setting (as is likely with *takharraja*).

Because of his emphasis on the knowledge carried in books and its connection to certifications in learning, Ibn Qāḍī Shuhbah clearly attributes a deeper level of learning to *qaraʾa*. He would appear, however, to see it as less important in learning legal rules than in the study of theoretical subjects. Why this is the case is not immediately clear. What is significant is that while *ijāzah*s are mentioned frequently in conjunction with *qaraʾa*, certifications for the issuance of legal opinions (*ijāzah bi ʾl-iftāʾ*), which is the primary purpose of legal education, are not mentioned. *Ijāzah*s for the issuance of legal opinions (described in the text both as *ijāzah bi ʾl-iftāʾ* and simply as *iftāʾ*) are almost exclusively mentioned in conjunction with *darasa* and *darrasa* at a *madrasah*. Ibn Qāḍī Shuhbah indicates that while the quality of legal education gained from *darasa* at a *madrasah* is lower than the legal education gained from *tafaqqaha*, the issuance of certifications to issue legal opinions appears to come almost solely from work at a legal school. Ibn Qāḍī Shuhbah, therefore, indicates that legal institutions were important for the functioning of the legal system, especially for maintaining a system of law that regulated society, but education in law and other religious sciences could occur, and likely did occur on a deeper level outside the 'classroom.' It also indicates that Ibn Qāḍī Shuhbah may have understood the learning of legal rules to be different from acquiring the ability to issue legal rulings. Indeed, he seems to prize the ability to issue opinions—he uses the infinitive of the fourth form verb (*iftāʾ*) much in the same way as he does *ishtaghala*, as a signifier of elevated status. His use of *iftāʾ* as a sign of status would seem to create a model of scholarship whereas his discussion of *tafaqqaha*, with the praise he gives those who engage in it, creates a model for scholars. As is demonstrated in chapter five, Ibn Qāḍī Shuhbah sees the increasing levels of specialization in religious sciences as a cause of legal decline. Scholars, he implies through the rhetorical shaping of their biographies, were drawn away from the study of law that *tafaqqaha* typifies and moved into professions that he sees as ancillary to maintaining legal norms. His text is, on one level, a description of this process and on another, more fundamental level, a model for the return to more basic kinds of legal instruction that *tafaqqaha* represents.

Progression

Repetition exposes larger historical and normative claims that authors seek to make. But looking at repetition alone creates a synchronic picture and implies that authors did not understand the importance of historical change on the development of the Islamic tradition. Repetition is used by authors to create models of and models for various intellectual fields but writers were also sensitive to the impact that historical events had on the ways these models were understood and actualized at different times and places. The authors of *ṭabaqāt* texts were historical thinkers and they sought to create histories that reflected not only their understanding of the past but also projected onto those histories normative claims about how things ought to be. To understand the claims that lie hidden in *ṭabaqāt* works it is necessary to look at how terms and allied concepts are repeated as they ebb and flow over the course of the text. Patterns of repetition thus become evident as they 'progressively develop.' The progressive development of terms is frequently linked to the chronological arrangement of the text. In order to understand the progressive development of ideas one must plot repetitions and associate them with the chronology of the text; once this is done attitudes and theories about the expansion of disciplines of knowledge become apparent.

Tables 4.8a and 4.8b show how the terms for the acquisition of knowledge discussed in the previous section progressively develop over the course of the text.

Table 4.8a. Progressive development of terms for learning in Ibn Qāḍī Shuhbah's text

Generation (# of Bios in Generation)	*Akhadha*	*Ishtaghala Ashghala*	*Qara'a*	*Takharraja*
1	7		2	
(17)	(41%)		(12%)	
2	4		1	
(12)	(33%)		(8%)	
3	11	1		
(19)	(58%)	(5%)		
4	8		2	
(19)	(42%)		(11%)	
5	6	1		1
(20)	(30%)	(5%)		(5%)
6	9			
(21)	(43%)			
7	8		1	
(16)	(50%)		(6%)	
8	12	2	1	5
(30)	(40%)	(7%)	(3%)	(17%)
9	6	2	1	
(20)	(30%)	(10%)	(5%)	
10	3	1	1	1
(17)	(18%)	(6%)	(6%)	(6%)
11	10	1	3	
(21)	(48%)	(5%)	(14%)	
12	3	2	1	
(22)	(14%)	(9%)	(5%)	
13	4	1	5	1
(20)	(20%)	(5%)	(25%)	(5%)
14	11		1	
(19)	(58%)		(5%)	
15	3	1	1	1
(16)	(19%)	(6%)	(6%)	(6%)
16	6	4	3	2
(18)	(33%)	(22%)	(17%)	(11%)
17	6	4	3	3
(28)	(21%)	(14%)	(11%)	(11%)
18	4	2	4	2
(18)	(22%)	(11%)	(22%)	(11%)
19	9	9	6	2
(31)	(29%)	(29%)	(19%)	(6%)
20	7	4	8	1
(26)	(27%)	(15%)	(31%)	(4%)
21	8	11	7	4
(29)	(28%)	(38%)	(24%)	(14%)
22	14	14	10	5
(40)	(35%)	(35%)	(25%)	(13%)
23	11	10	7	2
(26)	(42%)	(38%)	(28%)	(8%)
24	20	23	13	7
(49)	(41%)	(47%)	(27%)	(14%)
25	24	21	22	9
(57)	(42%)	(37%)	(39%)	(16%)
26	24	24	15	5
(44)	(55%)	(55%)	(34%)	(11%)
27	16	23	13	3
(33)	(48%)	(70%)	(39%)	(9%)
28	25	28	15	9
(45)	(55%)	(62%)	(33%)	(20%)
29	18	19	6	2
(25)	(72%)	(76%)	(24%)	(8%)

Source: Ibn Qāḍī Shuhbah, *Ṭabaqāt al-fuqahā' al-shāfi'īyah*, ed. al-Ḥāfiẓ 'Abd al-Alī Khān, 4 vols. (Beirut: 'Ālam al-kutub, 1987).

Table 4.8b. Progressive development of terms for learning in Ibn Qāḍī Shuhbah's text

Generation (# of Bios in Generation)	*Ḥaṣṣala*	*Baḥatha*	*Darasa* *Darrasa*	*Tafaqqaha*
1 (17)				3 (18%)
2 (12)				4 (33%)
3 (19)				4 (21%)
4 (19)			1 (5%)	4 (21%)
5 (20)			3 (15%)	4 (20%)
6 (21)			6 (29%)	1 (5%)
7 (16)			3 (19%)	5 (31%)
8 (30)			6 (20%)	12 (40%)
9 (20)	1 (5%)		3 (15%)	5 (25%)
10 (17)			4 (24%)	11 (65%)
11 (21)			3 (14%)	7 (33%)
12 (22)			3 (14%)	14 (64%)
13 (20)	1 (5%)		2 (10%)	8 (40%)
14 (19)	1 (5%)		3 (16%)	9 (47%)
15 (16)			4 (25%)	10 (63%)
16 (18)	1 (6%)		5 (28%)	10 (56%)
17 (28)	1 (4%)		9 (32%)	11 (39%)
18 (18)	2 (11%)		8 (44%)	7 (39%)
19 (31)	3 (10%)		13 (42%)	19 (61%)
20 (26)	3 (12%)		12 (46%)	12 (46%)
21 (29)	1 (3%)		16 (55%)	5 (17%)
22 (40)	2 (5%)		17 (43%)	11 (28%)
23 (26)	4 (15%)		19 (73%)	8 (31%)
24 (49)	3 (6%)		28 (57%)	18 (37%)
25 (57)	2 (4%)		29 (51%)	19 (33%)
26 (44)	5 (11%)		27 (61%)	16 (36%)
27 (33)	7 (21%)	2 (6%)	16 (48%)	5 (15%)
28 (45)	7 (15%)	2 (4%)	31 (69%)	15 (33%)
29 (25)	4 (16%)	2 (8%)	19 (76%)	2 (8%)

Source: Ibn Qāḍī Shuhbah, *Ṭabaqāt al-fuqahā' al-shāfiʿīyah*, ed. al-Ḥāfiẓ ʿAbd al-Alī Khān, 4 vols. (Beirut: ʿĀlam al-kutub, 1987).

The number in parentheses under 'generation' is the actual number of biographies in each *ṭabaqah*. The numbers in parentheses below the raw numbers for each category of learning reflect their percentage of occurrence in each generation. The number of biographies varies depending of the number of scholars who died in each generation. Percentages are therefore helpful in understanding trends because they help ameliorate the impact of sudden shifts in population in each generation. Tables 4.8a and 4.8b also provide important insights into how Ibn Qāḍī Shuhbah sought to depict the development of Islamic intellectual thought. The two earliest methods of learning that Ibn Qāḍī Shuhbah describes are *akhadha* and *tafaqqaha*. *Akhadha* is statistically more common in the first two generations that had contact with al-Shāfiʿī, but *tafaqqaha* is still clearly an important source of transmission. Ibn Qāḍī Shuhbah lists twenty-nine scholars in the first two generations (224/839–298/911). Eighteen of those listed are described as studying with al-Shāfiʿī or one of his companions. Eleven are described as having an *akhadha* relationship with a teacher; seven, as studying with al-Shāfiʿī directly. Law is listed as the subject of study in six of the eleven *akhadha* biographies, only one of which is described as studying law with al-Shāfiʿī and no one else.[35] *Darasa* is not used as a descriptor of study in any of the biographies and *tafaqqaha* is used seven times. In four of the biographies students are listed as studying (*tafaqqaha*) specifically with al-Shāfiʿī and no one else (see table 4.9).

We see in these early biographies the different functions of *akhadha* and *tafaqqaha* educative connections. It is significant that Ibn Qāḍī Shuhbah describes only one of the *fiqh*-centered *akhadha* relationships as exclusively between al-Shāfiʿī and a student whereas four of the *tafaqqaha* relationships are exclusive. *Akhadha* functions in these biographies to demonstrate the transference of authority from al-Shāfiʿī to his students, but not necessarily knowledge. As with the comparison of *darasa* and *tafaqqaha*, Ibn Qāḍī Shuhbah clearly sees *akhadha* and *tafaqqaha* as serving two important but different roles. Not only does *akhadha* buttress claims on cultural capital by establishing intellectual pedigrees that lead back to the eponym of the school, but it also serves to create intellectual legitimacy. For some scholars it is clear that the acquisition of knowledge had political and economic motives,

[35] Ibid., 63.

Table 4.9. Repetition of terms for 'study' in the first two generations of Ibn Qāḍī Shuhbah's text

Biography Number	*Akhadha*	Subject	*Qara'a*	Subject	*Tafaqqaha*
1	With al-Shāfiʿī and others	Law			With al-Shāfiʿī
2	With al-Shāfiʿī and others	Law			
3	With al-Shāfiʿī	Law			
7			With al-Shāfiʿī	The *Risālah*	
8	With al-Shāfiʿī	Law			
10	With al-Shāfiʿī	*ʿilm*			
11	With al-Shāfiʿī	Unlisted			
12					With al-Shāfiʿī
13	With al-Shāfiʿī	*ʿilm*			
14					With al-Shāfiʿī
20					With al-Shāfiʿī
21	With students of al-Shāfiʿī	Law			
22	With students of al-Shāfiʿī	*ʿilm*			
24			With students of al-Shāfiʿī	Unlisted	
25	With student of al-Shāfiʿī	Law			With students of al-Shāfiʿī
27					With students of al-Shāfiʿī
28	With students of al-Shāfiʿī	Unlisted			
29					With students of al-Shāfiʿī

Source: Ibn Qāḍī Shuhbah, *Ṭabaqāt al-fuqahā' al-shāfiʿīyah*, ed. al-Ḥāfiẓ ʿAbd al-Alī Khān, 4 vols. (Beirut: ʿĀlam al-kutub, 1987).

but for others, the top scholars who saw themselves as religious professionals responsible for the protection of Islam as a manifestation of God's will on earth, the acquisition of *ʿilm* was a religious duty that fell to the *ʿulamā'*. Charting *akhadha* thus not only served the purpose of supporting social needs of intellectual elites but also the very important purpose of establishing networks of legal authority.

As stated above, Ibn Qāḍī Shuhbah lists a number of scholars that under other circumstances would not be considered important enough to warrant mention. They are listed, however, because they studied, taught, and transmitted particular concepts or ideas that originated with earlier scholars. They thus serve as conduits for the transmission of knowledge and are necessary components in the structure of the school. Their authority to act as conduits furthermore does not reside in their own knowledge or abilities but in their claims to be the intellectual descendents of al-Shāfiʿī. There are over five thousand intellectual relationships described in the text between individuals across the generations. Ibn Qāḍī Shuhbah, with exacting care, establishes a chain of authority that originates with al-Shāfiʿī for all but 27 scholars.

Chains of authority are not, however, created equal. Studying law through an *akhadha* relationship creates a level of authority but not as strong as *tafaqqaha*. The claims to legitimacy that *tafaqqaha* infer are superior to all other educative relationships and are thus important in Ibn Qāḍī Shuhbah's attempts to map structures of juridical authority and the authority of certain legal and methodological views (see, for instance, the biographies of al-Muzanī and al-Rafiʿī above).

Figure 4.1 also shows that Ibn Qāḍī Shuhbah depicts a divergence in the frequency of *akhadha* and *tafaqqaha* relationships. It demonstrates that, for the most part, *tafaqqaha* remains a more dominant mode of learning until the 19th generation (622/1225–640/1243).

Figure 4.1. Comparison of *tafaqqaha* and *akhadha*

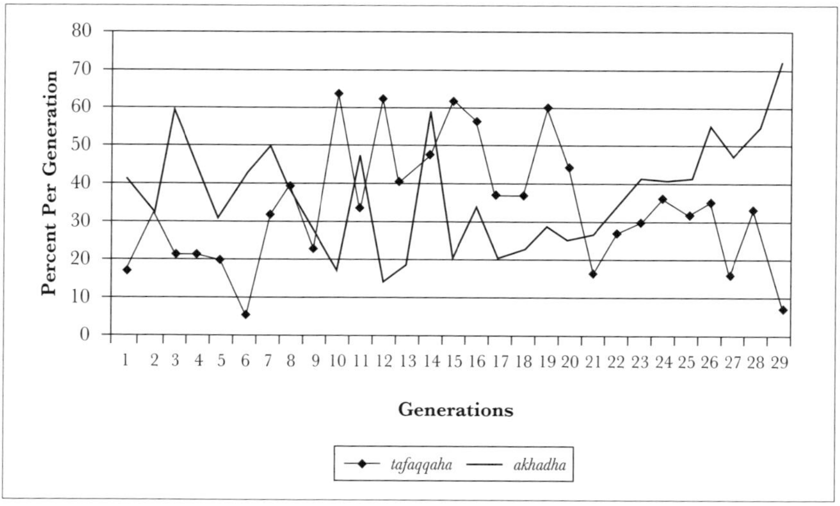

Source: Ibn Qāḍī Shuhbah, *Ṭabaqāt al-fuqahāʾ al-shāfiʿīyah*, ed. al-Ḥāfiẓ ʿAbd al-Alī Khān, 4 vols. (Beirut: ʿĀlam al-kutub, 1987).

Beginning in the 19th generation, a series of calamities are depicted as besieging the Muslim Middle East, most significantly the Mongol invasion that began in the early 7th/13th century. This is followed by the outbreak of plague in the 25th generation (741/1340–759/1358). The number of deaths recorded by Ibn Qāḍī Shuhbah beginning with the 19th generation nearly doubles that of the previous *ṭabaqah*, and, over the coming years, reaches a peak in 25th generation. As is made clear by figure 4.1, at the very time that these events overtake the major centers of Islamic learning in the Middle East, *tafaqqaha* educative relationships begin to decline and are replaced by less intellectually important *akhadha* connections.

Figure 4.2. Comparison of *tafaqqaha* and *darasa*

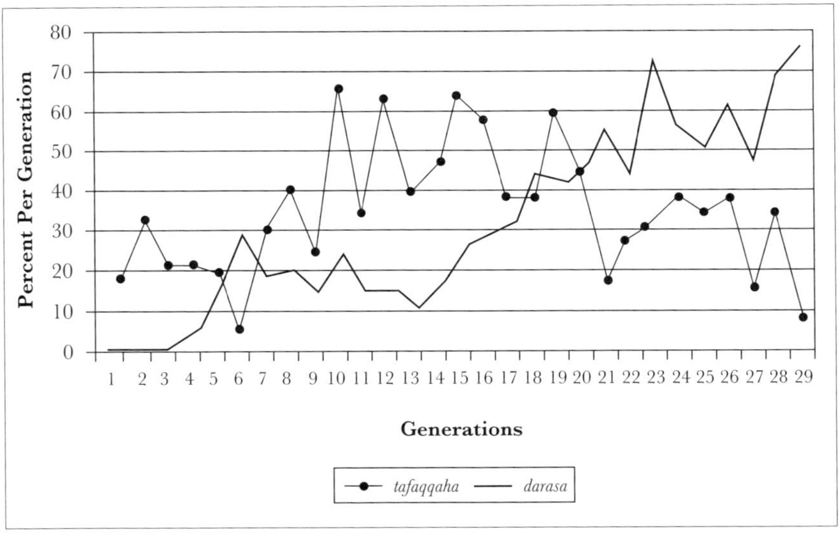

Source: Ibn Qāḍī Shuhbah, *Ṭabaqāt al-fuqahā' al-shāfi'īyah*, ed. al-Ḥāfiẓ 'Abd al-Alī Khān, 4 vols. (Beirut: 'Ālam al-kutub, 1987).

As figures 4.2–4.5 demonstrate, there were other important shifts in Islamic learning during this period. As with *akhadha* and *tafaqqaha*, there is an inverse relationship between *tafaqqaha* and *darasa/darrasa*. This trend indicates that, according to Ibn Qāḍī Shuhbah, there may have been a relationship between the decline in personal legal education and the rise of institutional legal education. It suggests a number of possibilities: 1) that as institutions developed, teachers became more preoccupied with 'classroom' instruction and had less time for independent individual instruction; 2) that, for reasons explained in chapter six, there were fewer teachers available to teach the ever increasing number of students that entered religious professions, forcing teachers and students to use institutionalized or group settings more frequently; and 3) because it appears that the permission to issue legal rulings was given almost exclusively through education gained at a *madrasah*, increasing numbers of students, in order to acquire the kinds of training and certifications necessary to enter the legal profession, studied in an institution and ignored the more traditional *tafaqqaha* relationship.

Figure 4.3. Comparison of *darasa, takharraja*, and *qara'a, ishtaghala*

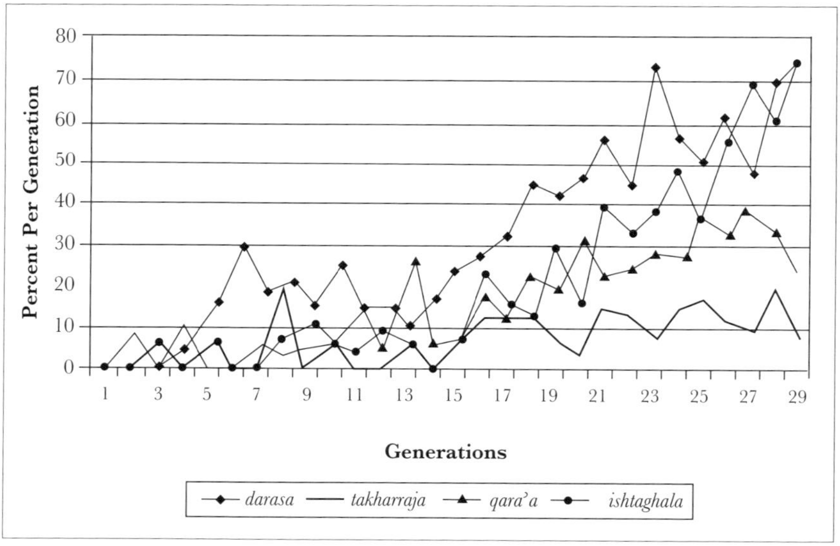

Source: Ibn Qāḍī Shuhbah, *Ṭabaqāt al-fuqahā' al-shāfi'īyah*, ed. al-Ḥāfiẓ 'Abd al-Alī Khān, 4 vols. (Beirut: 'Ālam al-kutub, 1987).

Figure 4.3 depicts trends in the development of *darasa/darrasa, takharraja, qara'a*, and *ishtaghala/ashghala*. Both *darasa* and *ishtaghala* increase at roughly the same rate and indicates that Ibn Qāḍī Shuhbah is attempting to draw a link between study at a *madrasah* and the broadening range of subjects students learn. It also indicates that while *qara'a* becomes more wide spread over time, it, and *takharraja*, decline in frequency in the last 3 to 4 generations (late 6th to early 9th/late 12th to early 15th centuries). Why this is the case is not immediately clear.

Figure 4.4. Comparison of *darasa* and *akhadha*

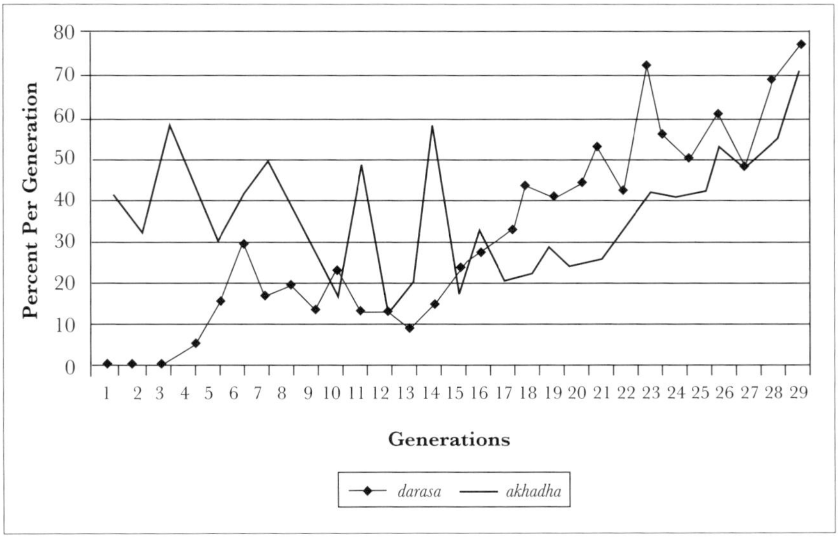

Source: Ibn Qāḍī Shuhbah, *Ṭabaqāt al-fuqahāʾ al-shāfiʿīyah*, ed. al-Ḥāfiẓ ʿAbd al-Alī Khān, 4 vols. (Beirut: ʿĀlam al-kutub, 1987).

Figure 4.4 shows an almost parallel increase in the frequency of *akhadha* and *darasa/darrasa*. The parallel development of the two forms of study suggests that as institutional methods of learning became more widespread so did the emphasis on personal and less formal educative contacts. While Ibn Qāḍī Shuhbah does not lavish praise on either *akhadha* or *darasa/darrasa* as the preferred method of learning he implies that as *tafaqqaha* became less common, *akhadha* and *darasa/darrasa* filled the void. It also suggests that, as *tafaqqaha* relationships became less common, other, less important forms of authority were required to augment the ability of jurists to claim the right to work in religious professions.

Ibn Qāḍī Shuhbah suggests a model for authority in the first two generations that implies that learning based on personal contact between teacher and student is the ideal. All of those listed in the first two generations attended either al-Shāfiʿī or one of his students personally. The most important of them had one-on-one contact as is implied by *akhadha* and *tafaqqaha*. With the decline of *tafaqqaha* as a source of one-on-one legal education and authority transference, *akhadha* appears to have become more important as a source of authority and the institutional *darasa* became more important as a source of legal knowledge. Ibn Qāḍī Shuhbah implies that instead of being opposite extremes, and in some sense in conflict (as both the institutionalists and social historians suggest), they worked in concert for the continuing maintenance of the law. Why *tafaqqaha* declines and other modes increase is hard to extrapolate from the text; but the theme of change in legal authority in the face of enormous political, economic, and environmental crises is central to the rhetorical purposes of his work.

CHAPTER FIVE

THE DEVELOPMENT OF TRENDS IN THE TRANSMISSION OF *'ILM*

Several authors have approached the issue of the decline of Islamic jurisprudence in the medieval period. One of the main areas of debate concerns the issue of *ijtihād*, whether it came to an end, and if so, in what period, and why. *Ijtihād* is generally defined as exhausting effort in the use of personal reason. The primary purpose of *ijtihād* is the discovery of new legal rules based on the texts of revelation (the Qurʾan and *sunnah*). *Ijtihād* is thought to have been restricted to jurists who have attained high levels of training in textual analysis and reason. Thus, *ijtihād* is personal reason guided by methods and methodologies developed over centuries of legal theoretical development.[1] Each legal school (*madhhab*) developed its own methods and methodologies of legal reasoning that were supposedly based on the opinions of the founding *Imāms*. Over time, however, the kinds of training necessary to use *ijtihād* became too extensive, and, according to some examinations of Islamic law, the use of *ijtihād* slowly disappeared.

Joseph Schacht, for instance, argues that the so-called 'gate of *ijtihād*' closed as early as the tenth century. He contends that *ijtihād* came to an end following the consolidation of the initial five, and later four, schools of law when, in the early years of the ʿAbbāsid

---

[1] There have been many Muslim jurists and legal theoreticians who wrote on *ijtihād* and its limits. For those that seem to have been most influential on Ibn Qāḍī Shuhbah see Muḥammad b. Idrīs al-Shāfiʿī, *al-Risālah*, ed. Aḥmad Muḥammad al-Shākir (Cairo: Muṣṭafā Bābī al-Ḥalabī, 1969), 487–503; Abū Isḥāq Ibrāhīm b. ʿAlī al-Shīrāzī, *Sharḥ al-lumaʿ*, ed. ʿAbd al-Majīd Turkī, 2 vols. (Beirut: Dār al-gharb al-islāmī, 1988), 1041–72; Jalāl al-Dīn Muḥammad b. Aḥmad al-Maḥallī al-Shāfiʿī, *Sharḥ al-waraqāt fī ʿilm uṣūl al-fiqh ʿalā waraqāt abī al-maʿālī imām al-ḥaramayn ʿabd al-mālik b. yūsuf b. muḥammad al-juwaynī al-shāfiʿī wa maʿahu ḥāshiyat al-shaykh aḥmad b. muḥammad al-dumayāṭī al-shāfiʿī* (Cairo: Maṭbaʿat Muḥammad ʿAlī Ṣubayḥ, 1965), 87–89; Ibn Ḥājib, *Kitāb mukhtaṣar al-muntahā al-uṣūl* (Cairo: Maṭbaʿat al-saʿada, n.d.), 122–31; al-Nawawī, *al-Majmūʿ*, vol. 1, 49–66.

Caliphate, "Islamic law had been elaborated in detail."[2] The perception that the law was fully articulated led jurists to deny the right of independent reasoning to scholars living after this period. Instead of *ijtihād*, Schacht argues that *taqlīd*—what he describes as the "unquestioning acceptance of the doctrines of established schools and authorities"—became the norm.[3]

Noel Coulson, following Schacht, argues that like other legal systems such as Roman law, Islamic law was based on a system of precedent that placed great emphasis on early juristic authority. As the schools of law were established by the early tenth century, the writings of their founders became the source of all later legal knowledge. The ability of think independently slowly disappeared because there was little need to find new legal solutions due to the rather static nature of Islamic society.[4] Although Schacht has been wrongly portrayed as giving rise to the idea that Islamic law lost its ability to be creative, his emphasis on the formation of schools of law and the desire of later jurists to be affiliated with one, has led scholars to argue, as does Coulson, that the need to be a member of a school meant that jurists gave up their right to independent thought.[5]

Wael Hallaq has argued, to the contrary, that *ijtihād*-like activities continued to be practiced well into the late medieval period, although debates about the disappearance of *mujtahid*s, which may have been prompted by millennial expectations, indicate that concerns about the continuing existence of legal speculation may have foreshadowed later decline.[6] He argues that in one way Schacht and Coulson were correct to argue that there were discussions concerning the closing

---

[2] Joseph Schacht, *An Introduction to Islamic Law* (Oxford: The Clarendon Press, 1964), 69. For another restatement of this idea see Schacht, "The Schools of Law and Later Development of Jurisprudence," in *Law in the Middle East*, ed. Majid Khadduri and Herbert J. Liebesny (Washington, D.C.: The Middle East Institute, 1955), 73–76.

[3] Schacht, *An Introduction to Islamic Law*, 69–71.

[4] Noel J. Coulson, *Conflicts and Tensions in Islamic Jurisprudence* (Chicago: University of Chicago Press, 1969), 41–44.

[5] Schacht, *Introduction to Islamic Law*, 71–73; Also see Norman Calder, "al-Nawawī's Typology of *Muftī*s and its Significance for a General Theory of Islamic Law," *Islamic Law and Society* 3 no. 2 (1996): 157.

[6] See his, "Was the Gate of *Ijtihād* Closed?" *International Journal of Middle Eastern Studies* 16 (1984): 3–41; also see *Authority, Continuity and Change in Islamic Law*, 81; and his "On the Origins of the Controversy about the Existence of Mujtahids and the Gate of Ijtihad," *Studia Islamica* 63 (1986): 133–35.

off of *ijtihād* in the tenth century. This discourse was primarily concerned with preventing new schools from forming and had little to do with the actual abilities of jurists to use independent reasoning. Hallaq differentiates between the absolute *ijtihād* that later scholars claimed was the sole activity of the school founders and 'affiliated' *ijtihād* that high level scholars in each of the schools claimed for themselves.[7]

Hallaq points out that most forms of independent thought were configured by jurists as *taqlīd*. *Taqlīd*, far from being the blind acceptance of authority as it is defined by Schacht, actually represents a broad range of legal reasoning that included *ijtihād*-like modes of reasoning to very restricted and almost blind kinds of legal adherence.[8] One who practices *taqlīd* is a *muqallid* ('an adherer') and is not certified to use individual reason in areas of law where he is deficient in training. Hallaq argues that the discourse over *taqlīd* has led modern scholars to assume that independent thought declined. In fact, he argues, forms of *ijtihād*-like activities continued until the nineteenth century.[9]

This chapter complicates the discussion of *ijtihād* by looking at how Ibn Qāḍī Shuhbah develops ideas specifically related to the discovery of law. He was not primarily interested in the discourse about the survival of legal reasoning in the way that modern scholars are. Modern scholarship has tended to focus on the activities of high level jurists and not the low and mid-level scholars that were intimately involved in the day-to-day administration of law in society. Instead, Ibn Qāḍī Shuhbah focuses on the dissemination of legal knowledge to jurists across an entire range of abilities and authority and seeks to demonstrate that, by the ninth/fifteenth century, while *ijtihād* continued on a limited basis (for high ranking scholars), the majority of jurists had become memorizers of substantive legal dicta handed down from earlier times. In doing so, Ibn Qāḍī Shuhbah seeks to assert the authority of substantive legal texts containing divergent legal opinions (*ikhtilāf*) transmitted through the writings of, among others, Abū Isḥāq al-Shīrāzī (d. 476/1083), al-Rāfiʿī (d. 623/1226) and, al-Nawawī (d. 676/1277). According to Ibn Qāḍī Shuhbah,

[7] *Authority, Continuity and Change in Islamic Law*, 57–62.
[8] Ibid., 86–120.
[9] Ibid., 217–35.

these texts reach the highest level of authority because each ruling transmitted by these master jurists can be traced through an unbroken chain of scholars back to al-Shāfiʿī and ultimately to the Prophet Muḥammad. These authorities, therefore, provide a protective barrier for the *madhhab*, guarding it from the insertion of legal rulings by less-qualified jurists.

Ibn Qāḍī Shuhbah's reconstruction of Islamic legal history

Ibn Qāḍī Shuhbah pays exacting attention to the placement and ordering of concepts, terms, and information. Because of his attention to detail it is important to examine how and where he locates certain ideas central to the transmission of *ʿilm* in his text. The acquisition of *ʿilm* is the primary function of *ijtihād* and is perhaps the most important concept in all of Islamic law. *ʿIlm* means 'knowledge,' or sometimes 'science.' *ʿIlm* is always elusive because it can only be perfectly known by God. Knowledge exists 'out there' somewhere, and the job of a jurist (*faqīh*) is to discover (literally 'understand') God's knowledge. *Fiqh*, as is discussed in chapter four, is usually translated as 'law,' (or here 'substantive' law, or rules) but its literal meaning is 'understanding.' Therefore, *fiqh* is a jurist's understanding, with reasonable probability (*ẓann*), of God's knowledge (*ʿilm*). *ʿIlm*, in the sense of 'science,' means the pathways by which a scholar might locate knowledge. Thus, there are fields such as *ʿilm al-naḥw* (the science of grammar), or *ʿilm al-tafsīr* (the science of Qurʾanic commentary), all of which allow scholars to gain approximations to God's *ʿilm*.[10]

Understanding God's *ʿilm* involves the interpretation of the Qurʾan and *Sunnah* through the use of ones *ijtihād*.[11] The Qurʾan is thought to be composed of individual instances of revelation (*sharʿ*) that were 'sent down' by God through the Angel Jabrīl (Gabriel) to Muḥammad in response to specific problems or issues that he faced.[12] Revelation,

---

[10] For a detailed discussion of knowledge in Islamic thought see Franz Rosenthal, *Knowledge Triumphant: The Concept of Knowledge in Medieval Islam* (Leiden: Brill, 1970).

[11] The following discussion is meant to present a basic overview of *uṣūl al-fiqh* (methodologies for knowing the will of God) and is in no way designed to be comprehensive or exhaustive. It is based primarily on *Sharḥ al-lumaʿ* by Abū Isḥāq al-Shīrāzī and on the *Waraqāt* by Imām al-Ḥaramayn al-Juwaynī.

[12] Weiss, *The Search for God's Law*, 68–69; Mohammad Hashim Kamali, *Principles*

however, did not occur all at once but was sent down over a period of twenty-three years (610–632 CE). Understanding revelation is made more complicated by the fact that the text of the Qurʾan is not organized chronologically or by theme, but is arranged according on the length of each chapter (although the first chapter is quite short and the final ten chapters vary in length). Additionally, each chapter does not represent a single instance of revelation but in many cases is thought to be composed of individual *sharʿ* that were then combined by Muḥammad. In many instances, verses of the Qurʾan that appear together can individually originate from very different time periods and are in no specific chronological order.[13]

Understanding the context (the place, time, and issue that prompted it) in which an individual instance of *sharʿ* is thought to have occurred is considered one of the most important aspects of discerning the meaning of revelation. The study of the historical causes and contexts of revelation is referred to as '*asbāb al-nuzūl*' (frequently translated as the 'occasions of revelation' but it also has the connotation of the 'causes of revelation').[14] One of the reasons for the rise of the *asbāb al-nuzūl* genre was to explain apparent conflicts in the text of revelation. Over the course of several centuries scholars developed theories that explained these conflicts by emphasizing that because revelation occurs in time, and in response to particular circumstances, it is necessary to know the context of each revelatory event. Passages in the text of revelation that appear similar may in fact be responding to very different problems and thus the causative factor (*ʿillah*) that results from each instance of *sharʿ* may be quite dissimilar.[15]

One of the basic paradigms that arose from this theory of revelation was *naskh* (abrogation). *Naskh* occurs when the operative section of one *sharʿ* that is thought to imply a particular rule is abrogated by a rule contained in a later instance of revelation that is determined to have been sent down in response to a similar situation.[16]

---

of Islamic Jurisprudence (Petaling Jaya, Selangor Darul Ehsan: Pelanduk Publications, 1989; reprint Cambridge: The Islamic Texts Society, 1991), 14–16.

[13] For an interesting examination of this see Muṣṭafa Zayd, *al-Naskh fī al-qurʾān al-karīm dirāsat tashrīʿīyah tārīkhīyah naqdīyah*, 2 vols. (Cairo: Dār al-fikr al-ʿarabīyah, 1963).

[14] See for instance, Jalāl al-Dīn al-Suyūṭī, *Lubāb al-nuqūl fī asbāb al-nuzūl* (Beirut: Dār iḥyāʾ al-ʿulūm, 1978).

[15] Hallaq, *A History of Islamic Legal Theories*, 84–99.

[16] Weiss, *The Search for God's Law*, 503–05. Admittedly, this is an over simplification

Furthermore, although each *shar*ʿ is a manifestation of God's knowledge its meaning is not always clear. Because revelation reflects God's ultimate and universal knowledge it is frequently obscure and is thought, therefore, to contain explicit and implicit references that can only be understood when various hermeneutical methods are applied to the text.[17] Disciplines such as grammar (*naḥw*) and lexicography (*lughāh*) developed originally as a means of unearthing the hidden and obscure meanings of the text.

The text of the Qurʾan is itself quite short; consisting of 114 chapters and just under 6300 verses, very few of which actually contain material thought to have legal content.[18] As Islamic society developed, groups began to emerge that argued that the Qurʾan, because of its size and limited scope, needed to be supplemented by other sources. Debates about what kinds of supporting sources were permissible were at times heated and continued well into the eleventh century (in some respects they never ended and continue even today). By the ninth century a consensus emerged that Muḥammad-his actions and sayings as collected and transmitted in texts referred to as *ḥadīth*-should serve as a companion to the Qurʾan.[19]

The idea that an individual could serve as a living example for others predates Islam. Arabs had for centuries believed that people inherited the qualities and abilities of their ancestors.[20] This idea was referred to as '*Sunnah*' (literally 'example'), and with the formation of Islam became an important religious concept. There is some debate as to whether the early Muslim community believed that Muḥammad possessed something special that set him apart from others as a living example. There is evidence early in Islamic history, especially in Medinah, that his example was just one of many that the Muslim

of what was a very controversial and problematic legal theory. See John Burton, *The Sources of Islamic Law: Islamic Theories of Abrogation* (Edinburgh: University Press, 1990), for an excellent overview.

[17] Hallaq, *A History of Islamic Law*, 45; Weiss, *The Search for God's Law*, 138–41; Kamali, 91–94.

[18] Kamali, for instance, argues that there are only 350 verses with legal content (p. 14). Al-Bayhaqī (d. 458/1066), in his collection of Qurʾanically derived rules that he transmits from al-Shāfiʿī, claims that there are just over 500. See his *Aḥkām al-qurʾān*, 2 vols. (Beirut: Dār al-kutub al-ʿilmīyah, 1975).

[19] Bernard Weiss, *The Spirit of Islamic Law*, 12–14.

[20] Ignaz Goldziher, *Muslim Studies (Muhammedanische Studien)*, ed. S. M. Stern and trans. C. R. Barber and S. M. Stern, 2 vols. (Chicago: Aldine Publishing, 1971), vol. 2, 25–26.

community used to establish social and legal norms.[21] Over time, as a result of a number of political, religious, and social factors, the *sunnah* of Muḥammad became more important and came to be seen as a source of knowing the will of God.[22]

In early Islam there were literally hundreds of thousands of *ḥadīth* that purported to transmit the *sunnah* of the Prophet. One of the early complaints about the use of *ḥadīth* as a source of law was that many were fabricated by transmitters. As Ignaz Goldziher demonstrated a century ago, *ḥadīth* were manufactured for political, religious, and other motives.[23] Over the course of the first two to three centuries of Islamic history, a science of *ḥadīth* studies (*ʿilm al-ḥadīth*) developed that attempted to create methods of ensuring the veracity of *ḥadīth*. Usually, these methods focused on the chain of transmission (*isnād*) by which a *ḥadīth* was passed down over the generations and rarely focused on the authenticity of the text (*maṭn*) itself.[24]

The most authentic *ḥadīth* were those that were transmitted by four independent chains of transmission, although very few of these, so called, *mutawātir ḥadīth* actually existed. Most *ḥadīth* were transmitted by independent chains and many did not possess complete and uninterrupted *isnād*s. Because of the absolute emphasis on revelation as a source of *ʿilm*, even *ḥadīth* with incomplete *isnād*s could be used to discover the will of God in situations where no other revelatory text existed.[25]

Law, however, did not emerge *ex nihilo* with the development of legal schools in the tenth century.[26] Jurists, political leaders, and other individuals had, since the time of the Prophet, issued legal rulings or given advice on correct practice. Over time, as more people came

---

[21] Ibid., 26–37.

[22] John Burton, *An Introduction to Ḥadīth* (Edinburgh: University Press, 1994), 17–29.

[23] Goldziher, *Muslim Studies*, vol. 2, 89–144; Schacht, *Origins of Muhammadan Jurisprudence*, 58–81; Gautier H. A. Juynboll, *Muslim Tradition: Studies in Chronology, Provenance and Authorship of Early Ḥadīth* (New York: Cambridge University Press, 1983); Eerik Dickinson, *The Development of Early Sunnite Ḥadīth Criticism: The Taqdima of Abī Ḥātim al-Rāzī (240/845–327/938)* (Boston: Brill, 2001), vii–x.

[24] Dickinson, 57–79; Burton, *An Introduction to Ḥadīth*, 169–77; Muḥammad Zubayr Ṣiddīqī, *Ḥadīth Literature: Its Origins, Development and Special Features*, ed. Abdal Hakim Murad (Cambridge: Islamic Texts Society, 1993), 76–90; 113–16.

[25] Hallaq, *A History of Islamic Law*, 58–68.

[26] Much has been written about the rise of the law prior to the formation of the main schools of law. See Schacht, *The origins of Muhammadan Jurisprudence*; Hallaq, *A History of Islamic Legal Theories*, 7–21; Melchert, *The Formation of the Sunni Schools of Law*, 1–86.

to do things in particular ways, these practices became codified. Early legal texts, such as the *Risālah* by al-Shāfiʿī, are concerned with justifying practice that emerged in the century following the death of Muḥammad and came to be accepted as orthoprax and orthodox behaviors.[27] The need to justify the received practices of Muslims in such areas as prayer, fasting, and the pilgrimage led to the development of notions of consensus (*ijmāʿ*). *Ijmāʿ* came to be seen as a third form of revelation that was based on a *ḥadīth* that quotes Muḥammad as saying "my community will never agree on an error."[28]

Ijmāʿ came to include the consensus of the community (*ijmāʿ al-ʿamm*) and the specific consensus of the community of jurists (*ijmāʿ al-khaṣṣ*). *Ijmāʾ al-ʿamm* governed broad categories of practice and belief, especially the ritual necessities of prayer, fasting, giving alms to the poor, and pilgrimage to Mecca.[29] *Ijmāʿ* was justified by the legal fiction that, during the generation in which consensus is thought to have formed, no voice of dissent is recorded. The functional difficulties of this notion for *ijmāʿ al-ʿamm* are obvious. Because dissent was always a part of Muslim society, especially in its formative years, *ijmāʿ al-ʿamm* was thought to apply in cases only when those who 'counted' as representing othrodoxy and orthopraxy agreed on an issue. Thus dissenting groups such as the Shīʿah and the Khawārij were excluded from collective voices that counted in the establishment of consensus.[30]

Ijmāʿ al-khaṣṣ functioned in much the same way as general consensus. In the case of the *ijmāʿ* of the jurists, legal authorities qualified to deal directly with the texts of revelation (*mujtahids*) only counted in the formation of consensus. Even with this more restricted kind

---

[27] See, for instance, the discussion of inheritance and the role of pre-existing public attitudes on interpreting and devising rules of abrogation in *al-Risālah*, 136–46. Also see Wael Hallaq, "Considerations of the Function and Character of Sunnī Legal Theory," *Journal of the American Oriental Society* 104, no. 4 (Oct.–Dec., 1984): 679–689.

[28] "*Lā tajtamiʿu ammatī ʿalā ḍalālah.*" *Al-Waraqāt*, 11.

[29] It does not appear that all scholars recognized the *ijmāʿ al-ʿamm*, and certainly few if any would place it on the same level as the special *ijmāʿ* of the jurists. Al-Shāfiʿī, in his *Risālah* seeks to certify the consensus of the public, largely for reasons discussed above (see his discussion on pp. 471–72). Other scholars, such as Imām al-Ḥaramayn al-Juwaynī in their discussions of *ijmāʾ* restricted it to the jurists (*al-Waraqāt*, 11).

[30] Albert Hourani, "The Basis of Authority in Sunnite Consensus," *Studia Islamica* 21 (1964): 13–60.

of *ijmāʿ*, locating a rule on which all qualified jurists in a generation agreed, or one on which no one asserted dissent, was relatively rare. While claims that unanimity existed on various rules was common, most later jurists were able to pass over such assertions by locating *mujtahid*s in the same or in later generations that either ignored the claim or were unaware that one was supposed to have existed.[31]

Although the Qur'an, *sunnah*, and *ijmāʿ* came to be seen as manifestations of revelation and thus sources of knowing the will of God, they still were not comprehensive enough to allow them to serve as the foundation of *ʿilm* in all situations, especially as the Muslim world expanded to embrace many different cultures and social groups. Jurists developed modes of analogical reasoning (*qiyās*) that when applied to the texts of revelation (the Qur'an and *sunnah*) allowed for a much more flexible and diverse system of thought. Locating *ʿilm* in revelation became easier and allowed for the expansion not only of law, but of all areas of religious knowledge.

Qiyās also made the attempts by jurists to rationalize previous practice easier because it allowed them to create legal fictions about the differing methodologies of jurists before the rise of the schools. As was said above, jurists, after the rise of the schools, frequently were troubled by the received practice of early Muslims that appeared in later times to violate social and religious norms. Because of the stipulations of *ijmāʿ*, however, it was not possible for jurists in the tenth and eleventh centuries to condemn Muslims who lived in the seventh and eight centuries. Jurists had to devise methods that corrected current practice while still refraining from imputations of sin on earlier generations. *Qiyās* became the standard method.[32]

Qiyās can be a complicated activity that involves a number of factors that go beyond the scope of the present work. In its most basic form, scholars turn to *qiyās* when they are confronted with a problem for which no explicit rule can be found in revelation or in the body of previous rulings. Jurists, therefore, try to locate an analogous situation in revelation (hence the importance of understanding context) and if the causative factors (*ʿilal*, sing. *ʿillah*) in both the revelatory text and in the problem are analogous, the jurist takes the

[31] Hallaq, "On the Authoritativeness of Sunni Consensus," *International Journal of Middle East Studies* 18 (1986): 427–54; Weiss, *The Search for God's Law*, 240–58.
[32] Hallaq, "Considerations," 680.

rule derived from the original problem solved by revelation, and applies it to the new problem.[33] By using *qiyās* on the sources of revelation scholars thus expand the scope by which *ʿilm* (the authoritative knowledge of God) can be applied to various issues, both inside and outside the law.

Qiyās soon gave way to other kinds of interpretive strategies as jurists sought to rationalize previous practice. With *qiyās*, jurists were able to project back into time and 'recreate' previous legal rulings to justify practice. They were then able to argue against the analogical maneuvers of previous 'jurists' and propose 'new' rulings that fit changing circumstances.[34] Other methodologies, such as *istiḥsān* (juristic preference) and *istiṣlāḥ* (ruling in the public good) developed out of *qiyās* and expanded not only the abilities of jurists to rationalize previous practice but, in theory at least, find new solutions that responded to the changing needs of the community.[35]

Out of the initial attempt to rationalize previous practice a diverse discipline known as '*uṣūl al-fiqh*' (literally, 'the roots of understanding God's *ʿilm*') developed. What this discipline came to represent is directly connected to the debates about the closing off of *ijtihād* and will be taken up in the next chapter. That some forms of legal methodology are necessary for the discovery of *ʿilm* is not in dispute. It is not clear, however, whether all scholars agreed on the kinds and levels of *uṣūl* that were necessary to find *ʿilm* in the texts of revelation.[36]

Reading Ibn Qāḍī Shuhbah's text shows that he places great store in the kinds of *ʿilm* scholars discovered, received, and transmitted. An analysis of the progressive development of the text has isolated 36 variables repeated in Ibn Qāḍī Shuhbah's *Ṭabaqāt* that represent either *ʿilm* or authority structures associated with its transmission. Of these 36 variables, there are five broad categories of *ʿilm* (see figure 5.1) which seem important to Ibn Qāḍī Shuhbah: 1) speculative theology (*kalām*), 2) speculative legal methodologies (*uṣūl al-fiqh*), 3) sub-

---

[33] Hallaq, *A History of Islamic Legal Theories*, 83–95.

[34] Hallaq, "Considerations," 682.

[35] Ibid., 683–89.

[36] See for instance, Sherman Jackson, "Fiction and Formalism: Toward a Functional Analysis of *Uṣūl al-Fiqh*," in *Studies in Islamic Legal Theory*, ed. Bernard Weiss (Boston: Brill, 2002), 177–201; and Mohammad Fadel, "'*Istiḥsān* is nine-tenth of the Law:' The Puzzling Relationship of *Uṣūl* to *Furūʿ* in the Mālikī *Madhhab*," in *Studies in Islamic Legal Theory*, ed. Bernard Weiss (Boston: Brill, 2002), 161–76.

Figure 5.1. Categories of *ʿilm* and their practitioners

Categories of *ʿIlm*	Practitioners of *ʿIlm*
Kalām	*Mutakallimūn*
Uṣūl al-Fiqh	*Uṣūlīyah*
Fiqh, Furūʿ, Ikhtilāf	*Fuqahāʾ*
Ḥadīth	*Muḥaddithūn*
Adab	

Source: Ibn Qāḍī Shuhbah, *Ṭabaqāt al-fuqahāʾ al-shāfiʿīyah*, ed. al-Ḥāfiẓ ʿAbd al-Alī Khān, 4 vols. (Beirut: ʿĀlam al-kutub, 1987).

stantive legal rules (*fiqh, furūʿ*, and *ikhtilāf*), 4) traditions of the Prophet (*ḥadīth*), and 5) literary arts not formally studied under the other categories (*adab*).

In addition to *adab*, there are a number of other religious sciences that are listed in the text that will be referred to as 'non-primary' forms of *ʿilm*. These include Arabic, Qurʾan recitation, Qurʾan commentary, rhetoric, philosophy, medicine, historical studies, grammar, lexicography, and variant readings of the Qurʾan. Each of these areas of *ʿilm* become important over the course of Islamic history but serve as secondary areas of interest in Ibn Qāḍī Shuhbah's text.

Beyond areas of *ʿilm*, Ibn Qāḍī Shuhbah outlines classes of authority that are important in the discovery and transmission of knowledge (See table 5.1). He indicates that four primary classes of practitioners of *ʿilm* are important: 1) the speculative theologians (*mutakallimūn*, sing. *mutakallim*), 2) speculative jurists (*uṣūlīyah*, sing. *uṣūlī*), 3), substantive jurists (*fuqahāʾ*, sing. *faqīh*), and 4) traditionists (*muḥaddithūn*, sing. *muḥaddith*). These classes of practitioners represent specializations in *ʿilm* and are not mutually exclusive. In other words, a scholar could specialize in any category of knowledge, or have several specializations at the same time. For instance, one could be referred to as a specialist in theology and as a specialist in *ḥadīth*.

Subsumed under the four classes of *ʿilm* practitioners, Ibn Qāḍī Shuhbah lists five ranks of authoritative jurists as being important. These are: 1) the student companions of al-Shāfiʿī, (*aṣḥāb al-Shāfiʿī*) 2) student companions of the student companions of al-Shāfiʿī (*aṣḥāb aṣḥāb al-Shāfiʿī*), 3) the proponents of authoritative divergent points of view (*aṣḥāb al-wujūh*), 4) jurists qualified to engage in the expenditure of effort in the resolution of legal problems (*mujtahidūn*), and 5) memorizers/preservers of substantive law (*ḥuffāẓ*). Memorizers or preservers of substantive law are referred to in the text as memorizing law (*fiqh*), legal rules (*furūʿ*), divergent opinions (*ikhtilāf*), the authoritative doctrine of the school (*madhhab*) (but, in the analysis that follows excludes those who memorize *ḥadīth* and Qurʾan).

Figure 5.2. Ranks of authority in the discovery and transmission of *ʿilm*

1. *Aṣḥāb of al-Shāfiʿī*
2. *Aṣḥāb of the Aṣḥāb of al-Shāfiʿī*
3. *Aṣḥāb al-Wujūh*
4. *Mujtahidūn*
5. *Ḥuffāẓ*

Source: Ibn Qāḍī Shuhbah, *Ṭabaqāt al-fuqahāʾ al-shāfiʿīyah*, ed. al-Ḥāfiẓ ʿAbd al-Alī Khān, 4 vols. (Beirut: ʿĀlam al-kutub, 1987).

In the formation of substantive rules, Ibn Qāḍī Shuhbah mentions four different sources or bodies of authoritative knowledge (see figure 5.3): 1) the commonly held opinions in both method and rules that form the core Shāfiʿī doctrine (*madhhab*), 2) substantive legal rules which are transmitted from generation to generation through direct contacts between teachers and students (*furūʿ*), 3) authoritative disagreement which represents the range of permissible opinions allowed in the school on certain subjects (*ikhtilāf*, or sometimes *masāʾil*), and 4) the opinions of certain jurists which came to represent sub-schools (*ṭarīq*, or sometimes *ṭarīqah*) within the Shāfiʿī *madhhab*.

Figure 5.3. Sources or bodies of authoritative knowledge in the formation of substantive rules

1. *Madhhab*
2. *Furūʿ*
3. *Ikhtilāf/Masāʾil*
4. *Tarīq*

Source: Ibn Qāḍī Shuhbah, *Ṭabaqāt al-fuqahāʾ al-shāfiʿīyah*, ed. al-Ḥāfiẓ ʿAbd al-Alī Khān, 4 vols. (Beirut: ʿĀlam al-kutub, 1987).

It is important to emphasize that *furūʿ*, *fiqh*, and *ikhtilāf* are not necessarily different categories of law. *Furūʿ* and *fiqh* are both understandings of God's will as it is expressed in legal discourse. *Ikhtilāf* are *fiqh* or *furūʿ* on which jurists disagree. In other words, *ikhtilāf* is a comparative category which establishes the commonalities and differences between rules. If a jurist derives a rule which is different from another rule on the same issue, this is a form of *ikhtilāf*. The question becomes, how many rules actually diverge? Most of the jurists listed by Ibn Qāḍī Shuhbah in the early periods of legal formation were holders of *ikhtilāf*. This would indicate that when Ibn Qāḍī Shuhbah speaks of *furūʿ* and *fiqh*, he is most likely referring to rules which diverge from other rules. Ibn Qāḍī Shuhbah is very careful, however, in the terms he uses and we will not attempt to create meanings that he seems reluctant to indicate. The following refers to *ikhtilāf* only when it is clear that he intends this meaning (i.e., when he refers to it directly, or to texts that catalogue divergent opinions).

In many cases, Ibn Qāḍī Shuhbah, particularly in treating later periods in his history of the school, directly contrasts *madhhab* (commonly held opinions that rose to the level of doctrine) with *ikhtilāf* (authoritative dissenting opinions), further demonstrating the difference between the two, while at the same time maintaining that *furūʿ* results from the dynamic process between the two. In other words, '*madhhab*,' as is made clear below, refers to core doctrines on which authoritative jurists have agreed, while *ikhtilāf* are those points of law on which these same jurists have differed.[37] In traditional Islamic law there existed an important, and often overlooked, subjectivity in the law that allowed for differing points of view to carry the same level of correctness. Subjectivity arose out of the concept of probability (*ẓann*), which held that because only God can ultimately know what God's will actually is (i.e., 'truth'), if two jurists, both using sound legal methods of discovery, derive opposing opinions, both judgments are considered 'probable' reflections of God's will. The uncertainty that the concept of *ẓann* caused, while acceptable, was, however, not preferable. The need for consensus on legal rulings, and thus certainty (which is based on the concept of *ijmāʿ*), drove jurists to look again at previous rulings and to determine how they were originally established. This constant and dynamic process of reexamination is what drove jurists to find new legal rules and to refine earlier concepts.[38]

---

[37] For an excellent discussion of the different definitions of *madhhab* see, Hallaq, *Authority, Continuity and Change in Islamic Law*, 155–60.

[38] Weiss, *The Spirit of Islamic Law*, 113–44; Hallaq, *Authority, Continuity, and Change in Islamic Law*, 126–52.

Legal disputation was not the only area in which jurists developed interests that concerned *ṭabaqāt* authors. George Makdisi has pointed out, with regard to al-Subkī's *Ṭabaqāt al-shāfiʿīyah al-kubrā*, that debates between traditionalists and Ashʿarī theologians, and specifically al-Subkī's argument for the inclusion of the latter, is central to the purposes behind his bio-history.[39] Conversely, Makdisi argues that Abū Isḥāq al-Shīrāzī's *Ṭabaqāt al-fuqahāʾ* was written for the purposes of establishing the traditionalist triumph over rationalism.[40] Thus the composition of legal *ṭabaqāt* texts, according to Makdisi, came out of the traditionalist/rationalist struggle. If Ibn Qāḍī Shuhbah was writing in response to this debate then it would stand to reason that one school of authority (traditionalists or speculativists) would dominate his attention.

The main protagonists in this struggle, from Makdisi's point of view, are the *mutakallimūn* (their allies in the *madhhab*, the *uṣūlīyah*), and their opponents, the *muḥaddithūn*. Indeed, although the *muḥaddithūn* do not by necessity represent traditionalist consensus, if they were more central to a traditionalist point of view they should receive more attention than their enemies. Of the 784 jurists Ibn Qāḍī Shuhbah lists in his text, 65 are said to engage in some aspect of theological speculation, 202 are mentioned as studying or transmitting knowledge about speculative jurisprudence, and 483 are mentioned as transmitting, hearing, or otherwise engaging in the study of tradition. This suggests, at least on the surface, that Ibn Qāḍī Shuhbah leans away from speculative issues.

Of the 65 scholars who are described as being engaged in theological speculation, eight are said to have been Ashʿarites, and only three are referred to directly as *mutakallimūn*. The first is Ibn Kullāb (d. 240/852), who was "among the great theologians and among the people of the *sunnah*."[41] The second is Abū Ḥasan al-Ashʿarī (d. 324/935) himself, who is cited as having turned away from the Muʿtazilah.[42] The last *mutakallim* listed is Abū al-Fatḥ al-Miṣṣīṣī (d. 542/1147) who, while listed as an *uṣūlī*, is also said to have heard *ḥadīth*.[43] No Muʿtazilī is given a notice in the *Ṭabaqāt*. Of the rest, seven are said to have

[39] Makdisi, "Ashʿari and the Ashʿarites," 57–60.
[40] Makdisi, "*Ṭabaqāt*," 385–88.
[41] Khān, vol. 1, 47.
[42] Ibid., 84.
[43] Ibid., 315.

specific training in *'ilm al-kalām*, and 16 in *uṣūl al-dīn* ('sources of religion'), although exactly what this entailed, and how the two fields differed, is difficult to distinguish from the text.

Of the 202 jurists who had or dispensed specific training in *uṣūl al-fiqh*, 19 are referred to as '*uṣūlī*.' Five of these only were involved with *ḥadīth* in any capacity, and three of those are listed as being *muḥaddith* as well. Of the 483 jurists who engaged in *ḥadīth* in some manner, only 30 are referred to as *muḥaddith*, nine of whom also engaged in *uṣūl*.

Table 5.1. The progressive development of categories of law

Generation	*Furū'*	*Ikhtilāf*	*Ṭarīq*	*Ḥāfiẓ*	*Mujtahid*	*Madhhab*	*Aṣḥāb Wujūh*	*Aṣḥāb Aṣḥāb Shāfi'ī*	*Aṣḥāb Shāfi'ī*
1	10	11	–	–	1	–	–	–	8(16)
2	9	8	–	–	–	–	–	3(13)	–
3	13	12	–	–	2	–	2	–	–
4	8	10	–	–	–	–	2	–	–
5	13	12	–	–	–	–	1	–	–
6	19	17	–	–	–	1	1	–	–
7	15	15	–	–	–	–	4	–	–
8	24	19	–	2	1	4	2	–	–
9	11	11	–	1	1	4	2	–	–
10	11	9	–	–	1	3	2	–	–
11	16	14	–	–	1	4	4	–	–
12	13	12	–	1	2	4	1	–	–
13	12	10	–	1	–	5	–	–	–
14	11	14	–	–	–	3	–	–	–
15	7	4	–	1	–	3	–	–	–
16	4	4	–	–	–	2	–	–	–
17	9	7	–	–	–	6	–	–	–
18	4	5	–	1	1	3	–	–	–
19	13	9	–	5	2	4	–	–	–
20	6	7	–	2	1	7	2	–	–
21	6	4	–	6	2	9	–	–	–
22	8	5	–	8	1	10	–	–	–
23	3	2	–	5	1	1	–	–	–
24	12	6	2	9	1	5	–	–	–
25	18	8	2	7	1	5	–	–	–
26	15	7	2	8	2	5	–	–	–
27	7	2	3	11	2	–	–	–	–
28	15	2	4	13	1	2	–	–	–
29	11	5	2	15	1	–	–	–	–
Totals	322	251	15	99	25	83	23	3	8

Source: Ibn Qāḍī Shuhbah, *Ṭabaqāt al-fuqahā' al-shāfi'īyah*, ed. al-Ḥāfiẓ 'Abd al-Alī Khān, 4 vols. (Beirut: 'Ālam al-kutub, 1987).

This synchronic explanation of the text indicates that while Ibn Qāḍī Shuhbah placed greater emphasis on *ḥadīth* as an authoritative source of knowledge over *uṣūl al-fiqh* and lastly *kalām*, he seems to have struck a middle ground in the 'debate' over the inclusion of speculativists (rationalists) versus traditionalists. Those referred to as belonging to a specific 'camp' account for less than 10% of all jurists discussed, with speculativists and traditionalists receiving almost equal representation. If Ibn Qāḍī Shuhbah understood there to have been a historical conflict between camps, it seems to have made little difference to him.

Then what, as a matter of historical development, did concern Ibn Qāḍī Shuhbah? As mentioned above, Ibn Qāḍī Shuhbah lists nine classes of authority in the transmission of *ʿilm* (five ranks of authoritative jurists and four sources of authoritative knowledge). These classes, and the way Ibn Qāḍī Shuhbah arranges them chronologically, suggest a clear argument about the development of the Shāfiʿī *madhhab* (see table 5.1).

Mujtahid*s*

One of the first things that the progression on table 5.1 reveals is the relative paucity of *mujtahid*s. Although there is a fairly even distribution of *mujtahid*s across time, they account for just 25 out of 784, or approximately 3% of all jurists. It is clear, however, that Ibn Qāḍī Shuhbah may have considered many other jurists to be *mujtahid*s. For instance, Abū Isḥāq al-Shīrāzī, a jurist he holds in the highest esteem, is not listed as a *mujtahid*.[44]

In his book, *Authority, Continuity and Change in Islamic Law*, Wael Hallaq argues that the use of the term '*mujtahid*' by historians frequently indicated individuals that sought to develop their own independent schools of law, or at the very least sought to step outside school boundaries, but were later incorporated into the Shāfiʿī school. He bases his argument on juridical typologies that place ultimate hermeneutical authority solely in the hands of school founders. Claims to *ijtihād* challenged the authoritative structures of the schools and, by necessity, were reinterpreted to be derivative of the founder's legal

[44] Khān, 219–21.

Figure 5.4. *Mujtahids* and the production of *furūʿ*

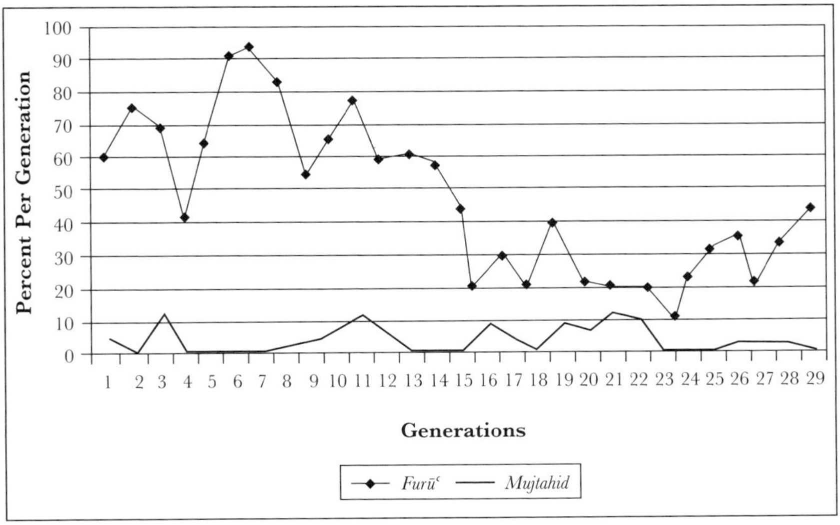

Source: Ibn Qāḍī Shuhbah, *Ṭabaqāt al-fuqahāʾ al-shāfiʿīyah*, ed. al-Ḥāfiẓ ʿAbd al-Alī Khān, 4 vols. (Beirut: ʿĀlam al-kutub, 1987).

method. Thus, the *mujtahids* that exist after the formation of the schools are by definition 'affiliated' scholars who depend on the method of the eponym. Hallaq is not arguing that affiliated *mujtahids* were not doing *ijtihād* in the same way the eponyms were, in fact he credits later jurists with far more skill and ability than al-Shāfiʿī, al-Mālik, and Abū Ḥanīfah. He contends, however, that the need to augment school authority was so great that later *mujtahids* were defined as affiliated so as to protect the reputation of the founders and thus ensure school loyalty.[45]

Regardless of whether a jurist is an affiliated or absolute *mujtahid*, Ibn Qāḍī Shuhbah, for reasons that are not yet clear, does not seem to indicate that they alone have the authority to produce legal rules. As figure 5.4 demonstrates above, there is extensive legal production that seems to exist outside the authority of the *mujtahids*. For instance, between generations four and seven, Ibn Qāḍī Shuhbah does not describe any jurist as being a *mujtahid* but, at the same time, depicts

[45] Hallaq, *Authority, Continuity and Change in Islamic Law*, 62–64.

Figure 5.5. Trends in the production and transmission of *furūʿ* and *ikhtilāf*

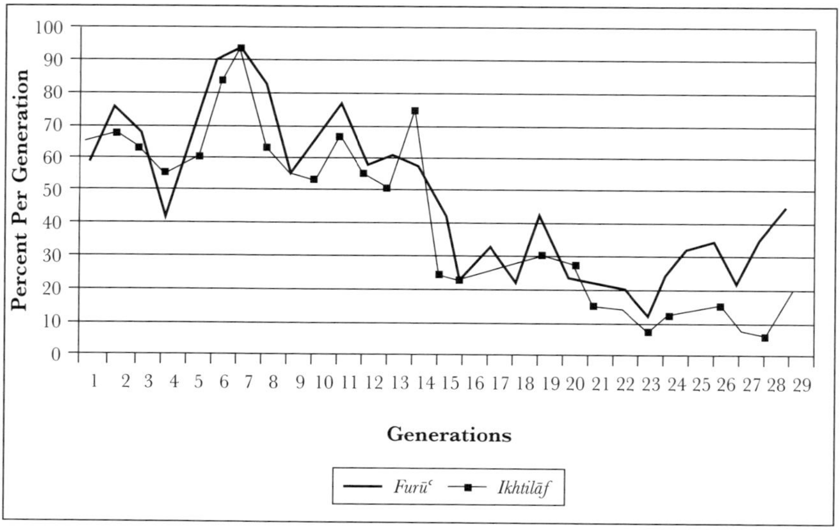

Source: Ibn Qāḍī Shuhbah, *Ṭabaqāt al-fuqahāʾ al-shāfiʿīyah*, ed. al-Ḥāfiẓ ʿAbd al-Alī Khān, 4 vols. (Beirut: ʿĀlam al-kutub, 1987).

the production of legal rules as being at their highest levels in school history. Who, then, was producing such a large volume of rules in the absence of *mujtahids*?

Furūʿ *and* ikhtilāf

The second aspect of the progression that stands out *is the absolute dominance* of substantive law in Ibn Qāḍī Shuhbah's depiction of legal history. As is depicted in figure 5.5, *furūʿ* was transmitted in every generation in fairly high numbers, with 41% (322) of all jurists being expressly involved in the transmission of substantive rules. Furthermore, since Ibn Qāḍī Shuhbah equates *fiqh* specifically with *furūʿ*, as opposed to equating it with *uṣūl al-fiqh*, this raises the number of scholars involved in the transmission of substantive rules to 750. The remaining 34, while not specifically mentioned as having training in substantive rules, are almost universally involved in the science of *ḥadīth*. *Furūʿ*, however, as an explicit category is second only to the transmission of *ḥadīth* (483). As stated above, the transmission of *ikhtilāf* is also an important area of *ʿilm*, with 251, or 32% of all jurists engaged in it in some way; it is the third most frequently occurring category. As figure 5.5 shows above, the study of *ikhtilāf* begins to decline sharply between the 14th and 15th generations (527/1132–560/1165) and nearly disappears in the 28th generation (801/1398–819/1417), before rebounding slightly in decade before Ibn Qāḍī Shuhbah wrote the book.

The three aṣḥābs

Three ranks of *'ilm* practitioners and transmitters stand out because of their importance in linking legal knowledge directly back to al-Shāfi'ī. Ibn Qāḍī Shuhbah uses the term *ṣāḥib* (pl. *aṣḥāb*, or *ṣaḥābah*), meaning 'fellow, disciple, or close student,' to indicate the beginning of the historical development of a cohesive community of jurists. Ibn Qāḍī Shuhbah points to the importance of this concept in his introduction when he states that the companion students of al-Shāfi'ī continued to live until the year 300/912. Ibn Qāḍī Shuhbah specifically applies the term to nine scholars among the first generation of al-Shāfi'ī's students. They are:

1. al-Muzanī, who is described as al-Shāfi'ī's first student in Egypt;[46]
2. al-Ḥārith b. Surayj (d. 236/852), who is said to have transmitted the *Risālah* while al-Shāfi'ī was in Baghdād;[47]
3. Ḥarmalah b. Yaḥyā al-Tujībī (243/859), who transmitted al-Shāfi'ī's opinion after his migration to Egypt;[48]
4. al-Rabī' b. Sulaymān b. Dāwūd (d. 256/872), who is credited with transmitting substantive rules directly from al-Shāfi'ī;[49]
5. al-Rabī' al-Murādī, who is described as the last and most faithful transmitter of al-Shāfi'ī's ideas;[50]
6. 'Abdallāh b. Zubayr al-Ḥumaydī (d. 219/835), who not only traveled with al-Shāfi'ī to Egypt but also studied with many of al-Shāfi'ī's teachers;[51]

---

[46] Khān, vol. 1, 58–59.
[47] Ibid., vol. 1, 60.
[48] Ibid., vol. 1, 61–62.
[49] Ibid., vol. 1, 64–65.
[50] Ibid., vol. 1, 65–66.
[51] Ibid., vol. 1, 66–67.

7. al-Buwayṭī, who succeeded al-Shāfiʿī as the leader of his teaching circle after 204/820, and who is reputed by al-Nawawī to be al-Shāfiʿī's greatest student;[52]
8. Yūnus b. ʿAbd al-Aʿlā (d. 264/876), who transmitted substantive rules from al-Shāfiʿī and succeeded al-Buwayṭī as leader of the school after his death;[53] and finally,
9. Aḥmad Ibn Ḥanbal (d. 241/855), who is said to have joined al-Shāfiʿī's *aṣḥāb*.[54]

Of these scholars, all but al-Buwayṭī and Yūnus b. ʿAbd al-Aʿlā are mentioned as transmitting substantive rules though the writings of al-Rabīʿ al-Murādī. Aḥmad Ibn Ḥanbal was imprisoned, and al-Buwayṭī died in prison, during the rationalist inquisition (*miḥnah*).

What distinguishes these scholars from the other eight jurists in the first generation, whom Ibn Qāḍī Shuhbah cites as studying with al-Shāfiʿī, is their close relationship to the eponym. The other scholars studied from al-Shāfiʿī (*akhadha ʿan*) or specifically studied law (*tafaqqaha ʿala*) with him, but they did not enjoy the intimacy indicated by the term '*aṣḥāb*' ('companions'). Describing an individual as being an *aṣḥāb* indicates a closeness that goes beyond the student/teacher relationship that *akhadha* and *tafaqqaha* imply. It refers to intimacy, to living in the presence of another individual, to long and close companionship. Thus the level of authority transmitted through an *aṣḥāb* relationship is far greater than any other kind.

Ibn Qāḍī Shuhbah mentions in the second generation, after the *aṣḥāb* of al-Shāfiʿī, three scholars who are specifically referred to as studying from the *aṣḥāb* (*akhadha ʿan aṣḥāb* or *tafaqqaha ʿala aṣḥāb*).

1. Muḥammad b. Aḥmad al-Tirmidhī (d. 295/907) is described as "*tafaqqaha ʿalā*" al-Rabīʿ and others among the *aṣḥāb* of al-Shāfiʿī;[55]
2. Muḥammad b. Ismāʿīl al-Bukhārī (d. 256/869) is referred to as "*akhadha ʿan*" the *aṣḥāb* including al-Ḥumaydī, al-Zaʿfarānī, al-Karābīsī, and Abū Thawr;[56] and
3. Muḥammad b. Naṣr al-Marwazī (d. 294/906) is described as both "*akhadha ʿan*" and "*tafaqqaha ʿalā*" the *aṣḥāb*.[57]

---

[52] Ibid., vol. 1, 70–72.
[53] Ibid., vol. 1, 72–73.
[54] Ibid., vol. 1, 56–58.
[55] Ibid., vol. 1, 82.
[56] Ibid., vol. 1, 83.
[57] Ibid., vol. 1, 84–85.

What sets these jurists apart from the others of their generation (other than their obvious fame in other areas) is that they are the first (and only, besides al-Karābīsī (d. 245/859) in the first generation) to be specifically described as transmitting *ikhtilāf* or questions (*masāʾil*) from al-Shāfiʿī or his *aṣḥāb* (al-Muzanī is the author of *ikhtilāf* and does not specifically transmit it from al-Shāfiʿī). From then, until the eighth/fourteenth century, *ikhtilāf* remains a central source of authoritatively transmitted knowledge. After the eighth/fourteenth century, *ikhtilāf* begins to fade out as an important source of knowledge in Ibn Qāḍī Shuhbah's presentation. However, of the approximately 600 jurists that fall in this range, 24% (251) are specifically referred to as transmitting *ikhtilāf*.

Beginning with the third, and continuing through the twelfth generation, another group of *aṣḥāb* becomes important, these being the *aṣḥāb al-wujūh* (the authoritative authors of divergent opinions). Hallaq argues that the *aṣḥāb al-wujūh* are a specific group of scholars who practiced a form of legal reasoning referred to as *takhrīj*. According to Hallaq, there where two types of *takhrīj* common in the early school. He states that,

> the first type became known as *al-takhrīj wal-naql*, while the second, being a relatively more independent activity, was given the unqualified designation *takhrīj*. This latter involves reasoning, among other things, on the basis of general principles, such as the principle that necessity renders lawful what is otherwise illicit, or that no legal obligation shall be imposed beyond the limit of endurance or optimal capability. In this type of activity, the limited *mujtahid*s take these principles as his rule of thumb and solves problems accordingly.[58]

Takhrīj wa ʾl-naql is a more restricted form of reasoning where rules are derived directly from material transmitted from the eponyms or their followers.[59]

Ibn Qāḍī Shuhbah refers to *takhrīj* as a mode of reasoning in six biographies only (he does not refer to *takhrīj wa ʾl-naql* in any biography). The most prominent is that of al-Muzanī discussed in chapter three. His case is so important for understanding how Ibn Qāḍī Shuhbah uses the term *takhrīj* that a re-examination of al-Muzanī's biography is in order. The author describes al-Muzanī as a *mujtahid*

[58] Hallaq, *Authority, Continuity and Change in Islamic Law*, 44.
[59] Ibid., 45.

and as studying legal methodologies. In discussing the controversy over whether al-Muzanī should be included in the *madhhab*, he quotes al-Rāfiʿī as saying

> (quoting al-Shāfiʿī) 'I consider every choice from to al-Muzanī to be derivative (*takhrījan*) [of my opinion/legal method],' for he does not contradict the jurisprudential method of al-Shāfiʿī. Unlike Abū Yūsuf and Muḥammad, for they contradict the jurisprudential method [of Abū Ḥanīfah] a great deal.

He then quotes al-Isnawī as saying

> I saw in *al-Nihāyah*, as if he, in the violation of rules for ritual ablutions, gave opposite what al-Rāfiʿī cited from him concerning divorce on the insistence of the wife. He said that he derived a subsidiary legal ruling, and his derivation (*takhrīj*) was more deserving than the derivation (*takhrīj*) of others besides him.

Ibn Qāḍī Shuhbah then adds parenthetically, "otherwise, he would be the master of an independent school of thought."[60]

It is unclear which kind of *takhrīj* al-Muzanī is supposed to have preformed. In the al-Rāfiʿī passage the more intensive kind of *takhrīj* is attributed to al-Muzanī, although it is likely that *takhrīj wa 'l-naql* is being referred to in the passage from al-Isnawī. Both passages seem to confirm Hallaq's interpretation of *takhrīj* and imply that it was a more common practice than Ibn Qāḍī Shuhbah indicates.

Hallaq also contends that *takhrīj* is the source of many divergent opinions (*ikhtilāf*) in the formation of the corpus of legal thought.[61] This is certainly the case with al-Muzanī, who is depicted by Ibn Qāḍī Shuhbah as the father of *ikhtilāf* in the school. One would expect, therefore, to find more references to *takhrīj* given the heavy emphasis on *ikhtilāf* in the text, but this is not the case.

Ibn Qāḍī Shuhbah does not refer to another scholar as practicing *takhrīj* for over 300 years, well after the end of the period in which *takhrīj* was supposed to have come to an end.[62] The famous historian and jurist Abū al-Qāsim Ibn ʿAsākir (d. 571/1176) is described as "working out derivative opinions" (*kharraja al-takhārīj*), but is not referred to as one of the *aṣḥāb al-wujūh* or as a particularly notable jurist; he is not described as being a *mujtahid*. He is, to the contrary,

---

[60] Khān, vol. 1, 58–59.
[61] Hallaq, *Authority, Continuity and Change in Islamic Law*, 45–54.
[62] Ibid., 75.

described as "the *Imām* of the people of *ḥadīth*" and is, for the most part, depicted not so much as a jurist but as a *ḥadīth* scholar.[63]

The situation is much different in the biography of Ibn al-Rifʿah (d. 710/1311) who is one of the most celebrated jurists in the text. He is described as studying with many of the most important scholars of his day, as being a prolific writer, as a teacher, and as excelling in many areas of legal knowledge. Ibn Qāḍī Shuhbah also says that Ibn al-Rifʿah was "a prodigy in knowledge of the texts of al-Shāfiʿī and a prodigy in the ability of *takhrīj*."[64] He is not depicted as one of the *aṣḥāb al-wujūh* or as being a *mujtahid*. The fact that he is depicted as a prolific writer may indicate that he ranks among the great jurists, maybe even a *mujtahid*,[65] but if Ibn Qāḍī Shuhbah understood him to be in that rank he does not say so.

In much the same way, Ibn Qāḍī Shuhbah describes Abū al-Ḥasan b. al-ʿAṭṭār (d. 724/1324), who is mentioned as an important jurist who studied (*tafaqqaha*) with such luminaries as al-Nawawī. He was a teacher, a practicing jurist and, like Ibn al-Rifʿah, a writer who produced a number of original works and commentaries, including a book on derivative opinions (*takhārīj*); although whether he was the author of these opinions or just the transmitter is not clear.[66]

Ibn Qāḍī Shuhbah also states that Abū ʿAbdallāh al-Ḥusaynī (d. 765/1364) "was among those who performed" *takhrīj*. As with Ibn ʿAsākir and al-ʿAṭṭār, al-Ḥusaynī is described as being a specialist in *ḥadīth*, as a writer, and a teacher. Also, like all of the others listed, he is not mentioned as being one of the *aṣḥab al-wujūh* or as being a *mujtahid*.[67]

The final reference to *takhrīj* occurs in the biography of Abū al-Rabīʿ al-Maqdisī (d. 789/1387). Al-Maqdisī is described as being a specialist in *ḥadīth*. He, too, is not mentioned as one of the *aṣḥāb al-wujūh*. In addition, and unlike the other scholars Ibn Qāḍī Shuhbah describes as doing *takhrīj*, al-Maqdisī is also described as studying broadly (*ishtighāl*) in a number of religious sciences. Ibn Qāḍī Shuhbah says that al-Maqdisī "worked out beneficial derivative opinions"

---

[63] Khān, vol. 2, 13–14.

[64] *Uʿjūbah fī maʿrifa nuṣūṣ al-Shāfiʿī wa-uʿjūbah fī quwwa al-takhrīj*. Khān, vol. 2, 211–13.

[65] Hallaq, *Authority, Continuity and Change in Islamic Law*, 168.

[66] Khān, vol. 2, 270–71.

[67] Ibid., vol. 3, 129–31.

(*kharraja takhārīj mufīdah*). Al-Maqdisī is similar to al-Muzanī in that he is described as "following the path of *ijtihād*."[68]

It is clear from Ibn Qāḍī Shuhbah's presentation of the material that he applies the term *takhrīj* in the way that Hallaq suggests. None of the six, however, is listed among the *aṣḥāb al-wujūh*; and only two, al-Muzanī and al-Maqdisī, are listed as practicing *ijtihād*. Furthermore, Ibn Qāḍī Shuhbah refers to four of the six as outside the standard time period Hallaq suggests was normative for the use of *takhrīj*. It is clear that Ibn Qāḍī Shuhbah understood *takhrīj* to be an elevated form of legal reasoning that falls within the general parameters of *ijtihād*. But, it is not explicitly connected to the *aṣḥāb al-wujūh*.

Ibn Qāḍī Shuhbah, however, through the progressive development of his text, demonstrates a clear relationship between the *aṣḥāb al-wujūh* and *ikhtilāf* (see figure 5.6 below). The production of *ikhtilāf* rises in accordance with the development of the *aṣḥāb al-wujūh* and drops precipitously following the end of their period. The relationship between *ikhtilāf* and the existence of the *aṣḥāb al-wujūh* would seem, in the end, to confirm part of Hallaq's contention. Why Ibn Qāḍī Shuhbah does not attribute *takhrīj* to any of the *aṣḥāb al-wujūh* is, however, not clear. It is possible that Ibn Qāḍī Shuhbah simply did not understand *takhrīj* to be the purview of the *aṣḥāb al-wujūh*.

Ibn Qāḍī Shuhbah describes the *aṣḥāb al-wujūh* as spanning ten generations only, and mentions them in just 21 biographies. The term occurs twice in the twentieth generation, but in each instance the text refers to the combined concept of *wujūh al-madhhab*. For instance, Ibn Qāḍī Shuhbah says that Aḥmad b. Kashāsib al-Dazmārī (d. 643/1245) was "a jurist, a pious [man], an expert in tradition (*naql*) and in the authoritatively divergent points of view in the corpus of received opinion (*wujūh al-madhhab*)."[69] The great jurist Ibn al-Ṣalāḥ (d. 643/1245) is also mentioned as "having an understanding of the corpus of received opinion (*al-madhhab*) and of the authoritatively divergent opinions of it (*wujūhihā*).[70] These men did not hold authoritatively divergent opinions; they were simply knowledgeable about them.

---

[68] Ibid., 152–54.
[69] Ibid., vol. 2, 100.
[70] Ibid., vol. 2, 113–14.

Figure 5.6. Comparison between the number of *aṣḥāb al-wujūh* to the production of *ikhtilāf*

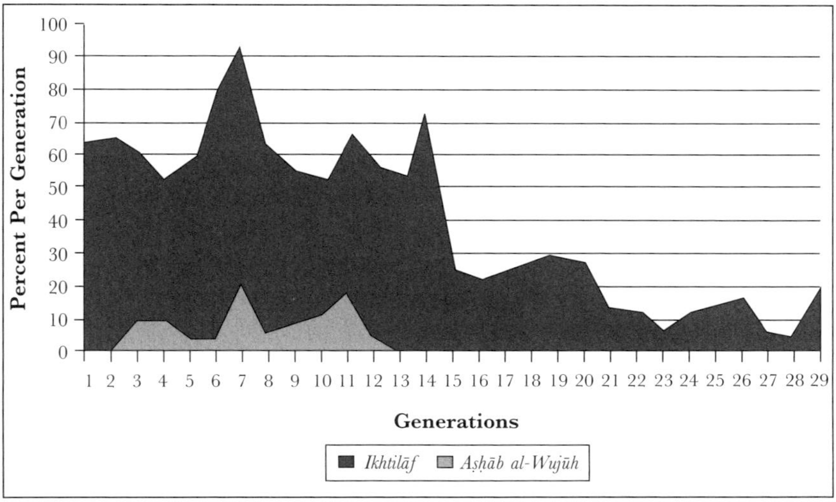

Source: Ibn Qāḍī Shuhbah, *Ṭabaqāt al-fuqahā' al-shāfiʿīyah*, ed. al-Ḥāfiẓ ʿAbd al-Alī Khān, 4 vols. (Beirut: ʿĀlam al-kutub, 1987).

The *aṣḥāb al-wujūh* thus form a select group. They are fewer in number than *mujtahids* and seem, given their clear role in the production *of ikhtilāf*, to be particularly important to Ibn Qāḍī Shuhbah. As is demonstrated below, their role in the development of Islamic legal history is central to the survival of the Muslim community.

Madhhab

According to Ibn Qāḍī Shuhbah, the next historical category to develop after the *aṣḥāb al-wujūh* (see figure 5.7) is the concept of *madhhab*. The term is used in three senses in the text. The first is also the most common usage in everyday parlance, namely that which refers to the school of law. Using this sense, Ibn Qāḍī Shuhbah says that the leadership (*ri'āsah*) of the Shāfiʿī school of law in Baghdād is said to have fallen to Abū al-Qāsim al-Dārakī (mentioned in chapter two) (*intahat ilayhī riyāsat al-madhhab bi-Baghdād*).[71] Secondly, the

[71] Ibid., vol. 2, 116.

term is used to mean the opinion of someone, and in this text, usually al-Shāfiʿī. Thus Abū al-Walīd al-Nīsābūrī (d. 349/960) is said to have written a book according the opinion of al-Shāfiʿī (*lahu . . . kitāb ʿalā madhhab al-Shāfiʿī*).[72] However, beginning in the sixth (362/972–380/991), and in full in the eighth generation (400/1009–420/1030), the term takes on the meaning of a corpus of received authoritative opinions that represents the doctrinal view of the Shāfiʿī school. In several early instances the concept is linked with the *aṣḥāb al-wujūh*. In Ibn Qāḍī Shuhbah's entry for Abū al-Qāsim al-Ṣaymarī (d. 386/996), the jurist is listed as being "one of the leaders of the Shāfiʿīs and of the professors of authoritatively divergent opinions" (*aḥad aʾimmat al-shāfiʿīyah wa-aṣḥāb al-wujūh*) and also as a "memorizer of the received corpus of authoritative opinions" (*ḥāfiẓan li l-madhhab*).[73] The concept occurs constantly from the eighth to the twenty-sixth generations (400/1009 to 780/1379), with nearly 20% of all jurists being linked with the idea. The high point of the concept occurred in the seventeenth through the twenty-second generations (581/1185 to 699/1300), with a sharp decline occurring in the twenty-third generation 701/1301–718/1319). Surprisingly, reference to the *madhhab* as a doctrinal unit nearly completely disappears in the final three generations. Its decline mirrors that of *ikhtilāf* and suggests that the same forces that brought about a reduction in divergent opinion also impinged upon the formation of doctrine.

Ḥāfiẓ

The root *ḥ f ẓ* means 'to remember,' and also 'to preserve,' or 'keep intact.' The concept of *madhhab* is linked with the idea of memorization (*ḥifẓ*) in 16 of 83 biographies. In fact, the first two instances of the term '*ḥāfiẓ*' occur in the context of one who memorizes the *madhhab*.[74] The concept of *ḥāfiẓ* develops substantially beginning with the nineteenth generation (beginning in 622/1225) and continues to increase up to the time of Ibn Qāḍī Shuhbah; with the decline of both *ikhtilāf* and *madhhab*, *ḥāfiẓ* increases dramatically (see figure 5.8).

[72] Ibid., vol. 2, 99.
[73] Ibid., vol. 2, 160–61.
[74] Ibid., vol. 2, 160–61; 174.

Figure 5.7. The development of the *madhhab* in comparison to *furūʿ* and *ikhtilāf*

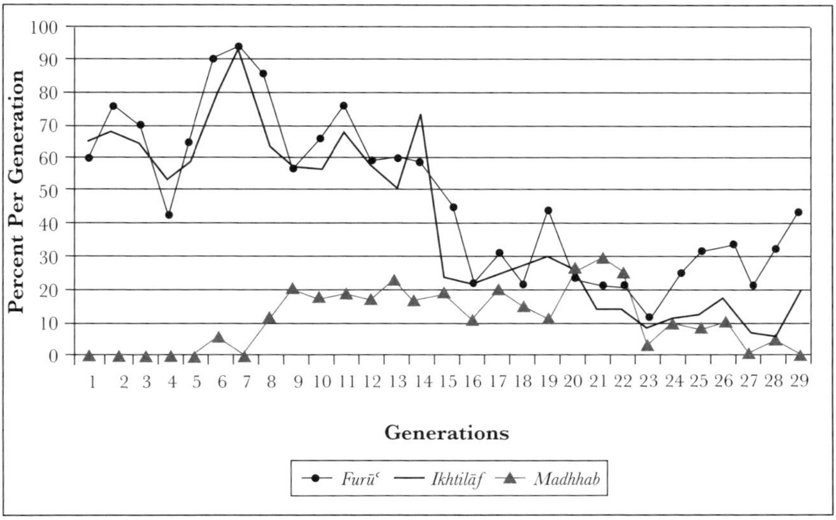

Source: Ibn Qāḍī Shuhbah, *Ṭabaqāt al-fuqahāʾ al-shāfiʿīyah*, ed. al-Ḥāfiẓ ʿAbd al-Alī Khān, 4 vols. (Beirut: ʿĀlam al-kutub, 1987).

Figure 5.8. *Ḥāfiẓ* in comparison with *madhhab* and *ikhtilāf*

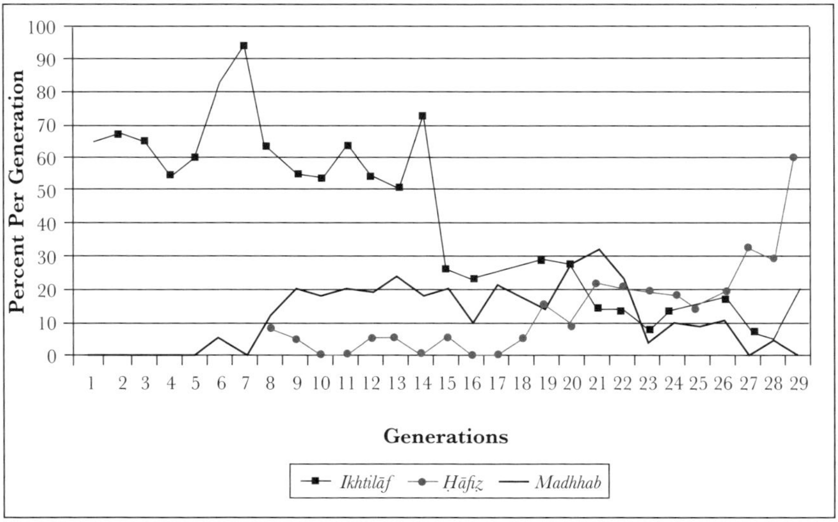

Source: Ibn Qāḍī Shuhbah, *Ṭabaqāt al-fuqahāʾ al-shāfiʿīyah*, ed. al-Ḥāfiẓ ʿAbd al-Alī Khān, 4 vols. (Beirut: ʿĀlam al-kutub, 1987).

Ṭarīq

The final concept that Ibn Qāḍī Shuhbah treats in his progressive development of the Shāfiʿī school of law is that of *ṭarīq*. The term *ṭarīq* (or sometimes *ṭarīqah*) means 'way/method,' or in this sense 'sub-tradition of law.' It arises late in Ibn Qāḍī Shuhbah's scheme; the first occurrence appears in the twenty-fourth generation (721/1221–740/1340), and it continues through the last generation. Each instance of the term is linked to a particular jurist, most commonly to al-Nawawī.[75] Sometimes there is a simple statement that the jurist followed an excellent path/method (*kāna ʿalā ṭarīqah ḥasanah*).[76]

A Model of Islamic Legal History

What should be made of Ibn Qāḍī Shuhbah's portrayal of the development of the school? It begins with the students of al-Shāfiʿī; then continues with their students; then progresses through the professors of authoritatively divergent opinions; overlaps with the development of the concept of *madhhab* as a corpus of received opinion; which in turn overlaps with the development of the memorization/preservation of those ideas; and finally culminates with the development of individual sub-legal traditions within the school.

The work of Muḥyī al-Dīn al-Nawawī (d. 676/1277) provides a crucial key to understanding Ibn Qāḍī Shuhbah's construction of Shāfiʿī legal history. For Ibn Qāḍī Shuhbah, al-Nawawī was one of the most important and influential jurists of all time. Of the five juridical texts Ibn Qāḍī Shuhbah wrote, two dealt with al-Nawawī's *Minhāj*.[77] In the *Ṭabaqāt* he cites al-Nawawī as an authority in the transmission of *ikhtilāf* over 75 times, second only to al-Rāfiʿī. His biography is also the longest Ibn Qāḍī Shuhbah wrote. Al-Nawawī's *al-Majmūʿ al-mudhahhab fī sharḥ al-muhadhdhab* is central to understanding how Ibn Qāḍī Shuhbah develops his history.[78]

---

[75] For instance, see the biography of Mahmūd b. Aḥmad al-Sarkhadī (d. 781/1379), vol. 2, 247. The term is used earlier, but in these previous instances it refers to Sufi brotherhoods or to concepts not specifically tied to the opinions of certain jurists.

[76] Ibid., vol. 2, 266.

[77] Al-Sakhāwī, *al-Ḍaw' al-lāmiʿ*, vol. 11, 21–23.

[78] Khān, vol. 1, 475–76.

In the introduction to the *Majmūʿ*, al-Nawawī includes a chapter entitled "*ādāb al-fatwā wa ʾl-muftī wa ʾl-mustaftī*" (Guidelines for the Issuance of Legal Rulings, the Issuing Jurist, and the Petitioner).[79] In this chapter al-Nawawī outlines the structure of legal authority in the Shāfiʿī *madhhab*, arguing that all jurists fall into three general conceptual categories: 1) *qawl*, 2) *wajh*, 3) *ṭarīq*.[80] Al-Nawawī states that *qawl* refers to the authoritative statements made by al-Shāfiʿī, while *wajh* refers to statements made by al-Shāfiʿī's companion students (*ṣāḥib*, pl. *aṣḥāb*) which, by virtue of the fact that they follow his methods of jurisprudence, are considered to be affiliated (*al-muntasibīn*) with al-Shāfiʿī's opinion.[81] *Ṭarīq* (path, school), on the other hand, refers to the different sub-traditions within the school which develop out of *ikhtilāf* between authoritative jurists concerning legal rulings. These differences grow out of the statements (*qawl*) made by a few jurists in matters concerning legal questions (*masʾalah*, pl. *masāʾil*), or in their differing authoritative points of view (*wajh*, pl. *wujūh*), or when different standards of evidence are applied to similar questions,[82] all of which prevents consensus from forming.

Norman Calder argues that overlaid on these general conceptual categories are three group rankings of jurists: independent *muftī*s (*mustaqill*), affiliated *muftī*s (*muntasib*), and deficient *muftī*s.[83] According to al-Nawawī, there have been no independent jurists since the death of al-Shāfiʿī,[84] with the vast majority of jurists falling in the middle category of those affiliated with either the opinions or methods of al-Shāfiʿī. The lowest category, 'deficient jurist,' refers to those who followed individual jurists other than al-Shāfiʿī.

In the affiliated group there are four ranks of jurists. The first rank are the *muftīs* who do not submit (*taqlīd*) to the founding *Imām*'s opinion (*madhhab*) on matters of substantive rules, or in proofs or indicators (*dalīl*), but who follow his path or method in matters of

---

[79] Al-Nawawī, *al-Majmūʿ*, vol. 1, 67.
[80] Ibid., 107.
[81] Norman Calder, "Al-Nawawī's Typology of *Muftī*s and its Significance for the General Theory of Islamic Law," 140.
[82] Al-Nawawī, *al-Majmūʿ*, vol. 1, 107.
[83] Calder, "Al-Nawawī's Typology," 143.
[84] "Al-Nawawī's Typology," 144; al-Nawawī, *al-Majmūʿ*, vol. 1, 71. In the following I will give citations for both Calder and al-Nawawī because the former, in his discussion of al-Nawawī, did not provide the Arabic terms for many of his concepts. In the discussion that follows, I want to make sure the reader has in mind what terms are active in al-Nawawī's discussion.

ijtihād (*ṭarīqah fī ijtihād*).[85] They are, therefore, submissive (*muqallid*) in matters of method only.

The second rank of affiliated jurists are those who are limited to the founding *Imām*'s opinions on substantive rules (*madhhab*) but not in matters regarding the discovery of proofs, which they locate using the founding *Imām*'s juridical method.[86] This rank of jurist is *muqallid* in that he must follow those rules already discovered by his founding *Imām*, and he must restrict himself to further discovery based solely on the juridical method of the *Imām*. The *aṣḥāb al-wujūh*, according to al-Nawawī, fall into this category. In al-Nawawī's scheme, if one is *muqallid* to one of the *aṣḥāb al-wujūh* he/she is not *muqallid* to them, but to the founding *Imām* (al-Shāfiʿī) because their rulings are either directly derived from the *Imām*'s substantive legal rulings, or are based solely on his method.[87]

The third rank of affiliated jurist "does not reach the level of the owners of divergent authoritative opinions but has a trained intelligence and has memorized/preserved the opinions of his *Imām*" (*lā yablughu rutbata aṣḥābi l-wujūhi lākinnahu faqīhu ʾl-nafs ḥāfiẓu madhhabi imāmihi*).[88] This group, which largely came to an end in the fifth/twelfth century, was the first to compile the opinions of al-Shāfiʿī and the *aṣḥāb al-wujūh* and collect them in comprehensive works. This rank of jurist continued to write legal rulings, but on average, did not meet the same standards of excellence as did the *aṣḥāb al-wujūh*.[89]

The fourth rank of affiliated jurist is a memorizer (*ḥāfiẓ*) of the *madhhab* (now as a corpus of received opinion and method) and must have extensive knowledge of substantive rules. He is limited by his general lack of training and is dependent on the legal rulings of previous generations of scholars. While he may practice some forms of analogical reasoning, these are rather limited. If a legal ruling is required, it is best to seek out a jurist of higher rank if the ruling will require the application of methods of jurisprudence.[90]

Below this there are three additional ranks of jurist which fall into the third category of deficient jurist. In this category (*ṭarīq*), jurists

---

[85] Calder, "Al-Nawawī's Typology," 144–45; al-Nawawī, *al-Majmūʿ*, vol. 1, 71.
[86] Calder, "Al-Nawawī's Typology," 145; al-Nawawī, *al-Majmūʿ*, vol. 1, 72.
[87] Calder, "Al-Nawawī's Typology," 146; al-Nawawī, *al-Majmūʿ*, vol. 1, 72–73.
[88] Al-Nawawī, *al-Majmūʿ*, vol. 1, 73.
[89] Calder, "Al-Nawawī's Typology," 146; al-Nawawī, *al-Majmūʿ*, vol. 1, 72–73.
[90] Calder, "Al-Nawawī's Typology," 147–48.

are generally considered by al-Nawawī to be weak in most areas and simply become memorizers of books and much of the received corpus of legal opinion that forms the *madhhab*. Here, since no form of *ijtihād* is possible, the jurist cannot add to the *madhhab* as a set of ideas[91] and does not contribute to its growth. These jurists simply follow the legal rulings of other jurists, forming sub-schools of tradition.

Calder maintains that al-Nawawī, while holding that *ijtihād* continued to exist up to his time, sought (through *al-Majmūʿ*) to distinguish between what Calder calls 'scholar jurists' and 'author jurists.' Scholar jurists were those theoreticians, like al-Nawawī himself, who engaged in contemplating and writing about theoretical issues but who did not actually take up the administration of law. Author jurists were the active *muftīs* who met with the public and had to write legal rulings on a daily basis. Author jurists did not need the high levels of legal training that the scholar jurists did. The scholar jurists, on the other hand, existed solely to act on the rare occasions when they were needed to handle questions requiring high levels of legal reasoning.[92]

Calder contends that al-Nawawī admits by this that the abilities of most jurists, by his time, required them to practice *taqlīd* on some level. This de facto narrowing of the 'gate' was the apparent reality, but al-Nawawī does not provide any clues as to when he believes this situation came about. Most of al-Nawawī's ranks and categories are synchronic, with virtually any rank of jurist potentially existing at any time since the beginning of the *madhhab*. While it is true that the second and third rank were largely closed off by the fifth/eleventh centuries, Calder argues that al-Nawawī held these divisions to be less rigid than they would appear in his text.[93]

Ibn Qāḍī Shuhbah attempts to make al-Nawawī's typologies diachronic by creating a history which mirrors al-Nawawī's hierarchies in almost every respect. Figure 5.9 (below) is a depiction of how Ibn Qāḍī Shuhbah portrays the history of the Shāfiʿī school using al-Nawawī's rankings of jurists as historical periods. His purpose is to describe the chain of authoritative knowledge going back

[91] Al-Nawawī, *al-Majmūʿ*, vol. 1, 74–75.
[92] Calder, "Al-Nawawī's Typology," 147–55.
[93] Ibid.

to *Imām* al-Shāfiʿī. He takes al-Nawawī's ranks and makes them historical periods which correspond with al-Nawawī's statement that the end of the fifth/twelfth century marked the end of the third rank of affiliated jurist. Ibn Qāḍī Shuhbah also makes this the end of the *aṣḥāb al-wujūh*. The intermediate period marks the era of the rise and eventual decline of the concept of *madhhab* as an evolving corpus of opinion. It is interesting to note that contrary to al-Nawawī, Ibn Qāḍī Shuhbah sees the *madhhab* continuing to develop and exist beyond the closing of the period of the *aṣḥāb al-wujūh*.

It is also interesting that Ibn Qāḍī Shuhbah sees the rise of the memorizers (*ḥāfiẓ*) of the *madhhab* as beginning with the latest of the authoritative *ikhtilāf* collections. Ibn Qāḍī Shuhbah places this slightly later than al-Nawawī's types would admit. For both al-Nawawī and Ibn Qāḍī Shuhbah, however, the end of the period of the *aṣḥāb al-wujūh* and the end of authoritative collections of *ikhtilāf* is marked by the lives of two great scholars: al-Shīrāzī and al-Rāfiʿī. Al-Shīrāzī died in 476/1083, seventeen years before the death of the last of the *aṣḥāb al-wujūh*. Al-Rāfiʿī, for both al-Nawawī and Ibn Qāḍī Shuhbah, marks the high point of authoritative substantive rules compilation. His death in 623/1226 marks the end of the golden age of law. After al-Rāfiʿī, while there may be a few great jurists (such as al-Nawawī), the vast majority of substantive rules are derivative of something handed down by or through al-Rāfiʿī.[94]

This is of course not to say that the decline in legal development meant the end of *ijtihād*. Ibn Qāḍī Shuhbah clearly argues that *mujtahid*s continued to exist, although they are few and far between. As al-Nawawī argues, however, for the school (and indeed Islam in general) to continue to exist there must be jurists who are capable of dealing with issues that lower-level jurists cannot. While Ibn Qāḍī Shuhbah clearly sees the inherited tradition as sufficient for most tasks, he must admit the existence of at least one *mujtahid* per generation, at least on average. As there are several generations, however, in which he did not designate a *mujtahid*, this requirement may not be as fixed in his view as al-Nawawī has it.

---

[94] Al-Nawawī's *Rawḍah* and al-Rāfiʿī's *ʿAzīz* are considered to be the most important divergent substantive rules texts of the Shafiʿī school. The *Rawḍah* is actually based on al-Rāfiʿī's *ʿAzīz*. Thus the most important texts of the school, and for Ibn Qāḍī Shuhbah, derive from al-Rafiʿī's collections (*Encyclopedia of Islam*, 2nd ed. s.v. "Al-Nawawī").

Figure 5.9. Graphic and chronological depiction of the periods of legal development

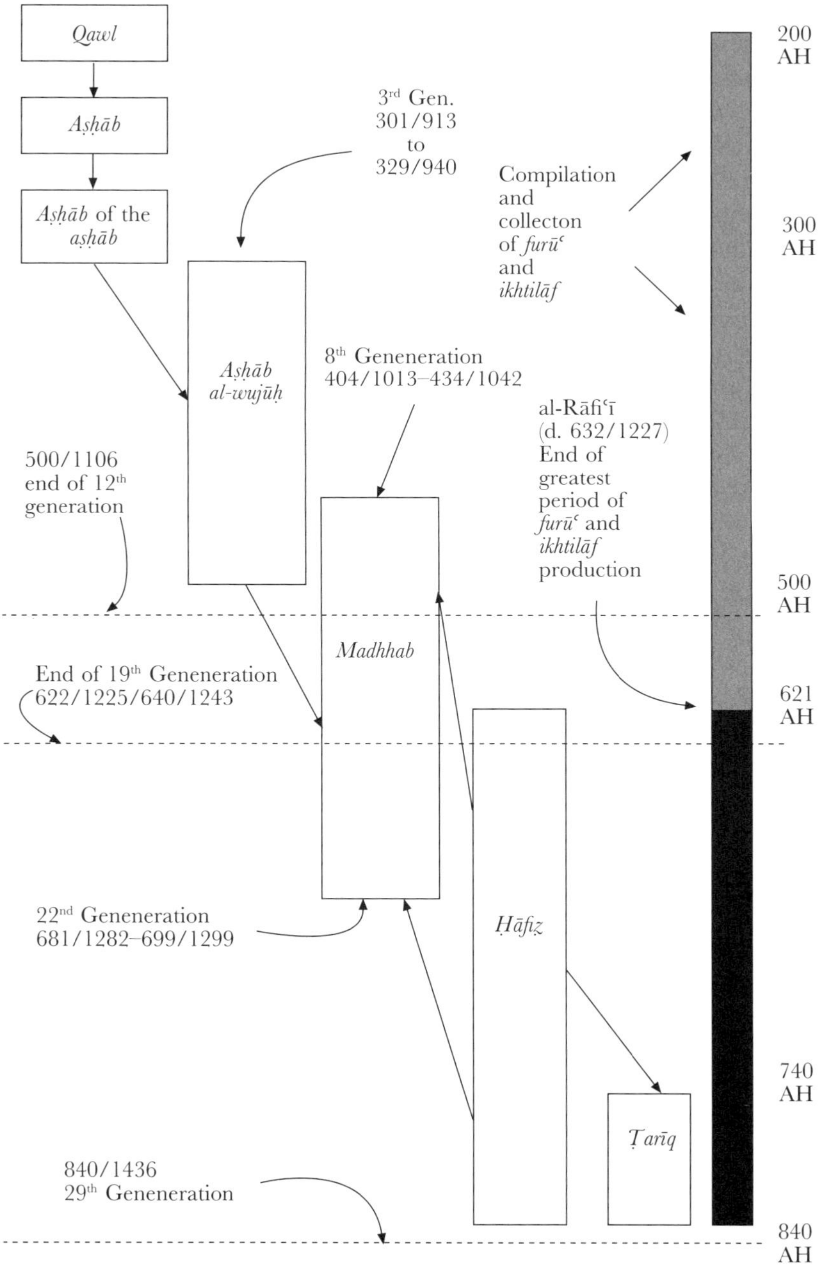

What clearly dominates for Ibn Qāḍī Shuhbah is the existence and transmission of divergent substantive rules. *Ikhtilāf* remains a constant in Ibn Qāḍī Shuhbah's history, although it declines after the end of the *aṣḥāb al-wujūh* period. Without the clear and constant transmission of divergent substantive rules, jurists would have no means for conducting legal affairs. Thus, while one may guess this decline to be distressing to Ibn Qāḍī Shuhbah, there is no hint of it in the text. There is simply the admission that decline has occurred and that the means of maintaining the law, given the lack of jurists of greater ability, is the continuing living divergent substantive legal tradition.

Conclusion

The preceding indicates that Ibn Qāḍī Shuhbah understood there to have been trends in legal training, and that while *ijtihād* continued to be practiced, the vast majority of jurists relied on divergent substantive rules as contained in the authoritative texts transmitted by the jurists he mentions. Ibn Qāḍī Shuhbah's text is not concerned with cataloguing *mujtahid*s as was al-Shīrāzī's, but in outlining those jurists who, given the decline of the *madhhab* in all of its senses, have been considered reliable transmitters of divergent substantive rules. Thus Ibn Qāḍī Shuhbah's text serves the double purpose of providing a historical picture of intellectual trends in the Shāfiʿī school (at least as Ibn Qāḍī Shuhbah understood them) and of giving jurists of his and later generations a reference work upon which they could authoritatively base legal rulings.

Not all *ṭabaqāt* texts are suitable for this type of analysis, but, given the proliferation of *ṭabaqāt* in the medieval period, they are an excellent source, when taken on their own merits, for understanding how jurists of the period understood the situation of the school. The central purpose of this chapter has been to understand how Ibn Qāḍī Shuhbah understood the historical development of the Shāfiʿī *madhhab*.

Progressive analysis has made Ibn Qāḍī Shuhbah's views important to the debates outlined in the introduction of this chapter. According to Ibn Qāḍī Shuhbah there never were many scholars who rose to the level of *ijtihād*. The greatest concentration of them, the *aṣḥāb al-wujūh*, disappeared after the twelfth century, but this does not appear to present a problem for the continuing discovery of law. The above analysis of Ibn Qāḍī Shuhbah's historical argument both confirms and qualifies aspects of Hallaq's view, while it also clearly disagrees with Schacht's view that *ijtihād* ended after the beginning of the tenth century.

Hallaq and Ibn Qāḍī Shuhbah argue that while *ijtihād* was rare, it did not disappear. Where Hallaq disagrees with Ibn Qāḍī Shuhbah is over the importance of *ijtihād*. Hallaq argues that jurists not normally qualified to be called *mujtahid*s continued to perform *ijtihād*-like activities without calling it such. Ibn Qāḍī Shuhbah, following al-Nawawī, seems to argue that God would not allow the community to go without proper guidance in times of need. *Mujtahid*s never fully disappear nor does the ability to perform *ijtihād* in the proper sense. He relies, therefore, on the faith that when the community needs a *mujtahid*, God will provide one. *Ijtihād*, at least in the way that most scholars seem to think of the practice, does not seem necessary to discover new rules. *Furūʿ* production, though declining, occurs in the absence of *mujtahid*s. They exist to respond to larger theoretical issues that author jurists cannot answer, but author jurists are still capable of functioning in their absence on other kinds of issues.

The larger issue that concerns Ibn Qāḍī Shuhbah has to do with the decline in the number of low and middle level scholars that can carry-out minimal levels of legal reasoning and still maintain the function of Islamic law in society. Comparing the way that he presents legal education with the production of *furūʿ* provides an important insight into the crisis that he sees as gripping the medieval legal community. Figure 5.10 shows that in early Islam there was a gap between *tafaqqaha* training and the production of *furūʿ*. In this period, there was, nevertheless, a relationship between the rise and fall in *furūʿ* and similar ebbs and flows in *tafaqqaha* relationships. Ibn Qāḍī Shuhbah suggests, therefore, that the decline in law had less to do with a supposed decline in *ijtihād* and more to do with a reduction in the intensive personal legal training that he prizes so highly.

The problem becomes more apparent when one compares trends in *furūʿ* with *akhadha* and *darasa/darrasa* training in *madrasah*s. Figure 5.11 shows that as *akhadha* relationships and *madrasah* training increase there is a decrease in the production of *furūʿ*. This even occurs given the sharp increase in the number of scholars who earn permissions to issue legal rulings as a result of training in the *madrasah* setting.

Figure 5.10. Comparison between *tafaqqaha* and *furūʿ*

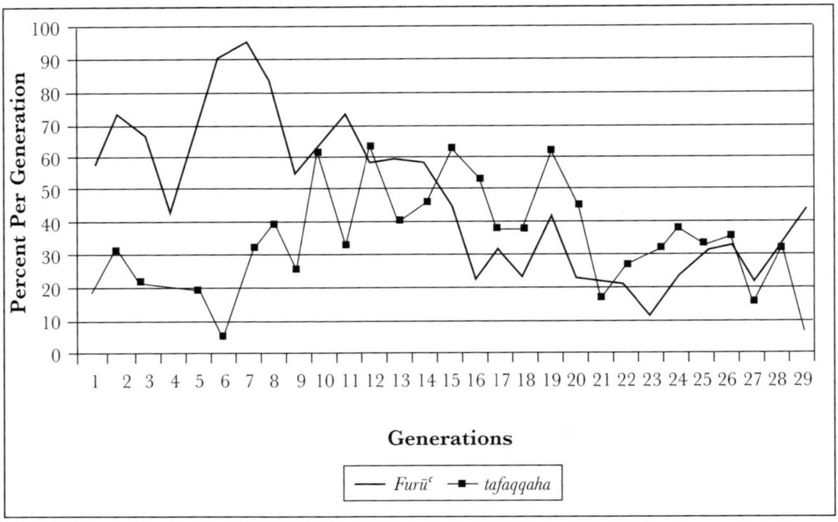

Source: Ibn Qāḍī Shuhbah, *Ṭabaqāt al-fuqahāʾ al-shāfiʿīyah*, ed. al-Ḥāfiẓ ʿAbd al-Alī Khān, 4 vols. (Beirut: ʿĀlam al-kutub, 1987).

Ibn Qāḍī Shuhbah indicates that the reduction in juridical abilities is tied directly to shifts in educational culture that prize individualized bonds of loyalty *and* certifications earned in group settings. Both lack the integrity of what he sees as traditional legal education that is exemplified in *tafaqqaha*. *Ijtihād*, or the lack thereof, is not the cause of decline, or even an issue for him. Basic knowledge of legal rules, and thus the need for attention to *ikhtilāf*, lies at the heart of the crisis.

Figure 5.11. Comparison between *furūʿ* production and *akhadha* and *darasa/darrasa*

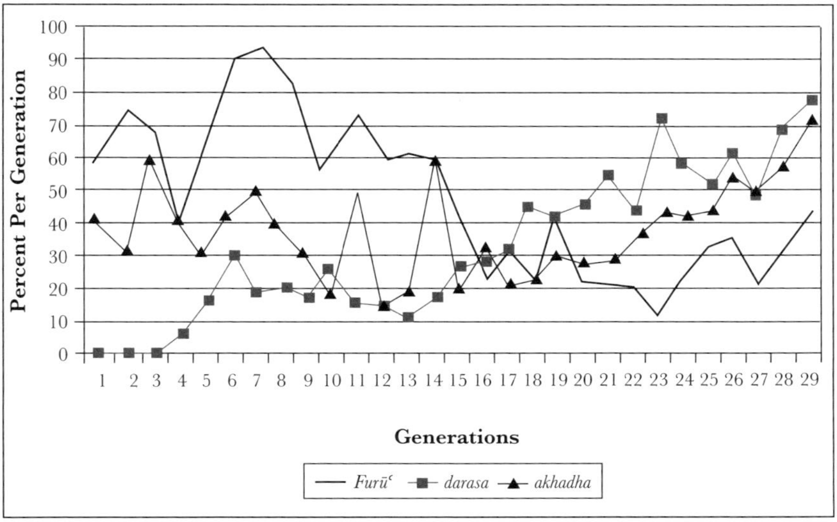

Source: Ibn Qāḍī Shuhbah, *Ṭabaqāt al-fuqahā' al-shāfiʿīyah*, ed. al-Ḥāfiẓ ʿAbd al-Alī Khān, 4 vols. (Beirut: ʿĀlam al-kutub, 1987).

CHAPTER SIX

THE DEVELOPMENT OF LEGAL METHODOLOGIES AND THE DECLINE OF LEGAL THINKING

The decline in legal thought that is exemplified by the drop in *furūʿ* production, prompted Ibn Qāḍī Shuhbah to point contemporary and future jurists to *ikhtilāf* texts from which author jurists could draw in order to discover new rules. It has been suggested, however, that 'decline' could not have taken place during the period because specialized training in *uṣūl al-fiqh* was too easy to obtain.[1] Many of the jurists in this period should not, according to this view, be understood as deficient and were in fact practitioners of *ijtihād*-like methods.[2] Indeed, on one level Ibn Qāḍī Shuhbah seems to have an ambiguous view of legal decline. He charts the continuing existence of *mujtahid*s, although how this is connected to the production of *furūʿ* is unclear. In fact, he never refers to the discourse, popular in his day, which so insistently claimed that those certified to discover law no longer existed.

Through the progressive development of the text, Ibn Qāḍī Shuhbah shows that at the very time memorization of *fiqh* became the norm, specializations in legal method became more common. Although he pays comparatively little attention to legal methodology as a discrete discipline, the majority of jurists engaged in *uṣūl al-fiqh* are active during the worst of the calamities of the Mamlūk period.

As figure 6.1 shows below, there was a general downward trend in the average lifespan of jurists beginning between the eighteenth and nineteenth generations (606/1209 to 640/1243) when the age at death began to decline from 72. This occurred at the same time that there was a marked increase in the number of scholars who specialized in *uṣūl al-fiqh* and allied sciences, from eleven to twenty-seven percent. The initial drop in age at death is due to the first incursions of the Mongols into central Asia and their destruction of

---

1 Wael Hallaq, "Was the Gate of *Ijtihād* Closed?," 3–5.

2 Hallaq, *Authority, Continuity and Change in Islamic law*, 218–41.

Figure 6.1. The average age of death (in years) for scholars listed in the text and percentage of scholars who engage in *uṣūl al-fiqh*

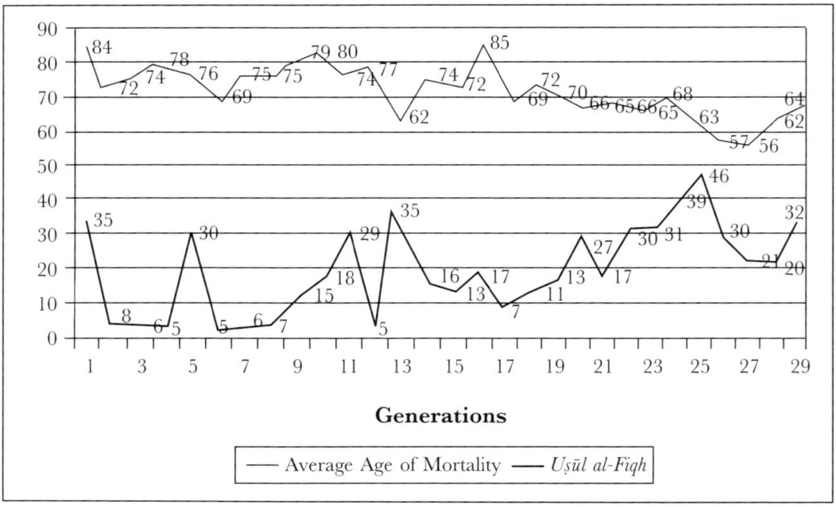

Source: Ibn Qāḍī Shuhbah, *Ṭabaqāt al-fuqahā' al-shāfi'īyah*, ed. al-Ḥāfiẓ 'Abd al-Alī Khān, 4 vols. (Beirut: 'Ālam al-kutub, 1987).
Note: Figures for practitioners of *uṣūl al-fiqh* and allied sciences are derived from the percentage of people in each generation who are described as being involved in one or more activities that would fall under the categories (see below for more details). The age of death is based on the average age at death for all biographies in each generation and is based on information in entries where an age is given, or more commonly, when a year and birth and death are provided.

many Muslim cities, most importantly Nīsāpūr (sacked in 618/1221). Arab chroniclers claimed that over 1,747,000 people were killed, a number that is obviously inflated, but nevertheless speaks to the fear and devastation that the Mongols caused.[3] This was followed by a second sudden drop between the twenty-fourth and twenty-sixth generations (721/1321 to 780/1379) when the average declined from 68 to 57. As will be explained below, the drastic die-off that occurred in the period is a result of the plague which devastated the ranks of the jurists during this period. The mortality rate during the plagues was so high, as is evident in the decline in average age, that educational lineages were severed in the majority of cases.

[3] David Morgan, *The Mongols* (New York: Basil Blackwell, 1986), 74–75.

Ibn Qāḍī Shuhbah links the sudden drop in average age at death with the rise of specializations in *uṣūl al-fiqh* and allied genres of knowledge, and its impact on the development of Islamic law. He, while explicitly arguing for the importance of a basic types of legal methods, nonetheless shows that the kinds of legal methods that developed later in Shāfiʿī legal history were nothing more than tangential specializations that took scholars away from the real object of the legal profession—the rules themselves. This idea is developed throughout his text by the progressive development of *uṣūl al-fiqh* from the basic, non-speculative method of *Imām* al-Shāfiʿī, to the rise of speculative forms of legal methodology. Through the use of rhetorical strategies such as 'terminological association,' Ibn Qāḍī Shuhbah describes a variety of sub-schools of legal methodology whose primary purpose was not the discovery of law, but evolved out of theologically inclined jurists' interests in theoretical problems. Over time, the interest in non-rules-based sciences overshadowed the legal profession, leading jurists away from legal rules just as social, political, environmental, and religious problems began depleting the ranks of the jurists. As a result, there occurred a general decline in the abilities of jurists and a reduction in the production of substantive rules.

The early development of legal method: al-Shāfiʿī's uṣūl

As mentioned in the last chapter, the development of *uṣūl al-fiqh* has become one of the primary fields of inquiry for historians of Islamic law. The development of a coherent and well-articulated methodology is understood to indicate the establishment of jurisprudence in the proper sense. Therefore, modern scholars, in seeking to locate the origins of law, have attempted to establish when a coherent and well-articulated methodology of jurisprudence first arose in order to define the historical boundaries of the existence of Islamic jurisprudence. The rationale for this argument originated in Joseph Schacht's *The Origins of Muhammadan Jurisprudence*.[4] Schacht argued that al-Shāfiʿī,

[4] *The Origins of Muhammadan Jurisprudence* (Oxford: Clarendon Press, 1950). The issue of al-Shāfiʿī's contribution to the development of a well-articulated and coherent legal method was first raised by Goldziher in 1884. He argued that al-Shāfiʿī was reacting to the method first established by Abū Ḥanīfah, thereby attempting to control the use of analogical reasoning on the part of jurists. See his *The Ẓahiris: Their Doctrine and Their History*, ed. and trans. Wolfgang Behn (Leiden: E. J. Brill, 1971).

through his *Risālah*, was the first to establish a coherent and well-articulated system of legal methods. Al-Shāfiʿī succeeded in this because he was the first to draw together various theoretical and theological ideas in such a way that allowed for the interpolation of certain basic forms of reason into a tradition (*ḥadīth*) centered legal philosophy.[5]

George Makdisi has argued that while the Islamic tradition sees al-Shāfiʿī as the founder of legal method, it actually dates to before the writing of the *Risālah*.[6] Early method, however, was not referred to as *uṣūl al-fiqh*, which did not come into vogue for several centuries after al-Shāfiʿī. Early on, Makdisi argues, *uṣūl* referred to *furūʿ* until as late as the fourth/tenth century. The early references to *uṣūl* indicated maxims, elements, and rules of law, not method in the proper sense. While methodological issues were discussed, this was not done in the systematized forms found in later methodological texts.[7]

Makdisi agrees with Schacht that the *Risālah* was a text on legal method. He, however, sees the text as al-Shāfiʿī's attempt to control the use of analogical reasoning (*qiyās*) and make it subservient to his pronounced focus on *ḥadīth* as the central source of Islamic law.[8] Then why was al-Shāfiʿī's text ignored by Shāfiʿī jurists for over two centuries, and why does the *Risālah* not examine many of the issues found in later *uṣūl al-fiqh* texts? Makdisi admits that the text was originally ignored but argues that the reason for the eventual rehabilitation of the *Risālah* as the founding *uṣūl* text has more to do with the anti-rationalist position of the work than its examination of legal method. Makdisi contends that a pro-traditionalist backlash began in the aftermath of the anti-traditionalist inquisition of the early ninth century. Over time traditionalists, needing to couch their anti-rationalist arguments in the authority of some prestigious scholar, latched onto the *Risālah* and its elevation of tradition over reason as

---

[5] Schacht, *Origins*, 4–7.

[6] This text has been published in various editions, in both English and Arabic. For an English edition, see Majid Khadduri, trans., *al-Shāfiʿī's Risāla* (Baltimore: Johns Hopkins Press, 1961; reprint Cambridge: The Islamic Texts Society, 1987). For an Arabic edition, see Muḥammad Idrīs al-Shāfiʿī, *al-Risālah*, ed. Aḥmad Muḥammad Shākir (Cairo: Maṭbaʿat Muṣṭafā al-Bābī al-Ḥalabī, 1940).

[7] George Makdisi, "The Juridical Theology of Shāfiʿī: Origins and Significance of Uṣūl al-Fiqh," *Studia Islamica* 59 (1984): 9–12.

[8] Ibid., 12.

a tool to suppress rationalism within the school.[9] The irony, according to Makdisi, of the success of the traditionalist suppression of rationalism, is that rationalist theologians were forced to go underground and resurface as neo-traditionalist specialists in legal methodology. In doing so, they created what later became to be known as the discipline of *uṣūl al-fiqh*.[10]

Wael Hallaq disagrees with Schacht's and Makdisi's contention that al-Shāfiʿī was the founder of a tradition-centered system of legal method. He argues that the *Risālah* does not present a legal method as such, but simply seeks to establish the primacy of revelation as the source from which jurists must discover law.[11] Furthermore, Hallaq disagrees with Makdisi's assumption that al-Shāfiʿī saw himself as the defender of tradition over reason. He argues that, while al-Shāfiʿī was later claimed by the traditionalists as their champion, he actually trained with Muʿtazilī rationalists. According to Hallaq, the actual founder of a well-articulated and coherent legal method was Ibn Surayj, who, in doing so, combined knowledge of theology with that of law.[12] Thus, Hallaq has the founding of the Shāfiʿī school occurring with Ibn Surayj and his students, who were the first to write *uṣūl* texts similar to the ones that came to dominate later methodological discourse.

Makdisi, however, differentiates between the method of al-Shāfiʿī and the methodologies of later *uṣūl* texts by citing Fakhr al-Dīn al-Rāzī (d. 606/1209), who argues that the science al-Shāfiʿī established was different from what developed in the tenth and eleventh centuries. According to al-Rāzī, al-Shāfiʿī's science was *ʿilm al-sharʿ*, or the 'science of revelation,' as opposed to later formulations of *uṣūl* which he referred to as *ʿilm al-ʿaql*, or the 'science of reason.' The science of reason was what the theologians who infiltrated the schools of law performed. This was a decidedly different operation from the science of revelation, which was focused on finding the rules of living from the texts of the Qurʾan and *sunnah*.[13] Throughout this chapter I will draw a distinction between the 'method' of al-Shāfiʿī and the

---

[9] Ibid., 12–14.
[10] Ibid., 45.
[11] Wael Hallaq, "Was Shāfiʿī the Master Architect of Islamic Jurisprudence?" *International Journal of Middle Eastern Studies* 25 (1993): 592.
[12] Ibid., 597–98.
[13] Makdisi, "Juridical Theology," 13.

'methodologies' of speculative jurisprudence. I will contend that al-Shāfiʿī's method, although rather simplistic, was designed specifically as a tool for jurists to use in discovering new substantive rules.[14] It is the simplicity of his method, in fact, that attracted initial notice and led to its use by jurists. The methodologies of the speculative scholars, however, were concerned more with explicating their assumptions about the nature of revelation and reason, and less with legal discovery.[15]

Ibn Qāḍī Shuhbah's depiction of uṣūl al-fiqh

With all of the attention paid by modern scholars to a coherent and well-articulated legal method as the *sine qua non* of Islamic law, it is surprising that Ibn Qāḍī Shuhbah would pay so little attention to it. Legal rules—not legal method—dominate his description of the Shāfiʿī school. He discusses the transmission of substantive rules (*furūʿ*) in 41% (322) of the biographies. When combined with jurists specializing in *fiqh* as a discrete discipline, the total number of biographies rises to 750. The study of *uṣūl al-fiqh* in any capacity is mentioned in only 202 biographies, and only 19 jurists are mentioned as being engaged in *uṣūl* as a discrete professional discipline of law. What Ibn Qāḍī Shuhbah says about legal method and methodology is revealing of his historical understanding of the role of *uṣūl al-fiqh* and its allied fields of study in the development of trends in Islamic law.

In the first generation of scholars who studied with al-Shāfiʿī, only al-Muzanī is specifically mentioned as being involved with legal method.[16] The passage, referred to in chapter three, concerns the debate as to whether al-Muzanī actually followed al-Shāfiʿī's method in the discovery of rules. The term '*uṣūl*' is used to define method.

---

[14] For an interesting discussion of the *Risālah* and its contents and purposes, see Joseph Lowry, "Does Shāfiʿī have a theory of 'Four Sources' of Law?," in *Studies in Islamic Legal Theory*, ed. Bernard Weiss (Boston: Brill, 2002), 23–50, especially 45–49. Also see David Vishanoff, "Early Islamic Hermeneutics: Language, Speech, and Meaning in Preclassical Legal Theory" (Ph.D. diss., Emory University, 2004), 31–48.

[15] See Mohammad Fadel, "'*Istiḥsān* is nine-tenth of the Law,' 164. Fadel mentions that prominent Shāfiʿī *uṣūlīs* were frequently more interested in legal theory than legal rules.

[16] Khān, vol. 1, 58–59.

Ibn Qāḍī Shuhbah concludes that al-Muzanī indeed followed al-Shāfiʿī's method even though his opinions as to the rules differed.

Abū ʿUbayd al-Baghdādī (d. 224/838–39) is also described as "studying the legal sciences" with al-Shāfiʿī,[17] and in the biographies of three other jurists it is implied they studied method with al-Shāfiʿī. These three, al-Ḥārith b. Surayj (d. 236/850–51),[18] al-Zaʿfarānī (d. 260/874),[19] and al-Rabīʿ al-Murādī[20] are said to have transmitted the *Risālah* from al-Shāfiʿī to other people.

Al-Karābīsī (d. 245/859–60) is described as having written many books of *uṣūl (al-fiqh)*. This, however, as Makdisi mentioned above, does not mean that his books were necessarily devoted to method. For instance, the second-generation jurist Muḥammad b. Aḥmad al-Tirmidhī (d. 295/907), is described as writing a book entitled *Ikhtilāf ahl al-ṣalāh* (The Disagreement of the People of Prayer), which Ibn Qāḍī Shuhbah says is a book on *uṣūl*. He goes on to say, however, that the text concerns *waqf*s (testamentary endowments) and is therefore, not a methods manual.[21]

In the third generation, only Ibn Surayj is mentioned as specifically being involved in *uṣūl*. Ibn Qāḍī Shuhbah describes him as being the "author of *uṣūl*" (*ṣāḥib al-uṣūl*).[22] This, in light of Hallaq's comments above, is an interesting statement. While none of Ibn Surayj's students are described as studying *uṣūl* from him, his intellectual descendants over the following seven generations account for 9 of 17 scholars mentioned as studying or writing about *uṣūl*.[23] All but two of the remaining eight jurists are intellectually descended from Ibn Surayj's teacher, al-Anmāṭī.[24] None, however, are described as studying *uṣūl* with an identified teacher. Why is this the case?

It may be that Ibn Qāḍī Shuhbah did not know with whom any of these scholars may have studied *uṣūl*. For instance, in the *ṭabaqāt* texts of Ibn al-Ṣalāḥ and al-Subkī, no teachers of *uṣūl* are mentioned

---

17 Ibid., vol. 1, 67.
18 Ibid., vol. 1, 60.
19 Ibid., vol. 1, 62.
20 Ibid., vol. 1, 65–66.
21 Ibid., vol. 1, 82–83. The work in not listed in the *Fihrist* of Ibn al-Nadīm, or in Brockelmann.
22 Ibid., vol. 1, 90.
23 Ibid., vol. 1, 105–06, 124–25, 126, 127, 132, 173, 225–26, 230–32.
24 Who is not mentioned as studying or otherwise being involved with method (ibid., vol. 1, 80).

for these jurists.[25] This is an important indicator of what later jurists' understanding of the early state of Shāfiʿī legal method was (not to mention how it may have actually been), and how it compares with later formulations of *uṣūl al-fiqh*. Ibn Qāḍī Shuhbah uses three verbs to describe education between the seventeen jurists and their teachers in the seven generations following Ibn Surayj. He states that they studied law (*tafaqqaha*, or *darasa*), or more generally studied legal rules (*akhadha fiqh*). Abū al-Ḥusayn al-Qaṭṭān (d. 359/970) is described as having al-Shīrāzī study legal science (*akhadha al-ʿilm*) from him.[26] There is no specific mention of method. This indicates that in the early period, at least for the jurists Ibn Qāḍī Shuhbah lists, rules and method were not separate disciplines in his portrayal. Ibn Qāḍī Shuhbah indicates that *uṣūl al-fiqh*, while explicitly different from *furūʿ* in terms of literary output (for instance, al-Qaṭṭān is described as writing books of *furūʿ* and *uṣūl al-fiqh*),[27] was not yet taught as a separate field, and no certificates or permissions were yet issued in methodological specializations.

So what was the method these jurists learned and applied? Ibn Qāḍī Shuhbah does not give a specific indication. When he characterizes early *uṣūl*, Ibn Qāḍī Shuhbah says it reflects the "opinion of al-Shāfiʿī" (*madhhab al-Shāfiʿī*),[28] or is based on commentaries on the *Risālah*.[29] As stated above, the kinds of terms Ibn Qāḍī Shuhbah combines indicate important networks of meaning; that Ibn Qāḍī Shuhbah does not characterize the legal method transmitted from al-Shāfiʿī through al-Muzanī and al-Rabīʿ to al-Anmāṭī and Ibn Surayj, and then to their students, as anything but that which is reflective of al-Shāfiʿī's methodological opinion, indicates that he understood these early jurists to have practiced the rudimentary forms of method outlined in the *Risālah*.

The kind of legal method these early jurists would have studied is based on al-Shāfiʿī's concept of '*bayān*.' According to Joseph Lowry, *bayān* rests on two sources of law, the Qur'an and the *sunnah*. Substantive rules can be discovered from these texts in five possible

[25] See Ibn al-Ṣalāḥ, *Ṭabaqāt al-fuqahā' al-shāfiʿīyah* and al-Subkī, *Ṭabaqāt al-shāfiʿīyah al-kubrā*, vol. 2.
[26] Khān, vol. 1, 124.
[27] Ibid.
[28] Ibid., 167.
[29] Ibid., 126.

combinations: 1) Qur'an alone, 2) Qur'an and *sunnah* together when they express an identical rule, 3) Qur'an and *sunnah*, when the *sunnah* explains what is in the Qur'an, 4) *sunnah* by itself, and 5) neither, which forces the jurists to fall back on some form of interpretation,[30] primarily driven by three basic forms of *qiyās*.[31] Lowry contends that al-Shāfiʿī does not develop a clear and coherent legal epistemology in any one section of the text, but does so in a disorganized fashion in several places. He concludes, however, that because al-Shāfiʿī's method relies entirely on the texts of revelation there are some legal questions that cannot be fully answered and can only be subjectively known. Thus, al-Shāfiʿī purposefully places limits on the kinds of speculation in which jurists may engage due to the frailties of human reason and the inexactness of the language of revelation.[32]

The rise of ʿulūm al-ʿaql *(the sciences of reason)*

Ibn Qāḍī Shuhbah contrasts the seventeen jurists who studied *ʿilm al-sharʿ* in the seven generations following Ibn Surayj, with five others he describes as being jurists (*fuqahā'*, sing. *faqīh*), practitioners of *uṣūl* (*uṣūlīyah*, sing. *uṣūlī*), and theologians (*mutakallimūn*, sing. *mutakallim*). In these biographies he draws specific associations between the three professional designations and thereby implies that these jurists developed a legal methodology distinct from that of al-Shāfiʿī. The first jurist in which there is an association between methodology and theology is Abū Bakr al-Shāshī (d. 365/976). He is described as "one of the leaders of the Muslims," who studied from Ibn Surayj. Ibn Qāḍī Shuhbah says that al-Shāshī also wrote a "good book about *uṣūl al-fiqh*" and a commentary on the *Risālah*, from which it "communicated (*intashar*) the *fiqh* (understanding) of al-Shāfiʿī in what it transmitted." He is also described as being the most knowledgeable of the people (*ahl*) in what was transmitted concerning *uṣūl*, in his age" (the sixth generation, 362/972–380/991).[33] Throughout the passage, Ibn Qāḍī Shuhbah indicates that al-Shāshī specialized in al-Shāfiʿī's method. He is listed as studying *kalām* and *uṣūl*, but is not

[30] Lowry, "The Legal-Theoretical Content of the *Risālah*," 19–20.
[31] Ibid., 211–18.
[32] Ibid., 317–59.
[33] Khān, vol. 1, 148–49.

mentioned as being a speculative theologian. To the contrary, he is described as being a student of *ḥadīth*, in which he was as expert as he was theology.[34]

Ismāʿīl b. Aḥmad al-Jurjānī (d. 396/1006, in the seventh generation) is also associated with method and theology. Unlike al-Shāshī, however, he is not associated by Ibn Qāḍī Shuhbah with *ḥadīth* or with al-Shāfiʿī's method. The influence of theology on al-Jurjānī's view of method cannot be discerned from the biography.[35]

The next jurist that Ibn Qāḍī Shuhbah mentions as combining theology and method is Abū Isḥāq al-Isfarāʾīnī (d. 418/1027, in the eighth generation). Ibn Qāḍī Shuhbah argues that al-Isfarāʾīnī is the founder of a theologically inclined legal methodology because all later speculative jurists are intellectually descended from him and his students. He is described as "a *mutakallim*, an *uṣūlī*, and a *faqīh* who was the master of the people of Khurāsān." Ibn Qāḍī Shuhbah, however, did not see al-Isfarāʾīnī in a favorable light. He begins his negative assertions by stating that "it is said that he rose to the level of *ijtihād*." By attributing the elevation to independent reason to an unspecified third party, Ibn Qāḍī Shuhbah implies that this should be doubted. In most cases Ibn Qāḍī Shuhbah would simply declare "he rose to the level of *ijtihād*" if he had meant to imply acceptance of the claim. In addition, Ibn Qāḍī Shuhbah does not list any of al-Isfarāʾīnī's teachers or mention any of the subjects he studied; he does not even discuss any of the books al-Isfarāʾīnī may have studied. This type of omission is extremely rare, and occurs in only about 6% of all biographies. Ibn Qāḍī Shuhbah seems to argue that al-Isfarāʾīnī developed his abilities and ideas *ex nihilo* and thus they cannot be traced to al-Shāfiʿī.[36]

Theologically, al-Isfarāʾīnī is described as being a contemporary of al-Bāqillānī (d. 403/1013) and Ibn Fūrak. Al-Bāqillānī, the more famous of the two, was a Mālikī jurist and leading Ashʿarite theologian. He wrote several books on theology that have come down to

---

[34] Ibid.

[35] Ibid., 154–55.

[36] Ibid., 170–71. There are, of course other possible reasons why al-Isfarāʾinī might not have studied with teachers. He may, for instance, have studied from books instead. The point here, however, is the way that Ibn Qāḍī Shuhbah uses the material to shape a particular view of the scholar and his relationship to other individuals.

present.[37] The three together are described as leading followers of the school of al-Ashʿarī (d. 324/935).[38] Al-Ashʿarī was a Mālikī jurist whom Ibn Qāḍī Shuhbah describes as a Shāfiʿī, and whom he includes in his *Ṭabaqāt*.[39] He is described as the "leader of the theologians," who was originally a member of the Muʿtazilī school of theology. Late in life, however, he rejected the rationalist ideas of the Muʿtazilah and, according to Ibn Qāḍī Shuhbah, devoted himself to refuting the views of the rationalists. Ibn Qāḍī Shuhbah quotes al-Isfarāʾīnī as saying that "al-Ashʿarī studied law with Abū Isḥāq al-Marwazī, who studied theology with al-Ashʿarī." Quoting al-Isfarāʾīnī, however, is meant to discredit the idea that al-Marwazī studied theology, which is not mentioned in his biography; this is important for Ibn Qāḍī Shuhbah given al-Marwazī's crucial role in the transmission of divergent opinions.[40]

Throughout the final section of his biography of al-Ashʿarī, Ibn Qāḍī Shuhbah stresses the close connection between Abū Isḥāq al-Isfarāʾīnī, Ibn Fūrak, and al-Ashʿarī, who are described as belonging to "the generations of theologians who are Shāfiʿite Ashʿarīs (*al-Ashʿarī Shāfiʿī*),"[41] meaning that they were theologians first and jurists second. This statement, however, is not a praise, especially when Ibn Qāḍī Shuhbah's quotation of al-Ṣāḥib b. ʿAbbād (d. 385/995) is considered. Using a strategy common throughout the text, Ibn Qāḍī Shuhbah seeks to damn individuals indirectly by quoting third party sources. In this instance, he quotes al-Ṣāḥib b. ʿAbbād, who says that "al-Bāqillānī is a sea that drowns, Ibn Fūrak is a viper with his head bowed ready to strike, and al-Isfarāʾīnī is a fire that burns."[42] Ṣāḥib b. ʿAbbād was a Būyid *wazīr* under Rukn al-Dawlah. He also studied literature and patronized a number of Shāfiʿī scholars. He was a

[37] For a full description see Richard Martin and Mark Woodward, *Defenders of Reason in Islam* (Oxford: Oneworld Publications, 1997), 33.
[38] Khān, vol. 1, 171. Al-Subkī, in his *Ṭabaqāt al-shāfiʿīyah al-kubrā* also lists al-Ashʿarī as a Shāfiʿī (vol. 2, 245) but Muḥammad b. Muḥammad al-Makhlūf includes him in his *Shajarat al-nūr al-zakīyah fī ṭabaqāt al-mālikīyah* (Beirut: Dār al-fikr li ʾl-ṭibāʿah wa ʾl-nashr wa ʾl-tawzīʿ, n.d.), vol. 1, 79. Also see Ibn al-ʿImād al-Ḥanbalī, *Shadharāt al-dhahab fī akhbār min dhahab* (Beirut: Dār al-kutub al-ʿilmīyah, 1998), vol. 2, 506–09.
[39] Khān, vol. 1, 113–14.
[40] Ibid., 105–06.
[41] Ibid., 114.
[42] Ibid., vol. 1, 171.

patron of the Muʿtazilīs and may have made the statement to condemn their views on a particular theological issue.[43] By closely associating al-Bāqillānī, Ibn Fūrak, and al-Isfarā'īnī with al-Ashʿarī, he condemns all with this quotation and therefore devalues not only theology, but theologically-inclined legal methodology as well. In effect, he argues that theology, especially when mixed with law, is destructive and ultimately leads to hell's fire.

The condemnation of the combination of theology and law is further established through Ibn Qāḍī Shuhbah's quotation from Ibn Surayj, who has the jurist saying "rarely have I seen among the students of law one who studied theology and succeeded. He neither excels in the law nor achieves knowledge of theology."[44] Given that Ibn Surayj is seen as one of the main transmitters of al-Shāfiʿī's basic method of legal analysis, this is a powerful disapproval of the insertion of theological speculation into legal method. In this respect, Ibn Qāḍī Shuhbah would seem to contradict the contention that Ibn Surayj combined theology and law to form a new style of legal method. Because of the central role Ibn Surayj played in both the transmission of al-Shāfiʿī's legal method and substantive rules (from al-Rabīʿ through al-Anmāṭī) and divergent rules from al-Muzanī, it is hardly surprising that Ibn Qāḍī Shuhbah would seek to insulate Ibn Surayj from the taint of theological speculation.

The development of sub-schools of legal method

By the eleventh generation (460/1068–480/1088) the study of methodology had become a standardized part of the 'curriculum' of Islamic legal education. Whether the study occurred in a *madrasah* or was acquired through the less formal *akhadha* relationship is not yet clear.[45] This legal methodology was not the kind that the earlier generations appear to have studied, but became a highly sophisticated and largely speculative enterprise. Many *uṣūl al-fiqh* texts claim that new rules can be discovered only through the use of speculative (meaning theologically inclined) legal method.[46] These statements have been taken

---

[43] See Ibn 'Abbād's full biography in al-Dhahabī, *Tārīkh al-islām*, vol. 26, 92–98.
[44] Khān, vol. 1, 90.
[45] Chamberlain, *Knowledge and Social Practice in Medieval Damascus*, 83–87; George Makdisi, *The Rise of Colleges*, 78.
[46] See Vishanoff, 22–30. Also see Aḥmad b. 'Alī al-Rāzī al-Jaṣṣāṣ, *al-Fuṣūl fī al-*

at face value by modern scholars who have assumed these jurists spoke for the legal profession as a whole. Frequently, the opinions of al-Shīrāzī, al-Ghazālī, and al-Āmidī are quoted as stating that *ijtihād* is a necessary obligation for the jurists to fulfill in all ages.[47] *Ijtihād* is directly tied to speculative methodology, stating that, in effect, specialization in speculative methodology leads to the ability of independent reasoning. This, however, exposes a basic contradiction, for as was seen above, it is argued on the one hand that *uṣūl al-fiqh* did not exist before the tenth century, but on the other hand, *mujtahid*s did; if so, how is it that they were able to discover law without methods of discovery? Devin Stewart, while disagreeing with the contention that *uṣūl al-fiqh* as a genre did not exist before the tenth century, nonetheless, sees speculative methodologies as a genre which,

> more than any other, defines and acts as a forum for the 'thought collective' of the jurists, a community of interpretation with shared goals, assumptions, and ways of thinking operating within particular institutional constraints. Despite the differences of opinion expressed therein, the genre of jurisprudence nevertheless set the boundaries and the framework for Islamic legal discourse from the tenth century on.[48]

Ibn Qāḍī Shuhbah indicates, however, that several different genres of legal methodology were studied, ranging from the rudimentary or practical method of al-Shāfiʿī to other forms of speculative methodologies, influenced by theology. If *uṣūl al-fiqh* was a necessary component of legal discovery, Ibn Qāḍī Shuhbah's presentation suggests that there was a range of methodologies and there was little consensus about the kinds of methodology that were necessary.

According to Ibn Qāḍī Shuhbah's presentation, the backbone of legal discovery was the method of al-Shāfiʿī. He indicates that this method was so basic that it was not taught as a field separate from that of legal rules, but was an aspect of specialization in *fiqh* itself. This is indicated in a number of ways: 1) Ibn Qāḍī Shuhbah refers to al-Shāfiʿī's method as being synonymous with his *fiqh,* that is, his understanding of law is tied directly to his method;[49] 2) he does not

Uṣūl (Kuwait: Wazārat al-awqāf wa 'l-shu'ūn al-islāmīyah, 1994), vol. 1, 40–49 and Ibn Imām al-Kāmilīyah, *Taysīr al-wuṣūl ijā minhāj al-uṣūl min al-manqūl wa 'l-maʿqūl "al-Mukhtaṣar,"* ed. ʿAbd al-Fattāḥ Aḥmad Quṭb al-Dukhmīsī (Cairo: al-Fārūq al-ḥadīthīyah li 'l-ṭibaʿah wa 'l-nashr, 2002), vol. 1, 278–307.

[47] Hallaq, "Was the Gate of *Ijtihād* Closed?," 6–7.

[48] Stewart, *Islamic Legal Orthodoxy*, 30.

[49] Khān, vol. 1, 149.

separate the study of method from law in the first ten generations of al-Shāfiʿī's intellectual descendants, indicating, rather, that they were two aspects of the same discipline; and 3) he points jurists to the texts of the *madhhab* which contain the rudimentary kinds of method necessary to discover law (see chapter seven).

This last point is particularly important and needs some clarification. As mentioned above, legal method for al-Shāfiʿī is limited to the texts of revelation, and in cases where there is silence as to the specific issue at hand, to rather basic forms of legal reasoning. In everyday life, for instance, al-Shāfiʿī argues that one can use personal reasoning to locate the direction of prayer or to figure out other things which one cannot know directly through revelation.[50] Likewise, Ibn Qāḍī Shuhbah argues that there are guidelines for how personal reasoning can be used in this manner in each of the texts of the *madhhab*. For instance, in al-Nawawī's *Minhāj*, there are guidelines for using personal reasoning (*ijtihād*) to ascertain the purity of water used for ritual ablution, or to find the correct direction of prayer, and so on.[51]

In addition, *fiqh* texts, due to their internal logic and argumentation, instruct jurists in basic legal methods in ways *uṣūl* texts simply do not. As Brannon Wheeler has suggested in his *Applying the Canon in Islam*, Ḥanafī *fiqh* texts teach jurists not only what the rules are, but also how to think about the law and how new rules can be discovered. He argues that *fiqh* texts are written in such a way that forces jurists to think about how legal rules were derived from the texts of revelation.[52] Teaching, in an academic environment, had no more to do with students' memorizing the rules than it did with learning how to interpret the texts of revelation in order to discover new rules. Ibn Qāḍī Shuhbah's conflation of al-Shāfiʿī's basic methods with the rules (*furūʿ*) in the term '*fiqh*,' shows that he understood this to be the purpose of legal training. This is also why Ibn Qāḍī Shuhbah differentiates between *fiqh*, *furūʿ*, and *uṣūl al-fiqh*, which he projects as different disciplines. *Furūʿ* refers to the rules themselves, *fiqh* to the rules and the method of al-Shāfiʿī necessary for new legal

[50] Al-Shāfiʿī, *Risālah*, 487–90.
[51] Al-Nawawī, *Minhāj*, 5–7; 15–17.
[52] Brannon Wheeler, *Applying the Canon in Islam: The Authorization and Maintenance of Interpretive Reasoning in Ḥanafī Scholarship* (Albany: State University of New York Press, 1996).

discovery, and *uṣūl al-fiqh* to the development of speculative disciplines of *uṣūl* that became important professionally during and after the eleventh century.

This is why jurists, the majority of whom Ibn Qāḍī Shuhbah does not mention as having specific training in *uṣūl*, can clearly function as *muftīs* responsible for discovering new rules from the texts of revelation. Of the 220 jurists that Ibn Qāḍī Shuhbah considered authoritative voices in *ikhtilāf*, and thus capable of using the texts of revelation as sources for their legal opinions, only 42 are mentioned as having specific training in *uṣūl*. All are described as being a *faqīh*, or having legal training (*tafaqqaha*, *darasa*, or *akhadha fiqh*). Thus he implies that legal training in *fiqh* alone is sufficient for qualified jurists to discover new rules. Then why does *uṣūl* become so important as an academic discipline?

Ibn Khaldūn (d. 808/1406), a contemporary of Ibn Qāḍī Shuhbah, gives the reason for the elevation of *uṣūl al-fiqh* as a discipline separate from *fiqh* studies. He states that the science of *uṣūl* was founded by al-Shāfiʿī, and provided jurists with the means of discovering the law. Later, theologians became involved and added methods of speculation to the basic approach of al-Shāfiʿī, importing theological questions into jurisprudence.[53] This confirms Makdisi's contention, discussed above, that theologians infiltrated the schools and appropriated legal methods as the field in which they could continue to develop sciences of speculation.

In addition to outlining the rise of *uṣūl* as a professional discipline separate from *fiqh*-centered legal studies, Ibn Khaldūn goes on to argue that there are two kinds of science: sciences that are necessary by their nature (*ʿulūm maqṣūdah bi ʾl-dhāt*), such as the religious sciences of Qurʾan commentaries, *ḥadīth*, and *fiqh*; and second order sciences which are expedient (*wasīlah*, literally, 'a means to an end'), though not necessary, such as Arabic philology, arithmetic, and others that are a subset of the religious sciences such as logic (which is a subset of philosophy), speculative theology, and *uṣūl al-fiqh* (meaning here the speculative approach, not al-Shāfiʿī's method).[54]

The problem for Ibn Khaldūn, and for Ibn Qāḍī Shuhbah, is that once they became part of the 'curriculum' of legal colleges, the

[53] Ibn Khaldūn, *al-Muqaddimah* (Beirut: Maktabat Lubnān, 1970), vol. 3, 21–23.
[54] Ibid., 28.

expedient sciences took on a life of their own. Ibn Khaldūn argues that many jurists began to focus on *uṣūl*, which for them became more interesting because of its difficulty and the challenge of its theoretical questions, and elevated it to a status equal with that of *fiqh*. Thus, according to Ibn Khaldūn, what began as a way to spend idle time became the focus of academic activity. This is why, Ibn Khaldūn says, *uṣūl al-fiqh*, not the method of al-Shāfiʿī, became so important to many scholars.[55]

Indeed, we see the developments described by Ibn Khaldūn in Ibn Qāḍī Shuhbah's text. Beginning with Abū Isḥāq al-Isfarāʾīnī and his contemporary Ibn Fūrak, *uṣūl al-fiqh*, as a speculative science based in theology, becomes a discipline of its own, separate from *fiqh*. According to Ibn Qāḍī Shuhbah, the scholars engaged in theologically-oriented *uṣūl* are

1. Abū Isḥāq al-Isfarāʾīnī, d. 418/1027–28.
   He was a *mutakallim, uṣūlī* and a *faqīh*. Wrote a commentary on *uṣūl al-dīn*. Was among the *aṣḥāb* of Abū al-Ḥasan al-Ashʿarī.[56]

2. Muḥammad b. al-Ḥusayn, Ibn Fūrak, d. 406/1015–16.
   He was a *mutakallim* and an *uṣūlī*. He studied (*akhadha*) the path (*ṭarīqah*) of Abū al-Ḥasan al-Ashʿarī from Abū al-Ḥasan al-Bāhilī (321/933).[57]

3. Abū al-Qāsim al-Isfarāʾīnī, d. 452/1060.
   He was a disciple of Abū Isḥāq al-Isfarāʾīnī and Imām al-Ḥaramayn in *kalām*. He was among the leaders of the *fuqahāʾ* and the *mutakallimūn*. He wrote a book on the two *uṣūls*.[58]

4. Abū al-Qāsim al-Qushayrī, d. 1072.
   He studied Ṣūfism with al-Daqqāq, and *kalām* with Ibn Fūrak and al-Isfarāʾīnī. He was knowledgeable in the *uṣūl* of the Ashʿarīs and the legal rules of the Shāfiʿīs.[59]

5. Sahl b. Aḥmad al-Arghayānī, d. 499/1105.
   He studied *tafsīr* and *uṣūl al-fiqh* in Ṭūs. He then studied the science of *kalām* with Imām al-Ḥaramayn.[60]

---

[55] Ibid., 29.
[56] Khān, vol. 1, 170–71.
[57] Ibid., 190. Al-Bāhilī wrote a book about divergent opinions in the legal sciences. He does not have a biography in the *Ṭabaqāt*.
[58] Ibid., vol. 1, 229.
[59] Ibid., vol. 1, 254–55.
[60] Ibid., vol. 1, 264–65.

6. Abū al-Fatḥ al-Miṣṣīṣī, d. 542/1147.
An Ashʿarite. He was a *faqīh, uṣūlī,* and a *mutakallim.*[61]

7. Abū al-Qāsim al-Rāzī, n.d.
One of the leaders in the science of *kalām.* Wrote a book on the excellent qualities of al-Ashʿarī. He also studied *kalām* with al-Anṣārī. In addition, he was a disciple of Imām al-Ḥaramayn. He was a *faqīh, uṣūlī,* and a *mutakallim.*[62]

8. Abū al-Qāsim al-Wāsiṭī, d. 592/1196.
Studied *kalām* with Abū Futūḥ al-Isfarā'īnī (d. 538/1143–44). He was unique (*tafarrad*) in his knowledge of *uṣūl al-fiqh* and *kalām.*[63]

9. Abū ʿAbdallāh al-Fārisī, d. 622/1225–26.
He was a Ṣūfī and a *mutakallim.* He had the gift (*ʿaṭīyah*) of reason (*al-ʿaql*) in *uṣūl* and *kalām.*[64]

10. Abū ʿAbdallāh al-Hindī, d. 715/1315.
He was a *mutakallim* in the *madhhab* of al-Ashʿarī. He also taught *uṣūl.* He was among the most knowledgeable in the texts of the *madhhab* of al-Ashʿarī. He was a *faqīh* and an *uṣūlī.* He also took part in the two *uṣūls.* He wrote books on *kalām* and *uṣūl.* He was also a Ṣūfī.[65]

11. Bahā' al-Dīn al-Ikhmīmī, d. 764/1363.
He compiled a book on *uṣūl al-fiqh* and *dīn.* He had a hand in *uṣūl al-fiqh.* He also wrote a book on *kalām.* He studied with Taqī al-Dīn al-Subkī *uṣūl* and *fiqh.* In addition, he was a disciple of al-Qūnawī. He was a leader and excelled in the science of *kalām* and *uṣūl.* He was among the *muḥaddithīn.*[66]

All of the jurists above can trace their intellectual genealogies in Shāfiʿite Ashʿarī *uṣūl* either to al-Isfarā'īnī or Ibn Fūrak, but not back to al-Shāfiʿī. In addition, one thing that is immediately apparent in the above list is the absence of Imām al-Ḥaramayn al-Juwaynī. Although Imām al-Ḥaramayn is described as teaching theology and *uṣūl* to other jurists, Ibn Qāḍī Shuhbah does not mention his connection to *kalām* in his biographical entry. Why would Ibn Qāḍī Shuhbah not describe Imām al-Ḥaramayn as an important part of

[61] Ibid., vol. 1, 326–27.
[62] Ibid., vol. 2, 15.
[63] Ibid., vol. 2, 47–48.
[64] Ibid., vol. 2, 82–83.
[65] Ibid., vol. 2, 228.
[66] Ibid., vol. 3, 103–04.

the theologically oriented *uṣūl* genre, especially given that other scholars, such as Ibn Khaldūn, understood him to be one of the fathers of the field?[67]

Ibn Qāḍī Shuhbah describes Imām al-Ḥaramayn as writing several texts on *uṣūl al-dīn* and as studying *uṣūl al-fiqh* and *uṣūl al-dīn* with Abū al-Qāsim al-Isfarāʾīnī. In Ibn Qāḍī Shuhbah's presentation, *uṣūl al-dīn* is clearly different from *kalām*, although how it is dissimilar is not immediately evident. He seems to indicate that *uṣūl al-dīn* is less speculative than *kalām* and therefore more acceptable; it is also likely to be more important.[68] Ibn Qāḍī Shuhbah mentions eight jurists who have a specialty in *uṣūl al-dīn*. Each of these is described as having heavy concentrations in *ḥadīth* science and/or Ṣūfism. These concentrations seem to indicate jurists who have less speculative orientations.[69] It is important for Ibn Qāḍī Shuhbah to soften the appearance of Imām al-Ḥaramayn and to distance him from al-Isfarāʾīnī and Ibn Fūrak because he composes one of the core texts of the curriculum and is one of the major contributors to al-Rāfiʿī's *ʿAzīz* (see chapter seven). Therefore, to protect the reputation of the divergent opinions Imām al-Ḥaramayn transmits, Ibn Qāḍī Shuhbah must attempt, to the extent that he can, to make him appear as far away from *kalām* and speculation as possible.

A second genre of theologically-oriented *uṣūl* is what Ibn Qāḍī Shuhbah configures as a sort of philosophical-*kalām* oriented *uṣūl*. This, according to Ibn Khaldūn, is more oriented toward the theology of the Muʿtazilah than the Ashʿarīs, and seeks to insert aspects of philosophical reasoning into theological speculation.[70] Ibn Qāḍī Shuhbah only mentions four jurists specifically connected with this genre. The following are:

1. Fakhr al-Dīn al-Rāzī, d. 606/1209.
   He was the Sulṭān of the *mutakallimūn* in his time. He was a *mutakallim*. He was also a skillful leader in the sciences of reason (*al-ʿulūm al-ʿaqliyah*). In addition, he was one of the leaders of the science of the *sharīʿah*. He used to memorize *al-Shāmil* by Imām al-Ḥaramayn, which was about *kalām*. His views of *kalām* were based on *al-Shāmil*. He studied widely

[67] Ibn Khaldūn, vol. 3, 22.
[68] See D. Gimaret, who argues that *kalām* and *uṣūl al-dīn* are synonymous. *Encyclopedia of Islam*, 2nd ed., s.v. "uṣūl al-dīn."
[69] Khān, vol. 1, 271; vol. 2, 202, 229–32; vol. 3, 96, 103–04, 119–20, 144–45.
[70] Ibn Khaldūn, vol. 3, 22, 42–43.

in the science of *kalām*. He also knew well the paths (*ṭuruq*) of *kalāmīyah* and of philosophy. Al-Nawawī transmitted from him in his *Rawḍah* on the chapter dealing with the *ijtihād* of the *muftī*. He wrote a book on *uṣūl al-dīn, uṣūl al-fiqh*, and on philosophy. He had a path in *khilāf*.[71]

2. Abū al-ʿAbbās al-Khūʾī, d. 637/1240.
Studied *uṣūl* with the students of al-Rāzī and studied *fiqh* with al-Rāfiʿī. Wrote a book on *uṣūl* and was a *faqīh* and a specialist or expert (*khabīran*) in the science of *kalām*.[72]

3. Abū ʿAbdallāh al-ʿAlawī, n.d.
He had a long hand in *uṣūl* and *naẓar* (speculative philosophy).[73]

4. Abū ʿAbdallāh al-Iṣfahānī, d. 688/1289.
He was an *uṣūlī* and a *mutakallim*. He was the leading *uṣūlī* of his day. He wrote extensively on *uṣūl al-fiqh*. He also wrote (lesser) works on *khilāf*, *manṭiq* (logic), and *jadal* (rhetorical debate). He wrote commentaries on al-Rāzī's *uṣūl al-fiqh* works. He also wrote on the two *uṣūl*s.[74]

Allied with the philosophical theological approach to *uṣūl* is what Ibn Qāḍī Shuhbah indicates to be a logic (*manṭiq*) oriented approach to *uṣūl*. These jurists are:

1. Sayf al-Dīn al-Āmidī, d. 631/1233.
He was the master of the *mutakallimūn* in his time. He studied the opinion of Imām Aḥmad Ibn Ḥanbal. He also studied the science of *khilāf* and excelled in it. He memorized the path of the Sharīf. He studied the *ṭarīqah* of Asʿad al-Mīhanī. He mastered the science of philosophical speculation (*naẓar*) and *kalām*. He also wrote books about them. He wrote on he two *uṣūl*s, *manṭiq* (logic), and *khilāf*.[75]

2. Jamāl al-Dīn Ibn Faḍlān al-Baghdādī, n.d.
He was very learned in *khilāf*, *uṣūl*, and *manṭiq*.[76]

3. Abū Muḥammad al-Sulamī, d. 660/1262.
He studied *uṣūl* with al-Amidī. He also excelled in the *madhhab*. He drew together from a variety of sciences, including *tafsīr*, *ḥadīth*, *fiqh*, *uṣūl*, Arabic, and the divergent statements in the texts and what can be taken

71 Khān, vol. 2, 65.
72 Ibid., vol. 2, 70.
73 Ibid., vol. 2, 121.
74 Ibid., vol. 2, 200–01.
75 Ibid., vol. 2, 79.
76 Ibid., vol. 2, 91.

from them. He rose to the level of *ijtihād*. He was knowledgeable in *uṣūl* and legal rules (*furūʿ*).[77]

4. Abū ʿAbdallāh al-ʿĀmirī, d. 680/1281–82.
He memorized the writings of al-Ghazālī and Ibn al-Ḥājib's book on *uṣūl*. He participated in *khilāf*, *ḥadīth*, *bayān* (rhetoric), and *manṭiq*.[78]

5. al-Nawawī, d. 677/1278.
He wrote the *Rawḍah*, which is based on the *ʿAzīz* by al-Rāfiʿī. He taught *manṭiq*, *uṣūl al-fiqh* sometimes based on *al-Lumaʿ* by al-Shīrāzī, and sometimes on the *Muntakhab* by al-Rāzī. He studied *uṣūl* from al-Tiflīsī. He also studied *uṣūl al-dīn* (although it is not associated with *uṣūl al-fiqh*).[79]

6. Ibn al-Nafīs al-Miṣrī, n.d.
He wrote a book on *uṣūl al-fiqh* and on *manṭiq*. He also wrote a book on *fiqh* and the roots of it.[80]

7. Abū al-Maʿālī al-Aykī, d. 699/1300.
He was a leader in the two *uṣūl*s. He also wrote a commentary on logic in the *Mukhtaṣar* of Ibn al-Ḥājib.[81]

8. Jamāl al-Dīn al-Ḥamawī, d. 697/1298.
He studied the *madhhab* and *uṣūl* with Ibn al-Khabbāz (d. 631/1233–34). He wrote many works in the two *uṣūl*s, *manṭiq*, and medicine. He wrote the *Mukhtaṣar al-arbaʿīn* about *uṣūl al-dīn*, and the *Sharḥ al-mūjaz* and the *Sharḥ al-jamāl*, both about *manṭiq*.[82]

9. Jamāl al-Dīn al-Ṭāʾī, n.d.
He studied *manṭiq* with his father. He was good at participating (*shārak*) in *fiqh* and *uṣūl*, and other fields besides that.[83]

10. Abū al-Thanāʾ, d. 682/1283–84.
He was the author of a commentary on the *Maḥṣūl* by al-Rāzī. He also wrote a short work on the *Arbaʿīn* on *uṣūl al-dīn*. In addition, he wrote two books on *manṭiq*.[84]

---

77 Ibid., vol. 2, 148–49.
78 Ibid., vol. 2, 148–49.
79 Ibid., vol. 2, 153–55.
80 Ibid., vol. 2, 187.
81 Ibid., vol. 2, 191.
82 Ibid., vol. 2, 194–95.
83 Ibid., vol. 2, 198–99.
84 Ibid., vol. 2, 202.

11. Abū al-Ḥasan al-Bājī, d. 714/1315.
He studied the two *uṣūls* with Taqī al-Dīn al-Subkī and was a high level student with him in *munāẓarah* (debate). He was the most knowledgeable of the people of the world in the *madhhab* of al-Ashʿarī. He was a leader in the two *uṣūls*, and *manṭiq*. He was also the best debater (*anẓar*) of the people of his age. He wrote a commentary on the *Maḥṣūl* by al-Rāzī. He also wrote a work on *manṭiq*.[85]

12. Muḥammad b. ʿAlī al-Bāranbārī, d. 717/1317–18.
Excelled in *fiqh, uṣūl,* and *manṭiq*. He studied *uṣūl* with al-Iṣfahānī. In addition, he wrote a commentary on the *Maḥṣūl* by al-Rāzī.[86]

13. Muḥammad b. Yūsuf al-Jazīrī, d. 711/1312.
He studied *kalām* with Taqī al-Dīn al-Subkī. He was knowledgeable in the two *uṣūls*, grammar, *bayān, manṭiq*, and medicine. He also wrote a commentary on al-Rāzī's *al-Maḥṣūl*.[87]

14. Badr al-Dīn al-Tustarī, n.d.
He was the leader of his time in the two *uṣūls*, and *manṭiq*. He wrote a commentary on the *Mukhtaṣar* of Ibn al-Ḥājib.[88]

15. Fakhr al-Dīn al-Miṣrī, d. 751/1350–51.
He was a high-level student in a variety of sciences. He studied *uṣūl* with al-Hindī. He also memorized the *Mukhtaṣar* of Ibn al-Ḥājib. He studied *manṭiq*.[89]

16. Ibn al-Rahāwī, d. 767/1365.
He studied *uṣūl* and *manṭiq* with al-Iṣfahānī.

17. Abū ʿAbdallāh al-Kirmānī, d. 786/1384.
He wrote books on various sciences, including Arabic, *kalām*, and *manṭiq*. He also wrote a commentary on the *Mukhtaṣar* of Ibn al-Ḥājib in three volumes.[90]

18. Badr al-Dīn al-Kinānī, d. 819/1416.
He was skilled in grammar, *al-maʿānī, bayān, manṭiq*, and he penetrated deeply (*tawaghghala*) into *kalām*, medicine, and anatomy. He was knowledgeable in the science of *adab*, rational sciences (*ʿaqlīyah*) and the two *uṣūls*. He wrote a commentary on *Jamʿ al-jawāmiʿ* by al-Subkī.[91]

---

[85] Ibid., vol. 2, 223–24.
[86] Ibid., vol. 2, 232.
[87] Ibid., vol. 2, 235–36.
[88] Ibid., vol. 2, 284–85.
[89] Ibid., vol. 3, 62–64.
[90] Ibid., vol. 3, 180.
[91] Ibid., vol. 4, 49–50.

One jurist conspicuous by his absence from the above list is al-Ghazālī. He is widely held to be the father of the interpolation of logic into theologically-inclined *uṣūl al-fiqh*.[92] Ibn Qāḍī Shuhbah, however, is silent on his contributions to the genre. He is described as writing several works on *uṣūl al-fiqh* and on *kalām*. Ibn Qāḍī Shuhbah makes it clear that al-Ghazālī held a negative view of theology by placing his discussion of it next to a comment concerning al-Ghazālī's refutation of the Bāṭinīyah (Ismāʿīli Shīʿīs) and the philosophers.[93]

Ibn Qāḍī Shuhbah, for the same reasons that he distanced Imām al-Ḥaramayn from theology, must make sure that al-Ghazālī does not appear tainted by giving rise to a new genre of methodological speculation. He is the author, after all, of *al-Wajīz*, most commented-on divergent rules text in the school.[94] For the validity of al-Ghazālī's text to be maintained, Ibn Qāḍī Shuhbah must make it appear as though al-Ghazālī is the paragon of centrist legal thought.

Ibn Qāḍī Shuhbah presents one last theologically-oriented genre of *uṣūl* in his text: the genre of the two *uṣūl*s (*uṣūlayn*). It is the largest genre of specifically identified theologically-influenced speculative methodology, appearing in connection with 31 jurists. It is also interesting that two of the greatest *uṣūl* specialists, al-Āmidī and Taqī al-Dīn al-Subkī, are among its practitioners.

1. Abū al-Qāsim al-Isfarāʾīnī, d. 452/1060.
   He was a disciple of Abū Isḥāq al-Isfarāʾīnī and Imām al-Ḥaramayn in *kalām*. He was among the leaders of the *fuqahāʾ* and the *mutakallimūn*. He wrote a book on the two *uṣūl*s.[95]

2. Abū Nizār, d. 568/1173.
   Studied *uṣūl al-fiqh* with Ibn al-Burhān and *uṣūl al-dīn* with Abū ʿAbdallāh al-Qayrawānī (not listed in the text). He also studied *khilāf* with Asʿad al-Mīhanī. Wrote a short work on the two *uṣūl*s.[96]

3. Abū ʿAlī al-ʿĀmirī, d. 606/1210.
   A *muḥaddith*, he was also an *ʿālim* in the two *uṣūl*s and *khilāf*. He was also knowledgeable in *tafsīr* and the *madhhab*.[97]

---

[92] Ibn Khaldūn, vol. 3, 41–42.
[93] Khān, vol. 1, 293–94.
[94] Abū Ḥāmid b. Muḥammad b. Muḥammad al-Ghazālī, *al-Wajīz fī fiqh al-imām al-shāfiʿī*, ed. ʿAlī Muḥammad Muʿawwaḍ and ʿĀdil Aḥmad ʿAbd al-Mawjūd, 2 vols. (Beirut: Dār al-arqām, 1997).
[95] Ibid., vol. 1, 229.
[96] Ibid., vol. 2, 7–8.
[97] Ibid., vol. 2, 68.

3. Sayf al-Dīn al-Āmidī, d. 631/1233.
   He was the master of the *mutakallimīn* in his time. He studied the *madhhab* of Imām Aḥmad Ibn Ḥanbal. He also studied the science of khilāf and excelled in it. He memorized the path of the Sharīf. He studied the *ṭarīqāh* of Asʿad al-Mīhanī. He mastered the science of philosophical speculation (*naẓar*) and *kalām*. He also wrote books about them. He wrote on he two *uṣūls* and *manṭiq* (logic) and *khilāf*.[98]

4. Ibn Tilimsānī, d. 658/1260.
   He was a leader in *fiqh* and the two *uṣūls*. He studied the two *uṣūls* with al-Maqtarah (d. 612). He also wrote a commentary on the proofs used by Imām al-Ḥaramayn al-Juwaynī (in legal arguments). He wrote a book on *khilāf* and had many *taʿlīq* on divergent legal opinions.[99]

5. Abū ʿAbdallāh al-Sulamī, d. 655/1257–58.
   He was among the excellent leaders in combining a variety of sciences, including *ḥadīth*, the science of the Qurʾan, *fiqh*, *khilāf*, the two *uṣūls*, grammar, and lexicography.[100]

6. Abū al-Maʿālī al-Aykī, d. 699/1300.
   He was a leader in the two *uṣūls*. He also wrote a commentary on logic in the *Mukhtaṣar* of Ibn al-Ḥājib.[101]

7. Muḥammad b. Aḥmad al-Khūʾī, d. 698/1299.
   He used to bring together a variety of sciences, such as *tafsīr*, the two *uṣūls*, *fiqh*, grammar, divergent opinions, the science of idea expression (*maʿānī*),[102] rhetoric, and arithmetic (*al-ḥisāb*).[103]

8. Jamāl al-Dīn al-Ḥamawī, d. 697/1298.
   He studied the *madhhab* and *uṣūl* with Ibn al-Khabbāz (d. 631/1233–34). He wrote many works in the two *uṣūls*, *manṭiq*, and medicine. He wrote the *Mukhtaṣar al-arbaʿīn* about *uṣūl al-dīn*, and the *Sharḥ al-mūjaz* and the *Sharḥ al-jamāl*, both about *manṭiq*.[104]

9. Ibn al-Ustādh, d. 681/1282.
   He was an *ʿālim* (scholar) in the two *uṣūls* and in *khilāf*.[105]

10. ʿAbd al-Karīm b. ʿAlī al-Anṣārī, d. 704/1304.
    He excelled in a variety of sciences. He studied the two *uṣūls* with al-Tilimsānī and al-Khasrūshāhī.[106]

---

98 Ibid., vol. 2, 79.
99 Ibid., vol. 2, 107.
100 Ibid., vol. 2, 122–23.
101 Ibid., vol. 2, 191.
102 Rosenthal, vol. 3, 399.
103 Khān, vol. 2, 193.
104 Ibid., vol. 2, 194–95.
105 Ibid., vol. 2, 203.
106 Ibid., vol. 2, 218.

11. Abū al-Ḥasan al-Bājī, d. 714/1315.
He studied the two *uṣūls* with Taqī al-Dīn al-Subkī and was a high level student with him in *munāẓarah* (debate). He was the most knowledgeable of the people of the world in the *madhhab* of al-Ashʿarī. He was a leader in the two *uṣūls*, and *manṭiq*. He was also the best debater (*anẓar*) of the people of his age. He wrote a commentary on the *Maḥṣūl* by al-Rāzī. He also wrote a work on *manṭiq*.[107]

12. Abū ʿAbdallāh al-Hindī, d. 715/1315.
He was a *mutakallim* in the *madhhab* of al-Ashʿarī. He also taught *uṣūl*. He was among the most knowledgeable in the texts of the *madhhab* of al-Ashʿarī. He was a *faqīh* and an *uṣūlī*. He also took part in the two *uṣūls*. He wrote books on *kalām* and *uṣūl*. He was also a Ṣūfī.[108]

13. Ibn al-Wakīl, d. 716/1317.
He studied the two *uṣūls* with al-Hindī and wrote a book in three volumes thoroughly studying *ḥadīth*, *fiqh*, and *uṣūl*. He was also knowledgeable of *kalām* of the *madhhab* of al-Ashʿarī.[109]

14. Muḥammad b. Yūsuf al-Jazīrī, d. 711/1312.
He studied *kalām* with Taqī al-Dīn al-Subkī. He was knowledgeable in the two *uṣūls*, grammar, *bayān* (rhetoric), *manṭiq*, and medicine. He also wrote a commentary on al-Rāzī's *al-Maḥṣūl*.[110]

15. Badr al-Dīn al-Tustarī, n.d.
He was the leader of his time in the two *uṣūls*, and *manṭiq*. He wrote a commentary on the *Mukhtaṣar* of Ibn al-Ḥājib.[111]

16. Muḥammad b. ʿAbdallāh al-ʿUthmānī, d. 738/1338.
He studied *fiqh* and the two *uṣūls* with Ṣadr al-Dīn al-Subkī. He was knowledgeable in *fiqh* and *uṣūl*. He wrote two books on *uṣūl*.[112]

17. Muḥammad b. ʿAbd al-Raḥman al-Qazwīnī, d. 739/1338.
Studied the two *uṣūls* with al-Aykī. He also wrote a book on *uṣūl*.[113]

18. al-Anṣārī, d. 749/1348.
He was a leader in *fiqh* and the two *uṣūls*.[114]

---

[107] Ibid., vol. 2, 223–24.
[108] Ibid., vol. 2, 228.
[109] Ibid., vol. 2, 233–34.
[110] Ibid., vol. 2, 235–36.
[111] Ibid., vol. 2, 284–85.
[112] Ibid., vol. 2, 285–86.
[113] Ibid., vol. 2, 286–87.
[114] Ibid., vol. 3, 15–16.

19. ʿAbdallāh b. Muḥammad al-Ḥusaynī, d. 743/1343.
He used to write compilations on the sciences of the two *uṣūl*s and the rational sciences (*al-maʿqūlāt*). He was well known everywhere and he participated in it in all kinds disciplines.[115]

20. Taqī al-Dīn al-Subkī, d. 749/1348 or 756/1355.
He studied legal rules with Ibn al-Rifʿah, the two *uṣūl*s with ʿAlāʾ al-Dīn al-Bājī, *manṭiq* and *khilāf* with Sayf al-Dīn al-Baghdādī (d. 705), and Ṣūfism with Taqī al-Dīn al-ʿAṭṭāʾ (d. 709). He is referred to as being a leader of the *muḥaddithīn*, jurists, and practitioners of the two *uṣūl*s.[116]

21. Abū Muḥammad al-Ardabīlī, d. 749/1348 (from plague).
He was an *uṣūlī* and a *faqīh*. He taught the rational sciences. He also wrote a text on the two *uṣūl*s.[117]

22. Shams al-Dīn Ibn al-Labbān al-Miṣrī, d. 749/1348 (from plague).
He was a Ṣūfī. He was knowledgeable in *fiqh*, the two *uṣūl*s, and Arabic.[118]

23. Ibn ʿAdlān, d. 749/1348 (from plague).
He studied *uṣūl* with al-Iṣfahānī (491) and al-Qarāfī (d. 684). He was knowledgeable in the two *uṣūl*s, grammar, and inheritance law.[119]

24. Abū al-Thanāʾ al-Iṣfahānī, d. 749/1348 (from plague).
He was a leader, excelled in the rational sciences (*ʿaqlīyāt*), and knowledgeable in the two *uṣūl*s. He wrote a short work on the *Mukhtaṣar* of Ibn al-Ḥājib.[120]

25. Ibn Qāḍī al-Qaram, d. 780/1379.
He was knowledgeable in *uṣūl*, variant readings of the Qurʾan, recitation, and *fiqh*. He was a leader and an *ʿālim* (scholar) in *tafsīr*, *fiqh*, the two *uṣūl*s, Arabic, *maʿānī*, and *bayān*.[121]

26. ʿAbd al-ʿAzīz b. Muḥammad al-Kinānī, d. 767/1366.
He was a leader of the *muftī*s, a *faqīh*, a teacher, and a *muḥaddith*. He wrote a text examining the *ḥadīth*s used by al-Rāfiʿī. He studied the two *uṣūl*s with ʿAlāʾ al-Dīn al-Bājjī.[122]

---

[115] Ibid., vol. 3, 31.
[116] Ibid., vol. 3, 37–42.
[117] Ibid., vol. 3, 46–47.
[118] Ibid., vol. 3, 52–54.
[119] Ibid., vol. 3, 54–55.
[120] Ibid., vol. 3, 71–72.
[121] Ibid., vol. 3, 93–94.
[122] Ibid., vol. 3, 101–02.

27. Ibn al-Durayhim, d. 772/1370.
He participated in legal science a number of fields including, *ḥadīth*, *uṣūl al-dīn*, *uṣūl al-fiqh*, variant readings of the Qur'an, and *tafsīr*.[123]

28. Abū al-Faḍl b. al-ʿAjamī, d. 777/1375.
He studied *uṣūl* with al-Iṣfahānī. He was a leader, and he excelled in *fiqh*, and was an *ʿālim* (scholar) in the two *uṣūl*s.[124]

29. Muḥammad b. al-Ḥasan al-Qurashī al-Umawī al-Isnāʾī, d. 764/1363.
He was a *faqīh* and a leader in the science of the two *uṣūl*s, *khilāf*, *jadal*, and the science of Ṣūfism.[125]

30. Badr al-Dīn al-Kinānī, d. 819/1416.
He was skilled in grammar, *al-maʿānī*, *bayān*, *manṭiq*, and he penetrated deeply (*tawaghghala*) into *kalām*, medicine, and anatomy (literally, 'autopsy'). He was knowledgeable in the science of *adab*, reason (*ʿaqlīyah*) and the two *uṣūl*s. He wrote a commentary on *Jamʿ al-jawāmiʿ* by al-Subkī.[126]

The study of the two *uṣūl*s seems to be an explicit attempt to interject certain basic theological assumptions into legal methodological speculation for the purposes of defending the religion against the encroachment of extra-Islamic modes of reasoning. For instance, al-Subkī's *Jamʿ al-jawāmiʿ* is self described as an *uṣūlayn* work.[127] But how it is different from other theologically-oriented works is not immediately clear. It places a heavy emphasis on logic, and it couches many of its postulates in theological argument. Ibn Qāḍī Shuhbah is not clear about how *uṣūlayn* is different from other genres. In discussing those who engage in the two *uṣūl*s, jurists are usually involved in other kinds of theoretical and logical speculation, more so than scholars involved in the other genres of speculative methodology to the exclusion of the two *uṣūl*s.

All of the jurists above trace their *isnād*s in speculative *uṣūl* back to al-Isfarāʾīnī and Ibn Fūrak only. In areas of *fiqh* some of them can trace the lineages back to al-Shāfiʿī, which presents an interesting problem: what method did they use? Ibn Qāḍī Shuhbah does

[123] Ibid., vol. 3, 107.
[124] Ibid., vol. 3, 108–09.
[125] Ibid., vol. 3, 120–21.
[126] Ibid., vol. 4, 49–50.
[127] Taqī al-Dīn ʿAbd al-Wahhāb al-Subkī, *Jamʿ al-jawāmiʿ* (Beirut: Dār al-kutub al-ʿilmīyah, 1994), 86.

not say exactly how speculative legal methodologies were used in legal discovery. Ibn Khaldūn's interpretation, if accepted, would imply that since speculative theologically-oriented legal methodologies were in the category of expedient science, they likely had little direct impact. Indeed, since many, if not most legal rules originated before the rise of speculative *uṣūl*, it likely had only a small influence of the discovery of law. Joseph Schacht maintained that most rules were already decided by 900 CE, which is why he concluded that *ijtihād* began to slowly fade out after this time.[128] In surveying the texts Ibn Qāḍī Shuhbah defines as the core texts of the curriculum (see chapter seven), this would indeed seem to be the case. The texts of the *madhhab* are largely based on the statements of al-Shāfiʿī, al-Muzanī, and al-Rabīʿ. A survey of *al-Tanbīh*, *al-Muhadhdhab* (both by Abū Isḥāq al-Shīrāzī), and *al-Minhāj* (by al-Nawawī) reveals that, although there is additional legal matter included from later scholars, it would appear that this accounts for only 10–15% of the rules. In the texts of divergent opinion (*ikhtilāf*) there is considerably more material included from later jurists. But very little of this is composed by jurists Ibn Qāḍī Shuhbah identifies as being involved in theologically-inclined speculative jurisprudence. Therefore, as a historical matter, we cannot definitively conclude that speculative methods contributed significantly to the development of Islamic law. However, before a final decision can be made, further research is needed.

The above lists do not conclude Ibn Qāḍī Shuhbah's catalog of jurists involved in *ʿilm al-ʿaql*. He includes the biographies of over 175 other jurists who received some form of training in *uṣūl al-fiqh*. Although these jurists covered the spectrum of attitudes toward theological speculation, all sought training in *uṣūl al-fiqh* as a separate field of professionalization because this had become expected by the late eleventh century. Furthermore, jurists could train in more than one field of *uṣūl*, and often taught different methods. For instance, al-Nawawī alternated teaching al-Rāzī's *al-Muntakhab*[129] with al-Shīrāzī's *al-Lumaʿ*,[130] which is telling in itself about the importance of the

[128] Schacht, *Introduction to Islamic Law*, 69–75.
[129] Brockelmann, SI, 921.
[130] Abū Isḥāq al-Shīrāzī, *al-Lumaʿ fī uṣūl al-fiqh* (Beirut: Dār al-kutub al-ʿilmīyah, 1985).

discipline in legal studies.[131] Al-Rāzī, as is noted above, was the founder of the philosophically-inclined school of *kalām*-oriented *uṣūl*. His works draw on speculative theology and attempt a synthesis between the two disciplines. Al-Shīrāzī, on the other hand, is the staunch supporter of non-speculation in the field of *uṣūl*. His text seeks to defend against attempts by scholars hoping to draw into *uṣūl* theologically-inclined modes of speculation.

Ibn Qāḍī Shuhbah indicates, by mentioning al-Nawawī's practice, that movement between genres was rather easy, as is evident from the multiple references to specialization in more than one genre, and that study of *uṣūl* was an aspect of professionalization more than a field in which the law was discovered. In other words, if training in more than one method was the norm, and Ibn Qāḍī Shuhbah indicates that it may have been, then how could speculative methods have been the source from which all jurists discovered rules? If speculative methodologies were the generative force for new legal rules, it is expected that jurists would specialize in one method and not train in methodologies so distinctly different.

Specializations in the expedient sciences and the decline of legal thought

One of the things that stand out in the lists above is the rather sharp increase in the number of disciplines jurists became involved in during the late ʿAbbāsid and Mamlūk periods. Few jurists during this period specialized in the law only; many jurists had at least three specializations, some five or more. This rapid rise in extra-*fiqh* areas of academic work has important ramifications for the development of Islamic law in both Ibn Khaldūn's and Ibn Qāḍī Shuhbah's discussions.

Ibn Khaldūn worried that the distractions caused by involvement in the expedient sciences would lead jurists away from the law itself. Studying expedient sciences had an enormous impact on jurists and the profession. Ibn Khaldūn states that jurists were distracted by specializations in expedient sciences, and that this situation was aggravated by the academic process that required teachers to write commentaries and explanatory texts to facilitate education. As time

[131] Khān, vol. 2, 154.

Table 6.1. A chronological table of *uṣūl* related genres

Gen.	*Uṣūl al-fiqh*	*Uṣūlayn*	*Kalām* Oriented *Uṣūl*	Philosophical *Kalām* Oriented *Uṣūl*	*Manṭiq*	*Uṣūl al-Dīn*	*Kalām*
1	6	0	0	0	0	0	0
2	1	0	0	0	0	0	1
3	1	0	0	0	0	0	0
4	1	0	0	0	0	0	1
5	6	0	0	0	0	0	0
6	1	0	1	0	0	0	0
7	1	0	1	0	0	0	1
8	2	0	2	0	0	0	0
9	3	0	0	0	0	0	0
10	3	1	1	0	0	0	0
11	6	0	1	0	0	0	1
12	1	0	1	0	0	1	0
13	7	0	0	0	0	0	1
14	3	0	0	0	0	0	1
15	2	0	1	0	0	0	2
16	3	1	1	0	0	0	0
17	2	0	1	0	0	0	2
18	2	1	0	1	0	0	2
19	4	1	1	1	2	0	3
20	7	2	0	1	1	0	1
21	5	0	0	0	2	0	0
22	12	4	0	1	6	2	2
23	8	5	1	0	4	1	4
24	19	3	0	0	1	0	0
25	26	7	0	0	1	0	1
26	13	6	0	0	1	2	3
27	7	0	1	0	1	1	2
28	9	1	0	0	1	0	1
29	8	0	0	0	0	0	0

Source: Ibn Qāḍī Shuhbah, *Ṭabaqāt al-fuqahā' al-shāfiʿīyah*, ed. al-Ḥāfiẓ ʿAbd al-Alī Khān, 4 vols. (Beirut: ʿĀlam al-kutub, 1987).

went on, professionalization became dependent on students' mastery of an ever-increasing number of commentaries and explanatory texts. Over time, the number of texts students needed to master to be considered 'professionalized,' also steadily increased.[132] This occurred at the same time when the number of expedient sciences ballooned from just a few in the early periods of Islamic law to over fifteen

[132] Ibn Khaldūn, vol. 3, 248–58.

Figure 6.2. The growth of *uṣūl* related genres

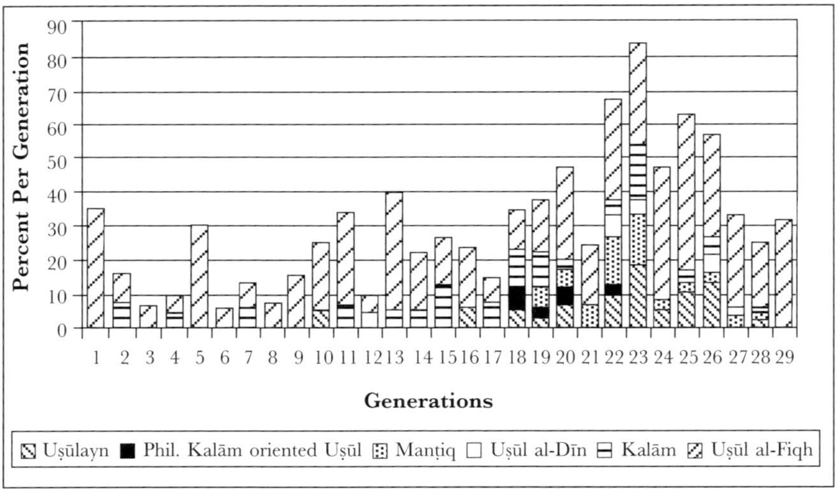

Source: Ibn Qāḍī Shuhbah, *Ṭabaqāt al-fuqahā' al-shāfi'īyah*, ed. al-Ḥāfiẓ 'Abd al-Alī Khān, 4 vols. (Beirut: 'Ālam al-kutub, 1987).

by the Mamlūk period. As we see in table 6.1 above and figure 6.2 below, in just the area of *uṣūl*, the number of genres expanded from one to at least six.

However, this occurred not only in *uṣūl*, but also in other expedient sciences. As tables 6.2a and 6.2b show below, there were 297 jurists described as being involved in 10 expedient sciences. These 297 jurists specialized in 371 non-legal fields. Furthermore, as figure 6.3 shows, specializations in expedient sciences remained fairly constant until the eleventh generation (460/1067–480/1088), when moderate increases began. Then, in the nineteenth generation (621/1224–640/1243), specializations in expedient disciplines exploded.

Table 6.2a. Chronological development of the expedient sciences

Generations	Qur'an	Arabic	Grammar Debate	Rhetoric	Lexicography
1	0	0	0	0	0
2	0	0	0	0	0
3	0	0	0	0	0
4	1	0	0	0	2
5	2	0	0	1	1
6	0	0	1	0	1
7	0	0	1	0	1

Table 6.2a. (*cont.*)

Generations	Qur'an	Arabic	Grammar Debate	Rhetoric	Lexicography
8	1	1	2	0	2
9	0	1	0	2	0
10	0	0	3	0	1
11	0	1	5	1	1
12	1	0	0	0	1
13	2	0	1	0	0
14	0	0	2	0	3
15	0	0	1	1	2
16	0	2	3	2	2
17	1	2	3	2	2
18	0	2	1	0	1
19	1	5	4	1	1
20	3	3	3	0	2
21	3	3	9	0	3
22	0	4	8	1	4
23	2	1	5	0	1
24	0	2	13	0	5
25	1	7	24	0	5
26	0	10	14	1	0
27	1	4	4	0	0
28	4	12	11	0	2
29	1	4	7	0	0

Source: Ibn Qāḍī Shuhbah, *Ṭabaqāt al-fuqahā' al-shāfi'īyah*, ed. al-Ḥāfiẓ 'Abd al-Alī Khān, 4 vols. (Beirut: 'Ālam al-kutub, 1987).

Table 6.2b. Chronological development of the expedient sciences

Generations	Variant Readings of the Qur'an	Qur'anic Recitation	History	Medicine	Philosophy	Total†
1	0	0	0	0	0	0
2	0	0	0	0	0	0
3	0	0	0	0	0	0
4	1	0	0	0	0	4
5	0	0	3	0	0	7
6	0	0	0	0	0	2
7	0	0	1	0	0	3
8	2	1	0	0	1	9
9	1	0	1	0	0	5
10	1	0	1	0	0	6
11	0	0	1	0	0	9
12	1	0	1	0	0	4
13	0	0	1	0	1	4
14	0	0	0	0	0	5

Table 6.2b. (*cont.*)

Generations	Variant Readings of the Qur'an	Qur'anic Recitation	History	Medicine	Philosophy	Total†
15	0	0	1	0	1	6
16	0	0	2	0	0	11
17	1	0	1	0	0	12
18	2	0	0	1	2	9
19	3	0	2	0	1	18
20	3	0	1	0	0	15
21	4	0	4	0	0	26
22	2	0	5	0	1	25
23	3	0	0	0	0	12
24	4	0	7	0	1	31
25	11	0	4	0	0	52
26	7	0	2	0	0	34
27	3	0	2	0	0	14
28	3	1	2	0	0	35
29	0	0	1	0	0	13

Source: Ibn Qāḍī Shuhbah, *Ṭabaqāt al-fuqahā' al-shāfiʿīyah*, ed. al-Ḥāfiẓ ʿAbd al-Alī Khān, 4 vols. (Beirut: ʿĀlam al-kutub, 1987).
† Totals are for all categories of expedient science.

The rise of professionalization and the expansion in expedient sciences is tied directly to the increases in education in *madrasahs* and personalized *akhadha* relationships. Figure 6.4 demonstrates below that Ibn Qāḍī Shuhbah links professionalization with *darasa* and *akhadha*. It is, however, unclear whether areas of study such as history would have occurred in a *madrasah*. Ibn Qāḍī Shuhbah specifically links the study of expedient sciences to *akhadha* education in 100 out of 269 biographies (37%). He indicates that not only were *akhadha* relationships important in the development of *aʿyān* claims to authority, but that the use of *ʿilm* as a cultural commodity was more closely attached to the acquisition of knowledge in the expedient sciences than law.

The increase in the study of the expedient sciences occurred during the period of the first Mongol invasions and the massive dislocations of jurists from Central Asia caused by the sack of virtually every town in Transoxania. Whether the two events are related is by no means certain. This period, however, is also the beginning of the decline of the *madhhab* as a consolidating institution, and the rise of the memorizers. This transition, it will be recalled, marks the near

Figure 6.3. The growth of expedient sciences

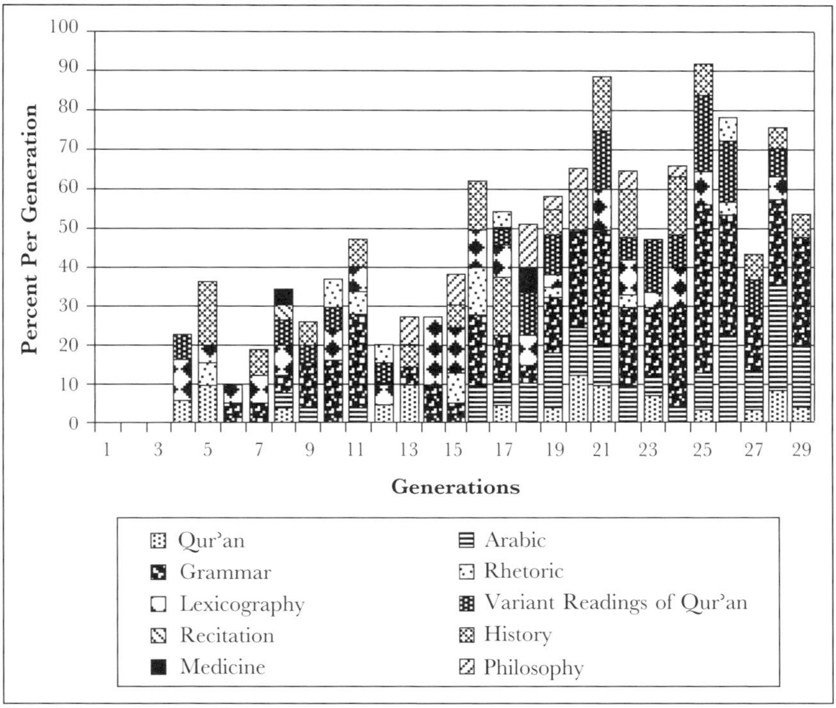

Source: Ibn Qāḍī Shuhbah, *Ṭabaqāt al-fuqahā' al-shāfi'īyah*, ed. al-Ḥāfiẓ ʿAbd al-Alī Khān, 4 vols. (Beirut: ʿĀlam al-kutub, 1987).

total disappearance of affiliated jurists and the rise of deficient jurists. Thus, this would seem to indicate, for Ibn Qāḍī Shuhbah, that the rise of expedient sciences meant an end to specializations in *fiqh*, which were necessary for original legal discovery to continue (see figure 6.5).

Figure 6.5 also shows that *uṣūl* genres track closely with the other expedient sciences throughout the period. As the other expedient sciences expand, so do the various genres of *uṣūl al-fiqh*. Therefore, as with grammar, lexicography, and Arabic phonology, the expansion of *uṣūl al-fiqh* genres indicate, and indeed are related to, the decline of legal thought in the period.

Figure 6.6 shows that with the outbreak of plague in 749/1348, all of the expedient sciences and *uṣūl*-related genres sharply decline before briefly rebounding, then declining in the generation before

Figure 6.4. Growth of expedient sciences compared to trends in *akhadha* and *darasa*

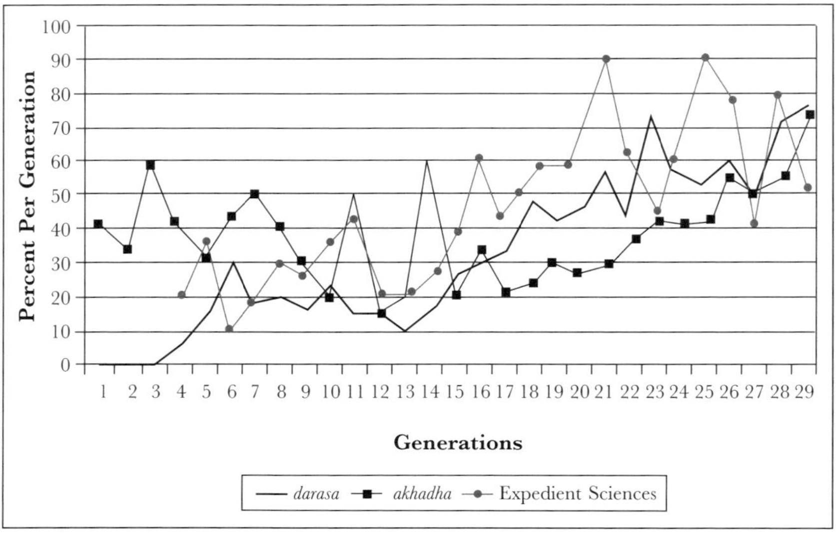

Source: Ibn Qāḍī Shuhbah, *Ṭabaqāt al-fuqahāʾ al-shāfiʿīyah*, ed. al-Ḥāfiẓ ʿAbd al-Alī Khān, 4 vols. (Beirut: ʿĀlam al-kutub, 1987).

Figure 6.5. Expedient sciences and *uṣūl* compared to *furūʿ* production

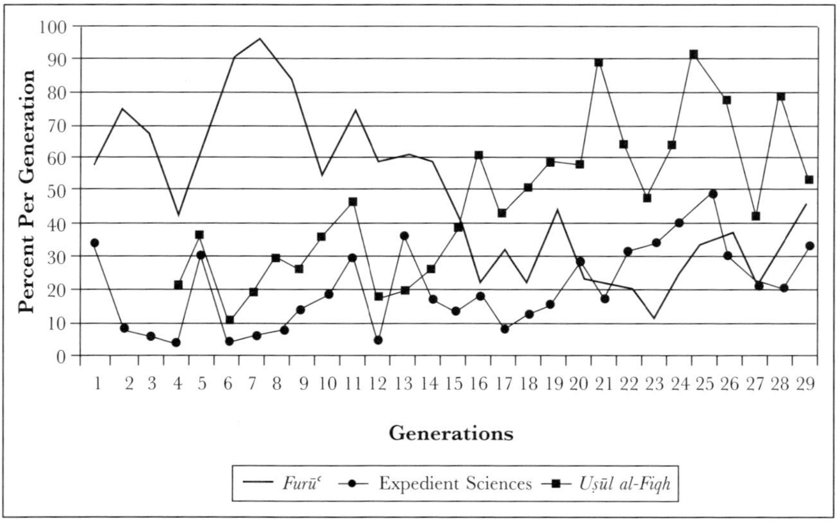

Source: Ibn Qāḍī Shuhbah, *Ṭabaqāt al-fuqahāʾ al-shāfiʿīyah*, ed. al-Ḥāfiẓ ʿAbd al-Alī Khān, 4 vols. (Beirut: ʿĀlam al-kutub, 1987).

Figure 6.6. Average age of mortality as compared with trends in expedient sciences and *uṣūl* genres

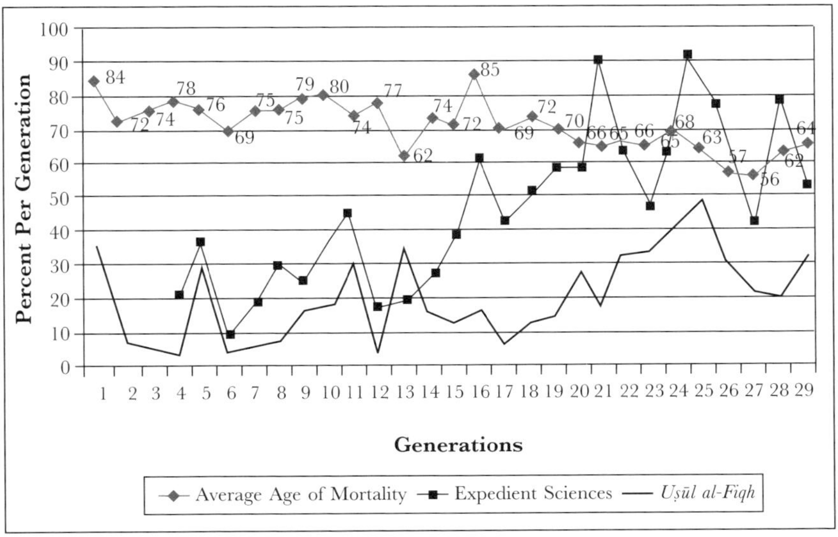

Source: Ibn Qāḍī Shuhbah, *Ṭabaqāt al-fuqahā' al-shāfiʿīyah*, ed. al-Ḥāfiẓ ʿAbd al-Alī Khān, 4 vols. (Beirut: ʿĀlam al-kutub, 1987).

Ibn Qāḍī Shuhbah composed his text. This is indicative of the enormous impact the plague had on the juridical community. All areas of law, even legal rules, were severely affected by the plague. The effect of the plague was most especially felt in the educative connections between the generations. Before the plague, approximately 70% of educative connections extended back to teachers two or more generations behind those of the students. As pointed out above, this occurred because, as both teachers and students lived longer, they were able to study with a broader range of scholars over longer periods of time. With the outbreak of plague, however, educative connections only reached back two or more generations for only 20% of jurists. The sharp reduction of educative connections indicates that education became more superficial because of the short time spent with teachers and the smaller number of lectures and study circles that students were able to attend.

As Figure 6.7 demonstrates, the impact of the decline on jurist longevity is most keenly felt in *tafaqqaha* educational relationships. Why this is the case is not clear in the text. Ibn Qāḍī Shuhbah implies, as with the case of al-Buwayṭī, that sudden and extra-ordinary

Figure 6.7. Average of mortality as compared to *tafaqqaha, darasa*, and *akhadha* educational relationships

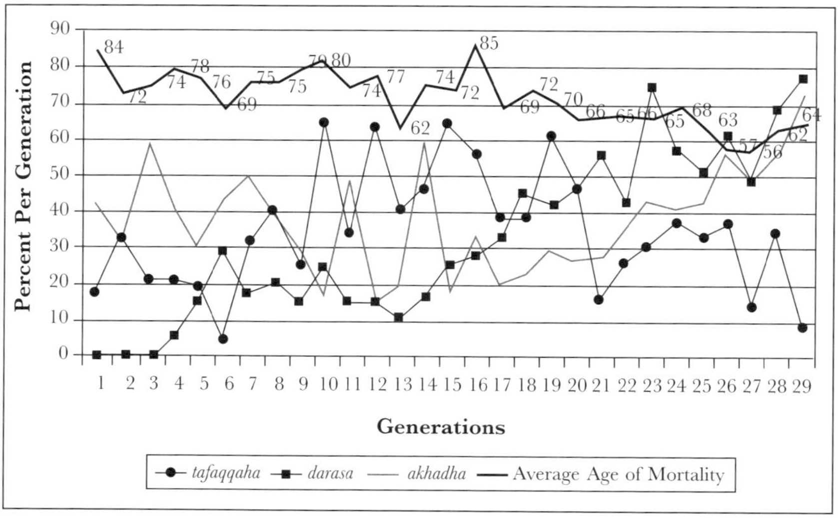

Source: Ibn Qāḍī Shuhbah, *Ṭabaqāt al-fuqahā' al-shāfiʿīyah*, ed. al-Ḥāfiẓ ʿAbd al-Alī Khān, 4 vols. (Beirut: ʿĀlam al-kutub, 1987).

death causes disruptions in the transmission of law. Since Ibn Qāḍī Shuhbah prizes *tafaqqaha* education over other means of transmitting knowledge it is only natural that he would seek to imply that the plague's impact was most keenly felt in this area.

The situation was so extreme that, in many cases, the generations became so compressed after the outbreak of plague that jurists are depicted as studying with scholars of their own generations more frequently than in previous times. This meant not only that few scholars received specializations in expedient sciences, but because so many scholars were drawn away from the law as a area of specialization, there was far less training in *fiqh* and *fiqh* legal method, virtually ensuring the near-complete disappearance of middle and low-level scholars who held certifications allowing them to solve legal problems.

The decline of jurists capable of using *fiqh* legal method is why the rise of specializations in expedient sciences is so troubling in Ibn Qāḍī Shuhbah's presentation. At the very time a wide number of scholars were needed for the discovery of *fiqh* to continue, the majority of jurists, many of whom Ibn Qāḍī Shuhbah describes as the best and the brightest, were distracted by speculative disciplines that had nothing to do with legal discovery. *Fiqh*, the combination of rules and al-Shāfiʿī's method, was nearly lost. Ibn Qāḍī Shuhbah's text calls for these jurists (deficient as a result of their own intellectual interests and the crises of the times) to turn to divergent opinions texts, which not only contained a wide array of legal rules from which deficient jurists could draw, but could also, in the way texts of the *madhhab* had originally done, train jurists in basic methods of legal discovery so that they could use the texts of revelation in the search for legal solutions. This, Ibn Qāḍī Shuhbah clearly hoped, would lead to a renaissance of legal thinking and a revitalization of the Islamic community.

CHAPTER SEVEN

CURATIVES FOR THE DECLINE OF LAW

Ibn Qāḍī Shuhbah wrote his *Ṭabaqāt* to achieve several ends. He sought to describe the trends in Shāfiʿī law that led to, and in many respects resulted from, the crises following the Mongol invasion in the 7th/13th century. In doing so, he attempted to depict changes in legal education that led to declines in juridical abilities. At the very moment when the community of jurists was needed most, the majority of scholars had become specialists in expedient sciences and speculative genres of *uṣūl al-fiqh*, and were mere memorizers of legal rules handed down from earlier periods. The vitality of legal thought and the interpretive ability of the majority of scholars, the ones actually responsible for the administration of Islamic law, had all but disappeared because the kinds of education necessary for judges and jurist-consults to think 'on their feet' no longer occurred in the majority of cases.

Ibn Qāḍī Shuhbah also wrote his text to show jurists a way out of the morass in which the juridical community found itself. As discussed above, he wrote his text to create *models of* and *models for* reality. For instance, in attributing excellence to the majority of *tafaqqaha* educational relationships, and by not doing so for *akhadha* and *darrasa/darasa*, he is pointing jurists toward the importance of the former as the preferred style of learning. The close and inter-personal mode of acquiring legal knowledge was clearly better in his view than *akhadha* (which had more to do with initiating people into the ranks of the *ʿulamāʾ*), or *darrasa/darasa* (which focused on credentialing scholars to issue opinions but not necessarily in teaching them how to do so). This is not to say that all educational styles did not have a place in medieval Islamic education, or that Ibn Qāḍī Shuhbah was criticizing those who engaged in the other modes of learning. Indeed, he is described as engaging in almost all forms of education at different points in his life, as a student and a teacher.[1] *Tafaqqaha*,

[1] See al-Sakhāwī's biography of Ibn Qāḍī Shuhbah for examples.

for Ibn Qāḍī Shuhbah, is simply better at communicating the kinds of legal ideas that jurists need to maintain the basic functioning of the law.

The daily maintenance and administration of the law, and not theories of idealized legal hierarchies, is what concerned Ibn Qāḍī Shuhbah above all else. One of the things that came to distinguish the *ṭabaqāt* genre from other kinds of literature that attempted to describe legal structures and assign ranks and responsibilities, is that *ṭabaqāt* always had one foot planted in reality. They dealt with describing the lives of individuals, and in doing so, to measure the reality of human endeavour against the theoretical structures that scholars argued should have existed in a perfect world. Works such as *Adab al-muftī wa ʾl-mustaftī* by Ibn al-Ṣalāḥ, or similar treatments found in *fiqh* and *uṣūl* texts are theoretical descriptions that create models for reality in an ideal situation.[2] They assume a legal context that is pristine, in which jurists are free from corruption, confusion, overwork, political coercion, fatigue, or human frailty. At the very least, they cast a jaundiced eye on the practical realities of working jurists. *In theory*, a jurist-consult (*muftī*), when given a question, was supposed to be able to look through the corpus of received opinion and decide if the problem he was dealing with had already been resolved by a higher-ranking scholar of a previous generation, or whether it had been resolved as a matter of consensus. If not, he was expected to be able to turn to the texts of revelation and discern a new rule on his own. *In theory*, judges were supposed to make recourse to trained *muftī*s who could advise the judge as to what the ruling should be in any particular case, based on the *muftī*'s *ijtihād*, or *ijtihād*-like effort. In either situation, *muftī*s were supposed to turn cases that they were not qualified to resolve over to higher-ranking jurists. *In theory, muftī*s were expected to exhaust every effort, look at every passage of revelation, to re-think every issue, on every case they were given; even if they had been given a similar case before. The ruling was to be original in every instance.[3]

[2] See Ibn al-Ṣalāḥ, *Adab al-muftī wa ʾl-mustaftī*, ed. Muwaffaq b. ʿAbd al-Qādir (Beirut: ʿĀlam al-kutub, 1986). Also see the chapter on *Adab al-muftī wa ʾl-mustaftī* in al-Nawawī, *al-Majmūʿ*, vol. 1, 68–85. For a discussion of the theoretical discussions of legal hierarchies see Hallaq, *Authority, Continuity, and Change*, 1–23.

[3] Also see Abū Bakr Aḥmad b. ʿAmr al-Shaybānī al-Khaṣṣāf, *Kitāb adab al-qāḍī*, ed. Farḥāt Zayādah (Cairo: Qism al-nashr bi ʾl-jāmiʿah al-amrīkīyah, 1978), 44–52;

The theoretical application of Islamic law would have been time consuming, even for jurists that possessed the necessary training to fulfil its requirements. In reality *muftīs* and judges did not have the time to return to the texts of revelation or to the corpus of received opinion. Jurists dealt with hundreds of cases in a day. They felt pressures from government officials and litigants; they were influenced by social expectations, family responsibilities, and professional necessities. The application of Islamic law in reality was a messy business that reflected the chaotic atmosphere of the times.[4]

Ibn Qāḍī Shuhbah wrote his text not to describe some theoretical vision of what the application of law should be in an idealized world, but to show jurists who had to deal with the ugly reality of law how to go about their business in an efficient and accurate manner. Thus, his target audience was not the few remaining high-level jurists, but those who did not have the high levels of training that theory suggested they should have possessed.

His experience as a deputy Shāfiʿī judge for over twenty years, as a deputy jurist in the Palace of Justice, as an assistant to Ibn Ḥijjī when he served as confidential secretary to Sulṭān Barsbāy, as a *muftī* to individuals seeking his private opinion, as a teacher, writer, and historian, shaped his view of the legal profession. He wrote his text in the context of his own rise to chief Shāfiʿī judge of Damascus, and its subsequent editions were produced in the midst of his involvement in the revolt against Sulṭān Jaqmaq, his removal from office, and his eventual rehabilitation and retirement. He lived in an environment

Ibn Abī al-Damm, *Kitāb adab al-qaḍāʾ*, ed. Muḥyī Hilāl al-Sarḥān (Baghdād: al-Jumhūrīyah al-ʿIrāqīyah, wazārat al-awqāf wa ʾl-shuʾūn al-dīnīyah, 1984), 203–09.

[4] There is little direct evidence of what jurists and judges endured. Much of what we do know is anecdotal and is, therefore, less reliable. It is clear that the juridical situation in Damascus during Ibn Qāḍī Shuhbah's life was highly chaotic. See Ibn Ṭūlūn, *Quḍat dimashq*, especially pages 129–57 for an indication on the turmoil surrounding the Damascene judiciary; and al-Subkī, *Muʿīd al-niʿam wa mubīd al-niqam*, 74–87. Also see Wael Hallaq, "The 'Qadi's Diwan (Sijill)' Before the Ottomans," *Bulletin of the School of Oriental and African Studies* 61, no. 3 (1998): 415–436, especially 418–25; N. J. Coulson, "Doctrine and Practise in Islamic Law: One Aspect of the Problem," *Bulletin of the School of Oriental and African Studies* 18, no. 2, (1956): 211–26, although this looks at the early Islamic period. For an interesting account of the process of judicial review and referral, see David Powers "A Court Case from Fourteenth-Century North Africa," *Journal of the American Oriental Society* 110, no. 2 (April-June, 1990): 237, 240. For one of the few detailed description of the political pressures put on judges also see Joseph H. Escovitz, *The Office of Qāḍī al-Quḍāt in Cairo under the Baḥrī Mamlūks*, 131–62.

that was shaped by social, political, and structural challenges to the administration of the law and he was keenly aware of the failures of the educational system and weaknesses in the administration of law. Although he may have believed that he was capable of disagreeing with al-Shāfiʿī's opinion he knew that he stood at the pinnacle of the legal profession and that the majority of the people who administered the law in major cities and small villages alike, did not have the training necessary to deal with many of the questions proffered to them according to the theory of Islamic jurisprudence.

The question that faced Ibn Qāḍī Shuhbah was how, in the face of the realities of decline and crisis, could Islamic law as a coherent and relevant system of thought survive? Was it enough to offer a model of education that most jurists no longer followed or was there more that needed to be done? In a system of professionalization that prioritized training in the expedient sciences and in speculative methods of legal discovery that had little real import for the discovery of legal rules, how could jurists who had little time or training in basic legal methods and rules learn the things they needed in order for the Muslim community to continue to exist?

Al-Nawawī, it will be recalled, argued almost 200 years before Ibn Qāḍī Shuhbah that Islamic law had declined because jurists had ceased to understand how legal rules were transmitted, who transmitted them, their situations and circumstances, and the kinds of principles that formed the basis of their opinions.[5] Although, he argues, that jurists had originally understood the importance of knowing the accuracy of early scholars and the reliability of their opinions, over time legal scholars forgot that historical knowledge was central to the maintenance of the law. In asserting this critique, al-Nawawī should not be understood to be speaking about the deficiencies of high-level jurists. As was demonstrated in chapter five, according to al-Nawawī's theory of juridical hierarchy, one of the qualifications for high ranking affiliated jurists, who are capable of turning to the texts of revelation, is their knowledge of the authoritative opinions of the previous generations. Instead, al-Nawawī is describing the lowest level of affiliated jurist and the ranks of deficient legal scholars who do not have training in, or knowledge of, the history of the

[5] Rosenthal, *The History of Muslim Historiography*, 303.

school or the transmission of rules.[6] He says in the *Majmūʿ*, that if they are presented with a legal question they must not answer, but, *in theory*, refer the question to a higher authority. The question is: how often were deficient jurists able to do this? Were there higher-ranking jurists available at all times to answer questions? What could a deficient jurist do when faced with a question he was not trained to resolve, but to which, because there were no better qualified jurists available, he was nevertheless forced to respond?

Ibn Qāḍī Shuhbah argued that the reality of the law in the Circassian Mamlūk period was that the majority of practicing jurists fell into the bottom categories of jurists, scholars whom al-Nawawī argued were not fit to issue legal opinions. It is interesting to note that al-Nawawī made his comments in the introduction to his revision of the *Ṭabaqāt al-shāfiʿīyah* originally written by Ibn al-Ṣalāḥ, and may indicate that he too was faced with the reality of a poorly trained cadre of jurists who did not measure up to his own theoretical constructions of authority. Ibn Qāḍī Shuhbah, taking up the critique of al-Nawawī, sought not only to provide a history of the transmission of rules, to give an overview of the lives of the great scholars of the past, but also to point deficient jurists to collections of rules that are necessary for the continuance of the law.

Substantive rules and madhhab: *Legal consensus and limited* Khilāf

Legal rules mattered to Ibn Qāḍī Shuhbah. There is, however, no single category or classification of substantive rules in his text. Rules are of different kinds—they represent the opinions of all jurists; of just a few; or are subject to dispute. Rules are depicted as applying to ritual and social life; and also to the discovery of the rules themselves. The fundamental issue before Ibn Qāḍī Shuhbah is the transmission of rules, in their plurality, from the founding of the school, through those qualified to differ and add to these rules, down to the memorizers of the rules in the ninth/fifteenth century.

As seen in chapter five, there are two primary categories of rules in Ibn Qāḍī Shuhbah's *Ṭabaqāt*. Some rules represent the *madhhab* and some stand outside it (*ikhtilāf*). *Madhhab*, it will be recalled, is used in three senses in Ibn Qāḍī Shuhbah's text: 1) the Shāfiʿī school

[6] Al-Nawawī, *al-Majmūʿ*, vol. 1, 72–75.

as a community of professional jurists (whether this be a guild or a corporation is not indicated), 2) the opinion of an individual, usually al-Shāfiʿī himself, and 3) the corpus of received authoritative opinion that represents the consensual doctrinal view of the Shāfiʿī school as it developed over the centuries.

With regard to the third category, there needs to be some clarification. George Makdisi, in his *The Rise of Colleges*, describes the *madhhab*, in the third sense, to indicate a kind of legal category on which all jurists agree. He states that the

> *madhhab* referred to those doctrines regarding which there were no differences of opinion. Used with a complement, for instance, the *madhhab* of a particular school of jurisprudence, it meant those doctrines having the consensus of that school's doctors.[7]

Taken at face value, this would seem to be an accurate representation of Ibn Qāḍī Shuhbah's opinion as well.

Ibn Qāḍī Shuhbah, throughout his *Ṭabaqāt*, points to a number of works that represent the core works of the *madhhab*. He mentions 2058 texts, of which only 32 are studied by, commented on, or memorized by more than the author of the original work. Of these 32 texts, four (the *Ṣaḥīḥ*s of al-Bukhārī[8] and Muslim,[9] and the *Musnad*s of al-Shāfiʿī[10] and Aḥmad Ibn Ḥanbal)[11] are *ḥadīth* works, one is a grammar text (the *Kitāb tashīl al-fawāʾid* by Ibn Mālik),[12] five are *uṣūl al-fiqh* texts, and one, *al-Iḥyāʾ* by al-Ghazalī,[13] does not fit any category. The 21 remaining works are *fiqh* texts. Of these, eight are construed as *fiqh* texts representing the *madhhab*. Additionally, Ibn al-Rifʿah's *al-Kifāyah* is a commentary on al-Shīrāzī's *al-Tanbīh*, and the *Minhāj al-ṭālibīn* by al-Nawawī is a commentary on the *Muḥarrar* by al-Rāfiʿī.

---

[7] Makdisi, *The Rise of Colleges*, 109.

[8] Khān, vol. 1, 67, 83, 84, 145, 150, 203, 206, 302; vol. 2, 164; vol. 4, 43, 45, 66, 78, 89, 98, 108, 112. Also see *Ṣaḥīḥ al-bukhārī*, ed. Muḥammad Munīr al-Dimashqī, 9 vols. (Beirut: ʿĀlam al-kutub, n.d.).

[9] Khān, vol. 1, 73, 126, 204, 263, 302, 309, 311; vol. 2, 35, 128, 156, 241; vol. 4, 42, 77, 98. See *Ṣaḥīḥ muslim*, ed. Muḥammad Fu'ād ʿAbd al-Bāqī, 5 vols. (Beirut: Dār iḥyāʾ al-turāth al-ʿarabī, n.d.).

[10] Khān, vol. 1, 134; vol. 2, 269, 274, 299; vol. 3, 25, 130. See *Musnad al-imām al-shāfiʿī* (Beirut: Dār al-kutub al-ʿilmīyah, n.d.).

[11] Khān, vol. 3, 42, 130, 131; vol. 4, 47.See Aḥmad Ibn Ḥanbal, *al-Musnad*, ed. Al-Ḥusaynī ʿAbd al-Majīd Hāshim and Aḥmad ʿUmar Hāshim, 22 vols. (Cairo: Dār al-maʿārif, 1985).

[12] Khān, vol. 2, 151; vol. 3, 7, 23, 69, 73, 78, 97, 99, 107; vol. 4, 57.

[13] Ibid., vol. 1, 294, 280, 307, 327; vol. 4, 32.

Figure 7.1. *Fiqh* texts representing the *madhhab*

	Text	Author	dod.
1.	*al-Umm*	al-Shāfiʿī	205/820
2.	*al-Tanbīh*	Abū Isḥāq al-Shīrāzī	476/1083
3.	*al-Muhadhdhab*	/	/
4.	*Al-Wajīz*	al-Ghazālī	505/1111
5.	*al-Muḥarrar*	al-Rāfiʿī	624/1227
6.	*al-Ḥāwī al-ṣaghīr*	ʿAbd al-Ghaffār	665/1266
7.	*Minhāj al-ṭālibīn*	Al-Nawawī	677/1278
8.	*al-Kifāyah fī sharḥ al-tanbīh*	Ibn al-Rifʿah	710/1311

Source: Ibn Qāḍī Shuhbah, *Ṭabaqāt al-fuqahā' al-shāfiʿīyah*, ed. al-Ḥāfiẓ ʿAbd al-Alī Khān, 4 vols. (Beirut: ʿĀlam al-kutub, 1987).

These works represent Ibn Qāḍī Shuhbah's view of the *madhhab*. They distill al-Shāfiʿī's opinion, and supplement it through the addition of rules discovered by later jurists. For instance, the most important text representing the *madhhab* for Ibn Qāḍī Shuhbah is al-Shīrāzī's *al-Tanbīh*. 73 jurists commented on, studied, or memorized this text, the last dying in 840/1437.[14] Ibn Qāḍī Shuhbah even wrote two commentaries on the text.[15] Al-Shīrāzī describes his text as "a short work on the main questions (*uṣūl*) of the opinion or doctrine of al-Shāfiʿī,"[16] and throughout the text al-Shīrāzī presents the *madhhab* as if it included no disagreement. Few jurists are ever mentioned by name, and for that matter, neither is al-Shāfiʿī. Al-Shīrāzī simply presents the rules in the text as representing either the direct opinion of al-Shāfiʿī or opinions which would be in accord with it. Throughout the text, al-Shīrāzī makes the argument that his work represents the consensus of the five schools of his time. He implies that there is little disagreement simply by neglecting to mention any.

Similarly, in his *Muhadhdhab*, al-Shīrāzī says,

> I mention in it, God willing, the main questions (*uṣūl*) of the opinion of al-Shāfiʿī according to the evidences of it and what is indicated by his method from the unsolved questions according to their occasioning factors.[17]

---

[14] Ibid., vol. 4, 111.

[15] Al-Sakhāwī, *al-Ḍaw' al-lāmiʿ*, vol. 11, 23.

[16] Abū Isḥāq al-Shīrāzī, *al-Tanbīh fī fiqh al-imām al-shāfiʿī* (Beirut: Dār al-ṭibāʿah wa 'l-nashr wa 'l-tawzīʿ, 1997), 66.

[17] Abū Isḥāq al-Shīrāzī, *al-Muhadhdhab fī fiqh al-imām al-shāfiʿī* (Beirut: Dār al-kutub al-ʿilmīyah, 1995), vol. 1, 13.

In other words, he bases his text on the rules on which al-Shāfiʿī had an opinion, and on issues where he is silent, on the discovery of rules based on his method. Unlike in the *Tanbīh*, al-Shīrāzī explicitly states that some of the opinions in the *Muhadhdhab* are his own, but, nevertheless, they do not diverge from what would have been al-Shāfiʿī's opinion because they are based on his method.

It may be that early in Shāfiʿī legal development '*madhhab*' was a synonym for '*ijmāʿ*.' However, the texts that Ibn Qāḍī Shuhbah refers to as representing the *madhhab* in the later development of the school seem to indicate that doctrinal views had become influenced by ideas that did not reflect received orthodoxy.[18] For instance, in the *Minhāj*, a text commented on, studied, or memorized by 22 jurists in Ibn Qāḍī Shuhbah's text, al-Nawawī states that his commentary on the *Muḥarrar* seeks to make several improvements on the original; most importantly, a) he attempts to mention divergent opinions not pointed out by al-Rāfiʿī, b) he cites, and makes plain, several instances where al-Rāfiʿī quotes opinions that are in *direct opposition to the doctrines of the school*,[19] c) he attempts to be more specific in the terminology used in the text so as to avoid misunderstandings that might indicate incorrect ideas,[20] and d) in instances where there is a divergence of opinion, he presents each point of view and the evidence used for each diverging position, using quotes from al-Shāfiʿī to indicate which of the opinions is most correct.[21]

These clarifications are significant because al-Nawawī implies that texts representing the *madhhab* began to include opinions that varied with the consensus of the school. More importantly, it indicates that by al-Nawawī's time, there was a recognition of the need to make divergent opinions explicit because corruptions had begun to creep into the *madhhab*. This signifies that by the late seventh/thirteenth

---

[18] See Hallaq's argument concerning the development of the concept of the *madhhab* in, *Authority, Continuity, and Change*, 155–60.

[19] *Wa minhā mawāḍiʿ yasīrah dhakarahā fī al-Muḥarrar ʿalā khilāf al-mukhtār fī al-madhhab kamā satarāhā inshāʾallāh taʿālā.*

[20] Terminological specificity is very important for understanding the changes in *fiqh* texts over time. See Hallaq, *Authority, Continuity, and Change* (pp. 121–65) for an excellent analysis of the importance of many terms and phrases. In this discussion, as in other areas of Hallaq's work, the value of the contribution is, however, tempered by the lack of a historical discussion of the changes in terminological uses over time.

[21] Al-Nawawī, *Minhāj al-ṭālibīn*, 3.

century, the third view of the *madhhab*, described above, began to change. Now it included not just the consensus of the school, and also those few conflicting rules on which jurists agreed were equally probable, but also rules that according to al-Nawawī, could no longer be considered orthodox Shāfiʿī law. The *Minhāj* represents a shift in thinking about the *madhhab* and a turn toward the prioritization of *ikhtilāf* as a means of preserving the school from corruption.

The transmission of ikhtilāf

For these reasons, Ibn Qāḍī Shuhbah argued that the *madhhab*—the collective opinion of the school—had begun to die-out by the end of the seventh/thirteenth century, at the very time that al-Nawawī makes the argument for the interpolation of distorted opinions into the texts of the *madhhab*. Ibn Qāḍī Shuhbah sees a direct link between the corruption of legal thinking and the events of the Mamlūk period. The end of the *madhhab* coincides with the rise of the Mamlūks and the devastations wrought by the plagues, economic decline, and political instabilities of the period. The failure of the jurists to prevent these calamities seems to have had an effect on his faith in the value of the received corpus of opinion. In effect, Ibn Qāḍī Shuhbah is arguing that jurists must 'think outside the box' if they are to be able to meet the challenges of rapidly changing social, economic, and environmental circumstances.

The interpolation of *ikhtilāf* into legal discourse expanded the range of opinions from which jurists could draw and allowed deficient jurists to judge the correctness of previous opinions for themselves. Instead of a limited range of opinions certified by the tradition as valid, jurists had the option of accessing a wide range of views that allowed for greater latitude in legal decision making. To be able to make the argument for a broader range of legal opinion, Ibn Qāḍī Shuhbah not only had to point to the texts which contained diverging opinions, but he had to establish the *isnād* (chain of transmission) for the authority of these opinions as ultimately originating with al-Shāfiʿī. He does this in three ways: 1) by listing those whose opinions count in the construction of divergent opinion, 2) by listing those who are certified by training to transmit those opinions, and 3) by listing and establishing the authority of the core texts containing diverging opinions.

The origins of ikhtilāf

Four jurists in the first generation are mentioned as transmitting divergent opinion to later generations through personal educative connections: Abū Thawr (d. 2540/854),[22] al-Muzanī,[23] al-Rabīʿ al-Murādī,[24] and Yūnus b. ʿAbd al-Aʿlā (d. 264/877–78).[25] Abū Thawr's chain of transmission dies out by the fifth generation (342/953–359/970),[26] and Yūnus b. ʿAbd al-Aʿlā's by the third (301/913–320/932).[27] Al-Rabīʿ's chain has four transmitters from him in the first three generations, none of whom continue to transmit divergent opinion through educative connections. Only al-Muzanī has educative connections that continue beyond the fifth generation. He has two primary scholarly descendants, Ibn Surayj and al-Marwazī. These two jurists account for over 80% of the transmission of divergent opinions through education in the first five generations.

Therefore, the *isnād* for the transmission of divergent opinions begins with al-Muzanī, who represents the voice of disagreement within the school. He is juxtaposed with al-Rabīʿ who is described as transmitting statements from al-Shāfiʿī.[28] If a full account of al-Shāfiʿī's intellectual descendants were presented above (all 784 jurists), it would show that al-Rabīʿ transmits al-Shāfiʿī's opinion to twelve disciples in the following three generations, who in the next generations transmit the *madhhab* to fifteen other jurists. Thus while al-Muzanī is the source of divergent opinion in the school, al-Rabīʿ is the source of the *madhhab*.

---

[22] Khān, vol. 1, 55–56.

[23] Ibid., 58–59.

[24] Ibid., 65–66.

[25] Ibid., 72–73.

[26] Ibn Qāḍī Shuhbah mentions three primary transmitters of *ikhtilāf* from Abū Thawr: 1) al-Ḥasan b. Sufyān al-Shaybānī (d. 303/916), who used to issue legal rulings based on the opinion (*madhhab*) of Abū Thawr (vol. 1, 92); 2) ʿAlī b. al-Ḥasan al-Baghdādī (d. 310/922), who is described as one of the *aṣḥāb al-wujūh*, and who used to follow the opinion of Abū Thawr before turning to al-Shāfiʿī (vol. 1, 96–97); and 3) Abū al-Sāʾib al-Hamdānī (d. 350/961), who was the first to be appointed a judge following the Shāfiʿī school (vol. 1, 129).

[27] Both of the jurists cited by Ibn Qāḍī Shuhbah as transmitting *ikhtilāf* from Yūnus are primarily known as *ḥadīth* scholars. The famous *ḥadīth* collector al-Nisāʾī (d. 303/915) is listed as having studied (*akhadha*) with Yūnus (vol. 1, 88) and ʿAbdallāh b. Muḥammad al-Qazwīnī (d. 315/927–28) is listed as taking *ḥadīth* from him (vol. 1, 95). Their importance as transmitters of divergent opinion seems to have more to do with their inclusion in the *ʿAzīz* by al-Rāfiʿī than their work with Yūnus.

[28] Khān, vol. 1, 65–66.

Transmission from al-Muzanī continues until the seventh/thirteen century when the chain of descent begins to break down. With the composition of the three most important *fiqh* texts cataloging divergent opinion, the *ʿAzīz sharḥ al-wajīz*, by al-Rāfiʿī, the *Rawḍat al-ṭālibīn* by al-Nawawī, and the *Maṭlab fī sharḥ al-wasīṭ* by Ibn al-Rifʿah (d. 710/1311), a coherent chain of transmission all but disappears.

The difference between the authority to espouse a divergent opinion and to debate divergent opinions

What then, does this mean for Ibn Qāḍī Shuhbah's history and the role of *ikhtilāf* in the survival of Islamic Law? With the near total breakdown of *ikhtilāf isnāds*, the authority to issue opinions that are at variance with the *madhhab* had all but disappeared. Only he, according to his own text, had the authority to voice opinions that disagreed with the received corpus of the *madhhab*. This may be why he felt he had the authority to hold opinions that disagreed with those of al-Shāfiʿī. But, what does it mean to disagree?

Ibn Qāḍī Shuhbah delineates three different modes of divergence in his description of the history of the school. There is first order *ikhtilāf* that diverges from the opinions of al-Shāfiʿī, such as that originating with al-Muzanī and Abū Thawr.[29] There is also second order dispute that diverges from the views of other jurists capable of using the texts of revelation. For instance, Abū al-Ḥasan al-Māwardī, in his discussion of ritual purity in his *Ḥāwī*, disputes al-Muzanī's claim to have transmitted from al-Shāfiʿī Qur'anic citations and *sunnah* outlining the importance of water in attaining *ṭahārah* (ritual purity). Al-Māwardī objects (*iʿtaraḍ*) to al-Muzanī's statement on the (rather specious) grounds that al-Shāfiʿī is not part of an *isnād* for transmitting the Qur'an (meaning that al-Muzanī erred by quoting al-Shāfiʿī's citation of the Qur'an), and the evidence used by al-Shāfiʿī in his opinion was evaluated differently (using a different set of evidence) than was done by al-Muzanī.[30] Finally, third order divergence is a dispute between jurists on legal questions originating not from an independent examination of the texts of revelation, but from disputes arising out of differing interpretations of already decided rules.

---

[29] Ibid., vol. 1, 58–59.
[30] Abū al-Ḥasan al-Māwardī, *al-Ḥāwī al-kabīr*, vol. 1, 35–36.

First order disagreement, that which diverges from the opinion of al-Shāfiʿī, is of a different quality than second order disagreement. First order disagreement means that the jurists have the authority to apply al-Shāfiʿī's methods of legal discovery to the texts of revelation and find solutions which he, as a result of some error, missed. This corresponds with the first rank of affiliated jurists in al-Nawawī's description of juridical levels.[31] Second order disagreement results from the examination of the texts of revelation that end in finding solutions that vary from other jurists, which is similar to the second rank of affiliated jurists outlined by al-Nawawī.[32] Third order disagreement is the purview of the lowest tier of affiliated jurists and of deficient jurists according to al-Nawawī's theoretical ranks.[33] First and second order disagreement requires the ability to apply personal methods of reason (*ijtihād*), while third order disagreement requires that the jurists only be *muqallid* to previous scholars.

Ibn Qāḍī Shuhbah's description of legal decline implies that after the closing of the period of legal vitalization, the late seventh/thirteenth century, only a handful of scholars were qualified to carry out *ijtihād* or *ijtihād*-like methods on the texts of revelation. The vast majority of jurists had become mere memorizers of legal rules and lacked the training and ability to analyze the texts of revelation in search of legal solutions. Ibn Qāḍī Shuhbah carefully separates those whom he describes as having voices in the creation and transmission of divergent opinion from those that merely debate divergent opinion (*khilāf*), or memorize and debate it. In his discussion of those active in the production of some form of divergence, he lists those whom al-Rāfiʿī, al-Nawawī, or Ibn al-Rifʿah mention as authorities, as well as those who authored their own texts containing disputed legal questions. Both of these groups would fall into either the first or second rank of affiliated jurist, with the *aṣḥāb al-wujūh* (the authoritative holders of divergent opinions) most likely being qualified to dispute al-Shāfiʿī, and most of the rest simply disputing each other. The remaining jurists, forty in all, are involved in *khilāf*, or a form of debate that examines which of the already decided rulings is most correct. This group is made up of low-level affiliated and deficient

---

31 Al-Nawawī, *al-Majmūʿ*, vol. 1, 71.
32 Ibid.
33 Ibid.

jurists who are not qualified to directly examine the texts of revelation, but are simply involved in sorting out the mass of already decided legal cases.

Ibn Qāḍī Shuhbah seems to create a functional hierarchy of jurists based on their abilities to access the texts of revelation as a means of deciding legal issues as he thought they existed in reality (see figure 7.2 below). At the top of the pyramid are the 'jurists with their own or independent *madhhab*s.' This would include not just al-Shāfiʿī, but also al-Muzanī and Abū Thawr, to both of whom Ibn Qāḍī Shuhbah attributes some level of independence (although since Shāfiʿī is the originator of the method of the school he would naturally stand higher).[34] It may be the case that al-Muzanī was thought by some scholars to fall outside the *madhhab*, but it is clear that Ibn Qāḍī Shuhbah is not one of them. For Ibn Qāḍī Shuhbah, independence is not an attribute that necessarily disqualifies one from inclusion in the school, although how one can be independent (meaning in terms of method and rule) and *muqallid* to al-Shāfiʿī at the same time is not clear.

Next are the jurists whom Ibn Qāḍī Shuhbah claims are *muṭlaq*, or 'unlimited' *mujtahid*s. He specifically attributes this status to only three jurists: Ibn al-Ṣabbāgh, Ibn al-Rifʿah, and al-Rāfiʿī. Ibn Qāḍī Shuhbah says that Ibn al-Ṣabbāgh is not only qualified to carry-out *ijtihād muṭlaq* (unlimited levels of personal reasoning on the texts of revelation), but he is also one of the *aṣḥāb al-wujūh*.[35] Likewise, Ibn Qāḍī Shuhbah says of Ibn al-Rifʿah, "I do not know among the Shāfiʿī's after al-Rāfiʿī a *muṭlaq* who equaled him;"[36] meaning that not only was Ibn al-Rifʿah an unlimited *mujtahid*, so was al-Rāfiʿī. After the unlimited jurists he places the *aṣḥāb al-wujūh*, or the authors of opinions that may potentially diverge from the opinions of al-Shāfiʿī.

After the unlimited jurists and the *aṣḥāb al-wujūh*, Ibn Qāḍī Shuhbah places those jurists from whom al-Rāfiʿī, al-Nawawī, and Ibn al-Rifʿah transmit. Highest in this group are those to whom he attributes an *isnād* going back to al-Muzanī as the authority for divergence. Historically, these groups, for the most part, come to an end by the

[34] Khān, vol. 1, 55–56; 58–59.
[35] Ibid., vol. 1, 251–52.
[36] Ibid., vol. 2, 213.

Figure 7.2. The hierarchy of practicing jurists according to Ibn Qāḍī Shuhbah

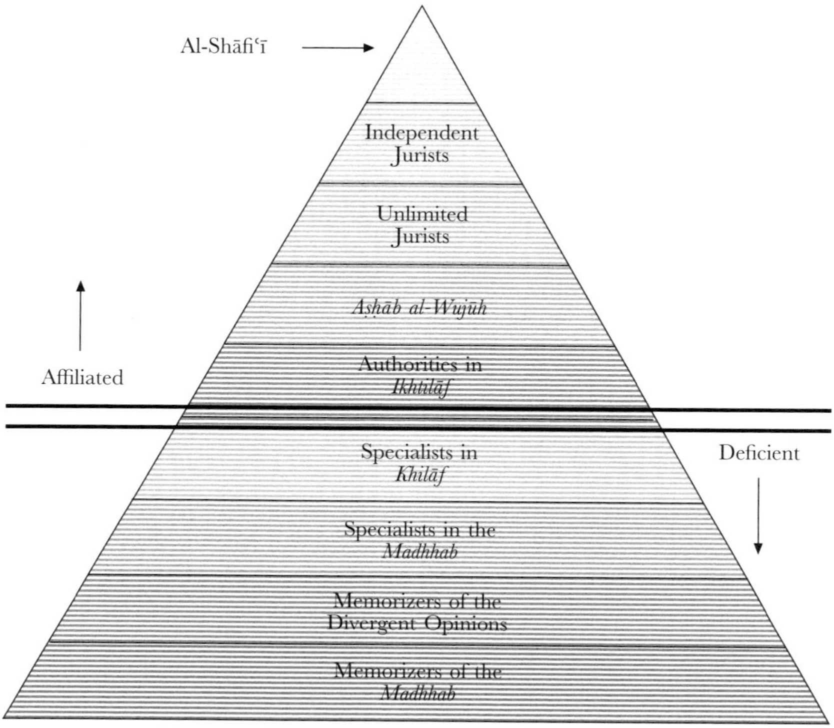

late seventh/thirteenth century for reasons mentioned in the last chapter. There are a few jurists (seven) to whom he attributes some level of *ijtihād*, but these are rare in the Mamlūk period.

The next groups of jurists are all deficient in that they are unqualified to examine the texts of revelation and must rely on the opinions of previous jurists. Highest among these are those jurists who specialize in *khilāf*, and are thus able to sort out differing opinions and weigh them against each other. However, there are only forty such jurists in the history of the school according to Ibn Qāḍī Shuhbah, and as such they do not carry much overall importance.

After the specialists in *khilāf*, according to Ibn Qāḍī Shuhbah, there are specialists in the *madhhab* who, nevertheless, do not represent a homogenous group. These are ranked according to the level of competence in their knowledge of the corpus of received opinion.

Ibn Qāḍī Shuhbah creates four primary levels of ability: 1) leaders (*a'immah*, sing., *imām*), 2) those who excel (*bara'a*), 3) those who are knowledgeable (*ma'rifah*), and 4) those who associate or participate (*shārak*).[37] In his historical progression, Ibn Qāḍī Shuhbah reduces the number of scholars in the first tier and increases the number of scholars in the lower tiers, indicating that as corruptions of *fiqh* seep into the texts of the *madhhab*, juridical competence declines.

After the specialists in the *madhhab*, Ibn Qāḍī Shuhbah presents two groups of memorizers, those of divergent opinions, and those of the *madhhab*. These jurists memorize the texts of each discipline and thereby serve an important role in the continuing function of the school. Ibn Qāḍī Shuhbah seems to recognize that in the period of legal decline, memorization is important. Since these scholars are limited to the rulings of previous jurists, his *Ṭabaqāt* is intended to encourage them to memorize and use specific texts. By focusing on certain texts, especially those containing widely ranging divergent opinions, jurists will have a larger store of decisions from which to draw.

The texts of ikhtilāf

As mentioned above, Ibn Qāḍī Shuhbah lists twenty-one texts that make up the core *fiqh* texts of the Shāfi'ī school. Eight of these texts represent the *madhhab*, but thirteen represent divergent opinions from the masters of the school. It is to these texts that Ibn Qāḍī Shuhbah sends deficient jurists as a protection for the school and against the insertion of errant opinion (see figure 7.3). The thirteen *ikhtilāf* texts are, by their nature, commentaries and collections of received legal dicta that, for the most part, coalesce around the works of two authors: al-Muzanī and al-Ghazālī. Their texts and the opinions that develop around, and often, in opposition to them, form the two central complexes of divergent opinion in the school.

[37] Ibn Qāḍī Shuhbah implies that this connotes someone who dabbles in various fields but does not master any.

Figure 7.3. The texts of divergent opinion

	Text	Author	dod
1.	*al-Jāmiʿ al-kabīr*	al-Muzanī	264/877
2.	*al-Mukhtaṣar*	/	/
3.	*al-Ḥāwī fī al-furūʿ*	Ibn Qāḍī	342/955
4.	*al-Shāmil*	Ibn al-Ṣabbāgh	447/1055
5.	*al-Ḥāwī*	al-Māwardī	450/1058
6.	*al-Nihāyah*	Imām al-Ḥaramayn	478/1085
7.	*al-Wasīṭ*	al-Ghazālī	505/1111
8.	*Mukhtaṣar al-wajīz*	al-Tabrīzī	621/1224
9.	*al-ʿAzīz sharḥ al-wajīz*	al-Rāfiʿī	624/1227
10.	*al-Taʿjīz fī mukhtaṣar al-wajīz*	Ibn Yūnus	671/1272
11.	*al-Rawḍat al-ṭālibīn*	al-Nawawī	677/1278
12.	*al-Maṭlab fī sharḥ al-wasīṭ*	Ibn al-Rifʿah	710/1311
13.	*Kitāb tamyīz al-taʿjīz*	Ibn al-Bārizī	738/1338

Source: Ibn Qāḍī Shuhbah, *Ṭabaqāt al-fuqahāʾ al-shāfiʿīyah*, ed. al-Ḥāfiẓ ʿAbd al-Alī Khān, 4 vols. (Beirut: ʿĀlam al-kutub, 1987).

The al-Muzanī complex of ikhtilāf *texts*

Al-Muzanī's *Mukhtaṣar* is the most important early text of divergent opinion. It is commented on, memorized, and studied twenty-four times in Ibn Qāḍī Shuhbah's *Ṭabaqāt* (the last occurring in the 8th/14th century).[38] Although Norman Calder has called into question the actual authorship of the text, it is clear that later scholars, Ibn Qāḍī Shuhbah among them, believed that al-Muzanī composed the text and was, therefore, an important source of expanding the range of al-Shāfiʿī's legal opinion.[39] According to Ibn al-Nadīm, the *Mukhtaṣar* was originally written in an extended version, known as the *Mukhtaṣar al-kabīr*, that had fallen out of use by the early 3rd/10th century. The text that came to be known simply as the *Mukhtaṣar* was the abridged version of the text.[40]

In the introduction to the text, al-Muzanī states that he composed the short work from the texts of al-Shāfiʿī (*ʿilm al-Shāfiʿī* literally, the knowledge of al-Shāfiʿī) and from opinions he heard directly from

[38] Khān, vol. 1, 75–76, 79, 102, 105–06, 107, 115, 117, 127, 130, 138, 140, 144, 167, 188, 211, 215, 216, 228, 281, 287; vol. 2, 253; vol. 3, 54.
[39] Calder, *Studies in Early Muslim Jurisprudence*, 86–104.
[40] Muḥammad b. Isḥāq Ibn al-Nadīm, *Fihrist*, ed. Gustav Flügel (Leipzig: Verlag von F. C. W. Vogel, 1872), 212.

the eponym.[41] As Calder has pointed out, however, there are frequent disagreements between characterizations and quotes that al-Muzanī asserts came from al-Shāfiʿī and those found in *Kitāb al-umm*, which the tradition came to see as composing al-Shāfiʿī's most authentic statements as transmitted by al-Rabīʿ. Because of this, al-Muzanī was always the subject of much discussion and distrust, particularly among those who identified more closely with the centrality of the *madhhab* (core doctrines of the school).[42]

Abū al-Ḥasan al-Māwardī's *al-Ḥāwī al-kabīr*, a commentary on the *Mukhtaṣar*, is one attempt to clarify the 'errors' committed by al-Muzanī and to defend the *madhhab* against divergent opinions that originated with his writings.[43] The *Ḥāwī al-kabīr* represented a full-fledged assault on the place of al-Muzanī in the Shāfiʿī school. Al-Māwardī not only attacked how al-Muzanī quoted al-Shāfiʿī, but also his method; arguing that, in many cases, al-Muzanī fell outside the parameters of the school.[44] Ironically, the *Ḥāwī al-kabīr* came to represent, for Ibn Qāḍī Shuhbah, a text that perpetuated the divergent opinion that originated with al-Muzanī, not as a guard against it, and was memorized, commented on, or studied by seven other jurists mentioned in the *Ṭabaqāt*.[45]

Al-Muzanī also wrote another text that became foundational in the formation of *ikhtilāf* in the school. His *al-Jāmiʿ al-kabīr* is mentioned in the *Ṭabaqāt* as being commented on or cited by only three jurists,[46] but its most important commentary, *al-Ḥāwī fī al-furūʿ*, written by Abū Aḥmad Ibn al-Qāḍī, was commented on, studied, or memorized by thirteen additional jurists.[47] Little is known about the *Jāmiʿ* of al-Muzanī. It is not mentioned by Ibn al-Nadīm, and does not appear to be extant, although Wüstenfeld erroneously argued that it was brought down to modern times as an edition of the *Mukhtaṣar*.[48]

---

[41] Ismāʿīl b. Ibrāhīm al-Muzanī, *al-Mukhtaṣar al-muzanī fī furūʿ al-shāfiʿī*, ed. Muḥammad ʿAbd al-Qādir Shāhīn (Beirut: Dār al-kutub al-ʿilmīyah, 1998), 7.

[42] Calder, *Studies in Early Muslim Jurisprudence*, 88–89.

[43] Al -Māwardī, *al-Ḥāwī al-kabīr*, vol. 1, 7.

[44] Ibid., 8–33.

[45] Khān, vol. 3, 14, 58, 95, 109, 138, 164.

[46] Ibid., vol. 1, 132, 139, 143.

[47] Ibid., vol. 1, 132; vol. 2, 214, 217–18, 239, 272, 299; vol. 4, 33, 38, 45, 56, 72, 79, 87, 112.

[48] See Ferdinand Wüstenfeld, "Der Imām el-Schāfʿī," *Abhandlungen der Königlichen Gesellschaft der Wissenschaften* 36 (1890): 17, 68–71. Also see W. Heffening, "al-Muzanī," in *Encyclopedia of Islam*, 2nd ed., and Ibn Kallikān, *Wafayāt al-aʿyān*, vol. 1, 217–18.

Al-Ḥāwī fī al-furūʿ, like the *Jāmiʿ*, does not appear to have survived.[49] It is likely, however, to have been critical of al-Muzanī. Ibn al-Qāḍī was a disciple of Abū Isḥāq al-Marwazī (d. 340/951) who wrote a text that sought to mediate between the opinions of al-Muzanī and al-Shāfiʿī, in which he raised a number of objections to the *Mukhtaṣar*.[50] Ibn al-Qāḍī was also a teacher of al-Māwardī, the author of the *Ḥāwī al-kabīr*.[51] *Al-Ḥāwī fī al-furūʿ* is particularly important in the *Ṭabaqāt* because it is listed as being used by eight jurists in Ibn Qāḍī Shuhbah's own time, thus bringing al-Muzanī down to the late Mamlūk period.[52]

The fact that two of the most important texts cited by Ibn Qāḍī Shuhbah as sources of *ikhtilāf* that transmitted the ideas of al-Muzanī are also critical of him should not indicate that Ibn Qāḍī Shuhbah did not understand the jurist to be central in the formation and transmission of divergent opinion. To the contrary, criticism of legal opinion was a key feature in the movement to make *ikhtilāf* a vital component in the development of a more inclusive definition of orthodoxy. As seen above, texts of the *madhhab* lacked rigorous judicial review and revision and became infused with ideas that were thought to be contrary to Shāfiʿī doctrine. Although it is clear that al-Muzanī was a problematic figure, he was also close to al-Shāfiʿī and had a large following in the school; his authority was such that he could not be dismissed by those who opposed him. Even though he was frequently accused of moving beyond the limits of al-Shāfiʿī's jurisprudential method, the fact that so much attention was focused on his opinions meant that discussions about how to find legal rulings based on the basic method of the eponym continued to take place. Al-Muzanī's importance for the school did not derive just from his opinion, or his legal method, but from the controversies that surrounded him and the attention to method that came with it. In many respects, al-Muzanī functions as a mirror against which the

[49] The text is not listed in Brockelmann, Ziriklī, Sezgin, Çelebi, nor in Ibn al-ʿImād. There is a reference to the text in ʿUmar Riḍā Kakhālah, *al-Mustadrak ʿalā muʿjam al-muʾallifīn tarājim muṣannifī al-kutub al-ʿarabīyah* (Damascus: Maktabat al-ʿarabīyah, 1957–61; reprint, Beirut: Dār iḥyāʾ al-turāth al-ʿarabī, 1983), vol. 10, 37, but there is no description of its contents.
[50] Khān, vol. 1, 106, 132.
[51] Ibid., vol. 1, 132.
[52] Ibid., vol. 4, 33, 38, 45, 47, 56, 76, 78, 87.

jurisprudential method of al-Shāfiʿī, and the opinions that supposedly developed out of it, came into full relief.

The al-Ghazālī complex of ikhtilāf *texts*

After the *Mukhtaṣar*, the most important work that forms the foundation of later *ikhtilāf* texts is the *Wajīz* by al-Ghazālī. The *Wajīz* is actually a text that, according to Ibn Qāḍī Shuhbah, came to represent the *madhhab* but was generated out of the divergent ideas emanating from Imām al-Ḥaramayn al-Juwaynī. The *Wajīz* is a condensation of al-Ghazālī's *al-Wasīṭ*, which, in turn, is an abridgment of his text *al-Basīṭ fī al-madhhab*.[53] The *Basīṭ* was a commentary on the *Nihāyah al-maṭlab fī dirāyah al-madhhab* by Imām al-Ḥaramayn al-Juwaynī.[54] Imām al-Ḥaramayn was an extremely important figure in the early school and Ibn Qāḍī Shuhbah juxtaposes him with Abū Isḥāq al-Shīrāzī as the opposite pole of authoritative thought in the eleventh generation (460/1068–480/1088). If al-Shīrāzī is characterized as the conduit of the transmission of the *madhhab* by Ibn Qāḍī Shuhbah, Imām al-Ḥaramayn is the channel for *ikhtilāf*. Both Imām al-Ḥaramayn and al-Shīrāzī are included in the eleventh generation (460/1068–480/1088) of the *Ṭabaqāt*. As mentioned in the pervious chapter, they are represented as occupying opposite ends of the spectrum in the use and application of *uṣūl al-fiqh*, although Ibn Qāḍī Shuhbah seeks to soften the appearance of Imām al-Ḥaramayn because of his central role as a transmitter of *ikhtilāf*.

In describing Imām al-Ḥaramayn, Ibn Qāḍī Shuhbah says that "without exception, he was the leader of the leaders" (*kānna imām al-aʾimmah ʿalā al-iṭlāq*), and describes the *Nihāyah* as his "most significant publication." [55] Al-Subkī, in his *Ṭabaqāt al-shāfiʿīyah al-kubrā* states that "there was no text like [the *Nihāyah*] in the school in what it authoritatively asserted."[56] He goes on to say that Imām al-Ḥaramayn took

[53] Abū Ḥāmid al-Ghazālī, *al-Wasīṭ fī al-madhhab*, ed. Aḥmad Maḥmūd Ibrāhīm and Muḥammad Muḥammad Tāmir (al-Ghūrīyah: Dār al-salām, 1997), vol. 1, 103.

[54] Khān, vol. 1, 294. Also see Ibn al-ʿImād, *Shadharāt al-dhahab*, vol. 4, 12, and Brockelmann, GI, 424.

[55] Khān, vol. 1, 256.

[56] Al-Subkī, *Ṭabaqāt al-shāfiʿīyah al-kubrā* (1999), vol. 3, 163.

> great care in the writing of the massive doctrinal text known as *al-Nihāyah*. . . . Until he edited it and he dictated it. [The text] resulted from intensive study (*baḥath*), teaching, formulation, investigation, close examination, and the precise determination of what quenches a burning thirst [in the] drought of the science of the *sharīʿah* and [in] the study of the law for the elite students. It clarifies the path (*al-sabīl*) and it teaches according to it.[57]

The *Nahāyah* also appears to have been a large text, stretching to approximately forty volumes.[58]

Al-Ghazālī was a student of Imām al-Ḥaramayn and wrote a number of texts that drew on the writings of his master. The *Basīṭ* appears to have followed the *Nihāyah* quite closely. The commentary, however, must have been quite large and does not seem to have inspired much notice by other scholars.[59] It was condensed in an abridged form by al-Ghazālī after 488/1095.[60] Although it is not clear how al-Ghazālī modified the text, the abridgement, known as *al-Wasīṭ fī al-madhhab* (the 'Middle' on the Opinion), contained much of the material of the original. For instance, Ibn Khallikān, in referring to jurists mentioned in the *Nihāyah*, frequently states that they were also listed in the *Basīṭ* and the *Wasīṭ* as well.[61]

Unfortunately, neither the *Nihāyah* nor the *Basīṭ* have been published and what we know about the texts can only be extrapolated from the *Wasīṭ*. The three texts drew on divergent opinions generated by a broad range of Shāfiʿī scholars including al-Muzanī, al-Buwayṭī, members of the *aṣḥāb al-wujūh*, and others who were considered authoritative holders of *ikhtilāf*,[62] as well as scholars outside the school, such as Abū Ḥanīfah and Abū Yusūf.[63] Although the *Nihāyah* and the *Basīṭ* mentioned a broader range of opinions and showed how these were derived using al-Shāfiʿī's method, the *Wasīṭ* continued to

[57] Ibid., 167.

[58] Kātip Çelebi, *Kashf al-ẓunūn*, vol. 2, 199.

[59] It seems that there were no commentaries written on the text. See Kātip Çelebi, *Kashf al-ẓunūn*, vol. 1, 245.

[60] Al-Dhahabī, *Siyār aʿlām al-nubalāʾ*, vol. 19, 334.

[61] See, for instance Ibn Khallikān, *Wafayāt al-aʿyān*, vol. 2, 134, 397; vol. 4, 200.

[62] Al-Nawawī, "al-Tanqīḥ fī sharḥ al-wasīṭ," in *al-Wasīṭ fī al-madhhab*, ed. Aḥmad Maḥmūd Ibrāhīm and Muḥammad Muḥammad Tāmir (al-Ghūrīyah: Dār al-salām, 1997), vol. 1, 79–80.

[63] For an excellent review of the sources for the *Nihāyah*, *Basīṭ*, and the *Wasīṭ*, see ʿAlī Muḥyī al-Dīn ʿAlī al-Qarah Dāghī's introduction to the 1984 edition of the *Wasīṭ* (Cairo: Dār al-iʿtiṣām, 1984), vol. 1, 7–280; especially, 243–46.

carry a significant number of divergent opinions and was considered by many scholars to be an extremely important text in its own right.[64]

The *Wasīṭ*, however, most usually sublimates the opinions of the various authorities into a group of unidentified 'others' whose opinions are then challenged. While there are references to individual scholars, as in the discussion of using *ijtihād* to ascertain the difference between pure and impure water for use in ritual ablutions, this is actually quite rare.[65] When al-Ghazālī wrote the abridgement to the *Wasīṭ* he continued the process of narrowing the range of *ikhtilāf* and removed almost all references to specific scholars. Comparing the *Wajīz* to the *Wasīṭ* we see how the process of narrowing occurred. In the chapter on ascertaining the purity or impurity of water for ritual ablution in the *Wasīṭ*, al-Ghazālī refers to specific scholars seven times and to unnamed others twice.[66] In his chapter in the *Wajīz*, he only refers to one scholar by name (Ibn Surayj) and he does not refer to any unnamed scholars or texts at all.[67]

Al-Maṭlab fī sharḥ al-wasīṭ

The *Wasīṭ* became the subject of many commentaries in the centuries following its completion, many of which continued to be used into the 1800s.[68] For Ibn Qāḍī Shuhbah, the most important commentary was Ibn al-Rifʿah's *al-Maṭlab fī sharḥ al-wasīṭ*, which ran to an enormous 60 volumes.[69] Unfortunately, the text has not been published and as of this writing, no analysis of the contents of the work has been produced. Al-Subkī, in his biography for Ibn al-Rifʿah, quotes several passages from the *Maṭlab* and states that he was "the Shāfiʿī of the period."[70] Ibn al-ʿImād, quoting al-Isnawī, states that the *Maṭlab* "was a marvel among the great texts and was the object of investigations."[71] Al-Isnawī goes on to say that "he did

---

64 Al-Nawawī, "al-Tanqīḥ fī sharḥ al-wasīṭ," 83–84.
65 Al-Ghazālī, *al-Wasīṭ fī al-madhhab* (1997), vol. 1, 214–28.
66 Ibid.
67 *ʿAzīz sharḥ al-wajīz*, vol. 1, 72–80.
68 Kātip Çelebi, *Kashf al-ẓunūn*, vol. 2, 2008–09, who lists the title as *Sharḥ al-wasīṭ*. Ibn Qāḍī Shuhbah and Ibn al-ʿImād states that the text was only 40 volumes. See Khān, vol. 2, 212 and *Shadharāt al-dhahab*, vol. 6, 163.
69 Ibid., 2008.
70 Al-Subkī, *Ṭabaqāt al-shāfiʿīyah al-kubrā*, vol. 5, 13.
71 Ibn al-ʿImād, *Shadharāt al-dhahab*, vol. 6, 163. For a very brief reference, see Wüstenfeld, "Der Imām el-Schāfiʿī," 17.

not complete [the text], but included sections from the congregational prayer to sale."[72] Although the text is described in the *Ṭabaqāt* as being commented on, studied, or memorized by three jurists only, this is due to the fact that it was written a little more than a century before Ibn Qāḍī Shuhbah. The *Maṭlab* is one of the three texts, along with the *ʿAzīz* and the *Rawḍah* that Ibn Qāḍī Shuhbah lists as authoritative for later jurists because of its comprehensive nature and the authority of its author.[73]

Al-Wajīz

With the *Wajīz*, however, al-Ghazālī completed the process of narrowing the range of divergent opinions transmitted through Imām al-Ḥaramayn and attempts to establish an orthodoxy for the school. He eliminates divergences and collapses the al-Juwaynī wing of Shāfiʿī opinion into a single authoritative view. He, in effect, reverses the process of expansion witnessed in texts of the *madhhab* and seeks to remove doubts and confusions by creating a doctrinal view that stands above all other Shāfiʿī texts. Were al-Nawawī sought to remove corruptions from the *madhhab* by introducing divergent opinions into doctrinal discussions, al-Ghazālī, a century earlier, attempted to remove confusions by purging the school of all but a few approved opinions.

In the centuries following its completion, the *Wajīz* became an extremely important text, not in and of itself, but for what it symbolized for the development of the school.[74] It was understood to distill all of the thought that originated with al-Muzanī and transmitted though al-Juwaynī, and to create out of it, a *madhhab* (body of authoritative thought) that stood alongside the *madhhab* originating with al-Rabīʿ and transmitted through al-Shīrāzī. The authors of *ikhtilāf* texts used it as the foundation for their works in order to regenerate a range of opinions that could unify, through their diversity, the collective opinion of the school over time.

The *Wajīz* served as the basis of five different divergent opinion works mentioned by Ibn Qāḍī Shuhbah, including the *ʿAzīz* and ultimately, the *Rawḍah*. *Al-Wajīz* was also commented on, studied, or

---

[72] Al-Isnawī, *Ṭabaqāt al-shāfiʿīyah*, vol. 1, 297.
[73] Khān, vol. 2, 212.
[74] According to Çelebi, there were over forty different commentaries on the *Wajīz*. See *Kashf al-ẓunūn*, vol. 2, 2002–04.

memorized by seven scholars in Ibn Qāḍī Shuhbah's text.[75] One of the most important commentaries was the *Mukhtaṣar al-wajīz* by Abū al-Khayr al-Tabrīzī, which was commented on, studied, or memorized by two scholars.[76] Al-Tabrīzī's work was also commented on by Ibn Yūnus, in his *al-Taʿjīz fī mukhtaṣar al-wajīz*. The *Taʿjīz* appears to have been an influential text that is described as being "astonishingly famous among the Shāfiʿīs,"[77] although why this is the case is not immediately clear. Ibn Yūnus was not a well known scholar and he does not receive a biography in Ibn Qāḍī Shuhbah's text. He is mentioned in a brief biography by al-Subkī, which says that Ibn Yūnus "prayed a great deal" and studied at the al-Ghazālīyah *madrasah*.[78] Ibn Qāḍī Shuhbah says that eleven jurists commented, memorized, or studied the *Taʿjīz*.[79] One commentary was written by Ibn al-Bārizī, whose *Kitāb tamyīz al-Taʿjīz* was memorized and studied by four jurists up to Ibn Qāḍī Shuhbah's time.[80] Including the *Rawḍah*, which is a based on the *ʿAzīz*, the *Wajīz* gave rise to over 80% of all divergent opinion works list by Ibn Qāḍī Shuhbah in the last 250 years that his text covers (see figure 7.4).

Al-ʿAzīz sharḥ al-wajīz

The *ʿAzīz sharḥ al-wajīz* is a monumental work that held immense importance for medieval Shāfiʿī scholars. Ibn Qāḍī Shuhbah, quoting al-Isnawī, says that "there is no publication in the Shāfiʿī school like it."[81] Al-Nawawī said,

> I know that there is no book in the school of al-Shāfiʿī, may God be pleased with him, about [his opinion] like what comes to you in everything of which it cites. [No book] is more perfect than al-Rāfiʿī's with its investigations. It is my belief and the belief of all, [that] a compilation of its like is not to be found in previous books or in [the works] of modern authors in what it refers to among the resolutions of the important issues.[82]

---

[75] Khān, vol. 2, 69, 75–77, 92, 137, 176, 202, 245.
[76] Ibid., vol. 2, 92, 232, 246. See Çelebi, *Kashf al-ẓunūn*, vol. 2, 1626.
[77] Çelebi, *Kashf al-ẓunūn*, vol. 1, 418.
[78] Al-Subkī, *Ṭabaqāt al-shāfiʿīyah al-kubrā* (1999), vol. 4, 344. His biography does not appear in Ibn al-ʿImād.
[79] Khān, vol. 2, 180–81, 226, 243, 247, 268, 289, 297, 299; vol. 3, 137, 145, 170.
[80] Ibid., vol. 3, 65, 145; vol. 4, 57, 91–92. See Çelebi, *Kashf al-ẓunūn*, vol. 1, 418.
[81] Khān, vol. 2, 76.
[82] Ibid., 77.

Figure 7.4. The genealogy of divergent opinion *fiqh* texts

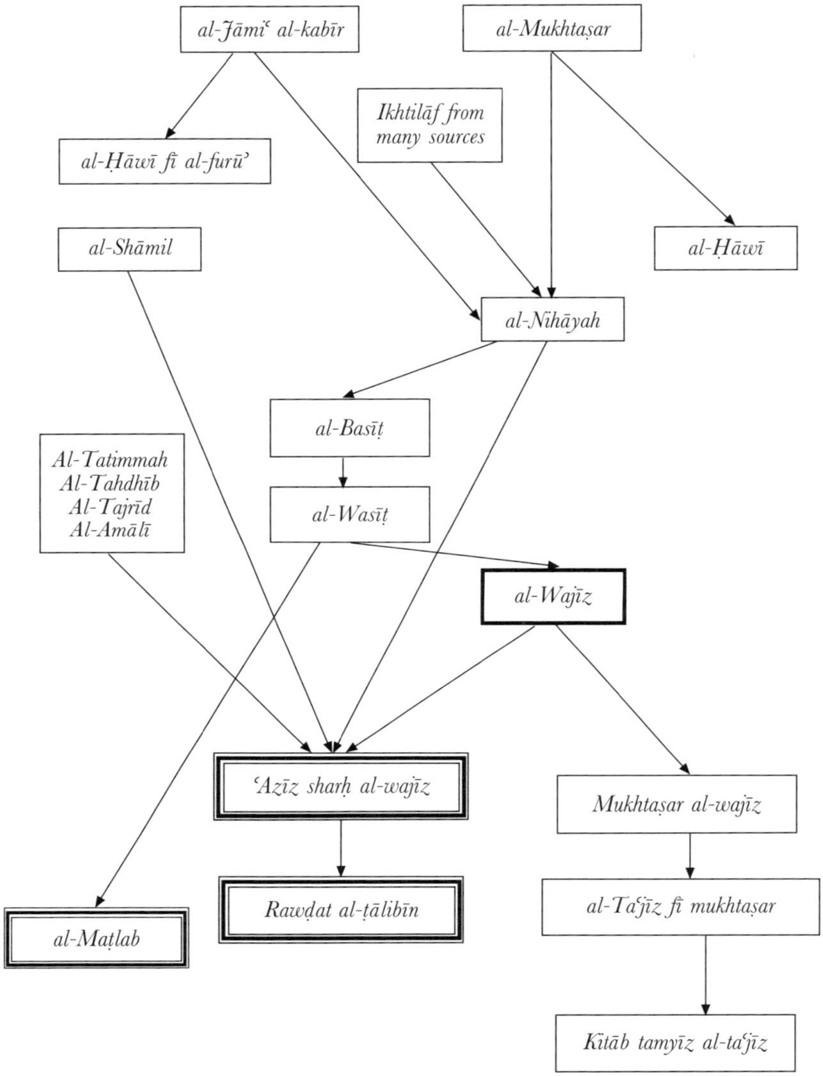

The value of the work for deficient jurists is demonstrated in almost every passage of the text. In virtually every legal category, the range of possible opinions from which deficient jurists can draw is dramatically increased compared to those found in the texts of the *madhhab*. Using the discussions of evaluating the purity of water for use in ritual cleansing as a touch-stone, al-Shīrāzī, in his *Muhadhdhab*, discusses only a few issues and cites eight scholars. Most of these authorities transmit statements from al-Shāfiʿī or are cited as forming a consensus position on particular legal issues. Difference of legal opinion is generally sublimated to the ethos of the text, which is to assert the view that the *madhhab* is a cohesive group of scholars who have agreed on a core set of doctrines formed around the method of the founding *Imām*.[83] While the *Wajīz* narrows the diversity even further to include just one scholar, al-Rāfiʿī expands the diversity of opinion to include thirty-six scholars (including himself, al-Shāfiʿī, and references to the *madhhab*), not to mention anonymous references to the 'companion students' of various authorities.[84] Throughout, he presses the point that there is divergence over many issues and he seeks to place them on the same level. Although he frequently asserts his views on a variety of issues concerning the opinions that he thinks are most sound, the correctness of the opinion is not fixed, but only applies in the circumstance of the problem mentioned in the text. It does not become a law in any concrete form, but is to be used as a basis for other legal rulings in situations that are analogous to the textual precedent.[85]

---

[83] Al-Shīrāzī, *al-Muhadhdhab*, vol. 1, 12–25.

[84] Al-Rāfiʿī, *ʿAzīz*, vol. 1, 7–56.

[85] Wael Hallaq is extremely important in understanding what he terms '*ijtihādic* pluralism,' although he goes too far in asserting that the purpose of "all legal works" was to reduce the "multiplicity [of views] to a single, authoritative opinion," which was "absolutely essential for achieving the highest possible degree of both consistency and predictability" (*Authority, Continuity, and Change*, 125–26). While it is true that many texts, especially those of the *madhhab*, or those with pretensions of creating *madhhab* as with the *Wajīz*, were concerned with reducing diversity in order to create "consistency and predictability," *ikhtilāf* texts, while seeking to present 'correct' opinions that were deemed to be the most sound, were equally intent on preserving diversity. Hallaq, in fact, points to the reason why *ikhtilāf* texts such as the *ʿAzīz* were so popular with jurists, especially in the crisis period of the Mamlūk age. Pluralism, while being acknowledged by legal theory, was nonetheless discouraged, while jurists 'on the ground' prized diversity because it provided them with more flexible tools for administering law (p. 127). Jurists such as Ibn Qāḍī Shuhbah focused on the transmission of diversity in *Ṭabaqāt* works because they were more concerned with the reality of legal work than with the theory of its formulation.

Ibn Qāḍī Shuhbah, quoting al-Isnawī, states that "the greater part of (the *ʿAzīz*) is taken from discussions of al-Ghazālī (in his *al-Wajīz*) and from commentaries on six books: the *Nihāyah*, the *Tatimmah*, the *Tahdhīb*, the *Shāmil*, the *Tajrīd* of Ibn Kajj, and the *Amālī* by al-Sarakhsī."[86] These six texts draw on over 90 other texts written by the masters of the school.[87]

The *Nihāyah*, discussed above, is referred to in the *Ṭabaqāt* as being used by four jurists[88] and the *Shāmil* by Ibn al-Ṣabbāgh is mentioned as having been memorized or studied by three jurists.[89] Both texts are also important because of the authority of their authors. Ibn al-Ṣabbāgh was one of the *aṣḥāb al-wujūh* and rose to the level of unlimited *ijtihād*,[90] and al-Juwaynī, as was mentioned above, was one of the greatest scholars of his time and the son of a *mujtahid*.[91] Al-Juwaynī's *al-Shāmil* was the subject of many commentaries that survived until the 19th century[92] and is described by Ibn Khallikān as one of the "better Shāfiʿī books."[93]

The *Tatimmah* was written by Abū Saʿd al-Mutawallī (d. 468/1076) who was also one of the *aṣḥāb al-wujūh*.[94] According to Ibn Qāḍī Shuhbah, the original text was never completed but was added to by other jurists so that the various editions of the text were very dissimilar.[95] According at al-Subkī, the text was based on a work written by his teacher Abū al-Qāsim al-Fūrānī (d. 461/1069) entitled *Tatimmat al-ibāna*.[96]

The *Tahdhīb fī furūʿ* was written by Abū ʿAlī al-Zajjājī (d. around 400/1009–10), who is not mentioned as either a practitioner of divergent opinion or as an *aṣḥāb al-wujūh*. It was a short text, about the

While it is true that al-Rāfiʿī frequently argues for a view that is most sound, the importance of his work for jurists was not his vetting of a particular opinion, but in the presentation of multiple views that they could use in various situations as new problems arose. For an excellent discussion of the process of vetting legal opinions in *Ikhtilāf* works, see Hallaq's discussion on pages 121–65.

86 Khān, vol. 2, 77.

87 ʿAlī Muḥammad Muʿawwaḍ, *Muqaddimat al-ʿazīz sharḥ al-wajīz* (Beirut: Dār al-kutub al-ʿilmīyah, 1997), 18–25.

88 Khān, vol. 1, 256, 286, 293, 309; vol. 2, 76.

89 Ibid., vol. 1, 252, 272, 290, 303; vol. 2, 76.

90 Ibid., vol. 1, 251.

91 Ibid., vol. 1, 255–56.

92 Çelebi, *Kashf al-zunūn*, vol. 2, 1025.

93 As quoted by Çelebi, *Kashf al-zunūn*, vol. 2, 1025.

94 Khān, vol. 1, 247–48.

95 Ibid., 248.

96 Al-Subkī, *Ṭabaqāt al-shāfiʿīyah al-kubrā* (1999), vol. 3, 123.

size of al-Shīrāzī's *Tanbīh*. Ibn Qāḍī Shuhbah says that it was a *furū*ʿ text which was an appendix to Ibn al-Qāṣṣ al-Ṭabarī's *al-Miftāḥ*.[97] Ibn al-Qāṣṣ (d. 335/946–47) is described by Ibn Qāḍī Shuhbah as being a student of Ibn Surayj and as being one of the leaders of "our companions." He was also the author of a number of important legal works, one of which was the *Miftāḥ*.[98] The *Miftāḥ* was an significant text that had dedicated to it a number of commentaries that survived into modern times, although the *Tahdhīb* does not appear to be extant.[99]

The *Tajrīd* was written by Yūsuf b. Aḥmad b. Kajj Abū al-Qāsim al-Dīnawarī, who was better known as Ibn Kajj (d. 405/1015). According to Ibn Qāḍī Shuhbah, Ibn Kajj was one of the *aṣḥāb al-wujūh* and the leader of the school in his time.[100] Besides its use in the *ʿAzīz* the text does not appear to have been widely used and it is not listed in Çelebi's *Kashf al-ẓunūn*.

Finally, the *Amālī* was written by Abū al-Faraj al-Sarakhsī (d. 494/1101), who is mentioned as an authority on divergent opinions. He was one the leaders of Islam in his time, although he is not mentioned as one of the *aṣḥāb al-wujūh*.[101]

What makes these texts important is the authority of their authors and the prestige of the jurists they cite. Throughout Ibn Qāḍī Shuhbah's text, he mentions those from whom al-Rāfiʿī transmitted divergent opinions. Al-Rāfiʿī drew his citations from the six texts above. They therefore represent the authoritative textual sources for the divergent opinions found in the *ʿAzīz*.

Al-Rāfiʿī's authority to write such a wide ranging *fiqh* text comes from his chain of educative connections that go back to both al-Shāfiʿī and al-Muzanī. He is intellectually descended from al-Shāfiʿī through al-Rabīʿ and al-Muzanī through Muḥammad b. ʿAbd al-Karīm al-Qazwīnī (314), Abū Muḥammad al-Baghawī (248), Abū ʿAlī al-Marwadhī (206), ʿAbdallāh b. Aḥmad al-Marwazī (144), Abū Zayd al-Fāshānī (103), Abū Isḥāq al-Marwazī (51), Abū Muḥammad al-Marwazī, who was better known as "ʿAbdān' (24), who studied with both al-Rabīʿ (10) and al-Muzanī (3). He is also an unlimited

[97] Ibid., vol. 1, 139–40. Also see Çelebi, *Kashf al-ẓunūn*, vol. 1, 517.
[98] Khān, vol. 1, 106–07.
[99] Çelebi, *Kashf al-ẓunūn*, vol. 2, 1769; Sezgin, vol. 1, 496–97.
[100] Khān, vol. 1, 198–99.
[101] Ibid., vol. 1, 266. Also see Çelebi, *Kashf al-ẓunūn*, vol. 1, 163.

mujtahid according to Ibn Qāḍī Shuhbah's biography of Ibn al-Rifʿah (mentioned above). Ibn Qāḍī Shuhbah says in his biography of al-Rāfiʿī that he was the "*mujtahid* of his time in the school."[102] He was, therefore, uniquely qualified to speak for the school and to present not only his view of legal authority, but also the kinds of legal dispute allowable in the school. Thus, he is presented as being positioned to define the broad boundaries of orthodoxy, much in the same way Ibn Qāḍī Shuhbah presents himself.

Al-Rawḍat al-ṭālibīn

The final text Ibn Qāḍī Shuhbah prioritizes is the *Rawḍah al-ṭālibīn* by al-Nawawī, although it is clearly derivative of the work written by al-Rāfiʿī. This text, he argues, is based on the *ʿAzīz* and adds only a few additional voices of divergent opinion not included by al-Rāfiʿī.[103] In his section on the purity of water used for ritual cleansing, al-Nawawī includes the opinions of over thirty-eight scholars (including himself, al-Shāfiʿī, and references to the *madhhab*).[104] He seeks to assert, as did al-Rāfiʿī, that the Shāfiʿī school was historically based not on core doctrines but on a commonly agreed upon method, that under changing circumstances different rulings can be found that take change into account, and that very few issues are ever completely closed.

Conclusion

Ibn Qāḍī Shuhbah prioritized texts containing divergent legal opinions over texts representing the *madhhab* because of his concern that the abilities of jurists in the Mamlūk period had declined to such a point that they were no longer capable of accessing the texts of revelation in the search for legal solutions. He does not simply list which texts are best for deficient jurists to use, but argues for the authority of the divergent opinions found in the texts by providing the *isnād*s for the authors of *ikhtilāf*. These *isnāds* argue that the author-

[102] Ibid., vol. 2, 76.
[103] Khān, vol. 2, 77.
[104] Al-Nawawī, *al-Rawḍat al-ṭālibīn*, ed. ʿĀdil Aḥmad ʿAbd al-Mawjūd and ʿAlī Muḥammad al-Muʿawwaḍ (Beirut: Dār al-kutub al-ʿilmīyah, 2000), vol. 1, 114–150.

ity to espouse divergent legal opinions originated with al-Muzanī. This is clearly demonstrated by Ibn Qāḍī Shuhbah's biographical citation for al-Muzanī, where he argues that although al-Muzanī held an independent opinion, his method nevertheless followed that of al-Shāfiʿī.

The *isnād*s of divergent authority also demonstrate that with the rise of the Mamlūk period coherent lines of intellectual descent all but disappear. Only Ibn Qāḍī Shuhbah's teacher al-Ṭaymānī, and by implication the author himself, continue to possess the authority to assert divergent legal opinions. Although most jurists were no longer sufficiently authorized to articulate legal opinions based directly on the texts of revelation, the ability to do so had not completely vanished.

CHAPTER EIGHT

IBN QĀḌĪ SHUHBAH, CRISIS, AND HIS AUTHORITY

In the winter and spring of 841/1437–38 Ibn Qāḍī Shuhbah sat in a cold dimly lit room and dictated his *Ṭabaqāt* to a select group of students. He was sixty years old and, as his hand writing suggests, he suffered from poor eyesight and tremors of the hand.[1] The cold of the late winter storm had killed many of the spring crops and caused water shortages in the city of Damascus, and although it is unknown if Ibn Qāḍī Shuhbah suffered deprivations as a result, it is clear he would have witnessed the hardships around him. Bubonic and pneumonic plague also ravaged the region, forcing people indoors, closing windows and shutting air vents to keep outside the bad humours that were thought to cause the disease.[2] If he heated the room in which he worked, it must have been filled with dank, smoke-laden air.[3]

Given the closed doors and windows, Ibn Qāḍī Shuhbah and his scribes would have worked by candle or oil lamp light.[4] The illumination would have been poor and the text hard to see. The feelings

[1] See the MS of his *Ṭabaqāt al-fuqahā' al-shāfiʿīyah*, Arabic Manuscript Collection, The British Library, Or. Mus. 3037, especially the *ijāzah* on the front cover. Also see his *Tarājim al-fuquhā' al-shāfiʿīyah min dhayl al-rawḍatayn li-abī shāmah*, Garrett Arabic manuscript Collection, Princeton University, MS 694.

[2] Dols, *The Black Death in the Middle East*, 47.

[3] There has been remarkably little research done on the heating systems of medieval Muslim architecture. See C. K. Wilkinson, "Heating and Cooking in Nishapur," *Bulletin of the Metropolitan Museum of Art*, no. 2 (1944): 282–91; Robert Hillenbrand, *Islamic Architecture: Form, Function, and Meaning* (New York: Columbia University Press, 1994), 461; K. A. C. Creswell, *A Short Account of Early Muslim Architecture* (Cairo: The American University in Cairo Press, 1989), 142. In E. De Boccard's *Les Monuments Ayyoubides de Damas* (Paris: Institut Français de Damas, 1932) there is no discussion or description of fireplaces in any of the *madrasahs* and Mosques build during the Ayyūbid period. Michael Burgoyne [*Mamluk Jerusalem* (London: British School of Archaeology in Jerusalem, World of Islam Festival Trust, 1987)] mentions two instances of fireplace heating in Jerusalem, but these were added during the Ottoman period (pp. 164, 234). It is likely that rooms in *madrasahs* were heated by small portable braziers that vented smoke into the room. See Finbarr Barry Flood, *The Great Mosque of Damascus: Studies on the Makings of Umayyad Visual Culture* (Brill: Boston, 2001), 38.

[4] See Doris Behrens-Abouseif, *Mamluk and Post-Mamluk Metal Lamps* (Cairo: Institut Français D'Archéologie Orientale, 1995).

of darkness, crisis, and turmoil were additionally heightened by rumours of the eschaton that began to circulate throughout the region. Sitting in that cold dim room, Ibn Qāḍī Shuhbah and his students must have felt that the world balanced on the brink of destruction.

As all of this was going on, Ibn Qāḍī Shuhbah was also engaged with the world outside. As news of the Sulṭān's illness and impending death arrived in Damascus, the viceroy Jakamī began to plot his rise to power. Given that Ibn Qāḍī Shuhbah rose to become chief Shāfiʿī judge of Damascus within a few months of Barsbāy's death, it is not unreasonable to suspect that the jurist must have engaged in discussions with Jakamī or his representatives and may have sought the position believing that a change of regime might create a space for his own advancement.

Based on what al-Sakhāwī tells us, it is likely that Ibn Qāḍī Shuhbah had even greater aspirations than simply become chief Shāfiʿī judge of Damascus. It seems that he wanted ultimately to be recognized as the leader (*raʾīs*) of the Shāfiʿī school, its intellectual head and guide; to be renowned as a *mujtahid* at a time when few could claim the title. Al-Sakhāwī says that when Ibn Qāḍī Shuhbah came across an opinion in a Shāfiʿī text he was capable of using *takhrīj* (the process of deriving a legal ruling using '*ijtihādi*c' methods), but that he did not do so because of fears of public reactions.[5] He thus felt he had the ability to be a *mujtahid* but was not publicly acclaimed as such.

Becoming chief Shāfiʿī judge was, among other things, a means to becoming recognized as a *mujtahid*. Although in earlier periods being a judge was not necessarily seen as an attribute of virtue or intelligence,[6] by the Mamlūk period, at least as Ibn Qāḍī Shuhbah understood it, being chief Shāfiʿī judge was a necessary component in the accumulation of intellectual status that made becoming *raʾīs* and a *mujtahid* possible.[7]

---

[5] Al-Sakhāwī, *al-Ḍawʾ al-lāmiʿ*, vol. 11, 23.

[6] N. J. Coulson, "Doctrine and Practise in Islamic Law: One Aspect of the Problem," 211–26.

[7] Devin Stewart, "Capital Accumulation," 356–60. Also see the biography of ʿAbd al-Raḥmān b. ʿUmar al-Bulqīnī for an example of how the accumulation of status, including being appointed chief Shāfiʿī judge, was important in being recognized as a *mujtahid* (Khān, vol. 4, 87–89).

Throughout his *Ṭabaqāt*, Ibn Qāḍī Shuhbah pays careful attention to the development of the Shāfiʿī judiciary in Damascus, and unlike with earlier generations of historians, he displays little repugnance for the position. His text presents an author who is, above all things, a realist interested in the actuality of life as a professional religious scholar. He is very much involved with the world, one that seems to be spinning toward greater hardship and decline.

The tension between crisis and the necessities of living, between the corruption of the law and the need to perpetuate its administration in society, and the quest for the authority and legitimacy to do so, are the dominant themes of the text. The book is both reflective and forward-looking. It seeks to describe the history of Shāfiʿī law, to point to the causes and examples of its decline, and also to show a way out of the crisis through simple education and divergent opinion.

Authority and the production of ṭabaqāt *texts*

Although it is commonly agreed that *ṭabaqāt* works are about describing authority, it should not be assumed that they only concern the authority of the scholars of they catalogue. Ibn Qāḍī Shuhbah, sitting in that dark, close room, was also interested in describing his own authority, as a scholar, a jurist, and a person descended from the tribe of the Prophet. His text, among other things, can be interpreted as a claim for his own authority to become chief judge and thus leader of the Shāfiʿīs of Syria and a *mujtahid*. Each time he was poised to become chief Shāfiʿī judge, the most important judicial position in all of Syria he returned to the classroom and produced an edition of the *Ṭabaqāt*. The construction of authority is, however, a complicated matter. The ability of a scholar to argue for his ownership of the highest levels of intellectual power stems from his claim to the accumulation of the various manifestations of authority. Biographies were, in many respects, designed to attest to the authority of a scholar by cataloguing his wealth, the numbers and reputations of his students and teachers, books he had written, his intellectual and physical lineage, his appointments to various positions, and other accoutrements of greatness.[8] While his *Ṭabaqāt* is about the history

[8] See Devin Stewart, "Capital Accumulation," 356–60; Mottahedeh, *Loyalty and Leadership in an Early Islamic Society*, especially the whole of chapter three.

of the Shāfiʿī school—the crises the community faced and the paths by which scholars can correct the decline of legal thought—it is also a self-conscious attempt to present its author as an heir to the great scholars of the past and as a leader uniquely qualified to lead the Syrian Shāfiʿī community in its hour of peril.

The *Ṭabaqāt* is a kind of autobiography that maps the sources of Ibn Qāḍī Shuhbah's authority, which he does by emphasizing the importance of lineage and intellectual pedigree. While he never directly asserts his own positive claims, they always lie in the background, and his authority as the leader of the school is elevated by the reflected importance of those his presents as being his ancestors.

Lineage

> Abū Bakr b. Aḥmad b. Muḥammad b. ʿUmar b. Muḥammad b. ʿAbd al-Wahhāb b. Muḥammad b. Dhuʾayb b. Musharraf Taqī al-Dīn b. Shihāb al-Dīn b. Shams al-Dīn b. Najm al-Dīn b. Sharaf al-Dīn al-Asadī al-Shuhbī al-Dimashqī al-Shāfiʿī

Ibn Qāḍī Shuhbah's name conveys important information about his cultural position in medieval Islamic society. Names communicate information about lineage, family, tribe, profession, specializations, and residency.[9] Names also speak to the authority of a person who is engaged in a religious profession, as they define one of the most important paths for the transmission of knowledge (*ʿilm*). Understanding the importance of names for medieval Arab Muslims is therefore an important step in contextualizing Ibn Qāḍī Shuhbah's claim to authority.

The first thing that one notices about Arab names is their length. Ibn Qāḍī Shuhbah's name contains nine generations of ancestors covering approximately 200 years of history. Nine generations of ancestors is common for names in Ibn Qāḍī Shuhbah's time, although

[9] There have been several works written in recent years on Muslim and Arabic names. For an informative, although not very useful reference, see Salahuddin Ahmed's *A Dictionary of Muslim Names* (New York: New York University Press, 1999). This text has limited use because it does not provide a transliteration of the Arabic into English. Also see Annemarie Schimmel, *Islamic Names* (Edinburgh: University Press, 1989). This text is very helpful in supplying transliterations for the often tricky names of Muslims who have non-Arabic *kunyah*s (surnames). It is also has a very interesting discussion of the symbolism of Muslim names and their meanings in Islamic society.

some scholars record names covering fifteen to twenty generations.[10] The length of a name is meant to demonstrate an individual's connection with the past, to outline his or her lineage (*nasab*). For scholars, it also communicates specific meanings about the reputation of the family, its longevity, and importance. Arabs in medieval Islamic society believed that a person inherited the qualities and abilities of his or her ancestors. The reputation of a person's family carried important cultural meaning. An individual was frequently thought to possess not only the qualities of his parents and grandparents, but also of his immediate clan group, as well as the more ancient tribes and great people from whom he was believed to descend.[11]

For scholars, descent appears to have functioned on two levels: 1) children inherited specific kinds of knowledge through direct study with fathers, grandfathers, and other relatives, thus acquiring their reputation, specializations, and authority, and 2) children inherited spiritual gifts that were thought by many medieval Muslims to pass down family lineages.

Ibn Qāḍī Shuhbah indicates in his text that in most instances (73% of the time) scholars initially study as children with their fathers. They frequently studied law,[12] but they also studied any of the Islamic sciences in which their fathers were expert. Descriptions of Ibn Qāḍī Shuhbah studying with his father are important, not for the number of subjects studied, nor the amount of time spent in study, but for establishing that Ibn Qāḍī Shuhbah sat with his father and thereby received his authority.[13] In doing so, he acquired not just the authority

---

[10] For instance, see the biography of Muḥammad b. ʿAlī al-Dimashqī (d. 765/1363) who has nineteen generations listed in his name. In addition, his name states that he is a descendant of the Prophet Muḥammad (*Sayyid*), a *ḥadīth* specialist, an author (*mu'allif*), and instructor (*al-mufīd*). Khān, vol. 3, 129–30.

[11] See Roy Mottahedeh, *Loyalty and Leadership in an Early Islamic Society*, 98–104.

[12] For instance, see the biography of Muḥammad b. Ismāʿīl al-Qalqashandī (d. 809/1406). Khān vol. 4, 52.

[13] It was not uncommon for children to be taken to sit with a *ḥadīth* scholar to learn a few traditions, and then to be given an *ijāzah* (permission) for the transmission of all of the *ḥadīth* the scholar had memorized and catalogued. The *ijāzah* was not meant to cover every line of *ḥadīth*, for these could easily be learned later, but for the position the child gained as being a link in the long line of transmission that went back to the Prophet. In a sense, what was transmitted had very little to do with the content of the lessons, but the almost intimate contact one gained with the presence of the Prophet that moved through the generations with the traditions. In the same way, study with a father had little to do with the legal rules or methods learned, but with the authority in those areas that moved from the

of his father, but also the authority of his family. Ibn Qāḍī Shuhbah mentions in the biography of his father Aḥmad b. Muḥammad that Aḥmad "studied a wide array of subjects with his father (Muḥammad b. ʿUmar) and the people of his generation."[14] Thus the knowledge that Ibn Qāḍī Shuhbah received was not just from his father, but also, through him, from his grandfather and from all of those with whom he had studied. Muḥammad b. ʿUmar, in turn, is mentioned as studying law and grammar from his paternal uncle ʿAbd al-Wahhāb b. Muḥammad (d. 726/1325).[15] In addition to these family members, Ibn Qāḍī Shuhbah also implies that he studied from his paternal uncle Yūsuf b. Muḥammad (d. 789/1387), who is cited as studying also with Ibn Qāḍī Shuhbah's grandfather Muḥammad b. ʿUmar.[16] Therefore, Ibn Qāḍī Shuhbah's *nasab* charts not only his lineage but also the chain of academic/scholarly authority that he inherited as a member of his family (see figure 8.1 below). It projects backward in time the familial connections by which authority has been passed from generation to generation (much in the same way that an *isnād* functions in the transmission of *ḥadīth* and the way that intellectual connections function in Ibn Qāḍī Shuhbah's *Ṭabaqāt*).

The fact that Ibn Qāḍī Shuhbah lists his father and other relatives in his text is an attempt to prop-up the reputation of his family and create a greater level of authority for himself. His father was in actuality a relatively minor scholar who is not mentioned by al-Maqrīzī or Ibn Taghrī Bidrī. He is mentioned by Ibn Ḥajar al-ʿAsqalānī in the *Inbāʾ al-ghumr* but the passage is an abbreviation of the biography given by Ibn Qāḍī Shuhbah in the *Ṭabaqāt.*[17] Likewise, the biography provided by Ibn al-ʿImād in the *Shadharāt al-dhahab* is taken completely from the *Ṭabaqāt.*[18]

Furthermore, while it appears that Muḥammad b. ʿUmar, Ibn Qāḍī Shuhbah's grandfather, was a fairly well known scholar, he only received a passing reference by al-Maqrīzī and is not men-

Prophet through the family of father and son connections. Study between fathers and sons therefore, conveyed sacred religious knowledge that would continue to elevate the family as long as the educative process continued. See Richard Bulliet, "The Age Structure of Islamic Education," *Studia Islamica*, no. 57 (1983): 105–17.

[14] Khān, vol. 3, 148.

[15] Ibid., vol. 2, 173.

[16] Ibid., vol. 3, 183.

[17] Compare *Inbāʾ al-ghumr*, vol. 2, 296 with the passage in Khān, vol. 3, 148.

[18] *Shadharāt al-dhahab*, vol. 7, 58–59.

Figure 8.1. Ibn Qāḍī Shuhbah's lineage according to his family's *nasab*

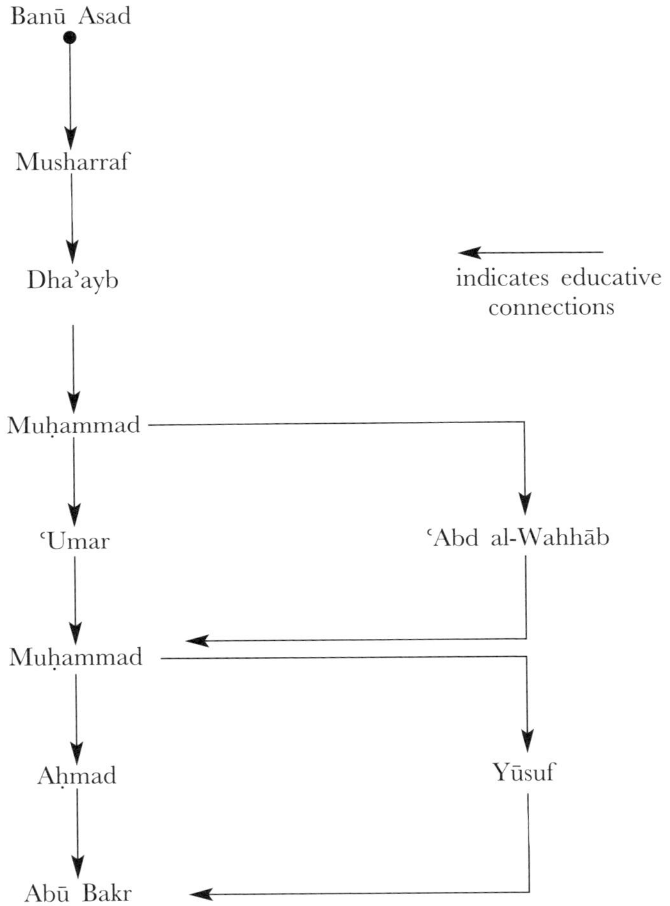

tioned at all by Ibn Taghrī Birdī.[19] Ibn Ḥajar's biography of him is based on the *Ṭabaqāt*, and the citation given in the *Shadharāt* is taken completely from Ibn Qāḍī Shuhbah.[20] Likewise, his uncle Yūsuf b. Muhammad's biography in Ibn 'Imād is based entirely on the *Ṭabaqāt*, while Ibn Ḥajar does not follow the *Ṭabaqāt*, but instead the *Tārīkh* of Ibn Qāḍī Shuhbah.[21]

[19] Al-Maqrīzī, *al-Sulūk*, vol. 3, 407. He is not mentioned in the *Manhal al-Ṣāfī*.
[20] *Inbā' al-ghumr*, vol. 2, 35–38; *Shadharāt al-dhahab*, vol. 7, 15–16.
[21] See *Shadharāt al-dhahab*, vol. 7, 56; *Inbā' al-ghumr*, vol. 2, 277; Ibn Qāḍī Shuhbah, *Tārīkh*, vol. 1, 237.

Only his ancestor ʿAbd al-Wahhāb b. Muḥammad appears to have attained any fame and is mentioned by al-Subkī in his *Ṭabaqāt* and by Ibn Kathīr in the *Bidāyah wa ʾl-nihāyah*.[22] Both biographies are very brief while the passage in Ibn Qāḍī Shuhbah's text is quite extensive and combines the biographies of al-Subkī, Ibn Kathīr, and references to other scholars to build a picture of an important and influential scholar.[23]

By including the biographies of his family members in his text, Ibn Qāḍī Shuhbah is attempting to create for himself an image of authority that he might not otherwise possess. It appears to have been successful, for by listing his father, grandfather, uncle, and great-granduncle in his book, he led other scholars to replicate his lineage in their works and to present them as authorities in their own right. Their reputations, reported almost entirely by Ibn Qāḍī Shuhbah, but quoted by his contemporaries and by later scholars, had the effect of creating for his family, and thus for him, an inheritance of esteem in legal knowledge that might have otherwise been unknown.

Establishing his credentials, however, involved not only the reputation of his immediate ancestors but also the prestige of this entire family. Part of establishing the lineal inheritance of an individual in medieval Muslim society was frequently focused on tying a person to a family, and for Arabs, a tribal group. As discussed in chapters three and four, prominent families used access to many kinds of knowledge as a means of social promotion in situations where wealth was controlled by absolutist state authorities. Elite families competed with one another for important state-paid positions in government and the judiciary, and therefore, for the favor of ruling political elites.

The 'Ibn Qāḍī Shuhbah' was one such family. The family is said to take its name from an ancestor known as Najm al-Dīn ʿUmar al-Asadī who was supposedly chief judge of the village of Shuhbah for over forty years,[24] although when he lived is known. Ibn Qāḍī Shuhbah's *nasab* also indicates that the Ibn Qāḍī Shuhbah family was a clan group in the larger Banū Asad tribe. Although there were

---

[22] Al-Subkī, *Ṭabaqāt al-shāfiʿīyah al-kubrā* (1999), vol. 5, 296–97; Ibn Kathīr, *al-Bidāyah wa ʾl-nihāyah*, vol. 14, 126.

[23] Khān, vol. 2, 267.

[24] Al-Ziriklī, *al-Aʿlām*, vol. 2, 35; al-Sakhāwī, *al-Ḍawʾ al-lāmiʿ*, vol. 11, 21. There are no dates given indicating when Najm al-Dīn might have lived. Furthermore, because many genealogies drop names over time in order to condense lists or are simply forgotten, it is not possible to accurately estimate his date of death.

several tribal groups with the name 'Banū Asad,' it appears that Ibn Qāḍī Shuhbah's family was descend from Quṣayy, a cousin of ʿAbd al-Muṭṭalib, the Prophet Muḥammad's grandfather.[25]

Descent from the tribe to which Muḥammad belonged carried with it a special status that other tribal groups did not possess. The Quraysh tribe was thought to be unique, to possess qualities and abilities that other groups could not claim. The innate qualities of the tribe gave its members specific kinds of authority to lead the community. The ideology of the Caliphate was based on the idea that only the descendents of the Quraysh tribe had the ability to lead the community according to God's design.[26] Although the Caliphs were, by the Mamlūk period, puppets of the Sulṭānate, the esteem given to members of the Quraysh tribe was still quite high.

Throughout his *Ṭabaqāt*, Ibn Qāḍī Shuhbah displays a general and telling interest in tribal affiliation. He mentions tribal affiliation in 244 biographies, or 31% of the time. Attention to tribal affiliation seems to be unusual for Shāfiʿī *ṭabaqāt* texts. For instance, Abū Isḥāq al-Shīrāzī, in his *Ṭabaqāt al-fuqahāʾ*, only mentions tribal affiliation in approximately 15% of biographies, usually in the citations for the companions and their successors. Al-Isnawī, in his *Ṭabaqāt*, includes tribal affiliation in the *nasab*s of jurists in only 6% of biographies (listing only 34 tribes), and in al-Subkī's al-*Ṭabaqāt al-shāfiʿīyah al-kubrā*, tribes are mentioned in fewer than 10% of the biographies (also listing 34 tribes). A comparison of Ibn Qāḍī Shuhbah's and al-Subkī's works is particularly telling in this regard. In the biographies of his own family members, al-Subkī does not list any tribal affiliation,[27] yet Ibn Qāḍī Shuhbah mentions al-Subkī's *nasab*, stating that he is affiliated with the al-Khazrajī al-Anṣārī tribe (one of the two Medinan tribes that welcomed Muḥammad after his flight from Mecca in 622).[28] Ibn Qāḍī Shuhbah's attention to descent in this instance implies that, 1) the al-Subkī family was descended from the 'helpers' of Muḥammad, and 2) that he is explicitly arguing that the 'Ibn Qāḍī Shuhbah' family has precedence and, therefore, more authority since it is descended from the Banū Quraysh.

[25] *Encyclopedia of Islam*, new ed., s.v. "Ḳurays," by Montgomery Watt.
[26] Ibid.
[27] Al-Subkī, *Ṭabaqāt al-shāfiʿīyah al-kubrā* (1964–76), vol. 9, 124, 167, 411; vol. 10, 89, 139, 391.
[28] Khān, vol. 2, 265, 300; vol. 3, 22, 38, 59, 104, 127, 134, 154.

Furthermore, al-Dhahabī, in his *Kitāb al-muʿīn fī ṭabaqāt al-muḥaddithīn*, mentions the tribal affiliation of only 268 of 2424 people listed in his text (11%). In his *Tārīkh al-islām*, however, tribal affiliation is mentioned in well over half of the biographies. Similarly, in Ibn ʿAsākir's *Tārīkh madīnat dimashq*, tribal affiliation is mentioned in the majority of biographies. Ibn ʿAsākir's focus on tribal identification may indicate that in historical writing genealogy is more important because it helps contextualize individuals against the long view of Islamic history. It brings to mind socio-cultural, as well as historical and religious meanings that are important for Arab Muslim historians, which should not be over looked. The importance of tribal identification in historiography may be another reason why Ibn Qāḍī Shuhbah cites such a high percentage of tribes in his text. Given his training in historiographical method with Shihāb al-Dīn Ibn al-Ḥijjī, it is natural that he would make recourse to methods in historiographical biographical citation. But, as with many aspects of his text, this may not be the only reason.

Ibn Qāḍī Shuhbah also explicitly links tribal affiliation and thus an individual's prestige with the transmission of divergent legal opinions. In over 80% of the biographies where he attributes the authority to discover, or to be mentioned as a source of divergent legal opinions, Ibn Qāḍī Shuhbah provides tribal affiliation. These tribes are primarily grouped into four tribal blocks (see table 8.1): 1) Quraysh (accounting for 85 jurists), 2) Qaḥṭānī, primarily Anṣārī (Khazraj) (accounting for 51 jurists), 3) Wā'il b. Qāsiṭ (accounting for 19 jurists), and 4) Muḍarī (accounting for 45 jurists). These four blocks account for 82% of all tribes mentioned in his text.

Table 8.1. Tribal blocks in Ibn Qāḍī Shuhbah's *Ṭabaqāt*

al-Muḍarī	#	Wāʿil b. Qāsiṭ	#	al-Qaḥṭanī	#	al-Quraysh	#
al-Ḍabbah	5	al-Taghlib	7	al-Ashʿarī	3	al-Quraysh	25
al-Tamīm	19	al-Thaʿlabah	5	al-Kalb	3	al-Ḥārith	2
al-ʿAmr	4	al-Shaybān	7	al-Khuzaʿah	1	al-ʿĀmir	2
al-Saʿd	9			al-Yāfiʿ	1	al-Makhzūm	7
al-Kinān	8			al-Lakhm	4	al-Quṣayy	5
				Al-Azd	5	al-Asad	7
				Al-Kindah	2	al-Umayyah	1
				al-Khazraj	32	al-Hāshim	2
						al-ʿUthmān	1
						al-Bakr[†]	7
						Ibn ʿAsākīr	4

Table 8.1. (*cont.*)

al-Muḍarī	#	Wāʿil b. Qāsiṭ	#	al-Qaḥṭanī	#	al-Quraysh	#
						al-ʿAbbās	3
						al-Ḥusaynī	9
						al-Khaṭṭāb	2
						al-Zuhr	6
						al-Ḥarīrī	2
Totals	45		19		51		85

Source: Ibn Qāḍī Shuhbah, *Ṭabaqāt al-fuqahā' al-shāfiʿīyah*, ed. al-Ḥāfiẓ ʿAbd al-Alī Khān, 4 vols. (Beirut: ʿĀlam al-kutub, 1987).
† There is an important tribe of the Wā'il b. Qāṣit group by the name 'al-Bakrī.' Ibn Qāḍī Shuhbah clearly does not mean this tribal group when he refers to al-Bakrī in his text. He mentions the al-Bakrī tribe seven times in his *Ṭabaqāt*. The first three biographies are referred to as 'al-Qurashī, indicating that this Bakrī group is a part of the Quraysh tribe. This is clarified in his biography for Abū al-Ḥasan al-Bakrī, whom he states was "among the descendants (*min wuld*) of ʿAbd al-Raḥman b. Abū Bakr al-Ṣiddīq," the son of the first Caliph (vol. 2, 274).

Obviously, the Quraysh and the Anṣār (Banū Khazraj) were important and early transmitters of Muḥammad's traditions. Abū Isḥāq al-Shīrāzī speaks to the importance of these two groups in the transmission of proto-law from Muḥammad to the eponymous founders of the then five major schools of law.[29] Abū Isḥāq states in the introduction to his discussion of the Companions of the Prophet that there are three sources of law, the utterance (*khiṭāb*) of God, the utterance (*khiṭāb*) of the Prophet, and the actions (*afʿāl*) of the Prophet. These sources must be subjected to reason (*ʿaql*) by jurists so that they can be applied to different situations. Therefore, what is transmitted by the Companions and their Successors is not just the traditions of the Prophet, but also legal method and legal rules that they developed over time.[30]

The Quraysh and their affiliated clans are particularly important figures in the first generations of legal transmitters; accounting for 45% of all jurists listed in the generations leading up to the founding of the five schools (*madhhabs*).[31] Muḍarī tribes account for 7%,

[29] In Abū Isḥāq's text, the al-Zahirī school is included in the collection of orthodox Sunni schools of law. The Zahirī school died out in the late eleventh century. See George Makdisi, *The Rise of Colleges*, 8.
[30] Abū Isḥāq, *Ṭabaqāt*, 35.
[31] Abū Isḥāq lists 110 jurists in the generations leading to the founding of the five schools. Of these jurists he mentions 33 tribes, although there are many where no tribal affiliation is discernable.

Qaḥṭanī tribes for 14%, and Wā'il for just 1%, with the total number of tribes in the four blocks listed in biographical citations being 71 out of 110 jurists (or 65% of all jurists). Not all of the tribes in the four blocks are mentioned: the Yāfiʿī and Lakhmī tribes of the Qaḥṭanī block, the ʿAmr and Kinānī of the Muḍarī block, the Taghlib and Thaʿlabī of the Wā'ilī block, and the Quṣayy from the Qurashī block are omitted. Only two tribes (Tanūkh and the al-Ḥārith) are mentioned that do not fall in one of the four blocks, and they are referred to only once.[32] The remaining 39 jurists do not have a tribe affiliation (or one that can be ascertained) cited, and in the discussion of the schools, very few tribal affiliations are mentioned.

The use of tribal affiliation indicates that Ibn Qāḍī Shuhbah is seeking to make an important argument about the nature of legal authority and the role that descent plays in it. He is, in effect, arguing that the specialized knowledge that originated with the Prophet and the first generations of his followers was not only transmitted to the eponymous founders of the schools but continues to be transmitted in lines of descent. In addition, he argues that an important qualification for authority in holding divergent legal opinions is the inheritance of specialized family knowledge.

On a deeper level, Ibn Qāḍī Shuhbah is making an argument for his own authority, to speak on the issues he raises in the *ṭabaqāt*, and to lead the community. By claiming descent from the Banū Quraysh, Ibn Qāḍī Shuhbah is claiming that he has access to special knowledge which gives him clarity and insight, and, therefore, the authority to draw lines around the Shāfiʿī *madhhab*. It gives him the authority to narrow to a select few those whose voices count in the formation and transmission of *ikhtilāf*. Thus, descent from the Quraysh gives him the authority to speak for all jurists in the history of the *madhhab*. Ibn Qāḍī Shuhbah does not claim that this is the only source of authority that is needed or that he possesses. Physical descent is the first layer of authority that Ibn Qāḍī Shuhbah asserts in making his argument for the decline of legal thought and the importance of *ikhtilāf* in the preservation of the school.

[32] Abū Isḥāq, *Ṭabaqāt*, 76.

Intellectual Pedigree

Along with, and even more important than physical descent, intellectual pedigree was an important aspect of claims to authority. As with physical descent, it was assumed that specific kinds of authority were transmitted down lines of student/teacher relationships and created, over time, the accumulation of knowledge and power. An individual inherited some of the authority of one's teachers, and all of the generations of teachers that came before them in their intellectual lines of transmission, over time, back to the Prophet Muḥammad.

After the rise of the schools, establishing lines of intellectual descent to the Prophet was very important. As mentioned above, Abū Isḥāq al-Shīrāzī, in his *Ṭabaqāt*, attempted to create clear lines of transmission from the Prophet to the eponymous founders of the schools of law. The Shāfiʿī *ṭabaqāt* that followed began with the assumption that the lines of transmission established by al-Shīrāzī were sound and did not seek to replicate or recreate his work. The goal of the Shāfiʿī biographical tradition from that point on was to establish new lines of transmission from al-Shāfiʿī to later generations of scholars. Not all texts, however, were interested in establishing the same lines of transmission, but were concerned instead with mapping out the paths by which knowledge of particular kinds of legal disciplines were passed down on the authority of al-Shāfiʿī. The point was not to argue that al-Shāfiʿī was necessarily the originator of the idea being transmitted, but that the authority to transmit the information originated with the eponym and thus ultimately with Muḥammad.

As has been pointed out, Ibn Qāḍī Shuhbah was interested in mapping the transmission of *ikhtilāf*, but he was also concerned with describing the paths by which various genres of legal knowledge were also passed on over time. His authority as a jurist was based on the sum total of his legal authority across the many areas of legal knowledge that medieval scholars thought were important. He thus not only had to claim an intellectual pedigree for legal rules (*fiqh* and/or *furūʿ*), but also divergent opinion, basic legal methods that he characterizes as being transmitted along with the study of *fiqh*, speculative legal methods, various genres of expedient sciences, and *ḥadīth*.

Ibn Qāḍī Shuhbah uses his *Ṭabaqāt* to establish his pedigree by listing many of his teachers in his text and then listing in their biographies the scholars with whom they studied and the subjects in which they specialized. By reading the *Ṭabaqāt*, scholars were able to construct the lines by which knowledge and authority was passed from individual to individual and ultimately to the author. As with his presentation of physical descent, Ibn Qāḍī Shuhbah does not directly stake a claim to certain kinds of authority. It was understood, however, that the readers of the text would understand the implications of the presentation of his lineage for his own position in the school.

In the last three generations of the text, Ibn Qāḍī Shuhbah lists eleven of his teachers, including his father and grandfather, Shihāb al-Dīn Ibn Ḥijjī, al-Ṭaymānī, al-Malkāwī, al-Qurashī, al-Ṣarkhadī, al-Zuhrī, al-Sharīshī, Ibn Maktūm, and al-Ghazzī.[33] By looking at the teachers listed in those biographies, and then mapping their teachers and so on, it is possible to construct a intellectual genealogy for Ibn Qāḍī Shuhbah that goes back to al-Shāfiʿī (see figure 8.2; the figure is provided to demonstrate the complexity of the genealogy and it is understood that it would not be possible, given the space allowed, to present a full size and easily readable table). His genealogy includes 180 scholars who specialized and transmitted knowledge of a wide array of disciplines.

Ibn Qāḍī Shuhbah claims descent from many important Shāfiʿī scholars including, Taqī al-Dīn al-Subkī,[34] al-Isnawī,[35] al-Mizzī,[36] Ibn al-Rifʿah,[37] al-Nawawī,[38] Ibn al- Ṣalāḥ,[39] Fakhr al-Dīn al-Rāzī,[40] Ibn ʿAsākir,[41] al-Ghazālī,[42] Abū Isḥāq al-Shīrāzī,[43] Imām al-Ḥaramayn al-Juwaynī,[44] Abū al-Ṭayyib al-Ṭabarī,[45] Abū Isḥāq al-Marwazī,[46] Ibn

[33] Because there appears to be a dispute as to whether Ibn Qāḍī Shuhbah studied directly with al-Bulqīnī or simply with his disciple al-Ṭaymānī, the following genealogical figures will not list al-Bulqīnī as a teacher of Ibn Qāḍī Shuhbah, but as his intellectual 'grandfather.'
[34] Khān, vol. 3, 37–42.
[35] Ibid., vol. 3, 98–101.
[36] Ibid., vol. 3, 74–76.
[37] Ibid., vol. 2, 211–13.
[38] Ibid., vol. 2, 153–57.
[39] Ibid., vol. 2, 113–15.
[40] Ibid., vol. 2, 65–67.
[41] Ibid., vol. 2, 54–55.
[42] Ibid., vol. 1, 293–94.
[43] Ibid., vol. 1, 238–40.
[44] Ibid., vol. 1, 255–56.
[45] Ibid., vol. 1, 226–28.
[46] Ibid., vol. 1, 105–06.

Figure 8.3. Ibn Qāḍī Shuhbah's complete fiqh genealogy

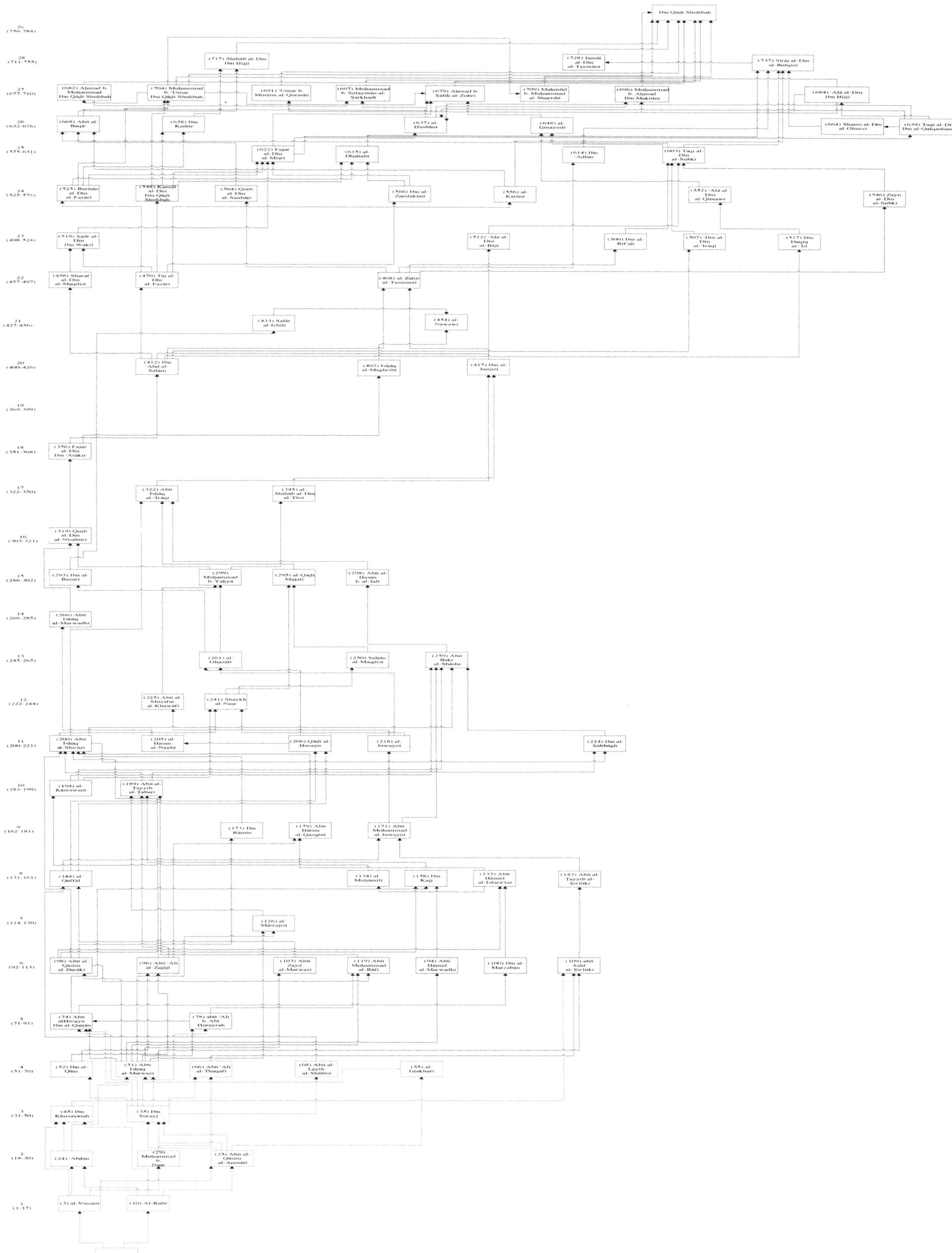

Source: Ibn Qāḍī Shuhbah, *Ṭabaqāt al-fuqahā' al-shāfi'iyah*, ed. al-Ḥāfiẓ ʿAbd al-Alī Khān, 4 vols. (Beirut: ʿĀlam al-kutub, 1987).

Figure 8.2. Complete intellectual genealogy for the Qāḍī Shuhbah according to his text

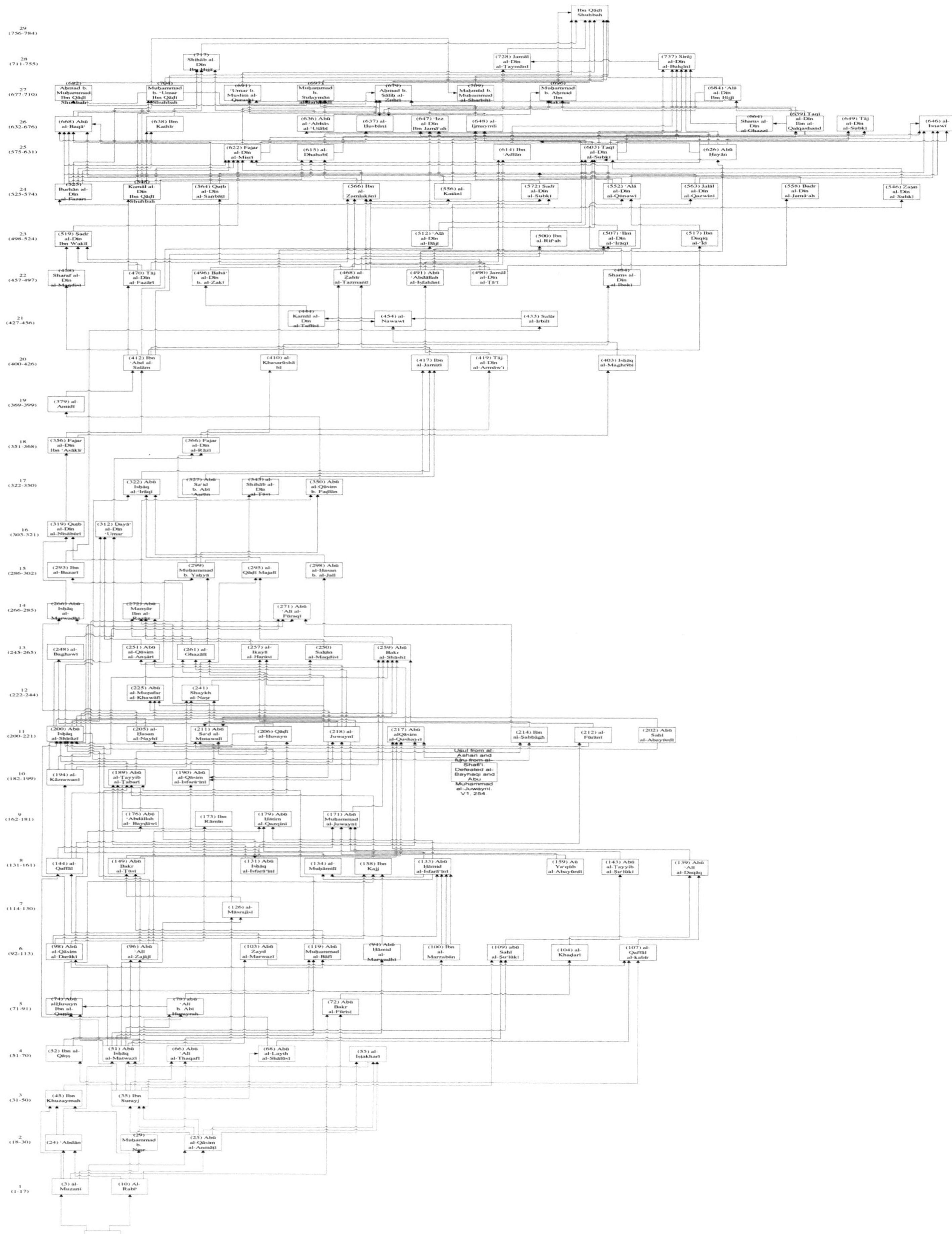

Source: Ibn Qāḍī Shuhbah, *Ṭabaqāt al-fuqahā' al-shāfi'iyah*, ed. al-Ḥāfiẓ ʿAbd al-Alī Khān, 4 vols. (Beirut: ʿĀlam al-kutub, 1987).

Surayj,[47] Abū al-Qāsim al-Anmāṭī,[48] al-Muzanī,[49] and al-Rabīʿ al-Murādī.[50]

He also claims descent from five members of the *aṣḥāb al-wujūh*, including Ibn al-Ṣabbāgh,[51] and from rather infamous scholars such as Ibn Fūrak[52] and Abū Isḥāq al-Isfarāʾīnī.[53]

The genealogy represented in figure 8.2 signifies Ibn Qāḍī Shuhbah's intellectual inheritance across a spectrum of disciplines, not just genres of *fiqh*. If the lines of descent are removed that do not refer to any discipline except the transmission of *fiqh*, *furūʿ*, or *ikhtilāf*, Ibn Qāḍī Shuhbah presents a lineage that includes 90 scholars (see figure 8.3).

His genealogy of *fiqh*, *furūʿ*, and *ikhtilāf* is quite important for establishing his credentials as a Shāfiʿī scholar and leader of his school. All of his intellectual genealogies begin with just two students of al-Shāfiʿī: al-Muzanī and al-Rabīʿ. In terms of law, their location as the sources of his authority implies that he is certified to speak about orthodox Shāfiʿī opinion as represented by the texts of the *madhhab* and divergent opinion that originates with al-Muzanī. From there, these two intellectual traditions are transmitted and developed through Abū Isḥāq al-Shīrāzī and Imām al-Ḥaramayn al-Juwaynī, both of whom are included in his transmissive line. Interestingly, al-Ghazālī does not appear in his legal genealogy, and al-Rāfiʿī does not appear in his intellectual line of descent at all. His authority to discuss and transmit the tradition of *ikhtilāf*, as it is represented in the great texts of the later school, is derived from al-Nawawī and Ibn al-Rifʿah.

In order to claim the highest levels of professional authority, Ibn Qāḍī Shuhbah also had to possess a pedigree in intellectual traditions that were important in the professionalization of law. As discussed in chapter one, Ibn Qāḍī Shuhbah, however, does not appear to have studied disciplines such as theology, logic, rhetoric, speculative legal method, or areas such as Qurʾanic recitation. He did study, and wrote a *ṭabaqāt* on, grammar and lexicography, but that appears

47 Ibid., vol. 1, 89–91.
48 Ibid., vol. 1, 80–80.
49 Ibid., vol. 1, 58–59.
50 Ibid., vol. 1, 65–66.
51 Ibid., vol. 1, 251–52.
52 Ibid., vol. 1, 190–91.
53 Ibid., vol. 1, 170–71.

to have been the extent of any kind of detailed work in expedient science or *uṣūl*.

The fact that he was not known for his knowledge in these areas does not mean that he did not possess a pedigree that certified him as expert in them; in fact, it would have made it all the more necessary. Through his work with Shihāb al-Dīn Ibn Ḥijjī and al-Ṭaymānī he was able to claim a line of descent in *uṣūl* and the expedient sciences that placed him in the elite of the school (see figure 8.4). Most of his authority rested on his examination of the writings of Sirāj al-Dīn al-Bulqīnī who was the teacher of al-Ṭaymānī. Al-Sakhāwī states that Ibn Qāḍī Shuhbah studied the texts of al-Bulqīnī with al-Ṭaymānī and it appears that they greatly influenced the scholar and were a major source for his claim to intellectual authority.[54]

One of the most interesting aspects of Ibn Qāḍī Shuhbah's lineage in *uṣūl* and related genres is that he claims a genealogy that begins with Abū Isḥāq al-Isfarā'īnī and then runs through Imām al-Ḥaramayn al-Juwaynī and al-Ghazālī. He does not list such scholars as Abū Isḥāq al-Shīrāzī who he presents as representing a more conservative understanding of *uṣūl al-fiqh*, or al-Ashʿarī, the founder of the orthodox Sunnī school of theology. Most importantly, he does not possess a genealogy in *uṣūl* or allied sciences that goes back to al-Shāfiʿī. The fact that Ibn Qāḍī Shuhbah presents a lineage in speculative legal methods and expedient sciences that do not originate with al-Shāfiʿī is a powerful rhetorical statement about the place of these sciences in the Shāfiʿī school. By truncating his lineage and beginning it with Abū Isḥāq al-Isfarā'īnī, Ibn Qāḍī Shuhbah is stating that the authority for these ideas do not originate with the eponym, but with the fifth/eleventh century scholar.

Abū Isḥāq al-Isfarā'īnī is a problematic figure for Ibn Qāḍī Shuhbah and it is interesting that he chose to include him in his genealogy at all, let alone that he decided to begin his lineage in speculative methods and expedient sciences with him. Although he characterizes Abū Isḥāq al-Isfarā'īnī as a specialist in theology and speculative legal method, it is clear that Ibn Qāḍī Shuhbah wanted to

[54] Khān, vol. 4, 36–43; al-Sakhāwī, *al-Ḍaw' al-lāmiʿ*, vol. 11, 21–22; also see al-Suyūṭī, *Naẓm al-ʿiqyān*, 94 for the possibility the Ibn Qāḍī Shuhbah studied directly with al-Bulqīnī.

diminish the esteem of Abū Isḥāq al-Isfarā'īnī without completely removing him from his text. He states that Abū Isḥāq al-Isfarā'īnī

> was a theologian, a specialist in speculative methods, and a jurist. He was the master of the people of Khurāsān. It is said that he rose to the level of *ijtihād*. He wrote many books, among them *Jāmiʿ al-ḥalā* on *uṣūl al-fiqh*, a refutation of the heretics in five volumes, and a graduate synopsis (*taʿlīq*)[55] on *uṣūl al-fiqh*. Al-Rāfiʿī mentions in his chapters on usurpation and marriage that he wrote a commentary on the legal rules of Ibn al-Ḥaddād and that he had other, similar, books. ʿAbdallāh al-Ḥākim graduated from him with ten different permissions to teach. He (al-Ḥākim) mentions him in his excellent history, although al-Ḥākim died before him. He states that he was "a jurist, a practitioner of speculative legal method, and a theologian; and he was well advanced in this science. He left from ʿIrāq and the community of scholars acknowledged his advancement". . . . The *shaykh* Abū Isḥāq said, "our master Abū al-Ṭayyib (al-Ṭabarī) studied law with him and from him (al-Isfarā'īnī) the community of scholars of Nīsabūr took (*akhadha*) knowledge in theology and legal method." Abū al-Qāsim Ibn ʿAsākir said, "it has been reported to me from one in whom I have confidence, that al-Ṣāḥib b. ʿAbbād used to refer to Ibn al-Bāqillānī, Ibn Fūrak, and al-Isfarā'īnī as being contemporaries among the students of al-Ḥasan al-Ashʿarī. Of these students, he said that 'al-Bāqillānī is a sea that drowns, Ibn Fūrak is a snake that strikes, and al-Isfarā'īnī is a fire that burns.'" He died on the day of *ʿāshūrā'* (Muḥarram 10) in the year 418 in Nīsābūr. His family originated in Isfarā'īn and he was buried in a tomb there. Al-Rāfiʿī transmitted from him in his discussion of menses, in the discussion of the use of *ijtihād* in ascertaining the time for the beginning of the communal prayer and in the direction of prayer, and in the discussion of inattentiveness while bowing in prayer. He then refined the transmission from him.[56]

In shaping the biography of al-Isfarā'īnī, Ibn Qāḍī Shuhbah goes to great lengths to qualify his importance and the level of his influence in legal method, while at the same time diminishing him as a jurist.

One important rhetorical strategy used in *ṭabaqāt* works is ordering material and linking ideas and concepts so that an author can shape the impression of the individual discussed. Ibn Qāḍī Shuhbah lists al-Isfarā'īnī as a theologian first, meaning that theology (*kalām*) was his primary preoccupation and claim to fame. Second, he lists speculative legal method and lastly, law. He does this to show that legal discovery was only a tertiary concern for Abū Isḥāq al-Isfarā'īnī.

---

[55] See Makdisi, *The Rise of Colleges*, 114 for a discussion of *taʿlīq*.
[56] Khān, vol. 1, 170–71.

Ibn Qāḍī Shuhbah then goes onto say that he was the master (*shaykh*) of the people of Khurāsān. This comment is meant to evoke the idea that in the early formation of the school there were two paths in legal scholarship, the ʿIrāqī school and that of Khurāsān. For instance, Ibn Qāḍī Shuhbah states in his biography of Abū al-Ḥasan al-Dāwūdī (d. 467/1075) that he studied (*akhadha*) law with the "masters of the two paths" Abū Bakr al-Qaffāl and Abū Ḥāmid al-Isfarāʾīnī.[57] Ibn Qāḍī Shuhbah refers to al-Qaffāl (d. 417/1026) as a "master of the path of Khurāsān"[58] and Abū Ḥāmid (discussed in some detail in chapter two) as a "master of the Shāfiʿīs of ʿIrāq."[59] While Ibn Qāḍī Shuhbah mentions a few scholars that were authorities of both approaches to law,[60] in most cases, scholars are referred to as practitioners of one regional *ṭarīqah*. Over time, the regional approaches became identified with Abū Isḥāq al-Shīrāzī as representative of the school of ʿIrāq[61] and Imām al-Ḥaramayn al-Juwaynī as representing the school of Khurāsān.[62] Later, the Khurāsānī tradition of *uṣūl* was transmitted by Fakhr al-Dīn al-Rāzī, who, as seen in chapter six, was the primary practitioner of a theologically-oriented form of *uṣūl al-fiqh*.[63] Al-Rāzī is also listed in Ibn Qāḍī Shuhbah's genealogy for *uṣūl* and expedient sciences. In most cases, those scholars identified with the Khurāsānī school are closely associated with speculative methodologies and expedient science, while those in the ʿIrāqī school are most usually referred to in the transmission and production of *fiqh* and *furūʿ*. Ibn Qāḍī Shuhbah's lineage in *fiqh*, *furūʿ*, and *ikhtilāf* includes representatives of both schools, but his genealogy in *uṣūl* and allied disciplines list, for the early generations, only those belonging to the Khurāsānī group.

Although it t is clear that Ibn Qāḍī Shuhbah is attempting to link himself with the Khurāsānī path of speculation, he seeks to do so with qualifications. As the progenitor of speculative methods in his lineage, al-Isfarāʾīnī is also described as rising to the level of *ijtihād*. But because Ibn Qāḍī Shuhbah attributes this designation to an un-

---

[57] Ibid., vol. 1, 249–50.
[58] Ibid., vol. 1, 182.
[59] Ibid., vol. 1, 172.
[60] Ibid., vol. 1, 188, 207, 244, 263–64, 319–20, vol. 2, 122–23.
[61] Ibid., vol. 2, 18, 81, 94.
[62] See vol. 2, 70 for a link between *uṣūl al-fiqh* and study in Khurāsān.
[63] Ibid., vol. 2, 65–67. Also see references to this in the biography of Quṭb al-Magribī (vol. 2, 50).

named source, he is seeking to diminish the idea that he was a leader in legal reasoning. Ibn Qāḍī Shuhbah seeks to emphasize this by placing the comment next to a discussion of al-Isfarāʾīnī's works on *uṣūl al-fiqh*. He does refer to Abū Isḥāq al-Isfarāʾīnī's works on law, but almost as an aside.

He then quotes ʿAbdallāh al-Ḥākim's *Tārīkh nīsābūr*, which states that Abū Isḥāq al-Isfarāʾīnī was "a jurist, a practitioner of speculative legal method, and a theologian; and he was well advanced in this science. He left from ʿIrāq and the community of scholars acknowledged his advancement." Ibn Qāḍī Shuhbah treats al-Ḥākim's quote as a polemical statement about the qualifications of Abū Isḥāq al-Isfarāʾīnī. By placing law first, Ibn Qāḍī Shuhbah implies that al-Ḥākim is asserting Abū Isḥāq al-Isfarāʾīnī's expertise as a jurist over his study of *uṣūl* and theology. Furthermore, he takes the comment that Abū Isḥāq al-Isfarāʾīnī left ʿIrāq to imply that he moved beyond the ʿIrāqī school of jurisprudence and that this was acknowledged by the scholars of the day as a great step forward. Ibn Qāḍī Shuhbah, however, overtly criticizes al-Ḥākim's judgement of Abū Isḥāq al-Isfarāʾīnī by stating that the historian died before the theologian. In fact, al-Ḥākim died thirteen years before al-Isfarāʾīnī and Ibn Qāḍī Shuhbah implies that because al-Ḥākim's opinion of Abū Isḥāq al-Isfarāʾīnī was formed early in his career, he is not well placed to judge his specialties or abilities.

Ibn Qāḍī Shuhbah then turns to the appraisal of al-Isfarāʾīnī found in the *Ṭabaqāt al-fuqahāʾ* of Abū Isḥāq al-Shīrāzī, who says that Abū al-Ṭayyib al-Ṭabarī studied law (*darasa*) with Abū Isḥāq al-Isfarāʾīnī. Al-Ṭabarī, who is located in Ibn Qāḍī Shuhbah's genealogy for *fiqh*, *furūʿ*, and *ikhtilāf* but not in the lineage for *uṣūl* and the expedient sciences, is described in his biography by Ibn Qāḍī Shuhbah as "the master of ʿIrāq . . ., and the seal of this (meaning the tenth) generation;" in order words, the seal Abū al-Ṭayyib's generation of the ʿIrāqī school.[64] Ibn Qāḍī Shuhbah quotes al-Shīrāzī, who says of Abū al-Ṭayyib, "I do not consider anyone among those whom I saw more perfect in *ijtihād*, more intense in judicial inquiry, and more serious in study than was he."[65] Although Ibn Qāḍī Shuhbah says further that Abū al-Ṭayyib was "a master in *uṣūl*," he does not mention Abū Isḥāq al-Isfarāʾīnī in his biography.

[64] Ibid., vol. 1, 227.
[65] Ibid., vol. 1, 228.

The hypertextual nature of the *Ṭabaqāt* indicates that Ibn Qāḍī Shuhbah intended, by mentioning al-Ṭabarī in the biography in Abū Isḥāq al-Isfarāʾīnī, but not the other way around, for readers to compare the two scholars and for the greatness he ascribes to Abū al-Ṭayyib to reflect poorly on the image of Abū Isḥāq al-Isfarāʾīnī. While Abū Isḥāq is described dismissively as rising to the level of *ijtihād*, Abū al-Ṭayyib is pictured as one of the great *mujtahid*s of his time. By not mentioning Abū Isḥāq al-Isfarāʾīnī in the biography of al-Ṭabarī, Ibn Qāḍī Shuhbah also implies that the greatness of Abū al-Ṭayyib has nothing to do with his study of law with Abū Isḥāq al-Isfarāʾīnī. Finally, by stating that Abū al-Ṭayyib was a master of *uṣūl*, Ibn Qāḍī Shuhbah seeks to create a picture of Abū Isḥāq al-Isfarāʾīnī has having no influence on the development of the ʿIrāqī approach to law.

Most provocatively, Ibn Qāḍī Shuhbah's quote from al-Ṣāḥib b. ʿAbbād, stating that Abū Isḥāq al-Isfarāʾīnī was a "fire that burns," is meant to equate his teachings with the inferno of hell; in other words, to follow and replicate the views of al-Isfarāʾīnī leads to damnation.

Ibn Qāḍī Shuhbah tempers the negative influence of Abū Isḥāq al-Isfarāʾīnī by listing Abū al-Qāsim al-Isfarāʾīnī, Imām al-Ḥaramayn and then al-Ghazālī as the next three scholars in his lineage. Abū al-Qāsim (d. 452/1060) is described as a disciple of Abū Isḥāq al-Isfarāʾīnī and Imām al-Ḥaramayn in the study of theology. He also says that Abū al-Qāsim wrote books on the two *uṣūl*s. Ibn Qāḍī Shuhbah then states that Abū al-Qāsim used to issue legal opinions by "following the path of the pious ancestors (*salaf*) who were ascetic and pious."[66] By referring to his following the *salaf* in the issuance of rules, Ibn Qāḍī Shuhbah seeks to ameliorate the negative influences of Abū Isḥāq al-Isfarāʾīnī by having his ideas past through the pious and ascetic hands of Abū al-Qāsim. Rhetorically, he is arguing that while Abū al-Qāsim may have studied the damning theology of Abū Isḥāq al-Isfarāʾīnī, he was nevertheless unchanged by the experience.

The role that Imām al-Ḥaramayn and al-Ghazālī play in Ibn Qāḍī Shuhbah's depiction of Shāfiʿī history have already been discussed in some detail and will not be repeated here. It needs to be reiterated, however, that in his effort to soften the image of Imām al-Ḥaramayn,

[66] Ibid., vol. 1, 229.

to distance him from some of the more speculative ideas that were later attributed to him, Ibn Qāḍī Shuhbah not only does so because he transmitted *ikhtilāf* but also because he is listed in his own intellectual genealogy.

Why, then, include Abū Isḥāq al-Isfarā'īnī as the source of his lineage in *uṣūl* and expedient sciences? Why not just begin with Abū al-Qāsim or Imām al-Ḥaramayn? As George Makdisi has pointed out, Abū Isḥāq al-Isfarā'īnī was an important figure in that section of the Shāfiʿī school that placed greater emphasis on the interpolation of Ashʿarite theology into law.[67] Scholars such as Tāj al-Dīn al-Subkī used the memory of Abū Isḥāq al-Isfarā'īnī to argue for the inclusion of Ashʿarī theology in to the Shāfiʿī school. His biography of Abū Isḥāq al-Isfarā'īnī is replete with glowing assessments of the scholar and critiques of those such as al-Dhahabī and Abū Isḥāq al-Shīrāzī who were critical of the theologian.[68] For Ibn Qāḍī Shuhbah to have legitimacy with the majority of jurists who by his time specialized in *uṣūl* and related disciplines, he had to cite Abū Isḥāq al-Isfarā'īnī in his lineage. Given his clear distaste for speculative sciences, however, he shaped the biography in such a way that gave clear indications of his views while at the same time listing Abū Isḥāq al-Isfarā'īnī as an intellectual ancestor. That he begins the genealogy with Abū Isḥāq al-Isfarā'īnī and not with al-Shāfiʿī is further evidence of his desire to claim an inheritance in the discipline while at the same time keeping the taint of it away from the founder of the school.

Although the more conservative ʿIrāqī school is not mentioned in his intellectual genealogy of *uṣūl* and related sciences, it is prominent in his general genealogy of *fiqh*, *furūʿ*, and *ikhtilāf*, and especially in his more narrow lineage defined solely by *akhadha* and *tafaqqaha* educational relationships. While Ibn Qāḍī Shuhbah implies that *akhadha* was not as important as *tafaqqaha* in transmitting knowledge of basic law and legal methods, it was nevertheless central to the transference of authority from teacher to student. As figure 8.5 shows, Ibn Qāḍī Shuhbah constructed a very narrow and limited lineage depicting the transmission of legal authority and basic legal ideas from al-Shāfiʿī, through both al-Muzanī and al-Rabīʿ, through such

[67] Makdisi, "Ashʿari and the Ashʿarites in Islamic Religious History," 74–75.
[68] Al-Subkī, *Ṭabaqāt al-shāfiʿīyah al-kubrā* (1999), vol. 2, 509–12.

important figures as al-Anmāṭī, Ibn Surayj, Abū Isḥāq al-Marwazī, Abū Ḥāmid al-Isfarā'īnī, Ibn Rif'ah, and al-Bulqīnī.

Although Abu Isḥāq al-Shīrāzī is not listed, Abū Ḥāmid al-Isfarā'īnī fills the void as one of the most important early authors of the 'Irāqī school. He has the added advantage of not only being a propagator of the basic legal method of al-Shāfi'ī, but he also wrote a commentary on the *Mukhtaṣar* of al-Muzanī and was thus also a transmitter *ikhtilāf*.[69] This also explains why Ibn Qāḍī Shuhbah constructed the biography of Abū al-Qāsim al-Dārakī (discussed in chapter two) as he did. Al-Dārakī is the only *tafaqqaha* link Ibn Qāḍī Shuhbah mentions between Abū Ḥāmid al-Isfarā'īnī and Abū Isḥāq al-Marwazī and is thus an important association in his own lineage in *tafaqqaha* and *akhadha* going back to al-Shāfi'ī. Ibn Qāḍī Shuhbah presents al-Dārakī as being part of the mainstream of the school, as a reputable scholar who is distanced from accusations that he deviated from the opinion and methods of the eponym. Ibn Qāḍī Shuhbah needs al-Dārakī to appear reputable so that his own pedigree in the two most basic forms of legal education are not sullied by imputations that might reflect on his own standing in the school. The combination of the kinds of legitimacy given to Ibn Qāḍī Shuhbah in his lineages of *fiqh, furū', ikhtilāf, uṣūl al-fiqh,* expedient sciences, as well as the authority imparted to him through his genealogy of *akhadha* and *tafaqqaha* relations going back to al-Shāfi'ī, were important aspects of his claims to the accumulation of intellectual clout that made him suitable to become the leader of the Shāfi'ī school in Syria. His pedigree was, by his own formulation, ideal for any claimant to the position of chief Shāfi'ī judge and thus leader of the school.

In many respects it appears that Ibn Qāḍī Shuhbah was successful in his quest to become the leader of the Shāfi'ī school in Syria. His student al-Sakhāwī, and the historians al-Suyūṭī, Ibn Ṭūlūn, and Ibn 'Imād all refer to him as the *ra'īs* of the Syrian community. His esteem in the eyes of later scholars, however, had more to do with his historical works, especially his *Ṭabaqāt* and the *Dhayl* on the history begun by Ibn Ḥijjī. He is heavily quoted by Ibn Ṭūlūn and al-Nu'aymī, and his influence on modern understandings of Mamlūk period Damascus is profound.

[69] Khān, vol. 1, 172–73.

Figure 8.5. Ibn Qāḍī Shuhbah's genealogy according to *akhadha* and *tafaqqaha* relationships

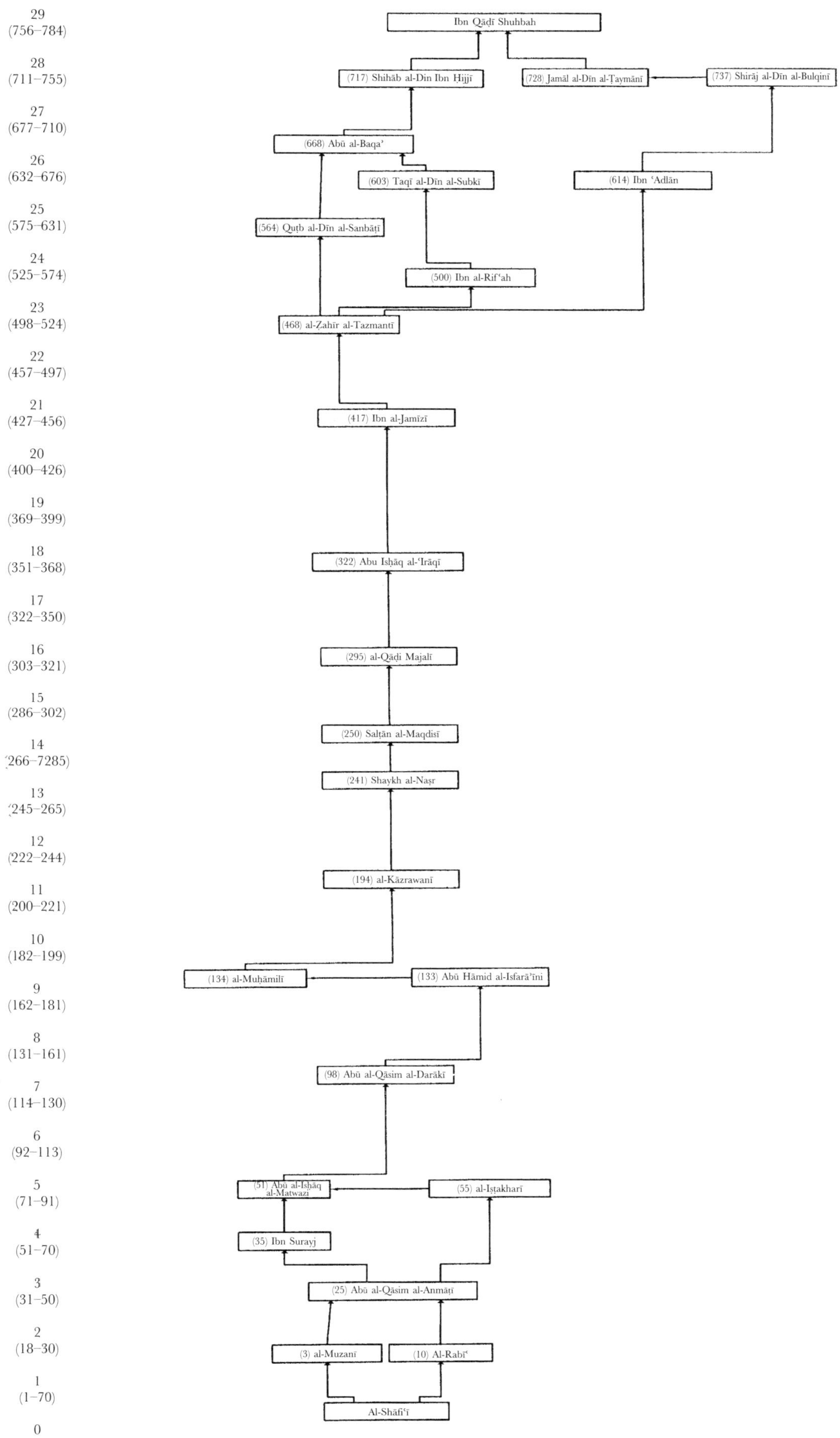

Source: Ibn Qāḍī Shuhbah, *Ṭabaqāt al-fuqahā' al-shāfiʿīyah*, ed. al-Ḥāfiẓ ʿAbd al-Alī Khān, 4 vols. (Beirut: ʿĀlam al-kutub, 1987).

Figure 8.4. Ibn Qāḍī Shuhbah's complete genealogy for *uṣūl al-fiqh* and expedient sciences

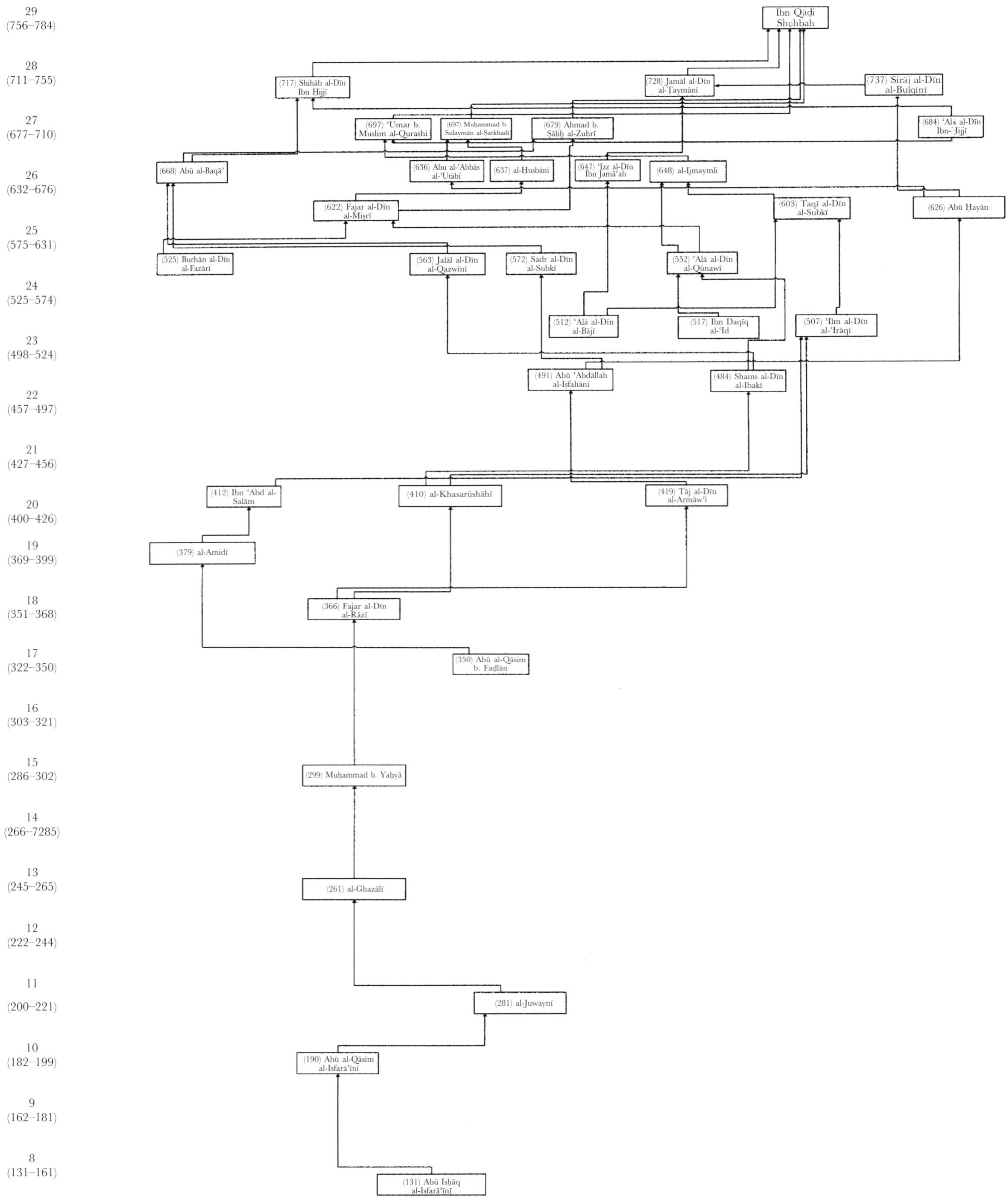

Source: Ibn Qāḍī Shuhbah, *Ṭabaqāt al-fuqahā' al-shāfi'īyah*, ed. al-Ḥāfiẓ 'Abd al-Alī Khān, 4 vols. (Beirut: 'Ālam al-kutub, 1987).

While Ibn Qāḍī Shuhbah saw himself as a historian, the main purpose of his work was to demonstrate to Shāfiʿī jurists their own history, and he was thus preoccupied with the importance of law and legal development. He understood his own abilities to reflect the great scholars of the past and in wanting to become the leader of the school he sought also to be proclaimed a *mujtahid*, as is evidenced by the colophon of the 841/1438 first edition of the text which refers to him as the *baqīyah al-mujtahidīn* (remnant of the *mujtahid*s).[70]

If this was his aspiration he appears to have failed to realize the goal. No contemporary or later historian referred to him as a *mujtahid* and in the colophons of the final three editions of the text there are no references to him as such.[71] Whether his talents as a jurist were not as great or as extensive as those of his contemporaries whom he refers to as *mujtahid*s, or whether his rather tragic and ill conceived involvement in the political upheavals of the period diminished his stature in the eyes of later Shāfiʿīs, it is clear that while he was respected as a jurist and historian, he was nonetheless not a *mujtahid*.

As al-Sakhāwī points out in his biography of Ibn Qāḍī Shuhbah, within three years of completing the first edition of the *Ṭabaqāt*, he had tired of the rigors of public life and retired to teach and visit tombs in order to collect *ḥadīth*.[72] By the end of his life the crises that had marked the post Mongol invasion Mamlūk period had all but faded from memory. The remaining years of the Sulṭānate were, in comparison, tranquil until the short burst of violence surrounding the Ottoman invasion in the early sixteenth century. The revolt in which he played such a central role was to be one of the last major challenges to Sulṭānic authority for seventy-five years. In the centuries that followed, Damascus became a backwater to the larger forces shaping Islamic law and although his texts remained popular, the larger ideas and ideologies that he attempted to transmit were lost as his works became historical resources of a distant past.

In the end, Ibn Qāḍī Shuhbah wanted to leave to future generations an outline of time that, for him, represented the unfolding of sacred history. The Shāfiʿī school, as the most important legal guild

---

[70] Khān, vol. 4, 114.
[71] Ibid.
[72] Al-Sakhāwī, *al-Ḍawʾ al-lāmiʿ*, vol. 11, 23.

of the day, held the keys to the restoration of the greatness of the Muslim community. He wanted to bequeath to future generations of Muslims, emerging from the crises and travails of the period, a map to the revitalization of Islamic law that could only be found in the texts of the glorious past.

To that end, he wrote an *ijāzah* (a permission to teach) on the cover of the 843 edition of the text for his student ʿIzz al-Dīn Abū Yaʿlā al-Ḥusaynī. Al-Ḥusaynī was twenty-two years old and had studied a number of subjects with Ibn Qāḍī Shuhbah, including law and the *Ṣaḥīḥ* of al-Bukhārī.[73] His experiences inscribing the *Ṭabaqāt* must have been important to the young scholar because he went on to write an appendix (*dhayl*) to the text based on three notebooks he kept during the composition of the work.[74]

The *ijāzah* is important because it gives us a window on to how Ibn Qāḍī Shuhbah hoped his text would be used. Not only did he want it used by his students, but he sent it to Ibn Ḥajar al-ʿAsqalānī, the chief Shāfiʿī judge of Egypt, to read and, it is evident, in order to gain his approval so that his stature in the Shāfiʿī school would be elevated. In the end, the text represented the entirety of Ibn Qāḍī Shuhbah's life as a scholar, all that he had inherited from the great jurists of the past, as well as what he hoped to offer the future. The *ijāzah* says,

> Praise God with power! For He indeed delivers and His grace rewards. May God's blessing be on our lord Muḥammad, the unlettered Prophet, and on his house, his helpers, his companions, their successors, and on him be peace and acceptance.
>
> And now: I taught my son, the noble of descent, the noble of birth, the noble, the Qurʾān reciter, the *ḥadīth* expert, the jurist ʿIzz al-Dīn Abū Yaʿlā Ḥamzah son of the descendant of Muḥammad, the noble of birth, the noble and leader Shihāb al-Dīn Abū al-ʿAbbās Aḥmad son of the one in need of God most High, the descendant of Muḥammad, the noble of birth, the noble, the abstaining man of distinction of the successful descendants of Muḥammad in our [indecipherable], the leader of the pious descendants of Muḥammad ʿAlāʾ al-Dīn Abū al-Ḥasan ʿAlī[75] son of the *ḥadīth* expert, the author Shams al-Dīn Abū al-Maḥāsin

[73] Ibid., vol. 3, 163–64.

[74] Ibid.

[75] Ibn Qāḍī Shuhbah discusses Muḥammad b. ʿAlī al-Ḥusaynī (d. 765/1363) in his *Ṭabaqāt*. He describes al-Ḥusaynī as mostly a jurist and a *ḥadīth* expert. He also appears to have been a historian who wrote appendices (*dhayl*) to al-Dhahabī's *al-*

al-Ḥusaynī al-Dimashqī al-Shāfiʿī, May God Most High strengthen him with authority and adorn him with wisdom; may he make use of it, and by means of his knowledge from the learned doers what is mentioned in my entire book, *The Generations of the Shāfiʿī and Ḥanafī Jurists*. For it to be studied I put its passages in order, and I continued editing it, may God make it useful.

He departed with the aforementioned book (and went) to Egypt, stopping with it at the leader of the community of jurists, the *ḥadīth* memorizer of Egypt, the teacher of the [indecipherable], the Chief Judge Shihāb al-Dīn Abū al-ʿAbbās Ibn Ḥajar, may God grant the Muslims happiness, in order to visit him and to dwell with them among the clouds. He met with him and he improved among its passages and all of it benefited from the useful lessons. It was thus like the testimony for the book, for its integrity. So be He a God of Praise and Grace.

I license for the above mentioned descendant of Muḥammad to transmit from me my writings, what I was licensed to transmit, and my books. (Signed) Abū Bakr b. Aḥmad Ibn Qāḍī Shuhbah al-Asadī al-Shāfiʿī. Praise God, Bless Muḥammad, his Family, and there is no power and no strength save in God.[76]

ʿIbr and *Ṭabaqāt al-ḥuffāẓ*. Ibn Qāḍī Shuhbah does not mention his son Shihāb al-Dīn Abū al-ʿAbbās Aḥmad, or his father Shams al-Dīn Abū al-Maḥāsin. (Khān, vol. 3, 129–131).

[76] Ms Or. 3039, fol. 1a.

BIBLIOGRAPHY

Manuscripts

ʿAbd al-Bāsiṭ, al-Qāḍī. *Kitāb akhbār al-duwal wa athār al-uwal.* 2 vols. MS Hunt. 610. Bodliean Library Manuscript, Oxford University, Oxford.

Ibn Qāḍī Shuhbah, *Ṭabaqāt al-fuqahāʾ al-shāfiʿīyah.* (microfilm). Arabic Manuscript Collection, The British Library, Or. Mus. 3037.

——. *Tarājim al-fuquhāʾ al-shāfiʿīyah min dhayl al-rawḍatayn li-abī shāmah.* (microfilm). Garrett Arabic manuscript Collection, Princeton University, MS 694.

Arabic and Primary Sources

al-ʿAbbādī, Abū ʿĀṣim Muḥammad b. Aḥmad. *Kitāb ṭabaqāt al-fuqahāʾ al-shāfiʿīyah.* Edited by Gösta Vitestam. No. 21. Leiden: E. J. Brill, 1964.

al-ʿAsqalānī, Ibn Ḥajar. *Inbāʾ al-ghumr bi abnāʾ al-ʿumr.* Edited by Sayyid ʿAbd al-Wahhāb Bukhārī. 9 vols. Hyderabad: Dāʾirat al-maʿārif al-ʿuthmānīyah, 1975.

——. *Badhl al-māʿūn fī faḍl al-ṭāʿūn.* Riyad: Dār al-ʿāṣimah, 1991.

——. *Lisān al-mīzān.* Edited by ʿĀdil Aḥmad ʿAbd al-Mawjūd and ʿAlī Muḥammad Muʿawwaḍ. 7 vols. Beirut: Dār al-kutub al-ʿarabīyah, 1996.

al-ʿAynī, Badr al-Dīn Maḥmūd b. Aḥmad. *ʿIqd al-jumān fī tārīkh ahl al-zamān.* Edited by ʿAbdallāh al-Ṭanṭāwī al-Qarḥūṭ. Cairo: al-Zahrāʾ liʾ l-iʿlām al-ʿarabīyah, 1989.

al-Baghdādī, al-Khaṭīb. *Tārīkh baghdād aw madīnāt al-salām.* 16 vols. Beirut: Dār al-kutub al-ʿilmīyah, n.d.

——. *Kitāb al-faqīh wa ʾl-mutafaqqih.* 2 vols. Beirut: Dār al-kutub al-ʿilmīyah, 1980.

al-Bayhaqī, Abū Bakr. *Aḥkām al-qurʾān.* 2 vols. Beirut: Dār al-kutub al-ʿilmīyah, 1975.

——. *Manāqib al-shāfiʿī.* Edited by Aḥmad Ṣaqr. 2 vols. Cairo: Maktabat dār al-turāth, 1971.

al-Bukhārī, Abū ʿAbdallāh Muḥammad b. Ismāʿīl. *Ṣaḥīḥ al-bukhārī.* Edited by Muḥammad Munīr al-Dimashqī. 9 vols. Beirut: ʿĀlam al-kutub, n.d.

Çelebi, Kātip. *Kashf al-ẓunūn ʿan asāmī al-kutub wa ʾl-funūn.* 2 vols. London: R. Bentley for the Oriental Translation Fund of Great Britain and Ireland, 1835–1858.

Dāghī, ʿAlī Muḥyī al-Dīn ʿAlī al-Qarah, ed. "Muqaddimah." In *Wasīṭ fī al-madhhab.* Vol. 1, 277–80. Cairo: Dār al-iʿtiṣām, 1984.

al-Daylamī, al-Ḥasan b. Muḥammad. *Irshād al-qulūb fī al-mawāʿiẓ wa ʾl-ḥikam.* 2 vols. Najaf: al-Maṭbaʿah al-ḥaydarīyah, n.d.

al-Dhahabī, Shams al-Dīn Muḥammad b. Aḥmad b. ʿUthmān. *Tārīkh al-islām wa wafayāt al-mashāhīr wa ʾl-aʿlām.* Edited by ʿUmar ʿAbd al-Salām Tadmurī. 58 vols. Beirut: Dār al-kutub al-ʿarabī, 1999.

——. *Kitāb tadhkirat al-ḥuffāẓ.* 2 vols. n.p.: Dār al-fikr al-ʿarabī, n.d.

——. *Bayān zaghal al-ʿilm wa ʾl-ṭalab.* Edited by Muḥammad Zāhid al-Kawtharī. Damascus: al-Qudsī, 1929.

——. *Siyar aʿlām al-nubalāʾ.* 25 vols. Beirut: Muʾassasat al-risālah, 1984.

——. *Kitāb al-muʿīn fī ṭabaqāt al-muḥaddithīn.* Edited by Hammām ʿAbd al-Raḥīm Saʿīd. ʿAmmān: Dār al-furqān, 1984.

——. *al-Muqtamā fī sadr al-kunī.* Edited by Ayman Ṣālaḥ Shaʿbān. 2 vols. Beirut: Dār al-kutub al-ʿilmīyah, 1997.

——. *al-ʿIbar fī khabar man ghabar.* 4 vols. Beirut: Dār al-kutub al-ʿilmīyah, 1985.

al-Ghazālī, Abū Ḥāmid b. Muḥammad b. Muḥammad. *al-Wajīz fī fiqh al-imām al-shāfiʿī*. Edited by ʿAlī Muḥammad Muʿawwaḍ and ʿĀdil Aḥmad ʿAbd al-Mawjūd. 2 vols. Beirut: Dār al-arqām, 1997.
——. *al-Wasīṭ fī al-madhhab*. Edited by Aḥmad Maḥmūd Ibrāhīm and Muḥammad Muḥammad Tāmir. 7 vols. al-Ghūrīyah: Dār al-salām, 1997.
Ibn Abī al-Damm. *Kitāb adab al-qaḍāʾ*. Edited by Muḥyī Hilāl al-Sarḥān. 2 vols. Baghdād: al-Jumhūrīyah al-ʿIrāqīyah, wazārat al-awqāf wa ʾl-shuʾūn al-dīnīyah, 1984.
Ibn Abī Ḥātim. *Kitāb al-jarḥ wa ʾl-taʿdīl*. 9 vols. Hyderabad: Dāʾirat al-maʿārif al-ʿuthmānīyah, 1952–53. Reprint, Beirut: Dār iḥyāʾ al-turāth al-ʿarabī, np.
Ibn ʿAsākir. *Tārīkh madīnat dimashq*. Edited by Muḥibb al-Dīn Abī Saʿīd ʿUmar b. Gharāmah al-ʿAmrawī. 80 vols. Beirut: Dār al-fikr, 1995.
Ibn Ḥājib. *Kitāb mukhtaṣar al-muntahā al-uṣūl*. Cairo: Maṭbaʿat al-saʿada, n.d.
Ibn Ḥanbal, Aḥmad. *al-Musnad*. Edited by Al-Ḥusaynī ʿAbd al-Majīd Hāshim and Aḥmad ʿUmar Hāshim. 22 vols. Cairo: Dār al-maʿārif, 1985.
Ibn Ḥijjī, Shihāb al-Dīn. *Tārīkh ibn ḥijjī*. Edited by Abū Yaḥyā ʿAbdallāh al-Kazarī. 2 vols. Beirut: Dār Ibn Ḥazm, 2003.
Ibn al-ʿImād al-Ḥanbalī. *Shadharāt al-dhahab fī akhbār min dhahab*. 9 vols. Beirut: Dār al-kutub al-ʿilmīyah, 1998.
Ibn Imām al-Kāmilīyah. *Taysīr al-wuṣūl ijā minhāj al-uṣūl min al-manqūl wa ʾl-maʿqūl "al-Mukhtaṣar."* Edited by ʿAbd al-Fattāḥ Aḥmad Quṭb al-Dukhmīsī. 6 vols. Cairo: al-Fārūq al-hadithīyah li ʾl-ṭibaʿah wa ʾl-nashr, 2002.
Ibn Iyās al-Ḥanafī. Muḥammad b. Aḥmad. *Badāʾiʿ al-zuhūr fī waqāʾiʿ al-duhūr*. Edited by Muḥammad Muṣṭafā. 5 vols. Cairo: Dār iḥyāʾ al-kutub al-ʿarabīyah, 1972.
Ibn al-Jawzī. *al-Muntaẓam fī tārīkh al-mulūk wa ʾl-umam*. Edited by Muḥammad ʿAbd al-Qādir ʿAṭā. 18 vols. Beirut: Dār al-kutub al-ʿilmīyah, 1992.
Ibn Kathīr, Ismāʿīl. *al-Bidāyah wa ʾl-nihāyah*. ʿAlī Muḥammad Muʿawwaḍ et al. 14 vols. Beirut: Dār al-kutub al-ʿilmīyah, 1994.
——. *al-Nihāyah fī al-fitan wa ʾl-malāḥim*. Edited by Muḥammad Aḥmad ʿAbd al-ʿAzīz. 2 vols. Beirut: Dār al-kutub al-ʿilmīyah, 1988.
——. *Tafsīr al-qurʾān al-ʿaẓīm*. Edited by Muḥammad Ḥusayn Shams al-Dīn. 9 vols. Beirut: Dār al-kutub al-ʿilmīyah, 1998.
——. *Ṭabaqāt al-fuqahāʾ al-shāfiʿīyīn*. Edited by Aḥmad ʿUmar Hāshim. 3 vols. Cairo: Maktabah al-thaqāfah al-dīnīyah, 1993.
Ibn Khaldūn. *al-Muqaddimah*. 3 vols. Beirut: Maktabat Lubnān, 1970.
Ibn Khallikān, Abū al-ʿAbbās Aḥmad b. Muḥammad. *Wafayāt al-aʿyān wa anbāʾ al-zamān*. Edited by Iḥsān ʿAbbās. 6 vols. Beirut: Dār Ṣādir, 1977.
Ibn al-Mulaqqin, ʿUmar b. ʿAlī. *Ṭabaqāt al-awliyāʾ*. Cairo: Maktabat al-khānjī, 1973.
Ibn al-Nadīm, Muḥammad b. Isḥāq. *Fihrist*. Edited by Gustav Flügel. Leipzig: Verlag von F. C. W. Vogel, 1872.
Ibn Qāḍī Shuhbah, Taqī al-Dīn Abū Bakr b. Aḥmad. *Tārīkh*. Edited by ʿAdnān Darwīsh. 4 vols. Damascus: Institut Français de Damas, 1977–97.
——. *Ṭabaqāt al-fuqahāʾ al-shāfiʿīyah*. Edited by ʿAlī Muḥammad ʿUmar. 2 vols. Cairo: Maktabah al-thaqāfah al-dīnīyah, 1993–98.
——. *Ṭabaqāt al-fuqahāʾ al-shāfiʿīyah*. Edited by al-Ḥāfiẓ ʿAbd al-Alī Khān. 4 vols. Hyderabad: Dāʾirat al-maʿārif al-ʿuthmānīyah, 1978–80.
——. *Ṭabaqāt al-fuqahāʾ al-shāfiʿīyah*. Edited by al-Ḥāfiẓ ʿAbd al-Alī Khān. 4 vols. Beirut: ʿĀlam al-kutub, 1987.
——. *Kitāb manāqib al-imām al-shāfiʿī*. Edited by ʿAbd al-ʿAzīz Fayyāḍ Ḥarfūsh. Damascus: Dār al-bashāʾir li l-ṭibāʿah wa l-nashr wa l-tawzīʿ, 2003.
——. *Ṭabaqāt al-nuḥāh wa l-lughawīyīn*. Najaf: Maṭbaʿat al-nuʿmān, 1974.
Ibn Qudāmah, *Ṭabaqāt ʿulamāʾ al-ḥadīth*. Edited by Akram al-Būshī and Ibrāhīm al-Zaybaq. 4 vols. Beirut: Muʾassasat al-risālah, 1997.
Ibn Saʿd. *Ṭabaqāt al-kubrā*. 9 vols. Beirut: Dār al-masīrah, 1957–1968.

Ibn al-Ṣalāḥ. *Ṭabaqāt al-fuqahā' al-shāfi'īyah.* Edited by Muḥyī al-Dīn 'Alī al-Najīb. 2 vols. Beirut: Dār al-bashā'ir al-islāmīyah, 1996.
———. *Adab al-muftī wa 'l-mustaftī.* Edited by Muwaffaq b. 'Abd al-Qādir. Beirut: 'Ālam al-kutub, 1986.
Ibn Taghrī Birdī, Abū al-Maḥāsin. *al-Nujūm al-ẓāhirah fī mulūk miṣr wa 'l-qāhirah.* Edited by William Popper. 7 vols. Berkeley: The University Press, 1909–1912.
———. *Manhal al-Ṣāfī wa 'l-mustawfī ba'ad al-wāfī.* Edited by Sa'īd 'Abd al-Fattāh 'Āshūr. 6 vols. Cairo: np, 1984.
Ibn Tāwās, 'Alī b. Mūsā. *al-Malāḥim wa 'l-fitan.* Najaf: al-Maṭba'at al-ḥaydarīyah, 1946.
Ibn Taymīyah. *Majmū'at al-rasā'il wa 'l-masā'il.* 5 vols. Cairo: Lajnat al-turāth al-'arabī, 1976.
———. *al-Siyāsah al-shar'īyah.* Beirut: Dār al-kutub al-'arabīyah, 1966.
———. *Ma'ārij al-wuṣūl ilā anna uṣūl al-dīn wa furū' 'uhū qad bayyanahā' al-rasūl.* Cairo: Quṣayy Muḥibb al-Dīn al-Khaṭīb, 1968.
Ibn Ṭūlūn, Shams al-Dīn. *Quḍāt dimashq al-thaghir al-bassām fī dhikr man wullīya qaḍā' al-shām.* Edited by Ṣalāḥ al-Dīn al-Munajjid. Cairo: Maṭbū'āt al-majma' al-'ilmī al-'arabī, 1956.
———. *Mut'at al-adhhān min al-tamattu' bi 'l-iqrān bayna tarājim al-shuyūkh wa 'l-aqrān.* 2 vols. Beirut: Dār Ṣādir, 1999.
———. *I'lām al-warā bi-man wullīya nā'iban min al-atrāk bi-dimashq al-shām al-kubrā.* Edited by Muḥammad Aḥmad Duhmān. Damascus: al-Maṭba'at wa 'l-jarīdah al-rasmīyah, 1964.
Ibn Yūnus. *Tārīkh al-miṣrīyīn.* Edited by 'Abd al-Fattāḥ Fatḥī 'Abd al-Fattāḥ. Beirut: Dār al-kutub al-'arabīyah, 2000.
Ibn Zūlāq. *Kitāb akhbār sībawayhi al-miṣrī wa huwa ghayr sībawayhi al-nahwī 'ilm wa adab wa tārīkh.* Cairo: n.p., 1933.
al-Isnawī, 'Abd al-Raḥīm. *Ṭabaqāt al-shāfi'īyah.* Edited by Kamāl Yūsuf al-Ḥūt. 2 vols. Beirut: Dār al-kutub al-'ilmīyah, 1987.
al-Ja'dī, 'Umar b. 'Alī. *Ṭabaqāt al-fuqahā' al-yaman.* Edited by Fu'ād al-Sayyid. Beirut: Dār al-qalam, n.d.
al-Jaṣṣāṣ, Aḥmad b. 'Alī al-Rāzī. *al-Fuṣūl fī al-uṣūl.* 4 vols. Kuwait: Wazārat al-awqāf wa 'l-shu'ūn al-islāmīyah, 1994.
al-Juwaynī, Imām al-Ḥaramayn. *Sharḥ al-waraqāt fī uṣūl al-fiqh.* Cairo: Maṭba'at al-madanī, n.d.
Kakhālah, 'Umar Riḍā. *Al-Mustadrak 'alā mu'jam al-mu'allifīn tarājim muṣannifī al-kutub al-'arabīyah.* 15 vols. Damascus: Maktabat al-'arabīyah, 1957–61. Reprint, Beirut: Dār iḥyā' al-turāth al-'arabī, 1983.
al-Khalīlī, Khalīl b. 'Abdallāh, *Kitāb al-irshād fī ma'rifat 'ulamā' al-ḥadīth.* Edited by Muḥammad Sa'īd b. 'Umar. 3 vols. Riyad: Maktabat al-rushd, 1989.
al-Khaṣṣāf, Abū Bakr Aḥmad b. 'Amr al-Shaybānī. *Kitāb adab al-qāḍī.* Edited by Farḥāt Zayādah. Cairo: Qism al-nashr bi l-jāmi'ah al-amrīkīyah, 1978.
al-Maḥallī al-Shāfi'ī, Jalāl al-Dīn Muḥammad b. Aḥmad. *Sharḥ al-waraqāt fī 'ilm uṣūl al-fiqh 'alā waraqāt abī al-ma'ālī imām al-ḥaramayn 'abd al-mālik b. yūsuf b. muḥammad al-juwaynī al-shāfi'ī wa ma'ahu ḥāshiyat al-shaykh aḥmad b. muḥammad al-dumayāṭī al-shāfi'ī.* Cairo: Maṭba'at Muḥammad 'Alī Ṣubayḥ, 1965.
al-Makhlūf, Muḥammad b. Muḥammad. *Shajarat al-nūr al-zakīyah fī ṭabaqāt al-mālikīyah.* 2 vols. Beirut: Dār al-fikr li 'l-ṭibā'ah wa 'l-nashr wa 'l-tawzī', n.d.
al-Maqrīzī, Aḥmad b. 'Alī. *Kitāb al-sulūk li-ma'rifat duwal al-mulūk.* Edited by Sa'īd 'Abd al-Fattāḥ 'Āshūr. 4 vols. Cairo: Maṭba'at dār al-kutub, 1972.
al-Māwardī, Abū al-Ḥasan. *al-Ḥāwī al-kabīr fī fiqh madhhab al-shāfi'ī wa huwa sharḥ mukhtaṣar al-muzanī.* 'Alī Muḥammad al-Mu'awwaḍ et al. 20 vols. Beirut: Dār al-kutub al-'ilmīyah, 1994.
Mu'awwaḍ, 'Alī Muḥammad. *Muqaddimat al-'azīz sharḥ al-wajīz.* Beirut: Dār al-kutub al-'ilmīyah, 1997.

Muslim, Abū al-Ḥusayn. *Ṣaḥīḥ muslim*. Edited by Muḥammad Fu'ād ʿAbd al-Bāqī. 5 vols. Beirut: Dār iḥyā' al-turāth al-ʿarabī, n.d.
al-Muzanī, Ismāʿīl b. Ibrāhīm. *al-Mukhtaṣar al-muzanī fī furūʿ al-shāfiʿī*. Edited by Muḥammad ʿAbd al-Qādir Shāhīn. Beirut: Dār al-kutub al-ʿilmīyah, 1998.
al-Nawawī, Muḥyī al-Dīn b. Yaḥyā. *al-Majmūʿ al-mudhahhab fī sharḥ al-muhadhdhab*. 18 vols. Beirut: Dār al-kutub al-ʿilmīyah, 1996.
——. *Minhāj al-ṭālibīn*. Beirut: Dār al-kutub al-ʿilmīyah, 1996.
——. *al-Rawḍat al-ṭālibīn*. Edited by ʿĀdil Aḥmad ʿAbd al-Mawjūd and ʿAlī Muḥammad Muʿawwaḍ. 15 vols. Beirut: Dār al-kutub al-ʿilmīyah, 2000.
——. "Al-Tanqīḥ fī sharḥ al-wasīṭ." In *al-Wasīṭ fī al-madhhab*. Edited by Aḥmad Maḥmūd Ibrāhīm and Muḥammad Muḥammad Tāmir. Vol. 1, 77–98. al-Ghūrīyah: Dār al-salām, 1997.
——. *Tahdhīb al-asmā' wa 'l-lughāt*. 2 vols. Cairo: Idārat al-ṭabāʿah al-munīrīyah, 1927.
al-Nuʿaymī, ʿAbd al-Qādir b. Muḥammad. *al-Dāris fī tārīkh al-madāris*. 2 vols. n.p.: Maktabat al-thaqāfah al-dīnīyah, 1988.
al-Nuwayrī, Muḥammad b. Qāsim. *Kitāb al-ilmān*. Edited by ʿAzīz Suryl Atiya. 8 vols. Hyderabad: Osmania Oriental Publications Bureau, 1979.
al-Qaysī, Muḥammad b. ʿAbdallāh. *Tawḍīḥ al-mushtabih*. Edited by Muḥammad Nuʿaym al-ʿArqasūsī. 9 vols. Beirut: Mu'assasat al-risālah, 1993.
al-Rāfiʿī, Abū al-Qāsim. *ʿAzīz sharḥ al-wajīz*. Edited by ʿAlī Muḥammad Muʿawwaḍ and ʿĀdil Aḥmad ʿAbd al-Mawjūḍ. 13 vols. Beirut: Dār al-kutub al-ʿilmīyah, 1997.
al-Ṣafadī, Ṣalāḥ al-Dīn Khalīl b. Aybak. *Kitāb al-wāfī bi 'l-wafayāt*. Edited by Muḥammad Yūsuf Najm et al. 29 vols. Wiesbaden: Franz Steiner Verlag GMBH, 1971.
al-Sakhāwī, Shams al-Dīn Muḥammad ʿAbd al-Raḥmān. *al-Iʿlan bi 'l-tawbīkh li-man dhammah al-tārīkh*. Damascus: n.p., 1930.
——. *al-Ḍaw' al-lāmiʿ li-ahl al-qarn al-tāsiʿ*. 12 vols. Beirut: Manshūrat dār maktabat al-ḥayāh, 1966.
——. *al-Tibr al-masbūk fī dhayl al-sulūk*. Edited by Najwā Muṣṭafā Kāmil and Labībah Ibrāhīm Muṣṭafā. Cairo: Maṭbaʿat dār al-kutub wa 'l-wathā'iq al-qawmīyah, 2002.
al-Sakkākī, Abū Yaʿqūb Yūsuf b. Muḥammad. *Miftāḥ al-ʿulūm*. Beirut: Dār al-kutub al-ʿilmīyah, 2000.
al-Samʿānī. *Kitāb al-ansāb*. 13 vols. Hyderabad: Maṭbaʿat majlis dā'irat al-maʿārif al-ʿuthmānīyah, 1993.
al-Ṣaymarī, Abū ʿAbdallāh al-Ḥusayn b. ʿAlī. *Akhbār abī ḥanīfah wa aṣḥābihi*. Beirut: Dār al-kitāb al-ʿarabī, 1976.
al-Shāfiʿī, Muḥammad b. Idrīs. *al-Risālah*. Edited by Aḥmad Muḥammad al-Shākir. Cairo: Maṭbaʿat Muṣṭafā Bābī al-Ḥalabī, 1969.
——. *Musnad al-imām al-shāfiʿī*. Beirut: Dār al-kutub al-ʿilmīyah, n.d.
al-Shīrāzī, Ibrāhīm b. ʿAlī Abū Isḥāq. *Ṭabaqāt al-fuqahā'*. Beirut: Dār al-rā'id al-ʿarabī, 1980.
——. *Sharḥ al-lumaʿ*. Edited by ʿAbd al-Majīd Turkī. 2 vols. Beirut: Dār al-gharb al-islāmī, 1988.
——. *al-Lumaʿ fī uṣūl al-fiqh*. Beirut: Dār al-kutub al-ʿilmīyah, 1985.
——. *al-Tanbīh fī fiqh al-imām al-shāfiʿī*. Beirut: Dār al-ṭibāʿah wa 'l-nashr wa 'l-tawzīʿ, 1997.
——. *al-Muhadhdhab fī fiqh al-imām al-shāfiʿī*. 3 vols. Beirut: Dār al-kutub al-ʿilmīyah, 1995.
al-Subkī, Tāj al-Dīn ʿAbd al-Wahhāb b. ʿAlī. *Muʿīd al-niʿam wa mubīd al-niqam*. Cairo: Maktabat al-khanjī, 1993.
——. *Ṭabaqāt al-shāfiʿīyah al-kubrā*. Edited by Maḥmūd Muḥammad al-Ṭanāḥī and ʿAbd al-Fattāḥ Ḥulw. 10 vols. Cairo: ʿĪsā al-Bābī al-Ḥalabī, 1964–76. Reprint, Cairo: Dār ʿIḥyā' al-kutub al-ʿarabīyah, n.d.

——. *Ṭabaqāt al-shāfiʿīyah al-kubrā*, 6 vols. Beirut: Dār al-kutub al-ʿilmīyah, 1999.
——. *Jamʿ al-jawāmiʿ*. Beirut: Dār al-kutub al-ʿilmīyah, 1994.
al-Suyūṭī, Jalāl al-Dīn. *Lubāb al-nuqūl fī asbāb al-nuzūl*. Beirut: Dār iḥyāʾ al-ʿulūm, 1978.
——. *Kitāb al-radd ʿalā man akhlad ilā al-arḍ wa jahil ann al-ijtihād fī kull ʿaṣr farḍ*. Edited by Khalīl al-Mays. Beirut: Dār al-kutub al-ʿilmīyah, 1983.
——. *Naẓm al-ʿiqyān fī aʿyān al-aʿyān*. Edited by Phillip K. Hitti. New York: Syrian-American Press, 1927.
al-Yāfiʿī, ʿAbdallāh b. Asʿad b. ʿAlī. *Mirʾāt al-jinān*. 4 vols. Beirut: Dār al-kutub al-ʿilmīyah, 1997.
Zayd, Muṣṭafā. *al-Naskh fī al-qurʾān al-karīm dirāsat tashrīʿīyah tārīkhīyah naqdīyah*. 2 vols. Cairo: Dār al-fikr al-ʿarabīyah, 1963.
al-Ziriklī. *al-Aʿlam: qāmūs tarājim li-ashhar al-rijāl wa ʾl-nisāʾ min al-ʿarab wa ʾl-mustaʿribīn*. 11 vols. Beirut: Dār al-ʿilm li ʾl-malāyīn, 1990.

Secondary Sources

Abdel Haleem, M. A. S. "Grammatical Shift for Rhetorical Purposes: *Iltifāt* and Related Features in the Qurʾān," *Bulletin of the School of Oriental and African Studies* 55, no. 3 (1992): 407–432.
——. "Early Islamic Theological and Juristic Terminology: *Kitāb al-ḥudūd fī ʾl-uṣūl* by Ibn Fūrak." *Bulletin of the School of Oriental and African Studies* 54, no. 1 (1991): 5–41.
Ahmed, Salahuddin. *A Dictionary of Muslim Names*. New York: University Press, 1999.
Allouche, A. "The Establishment of the Four Chief Judgeships in Fatimid Egypt." *Journal of the American Oriental Society* 105 (1985): 317–20.
Auchterlonie, Paul. *Arabic Biographical Dictionaries: A Summery Guide and Bibliography*. Durham: Middle East Libraries Committee, 1987.
Baalbaki, Ramzi. "Reclassification in Arab Grammatical Theory." *Journal of Near Eastern Studies* 54, no. 1 (January, 1995): 1–13.
Behrens-Abouseif, Doris. *Mamluk and Post-Mamluk Metal Lamps*. Cairo: Institut Français D'Archéologie Orientale, 1995.
Berkey, Jonathan P. *The Transmission of Knowledge in Medieval Cairo: A Social History of Islamic Education*. Princeton: University Press, 1992.
——. "Women and Islamic Education in the Mamluk Period." In *Women in Middle Eastern History*, ed. Nikki Kedde and Beth Baron, 143–57. New Haven: Yale University Press, 1991.
Biegman, Nicalaas H. *Egypt: Moulids, Saints, Sufis*. The Hague: SDU and Kegan Paul International, 1990.
Bloch, Ariel A. *Studies in Arabic Syntax and Semantics*. Wiesbaden: Otto Harrassowitz, 1991.
Bonebakker, S. A. *Materials for the History of Arabic Rhetoric from the Ḥilyat al-Muḥāḍara of Ḥātimī*. Napoli: Istituto Orientale di Napoli, 1975.
Breure, Leen. "In Search of Mental Structures: A Methodological Evaluation of Computerized Text Analysis of Late Medieval Religious Biographies." *History and Computing* 11 (1999): 61–78.
Brinner, William M., trans. *ʿArāʾis al-majālis fī Qiṣaṣ al-anbiyāʾ or "Lives of the Prophets" as Recommended by Abū Isḥāq Aḥmad Ibn Muḥammad Ibn Ibrāhīm al-Thaʿlabī*. Boston: Brill, 2002.
Brockelmann, Carl. *Geschichte der Arabischen Litteratur*. 2 vols. Leiden: E. J. Brill, 1943–49. 3 supplements, Leiden: E. J. Brill, 1937–42.
Brockopp, Jonathan. *Early Maliki Law*. Boston: Brill, 2000.
Bulliet, Richard W. "A Quantitative Approach to Medieval Muslim Biographical Dictionaries." *The Journal of Economic and Social History* 13 (1970): 195–211.

——. *Conversion to Islam in the Medieval Period: An Essay in Quantitative History*. Cambridge: Harvard University Press, 1979.
——. *Islam: The View from the Edge*. New York: Columbia University Press, 1994.
——. *The Patricians of Nishapur: A Study in Medieval Islamic Social History*. Cambridge, Mass.: Harvard University Press, 1972.
——. "The Age Structure of Islamic Education." *Studia Islamica*, no. 57 (1983): 105–17.
Burton, John. *The Sources of Islamic Law: Islamic Theories of Abrogation*. Edinburgh: University Press, 1990.
——. *An Introduction to Ḥadīth*. Edinburgh: University Press, 1994.
Burgoyne, Michael. *Mamluk Jerusalem*. London: British School of Archaeology in Jerusalem, World of Islam Festival Trust, 1987.
Cachia, Pierre. *The Arch Rhetorician or the Schemer's Skimmer: A Handbook of late Arabic Badīʿ drawn from ʿAbd al-Ghanī an-Nābulsī's Nafaḥāt al-azhār ʿalā nasamāt al-asḥār*. Wiesbaden: Harrassowitz, 1998.
Cahen, Claude. "History and Historians." In *Cambridge History of Arabic Literature*, ed. M. J. L Young, et al., vol. 3, 188–233. Cambridge: University Press, 1990.
——. "Editing Arabic Chronicles: A Few Suggestions." *Islamic Studies* 1, no. 3 (1962): 1–25.
Calder, Norman. "Law." In *History of Islamic Philosophy*, ed. Seyyed Hossein Nasr and Oliver Leaman, vol. 1, 979–98. New York: Routledge, 2001.
——. "al-Nawawī's Typology of *Muftīs* and its Significance for a General Theory of Islamic Law." *Islamic Law and Society* 3 no. 2 (1996): 137–64.
——. *Studies in Early Islamic Jurisprudence*. Oxford: Clarendon Press, 1993.
Chamberlain, Michael. *Knowledge and Social Practice in Medieval Damascus, 1190–1350*. Cambridge: University Press, 1994.
Clanchy, M. T. *From Memory to Written Record: England 1066–1307*. Cambridge, Mass.: Harvard University Press, 1979.
Conrad, Lawrence I. "*Ṭāʿūn* and *Wabāʾ*: Conceptions of Plague and Pestilence in Early Islam." *Journal of the Economic and Social History of the Orient* 15, pt. 3 (1982): 268–307.
——. "Arabic Plague Chronologies and Treatises: Social and Historical Factors in the Formation of a Literary Genre." *Studia Islamica*, no. 54 (1981): 51–93.
Cook, David. *Studies in Muslim Apocalyptic*. Princeton: The Darin Press, 2002.
Cooperson, Michael. *Classical Arabic Biography: The Heirs to the Prophets in the Age of al-Maʾmūn*. Cambridge: University Press, 2000.
Coulson, Noel J. *Conflicts and Tensions in Islamic Jurisprudence*. Chicago: University of Chicago Press, 1969.
——. *A History of Islamic Law*. Edinburgh: University Press, 1964.
——. "Doctrine and Practise in Islamic Law: One Aspect of the Problem." *Bulletin of the School of Oriental and African Studies* 18, no. 2 (1956): 211–26.
Creswell, K. A. C. *A Short Account of Early Muslim Architecture*. Cairo: The American University in Cairo Press, 1989.
De Boccard, E. *Les Monuments Ayyoubides de Damas*. Paris: Institut Français de Damas, 1932.
Denny, Frederick M. "'God's Friends': The Sanctity of Persons in Islam." In *Sainthood: Its Manifestations in World Religions*, ed. Richard Kieckhefer, 69–97. Berkeley: The University of California Press, 1988.
Dickinson, Eerik. *The Development of Early Sunnite Ḥadīth Criticism: The Taqdima of Abī Ḥātim al-Rāzī (240/845–327/938)*. Boston: Brill, 2001.
——. "Ibn al-Ṣalāḥ al-Shahrazūrī and the Isnād." *Journal of the American Oriental Society* 122 (2002): 481–505.
Dols, Michael. "Plague in Early Islamic History." *Journal of the American Oriental Society* 94, no. 3 (1974): 371–83.

——. *The Black Death in the Middle East.* Princeton: University Press, 1977.
Eliade, Mircea. *The Sacred and the Profane: The Nature of Religion.* Translated by Willard R. Trask. New York: Harcourt Brace Jovanovich, 1987.
Endress, Gerhard. "The Language of Demonstration: Translating Science and the Formation of Terminology in Arabic Philosophy and Science." *Early Science and Medicine* 7, no. 3 (2002): 231–254.
Escovitz, Joseph. "The Establishment of the Four Chief Judgeships in the Mamlūk Empire." *Journal of the American Oriental Society* 102, no. 3 (July-October, 1982): 529–32.
——. *The Office of Qāḍī al-Quḍāt in Cairo under the Baḥrī Mamlūks* (Berlin: Klaus Schwarz Verlag, 1984).
Fadel, Mohammad. "'*Istiḥsān* is nine-tenth of the Law:' The Puzzling Relationship of *Uṣūl* to *Furūʿ* in the Mālikī *Madhhab*." In *Studies in Islamic Legal Theory*, ed. Bernard Weiss, 161–76. Boston: Brill, 2002.
Fähndrich, Hartmut. "The Wafayat al-Aʿyan of Ibn Khallikan: A New Approach." *Journal of the American Oriental Society* 93 (1973): 432–445.
Flood, Finbarr Barry. *The Great Mosque of Damascus: Studies on the Makings of Umayyad Visual Culture.* Brill: Boston, 2001.
Gibb, Hamilton A. R. "Islamic Biographical Literature." In *Historians of the Middle East*, ed. Bernard Lewis and P. M. Holt, 54–58. London: Oxford University Press, 1962.
——. *Studies on the Civilization of Islam.* Edited by Stanford J. Shaw and William R. Polk. Boston: Beacon Press, 1962.
Gilbert, J. "The 'Ulama' of Medieval Damascus and the International World of Islamic Scholarship." Ph.D. Diss., University of California-Berkeley, 1977.
——. "Institutionalization of Muslim Scholarship and Professionalization of the *'Ulamā'* in Medieval Damascus." *Studia Islamica* 52 (1980): 105–34.
Gottfried, Robert S. *The Black Death: Natural and Human Disaster in Medieval Europe.* New York: Free Press, 1983.
Goldziher, Ignaz. *Muslim Studies (Muhammedanische Studien).* Edited by S. M. Stern and translated by C. R. Barber and S. M. Stern. 2 vols. Chicago: Aldine Publishing, 1971.
——. *The Ẓahiris: Their Doctrine and Their History.* Edited and translated by Wolfgang Behn. Leiden: E. J. Brill, 1971.
Graham, William. *Beyond the Written Word: Oral Aspects of Scripture in the History of Religion.* Cambridge: University Press, 1993.
——. "Traditionalism in Islam." *Journal of Inter-disciplinary History* 23 (1992–93): 495–522.
Gully, Adrian. *Grammar and Semantics in Medieval Arabic: A Study of Ibn Hisham's 'Mughni l-Labib.'* Richmond, UK: Curzon Press, 1995.
——. "*Taḍmīn*, 'Implication of Meaning' in Medieval Arabic." *Journal of the American Oriental Society* 117, no. 3 (July-Sept., 1997): 466–80.
Hafsi, Ibrahim. "Recherches sur le genre Tabaqat dans la littérature arabe." *Arabica* 23 (September 1976): 227–65; 24 (February 1977): 1–41; 24 (June 1977): 150–86.
Hallaq, Wael. *A History of Islamic Legal Theories.* Cambridge: University Press, 1997.
——. *Authority, Continuity, and Change in Islamic Law.* Cambridge: University Press, 2001.
——. *The Origins and Evolution of Islamic Law.* Cambridge: University Press, 2005.
——. "Was the Gate of *Ijtihad* Closed?" *International Journal of Middle Eastern Studies* 16 (1984): 3–41.
——. "Notes on the Term *Qarīna* in Islamic Legal Discourse." *Journal of the American Oriental Society* 108, no. 3 (July-September, 1988): 475–80.
——. "*Takhrīj* and the Construction of Juristic Authority." In *Studies in Islamic Legal Theory*, ed. Bernard Weiss, 317–35. Boston: Brill, 2002.
——. "On the Origins of the Controversy about the Existence of Mujtahids and the Gate of Ijtihad." *Studia Islamica* 63 (1986): 129–41.

——. "Considerations of the Function and Character of Sunnī Legal Theory." *Journal of the American Oriental Society* 104, no. 4 (October-December, 1984): 679–689.

——. "On the Authoritativeness of Sunni Consensus." *International Journal of Middle East Studies* 18 (1986): 427–54.

——. "The 'Qadi's Diwan (Sijill)' Before the Ottomans." *Bulletin of the School of Oriental and African Studies* 61, no. 3 (1998): 415–436.

——. "Was Shāfiʿī the Master Architect of Islamic Jurisprudence?" *International Journal of Middle Eastern Studies* 25 (1993): 587–605.

Hillenbrand, Robert. *Islamic Architecture: Form, Function, and Meaning.* New York: Columbia University Press, 1994.

Hourani, Albert. "The Basis of Authority in Sunnite Consensus." *Studia Islamica* 21 (1964): 13–60.

Housley, Norman. *The Later Crusades 1274–1580: From Lyons to Alcazar.* New York, Oxford University Press, 1992.

Jackson, Sherman. *Islamic Law and the State: The Constitutional Jurisprudence of Shihāb al-Dīn al-Qarāfī.* New York: E. J. Brill, 1996.

——. "Fiction and Formalism: Toward a Functional Analysis of *Uṣūl al-Fiqh.*" In *Studies in Islamic Legal Theory*, ed. Bernard Weiss, 177–201. Boston: Brill, 2002.

——. "The Primacy of Domestic Politics: Ibn Bint al-Aazz and the Establishment of Four Chief Judgeships in Mamluk Egypt," *Journal of the American Oriental Society* 115, no. 1 (January-March, 1995): 52–65.

Johansen, Baber. *Contingency in a Sacred Law: Legal and Ethical Norms in the Muslim Fiqh.* Boston: Brill, 1999.

Juynboll, Gautier H. A. *Muslim Tradition: Studies in Chronology, Provenance and Authorship of Early Ḥadīth.* New York: Cambridge University Press, 1983.

Kamali, Mohammad Hashim. *Principles of Islamic Jurisprudence.* Petaling Jaya, Selangor Darul Ehsan: Pelanduk Publications, 1989. Reprint, Cambridge: The Islamic Texts Society, 1991.

Keats-Rohan, K. S. B. ed., *Resourcing Sources.* Vol. 7. *Prosopographica et Genealogica.* Oxford: Occasional Publications of the Unit for Prosopographical Research, 2002.

Kennedy, Hugh. *The Early Abbasid Caliphate.* London: Croon Helm, 1981.

Khadduri, Majid, trans. *al-Shāfiʿī's Risāla.* Baltimore: Johns Hopkins Press, 1961. Reprint, Cambridge: The Islamic Texts Society, 1987.

Khalidi, Tarif. *Arabic Historical Thought in the Classical Period.* Cambridge: University Press, 1994.

Kinberg, Naphtali and Fahid Abu-Khadra. "Casual and Adversative Meanings of the Particle Lakin in Arabic." *Journal of the American Oriental Society* 107, no. 4 (October-December, 1987): 761–65.

Kruk, Remke. "History and Apocalypse: Ibn al-Nafī's Justification of Mamluk Rule." *Der Islam* 72, no. 2 (1995): 324–37.

Lapidus, Ira. "State and Religion in Islamic Societies" *Past and Present,* no. 5 (May 1996): 3–27.

Larkin, Margaret. *The Theology of Meaning: ʿAbd al-Qāhir al-Jurjānī's Theory of Discourse.* New Haven, Conn.: American Oriental Society, 1995.

Lowry, Joseph. "Does Shāfiʿī have a theory of 'Four Sources' of Law?" In *Studies in Islamic Legal Theory*, ed. Bernard Weiss, 23–50. Boston: Brill, 2002.

——. "The Legal-Theoretical Content of the *Risālah* of Muḥammad b. Idrīs al-Shāfiʿī." Ph.D. diss., University of Pennsylvania, 1999.

Levin, Aryeh. "The Grammatical Terms *al-Musnad, al-Musnad ʾIlayhi* and *al-ʾIsnād.*" *Journal of the American Oriental Society* 101, no. 2 (April-June, 1981): 145–65.

Little, Donald P. *An Introduction to Mamluk Historiography: An Analysis of Arabic Annalistic and Biographical Sources for the Reign of an-Malik al-Nasir Muhammad ibn Qalaʾun.* Wiesbaden: Franz Steiner, 1970.

——. *History and Historiography of the Mamluks.* London: Variorum Reprints, 1986.

——. "Historiography of the Ayyubid and Mamluk Epochs." In *The Cambridge History of Egypt*, ed. Carl F. Petry, vol. 1: Islamic Egypt, 640–1051, 412–44. Cambridge: University Press, 1998.

Loth, Otto. "Die Ursprung und Bedeutung der Tabaqat." *Zeitschrift der Deutschen Morgenländischen Gesellschaft* 23 (1869): 593–614.

Makdisi, George. "*Ṭabaqāt*-Biography: Law and Orthodoxy in Classical Islam." *Islamic Studies* 32, no. 4 (1993): 371–96.

——. *The Rise of Humanism in Classical Islam and the Christian West: with Special Reference to Scholasticism*. Edinburgh: University Press, 1990.

——. *The Rise of Colleges*. Edinburgh: University Press, 1981.

——. "The Juridical Theology of Shāfiʿī: Origins and Significance of Uṣūl al-Fiqh." *Studia Islamica* 59 (1984): 5–47.

——. "Ashʿarī and Ashʿarites in Islamic Religious History." *Studia Islamica* 17 (1962): 37–80; 18 (1963): 19–39.

——. "The Significance of the Sunni Schools of Law in Islamic Religious History." *The International Journal of Middle Eastern Studies* 10 (1979): 1–18.

——. "The Guilds of Law in Medieval Legal History: An Inquiry into the Origins of the Inns Court." *Zeitschrift für Geshichte der Arabisch-Islamischen Wissenschaften* 1 (1984): 233–52.

Malamund, Margaret. "Sufi Organizations and Structures of Authority in Medieval Nishapur." *International Journal of Middle Eastern Studies* 26 (1994): 428–40.

Manz, Beatrice Forbes. *The Rise and Rule of Tamerlane*. Cambridge: University Press, 1989.

Martel-Thoumian, Bernadette. *Les Civils et l'Administration dans l'état militarie mamlūk (IX/XV Siécle)*. Damascus: Institut Français de Damas, 1991.

Martin, Richard and Mark Woodward. *Defenders of Reason in Islam*. Oxford: Oneworld Publications, 1997.

McGregor, Richard J. A. "A Sufi Legacy in Tunis: Prayer and the Shadhiliyya." *International Journal of Middle Eastern Studies* 29 (1997): 255–77.

Melchert, Christopher. *The Formation of the Sunni Schools of Law, 9th–10th Centuries C.E.* New York: Brill, 1997.

Morgan, David. *The Mongols*. New York: Basil Blackwell, 1986.

Mottahedeh, Roy. *Loyalty and Leadership in an Early Islamic Society*. New York: I. B. Tauris, 2001.

Muranyi, Miklos. *Materialien zur malikitischen Rechtsliteratur*. Wiesbaden: Harrassowitz, 1984.

Naphy, William and Andrew Spicer. *The Black Death: and the History of Plagues 1345–1730*. Charleston, S.C.: Tempus, 2000.

Owens, Jonathan. "Models for Interpreting the Development of Medieval Arabic Grammatical Theory." *Journal of the American Oriental Society* 111, no. 2 (April-June, 1991): 225–38.

Petry, Carl F. *The Civilian Elite of Cairo in the Later Middle Ages*. Princeton: University Press, 1981.

Popper, William. *Egypt and Syria under the Circassian Sultans: 1382–1468 A.D. Systematic Notes to Ibn Taghrī Birdī's Chronicles of Egypt*. Berkeley: University of California Press, 1955.

——, trans. *History of Egypt: An Extract from Abī l-Maḥāsin Ibn Taghrī Birdī's Chronicle*. New Haven: American Oriental Society, 1967.

Powers, David. *Studies in Qur'an and Hadith: The Formation of the Islamic Law of Inheritance*. Berkeley: University of California Press, 1986.

——. "A Court Case from Fourteenth-Century North Africa." *Journal of the American Oriental Society* 110, no. 2 (April-June, 1990): 229–54.

al-Qadi, Wadad. "Biographical Dictionaries: Inner Structure and Cultural Significance." In *The Book in the Islamic World: The Written Word and Communication in the Middle*

East, ed. George N. Atiyeh, 93–122. Albany: State University of New York Press, 1995.
Rabbat, Nasser O. "The Ideological Significance of the *Dār al-ʿAdl* in the Medieval Islamic Orient." *International Journal of Middle Eastern Studies* 27 (1995): 3–28.
Rahman, Fazlur. *Islam*. New York: Holt, Rinehart and Winston, 1966.
al-Rāzī, Najm al-Dīn. *The Path of God's Bondsmen from Origin to Return (Mersad al-ebad men al-maba ela'l-ma'ad)*. Translated by Hamid Algar. Delmar: Caravan Books, 1982.
Reinhart, Kevin. *Before Revelation: The Boundaries of Muslim Moral Thought*. Albany: State University of New York Press, 1995.
Reisman, David C. "A Holograph MS of Ibn Qāḍī Shuhbah's '*Dhayl*.'" *Mamluk Studies Review* 2 (1998): 19–49.
Robbins, Vernon. *Exploring the Texture of Texts: A Guide to Socio-Rhetorical Interpretation*. Valley Forge: Trinity Press International, 1996.
Robinson, Chase. *Islamic Historiography*. Cambridge: University Press, 2003.
——. "al-Muʿāfā b. ʿImrān and the Beginnings of the *Ṭabaqāt* Literature." *Journal of the American Oriental Society* 116, no. 1 (January-March, 1996): 114–120.
Roded, Ruth. *Women in Islamic Biographical Collections*. Boulder Co.: Lynne Rienner Publishers, 1994.
Rosenthal, Franz. *The History of Muslim Historiography*. Leiden: E. J. Brill, 1968.
——. "On Medieval Authorial Biographies: Al-Ya'qubi and Ibn Hajar." In *Literary Heritage of Classical Islam: Arabic and Islamic Studies in Honor of James A. Bellamy*, ed. Mustansir Mir, 255–74. Princeton: Darwin Press, 1993.
——. *Knowledge Triumphant: The Concept of Knowledge in Medieval Islam*. Leiden: Brill, 1970.
Schacht, Joseph. *An Introduction to Islamic Law*. Oxford: The Clarendon Press, 1964.
——. "The Schools of Law and Later Development of Jurisprudence." In *Law in the Middle East*, ed. Majid Khadduri and Herbert J. Liebesny, 57–84. Washington, D.C.: The Middle East Institute, 1955.
——. *Origins of Muhammadan Jurisprudence*. Oxford: Clarendon Press, 1950.
Schimmel, Annemarie. *Islamic Names*. Edinburgh: University Press, 1989.
Shaw, Stanford J. and William R. Polk, eds. *Studies on the Civilization of Islam*. Boston: Beacon Press: 1962.
Shehaby, Nabil. "*ʿIlla* and *Qiyās* in Early Islamic Legal Theory." *Journal of the American Oriental Society* 102, no. 1 (January-March, 1982): 27–46.
Ṣiddīqī, Muḥammad Zubayr. *Ḥadīth Literature: Its Origins, Development and Special Features*. Edited by Abdal Hakim Murad. Cambridge: Islamic Texts Society, 1993.
Smith, Jonathan Z. *Drudgery Divine: On the Comparison of Early Christianities and the Religions of Late Antiquity*. Chicago: The University of Chicago Press, 1994.
Stetkevych, Jaroslav. "Arabic Hermeneutical Terminology: Paradox and the Production of Meaning." *Journal of Near Eastern Studies* 48, no. 2 (April, 1989): 81–96.
Stern, S. M. "Petitions from the Mamluk Period: Notes on the Mamluk Documents from Sinai." *Bulletin of the School of Oriental and African Studies* 29, no. 2 (1966): 233–76.
Stewart, Devin. "Capital, Accumulation, and the Islamic Academic Biography." *Edebiyāt* 7 (1997): 345–62.
——. *Islamic Legal Orthodoxy: Twelver Shiite Responses to the Sunni Legal System*. Salt Lake City: University of Utah Press, 1998.
——. "The Doctorate of Islamic Law in Mamluk Egypt and Syria." In *Law and Education in Medieval Islam: Studies in Memory of Professor George Makdisi*, ed. Joseph E. Lowry, Devin Stewart, and Shawkat M. Toorawa, 45–90. Oxford: Gibb Memorial Trust, 2004.
Suleiman, M. Y. I. H. "On the Underlying Foundations of Arabic Grammar: A Preliminary Investigation." *Bulletin of the British Society for Middle Eastern Studies* 16, no. 2 (1989): 176–85.

Taylor, Christopher. *In The Vicinity of the Righteous: Ziyara and the Veneration of Muslim Saints in Medieval Egypt.* Leiden: Brill, 1999.
Tibawi, A. L. "Origin and Character of *al-Madrasah*." *Bulletin of the School of Oriental and African Studies* 25, no. 1/3 (1962): 225–38.
van Leeuwen, Richard. *Waqfs and Urban Structures: The Case of Ottoman Damascus.* Boston: Brill, 1999.
Versteegh, Kees. "Linguistic Contacts between Arabic and Other Languages." *Arabica* 68 (2001): 470–508.
Vishanoff, David. "Early Islamic Hermeneutics: Language, Speech, and meaning in Preclassical Legal Theory." Ph.D. diss., Emory University, 2004.
Weiss, Bernard. *The Spirit of Islamic Law.* Athens: University of Georgia Press, 1998.
——. "Subject and Predicate in the Thinking of Arabic Philologists." *Journal of the American Oriental Society* 105, no. 4 (October-December, 1985): 605–22.
——. *The Search for God's Law.* Salt Lake City: University of Utah Press, 1992.
Wensinck, A. J. "The Ideas of the Western Semites Concerning the Navel of the Universe." In *Mythology: Studies of A. J. Wensinck*, ed. Angelo Brelich, Joseph Campbell, and Mircea Eliade, 1–65. Johannes Muller, 1916. Reprint, New York: Arno Press, 1978.
Wheeler, Brannon. *Applying the Canon in Islam: The Authorization and Maintenance of Interpretive Reasoning in Ḥanafī Scholarship.* Albany: State University of New York Press, 1996.
Wilkinson, C. K. "Heating and Cooking in Nishapur." *Bulletin of the Metropolitan Museum of Art*, no. 2 (1944): 282–91.
Wüstenfeld, Ferdinand. *Academien der Araber und ihre Lehrer.* Göttingen: Vandenhoeck und Ruprecht, 1837.
——. "Der Imām el-Schāfiʿī." *Abhandlungen der Königlichen Gesellschaft der Wissenschaften* 36 (1890): 1–106.
Young, M. J. L. "Arabic Biographical Writing." In *The Cambridge History of Arabic Literature: Religion, Learning and Science in the ʿAbbasid Period*, ed. M. J. L. Young, J. D. Latham and R. B. Serjeant. 168–87. Cambridge: University Press, 1990.
Ziegler, Philip. *The Black Death.* Godalming: Bramley, 1998.

INDEX